X-O MANOWAR

PLANET DEATH

ROBERT VENDITTI | CARY NORD | TREVOR HAIRSINE | MOOSE BAUMANN

CONTENTS

Collection Cover Art: Clayton Crain

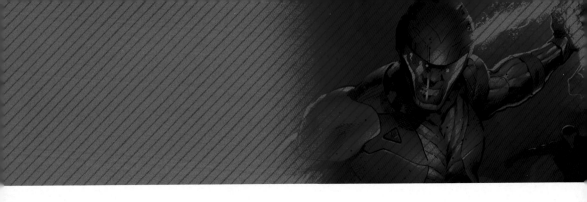

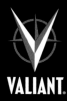

VALIANT

Peter Cuneo
Chairman

Dinesh Shamdasani
CEO and Chief Creative Officer

Gavin Cuneo
CFO and Head of Strategic Development

Fred Pierce
Publisher

Warren Simons
VP Executive Editor

Walter Black
VP Operations

Hunter Gorinson
Marketing and Communications Manager

Atom! Freeman
Sales Manager

Travis Escarfullery
Production and Design Manager

Alejandro Arbona
Associate Editor

Josh Johns
Assistant Editor

Peter Stern
Operations Coordinator

Ivan Cohen
Collection Editor

Steve Blackwell
Collection Designer

Rian Hughes/Device
Trade Dress and Book Design

Russell Brown
President, Consumer Products, Promotions & Ad Sales

Jason Kothari
Vice Chairman

X-O Manowar®: Planet Death. Published by Valiant Entertainment, LLC. Office of Publication: 424 West 33rd Street, New York, NY 10001. Printed in the USA. First Printing. ISBN: 9781939346087.

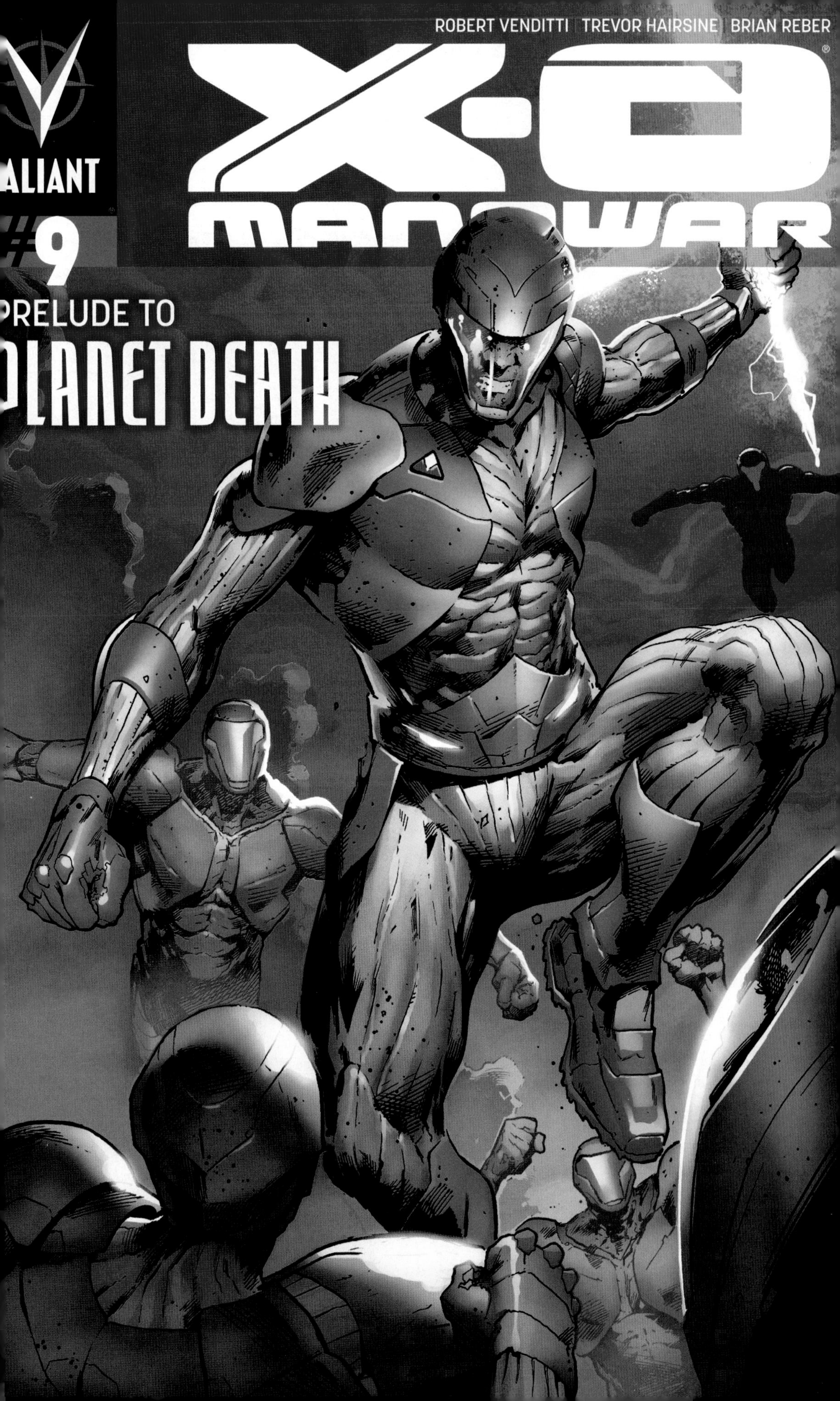

VALIANT
ROBERT VENDITTI | TREVOR HAIRSINE | BRIAN REBER
X-O MANOWAR
#9
PRELUDE TO
PLANET DEATH

OUR STORY SO FAR...

In 402 A.D., Aric of Dacia -- heir to the Visigoth throne -- suffered a crushing defeat at the hands of the Roman Empire, losing his father and his wife to the Roman legions. Soon after, Aric sought vengeance, attacking what he thought was a strangely garbed Roman patrol, but which was in fact a landing party from an alien race known as the Vine. The Vine captured Aric, along with warriors from across the globe who had the best chance of surviving as slave labor aboard their colony ships. The Vine also swapped their alien offspring with human infants, leaving perfect doppelgangers behind on earth. These "plantings" were raised by unsuspecting humans, allowing the Vine species to thrive on Earth for centuries.

Aboard the Vine colony ship, Aric endured years of brutal forced labor. After careful planning, he orchestrated a revolt and stormed the hallowed temple where the Vine kept their most sacred relic: Shanhara, the sentient X-O Manowar armor. Aric bonded with the armor, and with Shanhara's power at his command, he decimated his Vine captors and returned to Earth. Unfortunately, his trusted friend, Gafti, was lost during the escape.

On Earth, Aric discovered 1600 years had passed during his absence. The Vine plantings -- left behind in 402 A.D. -- had reproduced and spread around the globe, infiltrating every facet of humanity. With their power and influence, they attempted to retrieve the Manowar armor, but the Vine were betrayed by one of their own: Alexander Dorian, a descendant of the original Vine plantings, allied with Aric to thwart the Vine's plans.

Now the Vine Council has ordered that the armor be taken from Aric at any cost, even if it means the armor's destruction. A Vine invasion fleet speeds toward Earth, determined to eliminate the human threat...

And when they visit Earth this time, they will bring only death.

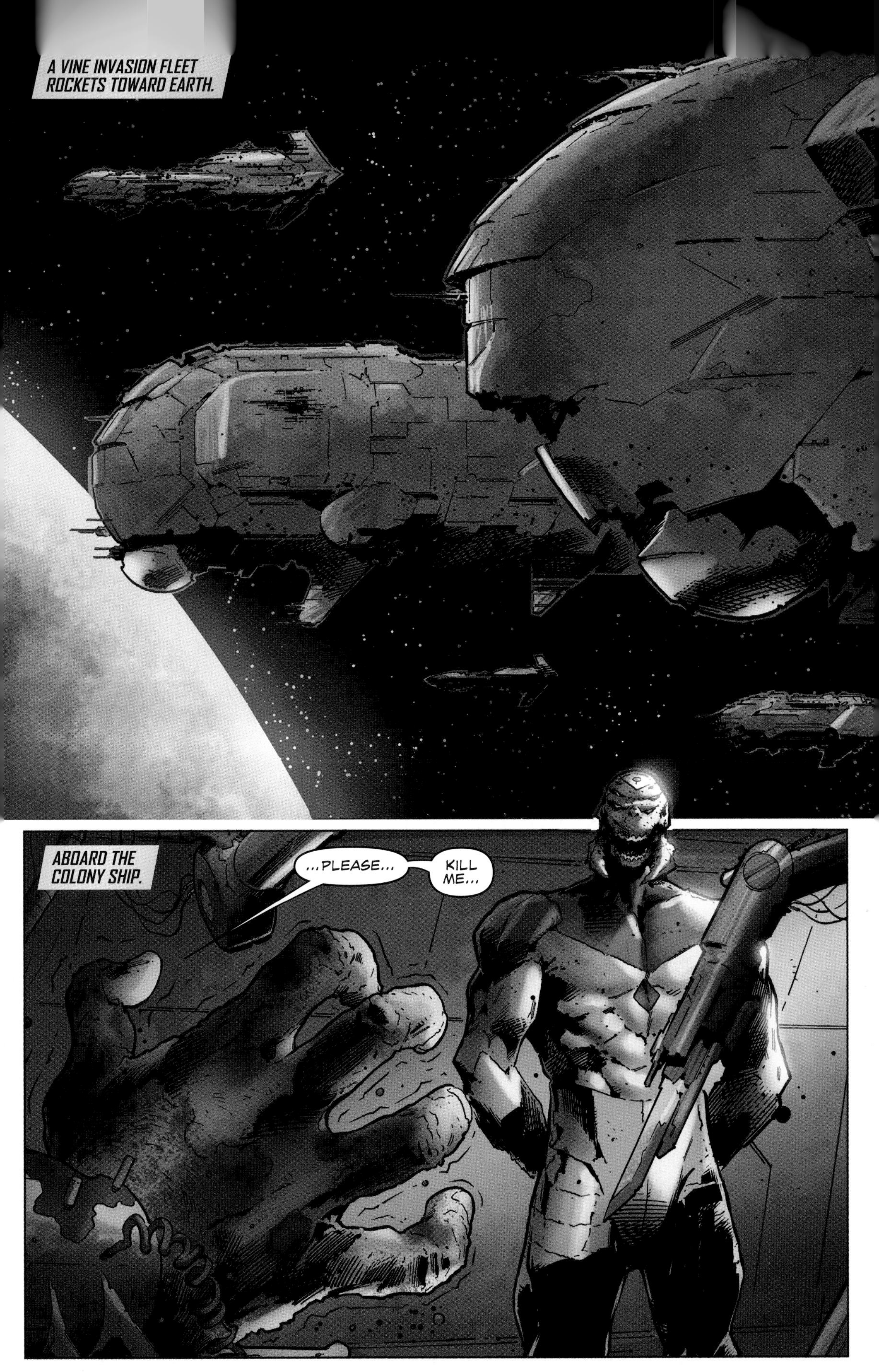
A VINE INVASION FLEET ROCKETS TOWARD EARTH.
ABOARD THE COLONY SHIP.
...PLEASE...
KILL ME...

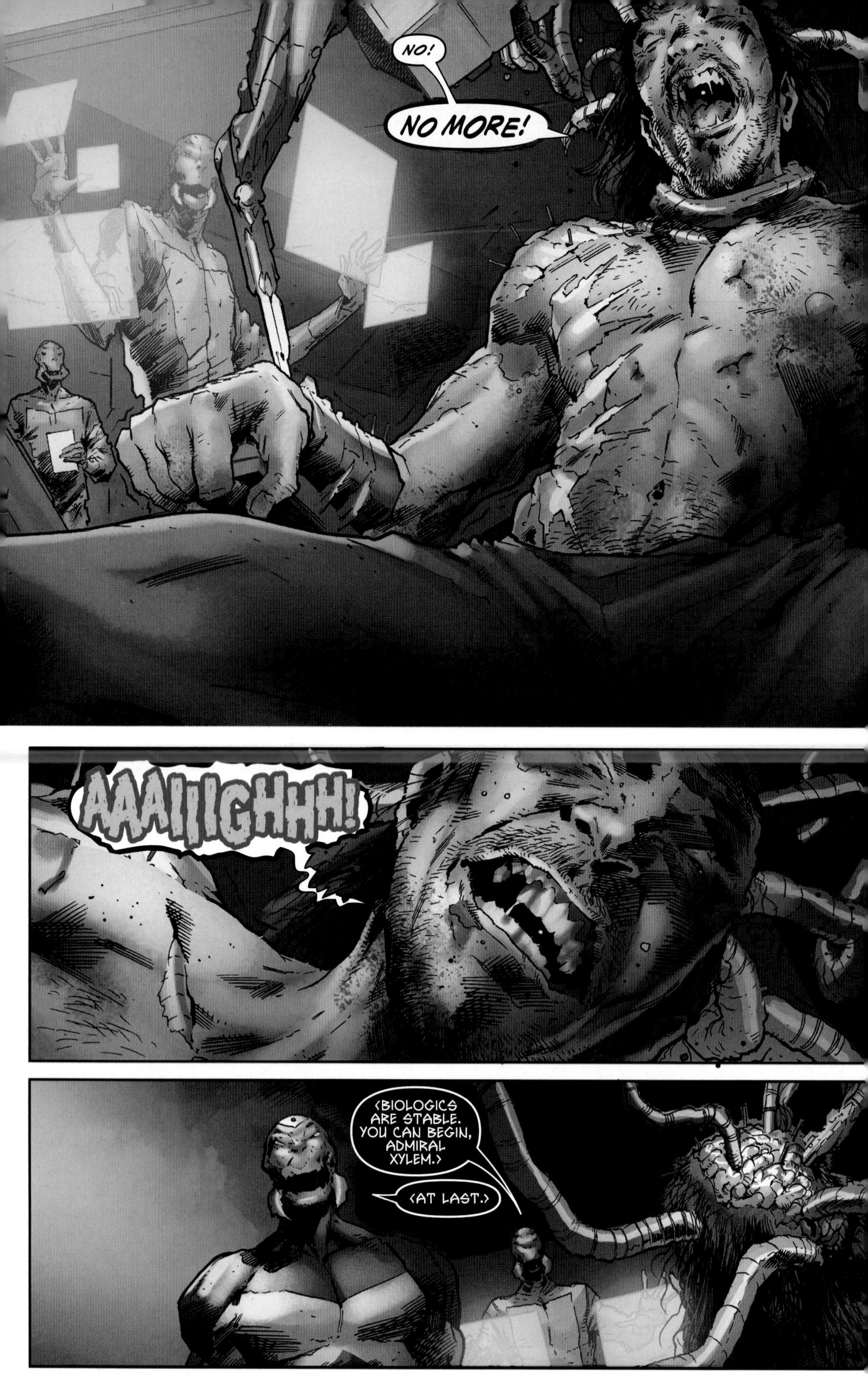
NO!
NO MORE!
AAAIIIGHHH!
<BIOLOGICS ARE STABLE. YOU CAN BEGIN, ADMIRAL XYLEM.>
<AT LAST.>

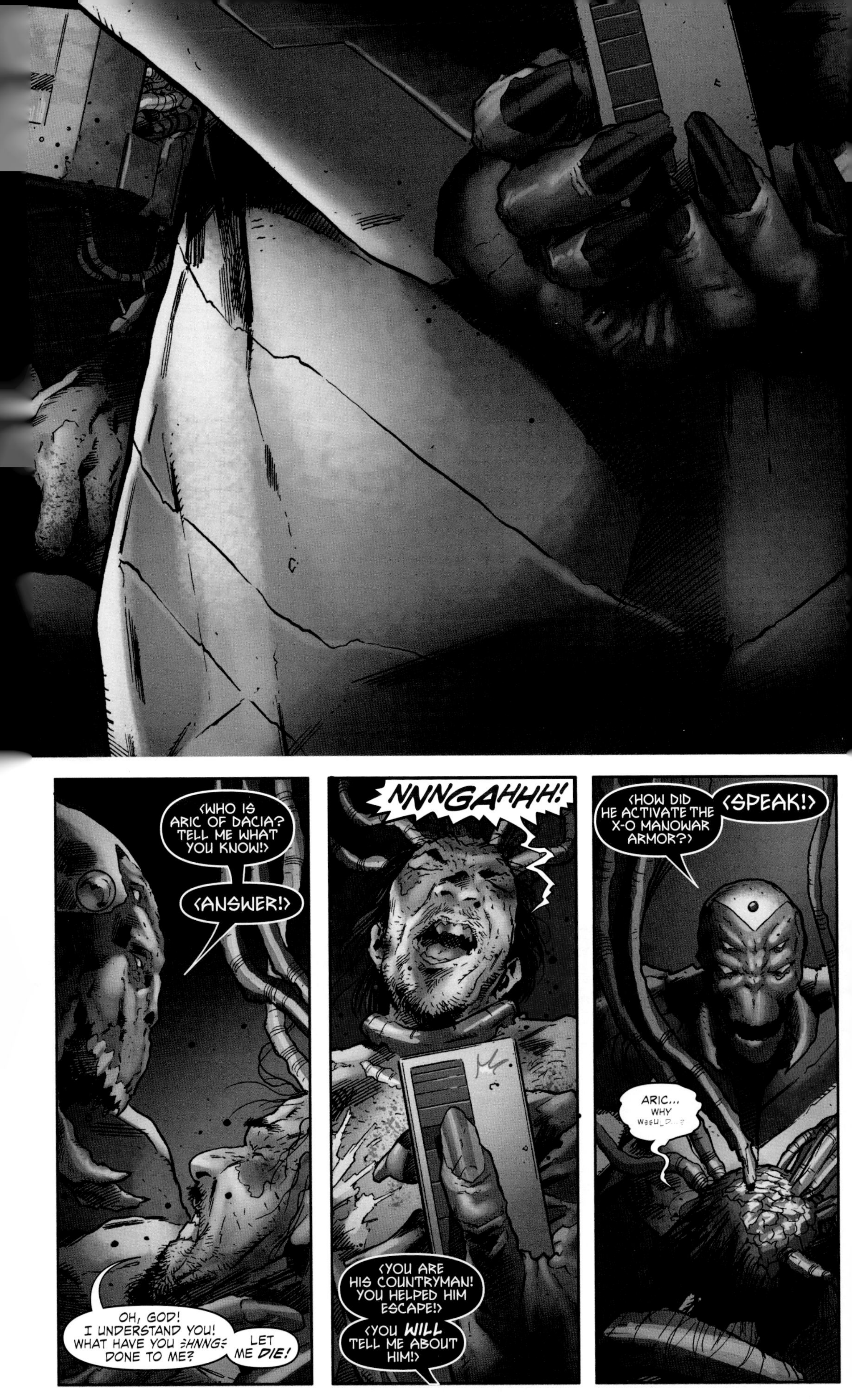
<WHO IS ARIC OF DACIA? TELL ME WHAT YOU KNOW!>
<ANSWER!>
OH, GOD! I UNDERSTAND YOU! WHAT HAVE YOU HNNG DONE TO ME?
LET ME *DIE!*
NNNGAHHH!
<YOU ARE HIS COUNTRYMAN! YOU HELPED HIM ESCAPE!>
<YOU *WILL* TELL ME ABOUT HIM!>
<HOW DID HE ACTIVATE THE X-O MANOWAR ARMOR?>
<SPEAK!>
ARIC... WHY WOULD...?

‹KEEP THE SLAVE CONSCIOUS, DOCTOR.›

‹PAIN ONLY SERVES ITS PURPOSE IF HE IS AWAKE TO FEEL IT.›

‹ADMIRAL--›

‹--THE PRIEST IS HERE.›

‹I SHOULD CHAIN THE PEST INSIDE HIS TEMPLE.›

‹SHOW HIM IN.›

‹ADMIRAL XYLEM--›

‹I HAVE SEEN THE STRIKE TEAM'S PREPARATIONS. THEY INTEND TO DESTROY THE SACRED ARMOR OF SHANHARA.›

‹THIS MADNESS... IT BORDERS ON BLASPHEMY!›

‹FOR A PRIEST, YOU HAVE A HIGH OPINION OF YOUR TACTICAL UNDERSTANDING.›

‹COMMANDER TRILL IS UNSTABLE! ORDER HIM AND HIS X-O COMMANDOS NOT TO HARM THE ARMOR.›

‹TRILL IS TO DO WHATEVER IS NECESSARY TO ENSURE THE MANOWAR ARMOR NO LONGER REMAINS AT THE HUMAN'S COMMAND.›

‹YOU OVERESTIMATE MY AUTHORITY.›

‹IT WAS THE COUNCIL WHO ORDERED THIS COURSE OF ACTION.›

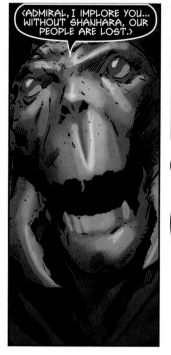

‹ADMIRAL, I IMPLORE YOU... WITHOUT SHANHARA, OUR PEOPLE ARE LOST.›

‹THE ANIMAL HAS REGAINED CONSCIOUSNESS.›

...ULLGH...

‹I HAVE NO TIME FOR ONE OF YOUR SERMONS, PRIEST.›

‹THERE IS AN INVASION TO PLAN.›

‹BEG THE COUNCIL TO RECONSIDER.›

‹THE MILITARY AND THE CLERGY DO NOT ALWAYS AGREE, BUT IN THIS, YOU KNOW I AM RIGHT.›

‹IF YOU THINK THE COUNCIL CAN BE SWAYED, I INVITE YOU TO TRY.›

‹IN PERSON.›

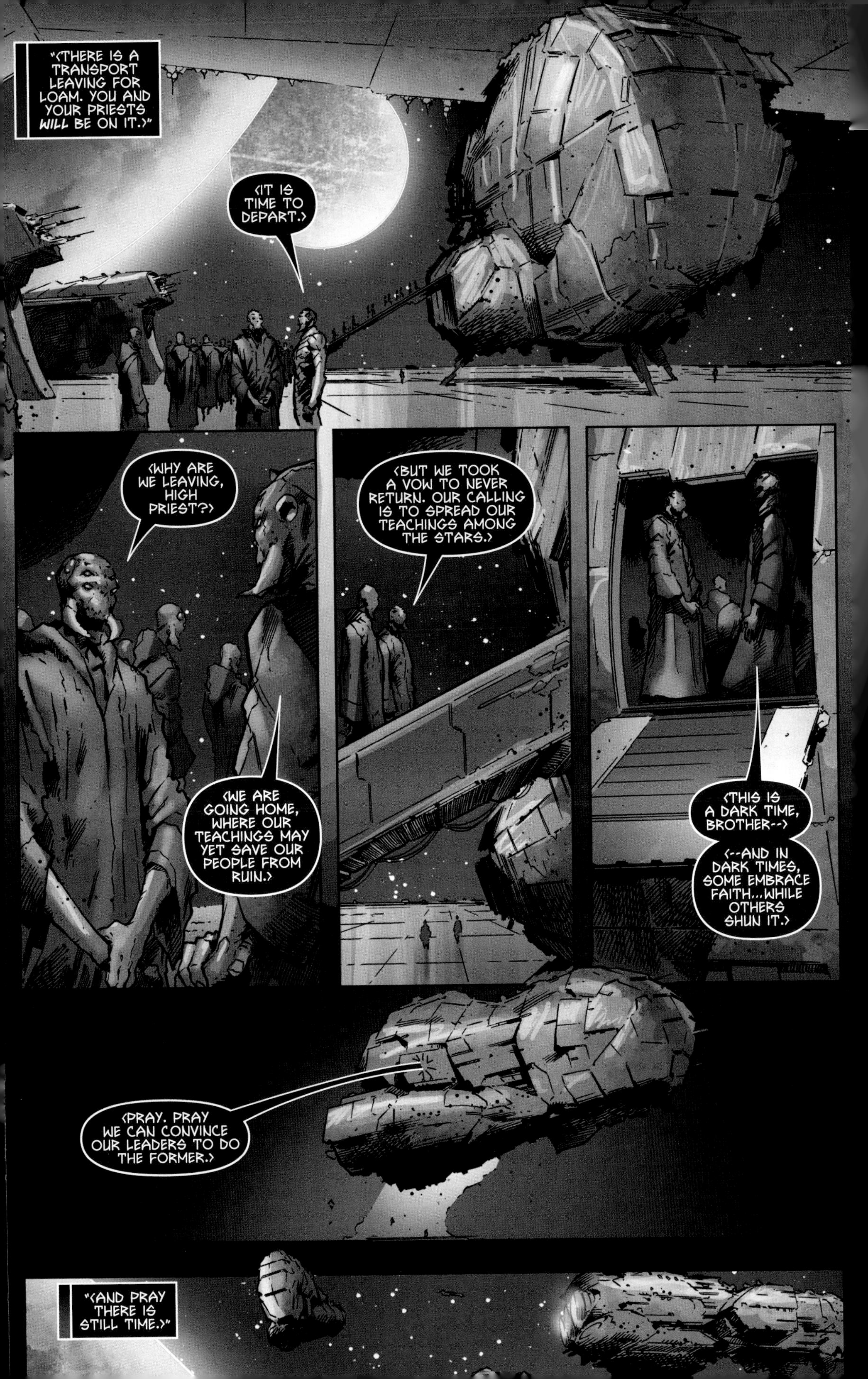
"‹THERE IS A TRANSPORT LEAVING FOR LOAM. YOU AND YOUR PRIESTS WILL BE ON IT.›"
‹IT IS TIME TO DEPART.›
‹WHY ARE WE LEAVING, HIGH PRIEST?›
‹WE ARE GOING HOME, WHERE OUR TEACHINGS MAY YET SAVE OUR PEOPLE FROM RUIN.›
‹BUT WE TOOK A VOW TO NEVER RETURN. OUR CALLING IS TO SPREAD OUR TEACHINGS AMONG THE STARS.›
‹THIS IS A DARK TIME, BROTHER--›
‹--AND IN DARK TIMES, SOME EMBRACE FAITH...WHILE OTHERS SHUN IT.›
‹PRAY. PRAY WE CAN CONVINCE OUR LEADERS TO DO THE FORMER.›
"‹AND PRAY THERE IS STILL TIME.›"

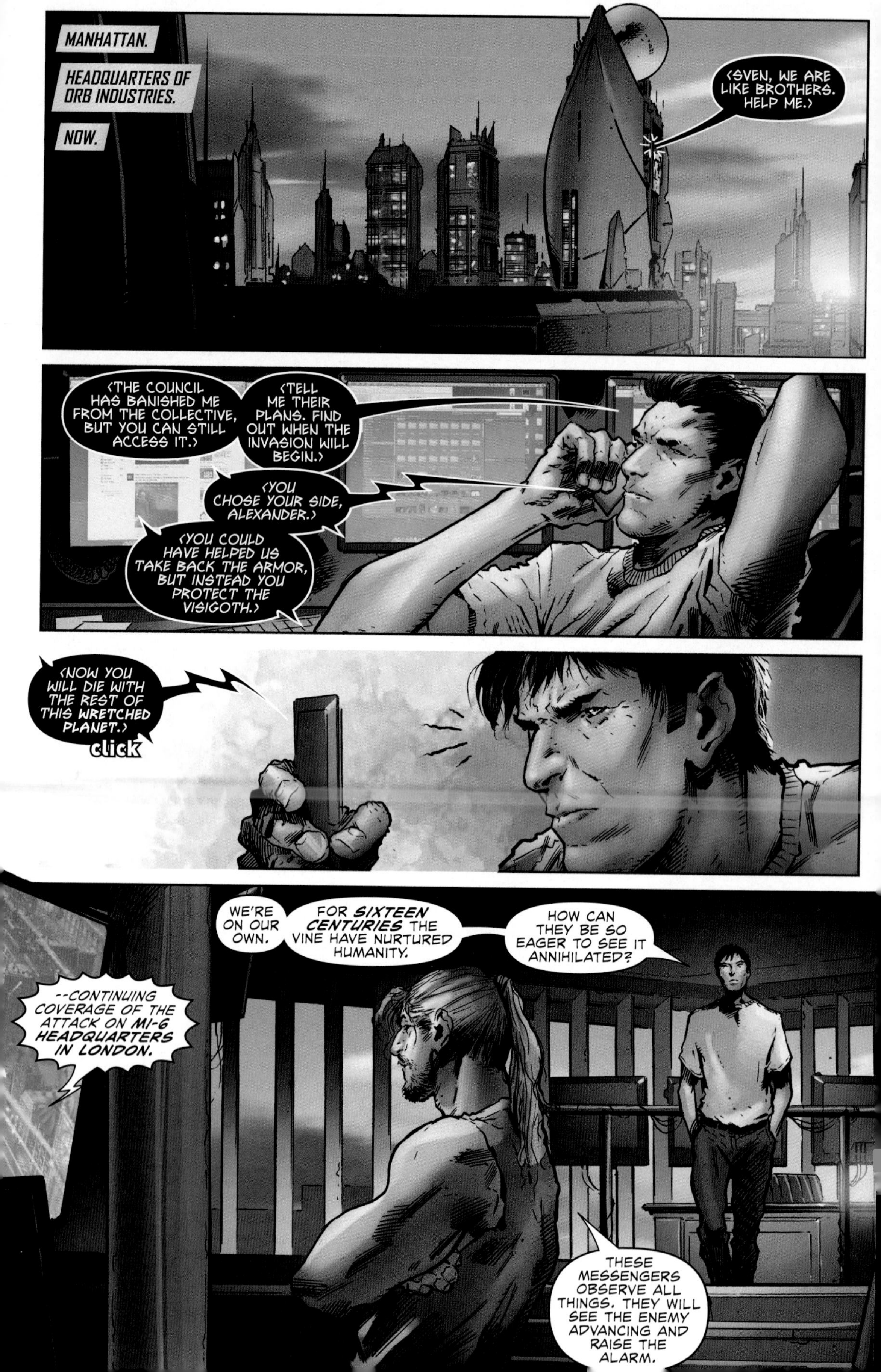
MANHATTAN.
HEADQUARTERS OF ORB INDUSTRIES.
NOW.
‹SVEN, WE ARE LIKE BROTHERS. HELP ME.›
‹THE COUNCIL HAS BANISHED ME FROM THE COLLECTIVE, BUT YOU CAN STILL ACCESS IT.›
‹TELL ME THEIR PLANS. FIND OUT WHEN THE INVASION WILL BEGIN.›
‹YOU CHOSE YOUR SIDE, ALEXANDER.›
‹YOU COULD HAVE HELPED US TAKE BACK THE ARMOR, BUT INSTEAD YOU PROTECT THE VISIGOTH.›
‹NOW YOU WILL DIE WITH THE REST OF THIS *WRETCHED* PLANET.›
click
WE'RE ON OUR OWN.
FOR *SIXTEEN CENTURIES* THE VINE HAVE NURTURED HUMANITY.
HOW CAN THEY BE SO EAGER TO SEE IT ANNIHILATED?
--CONTINUING COVERAGE OF THE ATTACK ON *MI-6 HEADQUARTERS IN LONDON.*
THESE MESSENGERS OBSERVE ALL THINGS. THEY WILL SEE THE ENEMY ADVANCING AND RAISE THE ALARM.

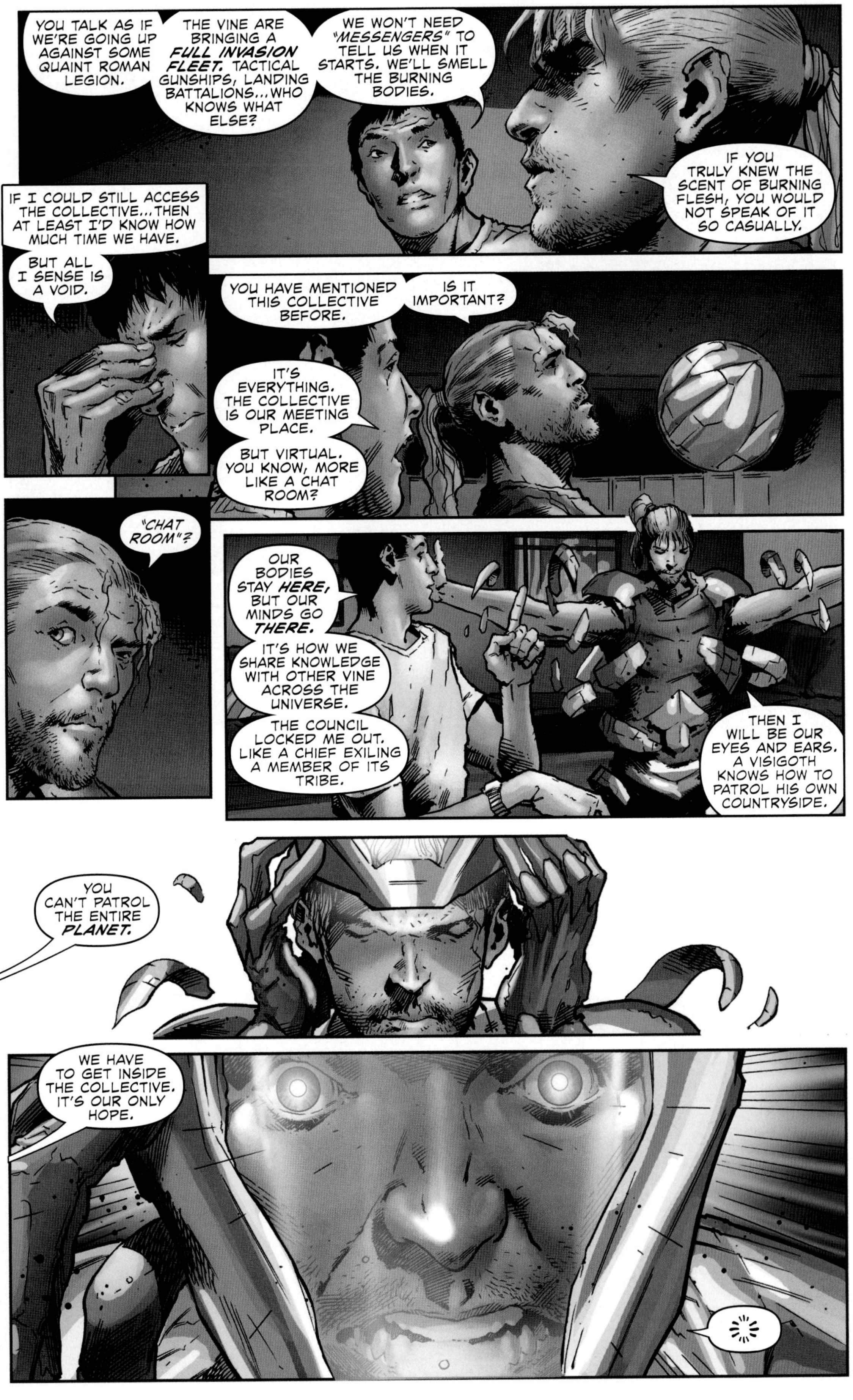
YOU TALK AS IF WE'RE GOING UP AGAINST SOME QUAINT ROMAN LEGION.
THE VINE ARE BRINGING A FULL INVASION FLEET. TACTICAL GUNSHIPS, LANDING BATTALIONS...WHO KNOWS WHAT ELSE?
WE WON'T NEED "MESSENGERS" TO TELL US WHEN IT STARTS. WE'LL SMELL THE BURNING BODIES.
IF YOU TRULY KNEW THE SCENT OF BURNING FLESH, YOU WOULD NOT SPEAK OF IT SO CASUALLY.
IF I COULD STILL ACCESS THE COLLECTIVE...THEN AT LEAST I'D KNOW HOW MUCH TIME WE HAVE.
BUT ALL I SENSE IS A VOID.
YOU HAVE MENTIONED THIS COLLECTIVE BEFORE.
IS IT IMPORTANT?
IT'S EVERYTHING. THE COLLECTIVE IS OUR MEETING PLACE.
BUT VIRTUAL. YOU KNOW, MORE LIKE A CHAT ROOM?
"CHAT ROOM"?
OUR BODIES STAY HERE, BUT OUR MINDS GO THERE.
IT'S HOW WE SHARE KNOWLEDGE WITH OTHER VINE ACROSS THE UNIVERSE.
THE COUNCIL LOCKED ME OUT. LIKE A CHIEF EXILING A MEMBER OF ITS TRIBE.
THEN I WILL BE OUR EYES AND EARS. A VISIGOTH KNOWS HOW TO PATROL HIS OWN COUNTRYSIDE.
YOU CAN'T PATROL THE ENTIRE PLANET.
WE HAVE TO GET INSIDE THE COLLECTIVE. IT'S OUR ONLY HOPE.

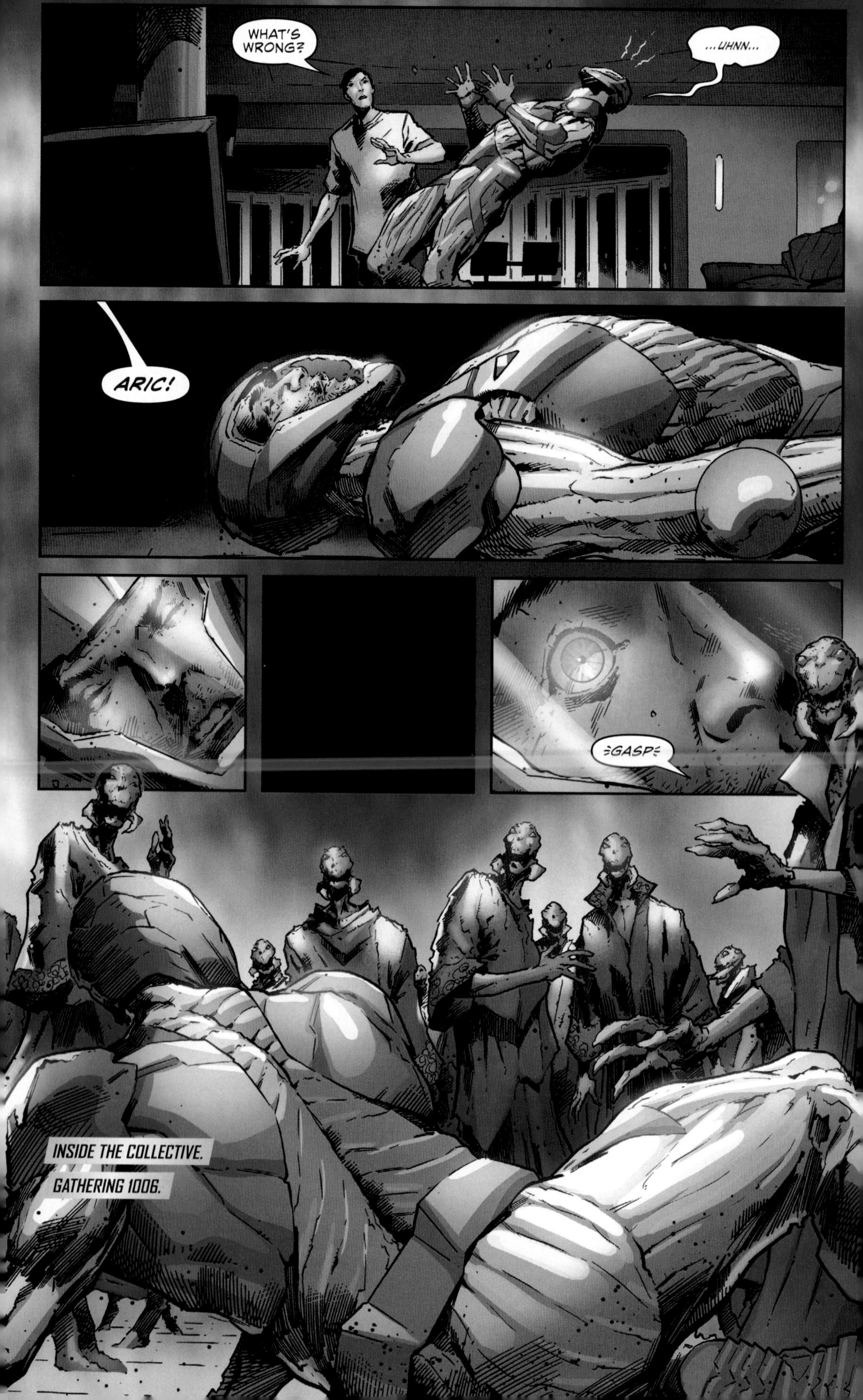
WHAT'S WRONG?
...UHNN...
ARIC!
GASP
INSIDE THE COLLECTIVE.
GATHERING 1006.

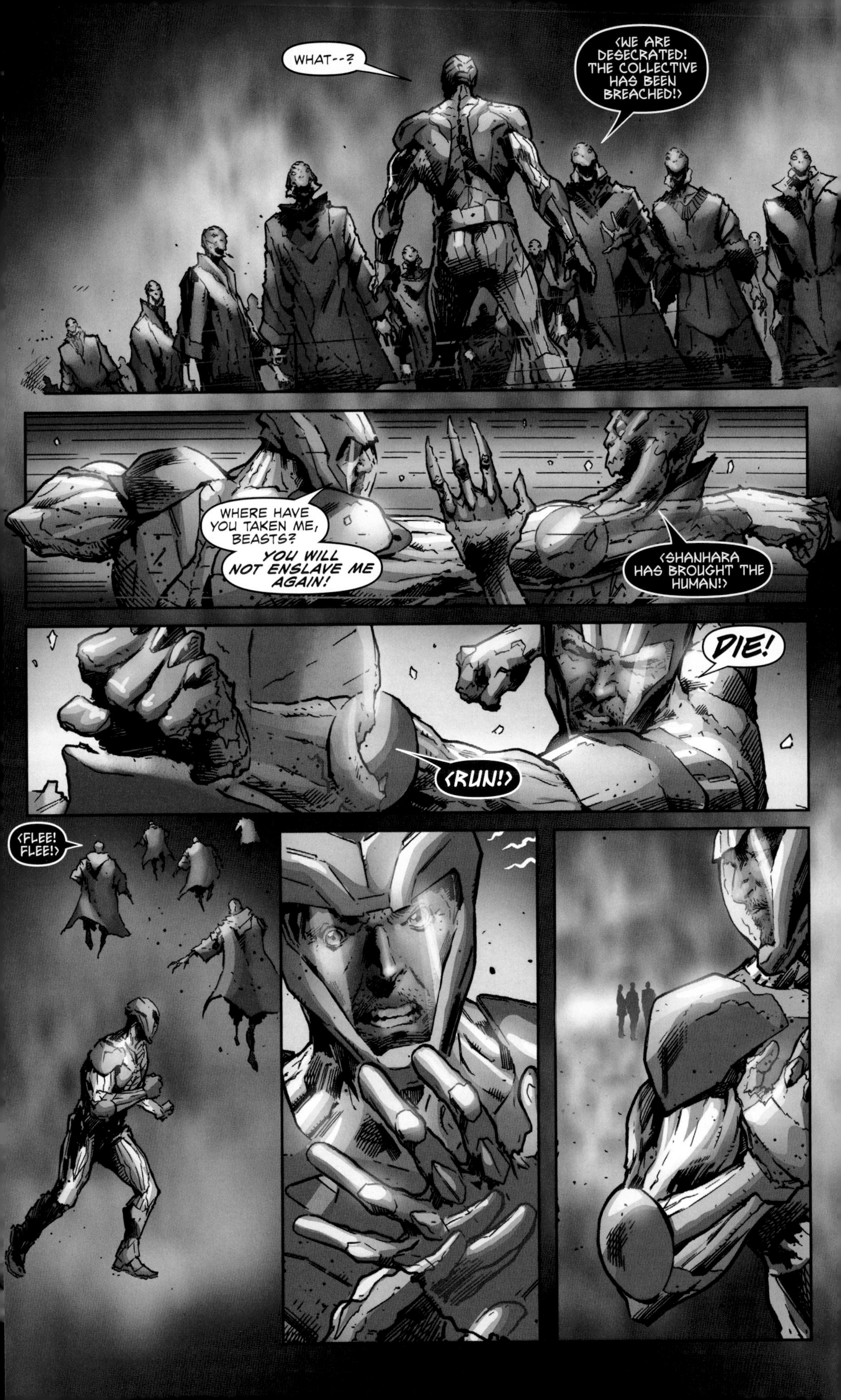
WHAT--?
<WE ARE DESECRATED! THE COLLECTIVE HAS BEEN BREACHED!>
WHERE HAVE YOU TAKEN ME, BEASTS? YOU WILL NOT ENSLAVE ME AGAIN!
<SHANHARA HAS BROUGHT THE HUMAN!>
DIE!
<RUN!>
<FLEE! FLEE!>

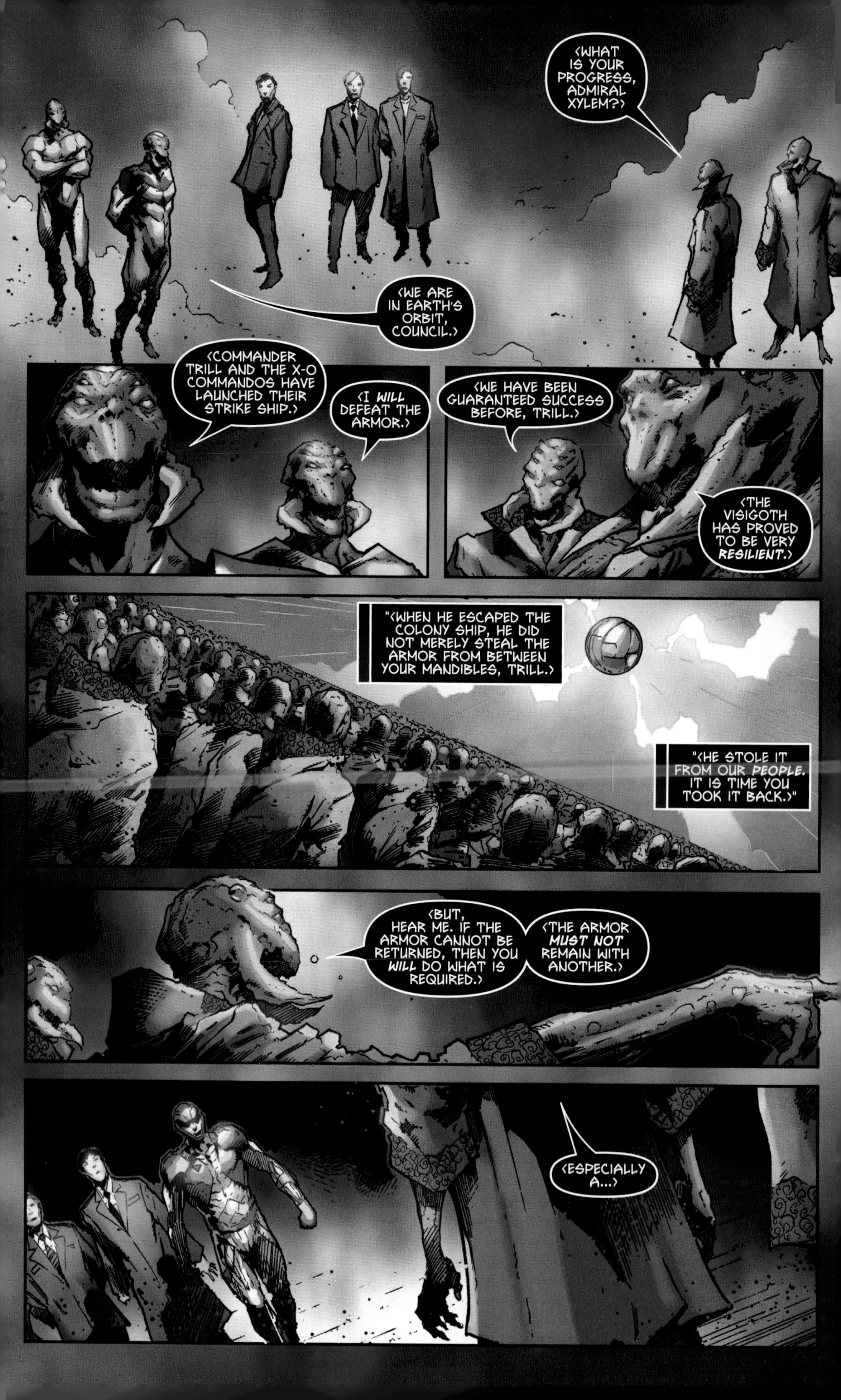

<WHAT IS YOUR PROGRESS, ADMIRAL XYLEM?>
<WE ARE IN EARTH'S ORBIT, COUNCIL.>
<COMMANDER TRILL AND THE X-O COMMANDOS HAVE LAUNCHED THEIR STRIKE SHIP.>
<I WILL DEFEAT THE ARMOR.>
<WE HAVE BEEN GUARANTEED SUCCESS BEFORE, TRILL.>
<THE VISIGOTH HAS PROVED TO BE VERY RESILIENT.>
"<WHEN HE ESCAPED THE COLONY SHIP, HE DID NOT MERELY STEAL THE ARMOR FROM BETWEEN YOUR MANDIBLES, TRILL.>
"<HE STOLE IT FROM OUR PEOPLE. IT IS TIME YOU TOOK IT BACK.>"
<BUT, HEAR ME. IF THE ARMOR CANNOT BE RETURNED, THEN YOU WILL DO WHAT IS REQUIRED.>
<THE ARMOR MUST NOT REMAIN WITH ANOTHER.>
<ESPECIALLY A...>

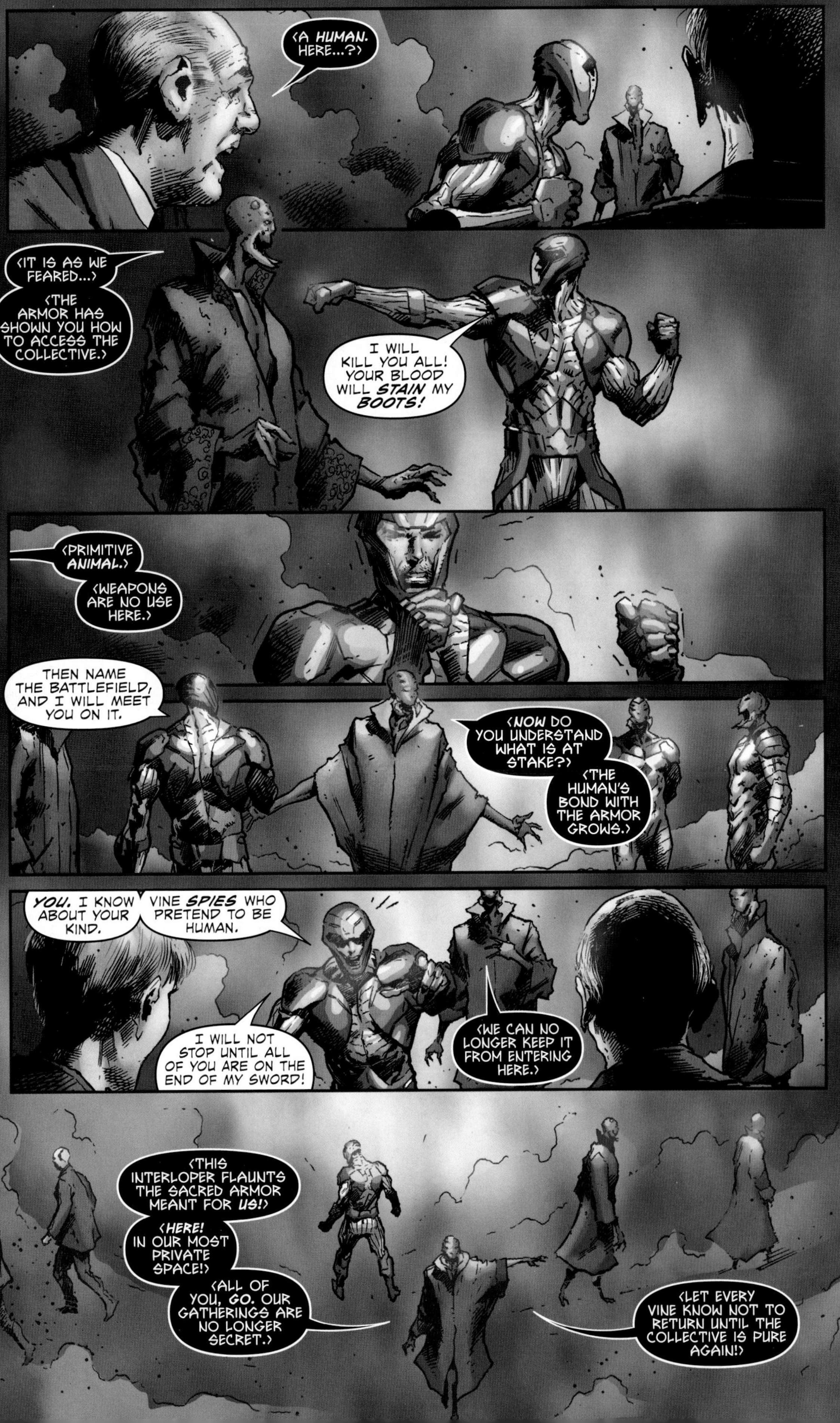

‹A HUMAN. HERE...?›
‹IT IS AS WE FEARED...›
‹THE ARMOR HAS SHOWN YOU HOW TO ACCESS THE COLLECTIVE.›
I WILL KILL YOU ALL! YOUR BLOOD WILL STAIN MY BOOTS!
‹PRIMITIVE ANIMAL.›
‹WEAPONS ARE NO USE HERE.›
THEN NAME THE BATTLEFIELD, AND I WILL MEET YOU ON IT.
‹NOW DO YOU UNDERSTAND WHAT IS AT STAKE?›
‹THE HUMAN'S BOND WITH THE ARMOR GROWS.›
YOU. I KNOW ABOUT YOUR KIND.
VINE SPIES WHO PRETEND TO BE HUMAN.
I WILL NOT STOP UNTIL ALL OF YOU ARE ON THE END OF MY SWORD!
‹WE CAN NO LONGER KEEP IT FROM ENTERING HERE.›
‹THIS INTERLOPER FLAUNTS THE SACRED ARMOR MEANT FOR US!›
‹HERE! IN OUR MOST PRIVATE SPACE!›
‹ALL OF YOU, GO. OUR GATHERINGS ARE NO LONGER SECRET.›
‹LET EVERY VINE KNOW NOT TO RETURN UNTIL THE COLLECTIVE IS PURE AGAIN!›

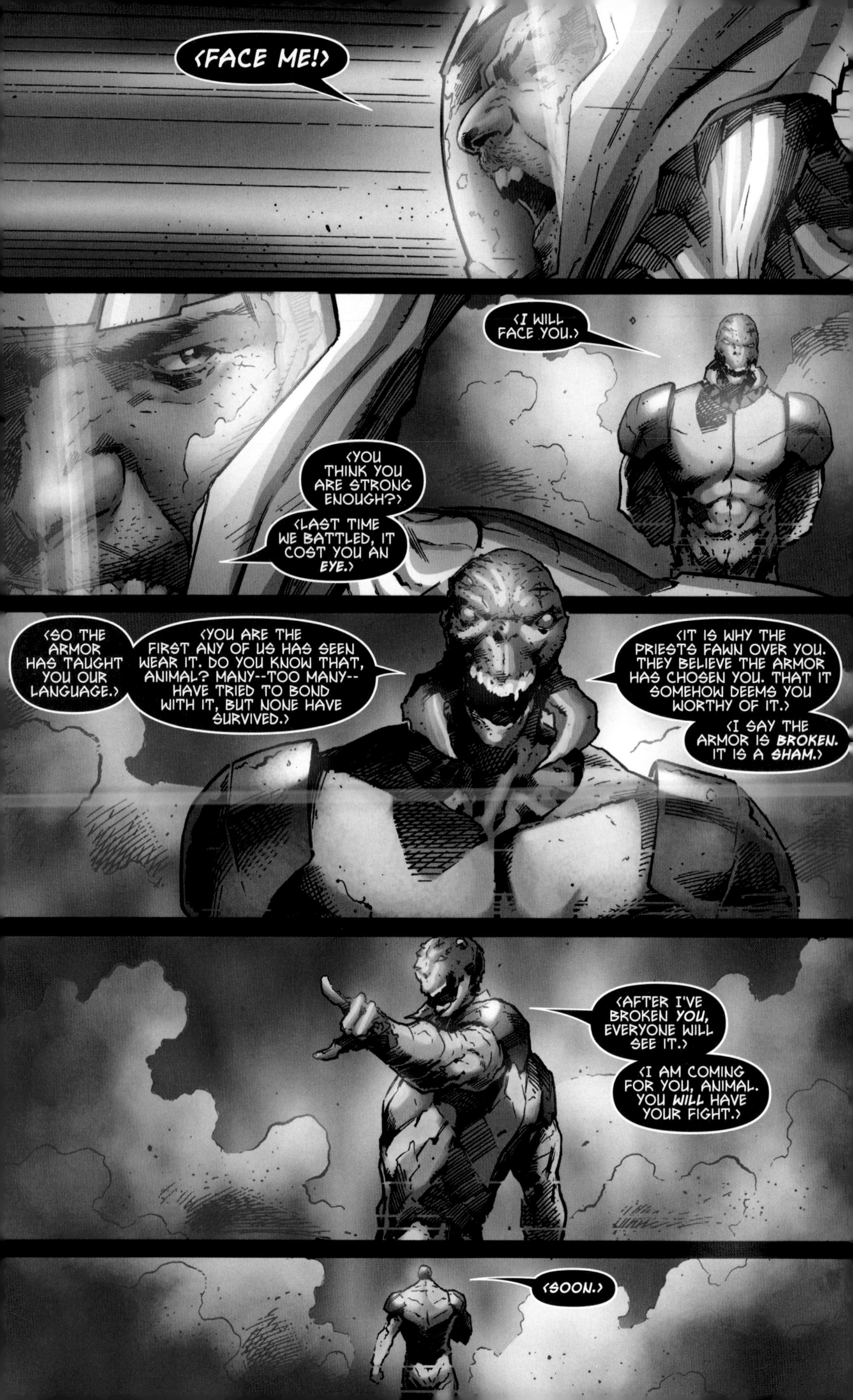
‹FACE ME!›
‹I WILL FACE YOU.›
‹YOU THINK YOU ARE STRONG ENOUGH?›
‹LAST TIME WE BATTLED, IT COST YOU AN EYE.›
‹SO THE ARMOR HAS TAUGHT YOU OUR LANGUAGE.›
‹YOU ARE THE FIRST ANY OF US HAS SEEN WEAR IT. DO YOU KNOW THAT, ANIMAL? MANY--TOO MANY--HAVE TRIED TO BOND WITH IT, BUT NONE HAVE SURVIVED.›
‹IT IS WHY THE PRIESTS FAWN OVER YOU. THEY BELIEVE THE ARMOR HAS CHOSEN YOU. THAT IT SOMEHOW DEEMS YOU WORTHY OF IT.›
‹I SAY THE ARMOR IS BROKEN. IT IS A SHAM.›
‹AFTER I'VE BROKEN YOU, EVERYONE WILL SEE IT.›
‹I AM COMING FOR YOU, ANIMAL. YOU WILL HAVE YOUR FIGHT.›
‹SOON.›

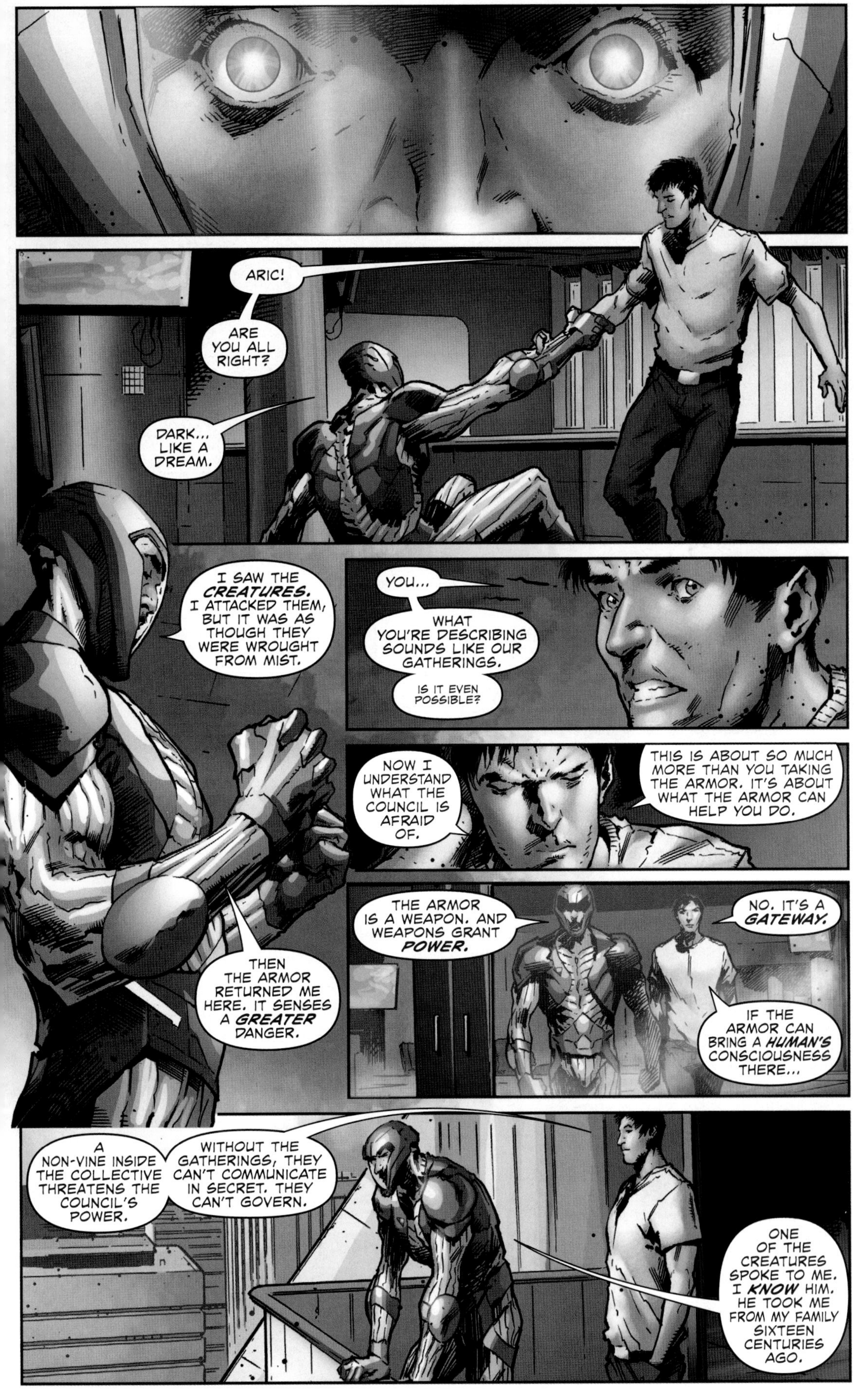
ARIC!
ARE YOU ALL RIGHT?
DARK... LIKE A DREAM.
I SAW THE CREATURES. I ATTACKED THEM, BUT IT WAS AS THOUGH THEY WERE WROUGHT FROM MIST.
YOU...
WHAT YOU'RE DESCRIBING SOUNDS LIKE OUR GATHERINGS.
IS IT EVEN POSSIBLE?
THEN THE ARMOR RETURNED ME HERE. IT SENSES A GREATER DANGER.
NOW I UNDERSTAND WHAT THE COUNCIL IS AFRAID OF.
THIS IS ABOUT SO MUCH MORE THAN YOU TAKING THE ARMOR. IT'S ABOUT WHAT THE ARMOR CAN HELP YOU DO.
THE ARMOR IS A WEAPON. AND WEAPONS GRANT POWER.
NO. IT'S A GATEWAY.
IF THE ARMOR CAN BRING A HUMAN'S CONSCIOUSNESS THERE...
A NON-VINE INSIDE THE COLLECTIVE THREATENS THE COUNCIL'S POWER.
WITHOUT THE GATHERINGS, THEY CAN'T COMMUNICATE IN SECRET. THEY CAN'T GOVERN.
ONE OF THE CREATURES SPOKE TO ME. I KNOW HIM. HE TOOK ME FROM MY FAMILY SIXTEEN CENTURIES AGO.

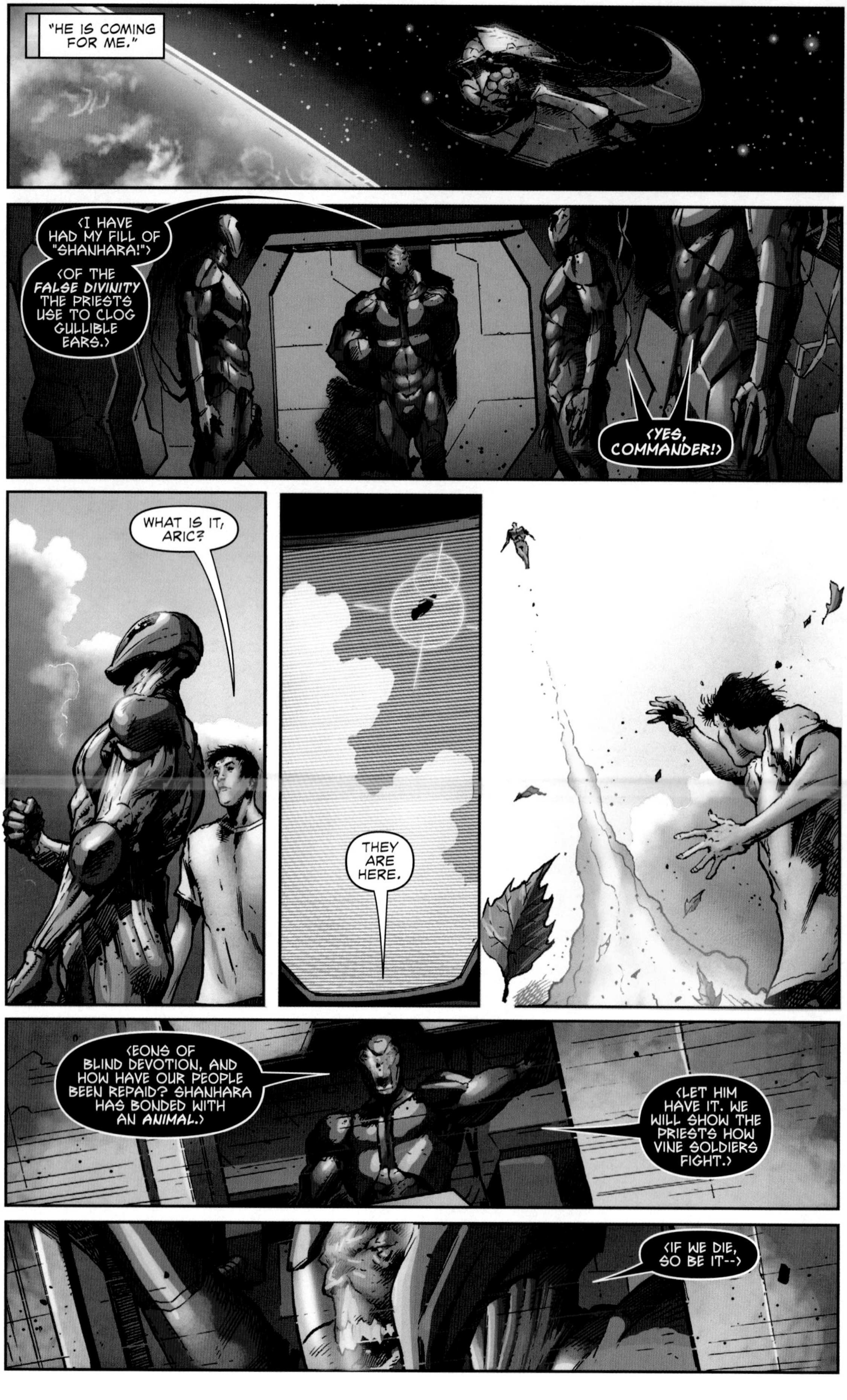
"HE IS COMING FOR ME."
<I HAVE HAD MY FILL OF "SHANHARA!">
<OF THE FALSE DIVINITY THE PRIESTS USE TO CLOG GULLIBLE EARS.>
<YES, COMMANDER!>
WHAT IS IT, ARIC?
THEY ARE HERE.
<EONS OF BLIND DEVOTION, AND HOW HAVE OUR PEOPLE BEEN REPAID? SHANHARA HAS BONDED WITH AN ANIMAL.>
<LET HIM HAVE IT. WE WILL SHOW THE PRIESTS HOW VINE SOLDIERS FIGHT.>
<IF WE DIE, SO BE IT-->

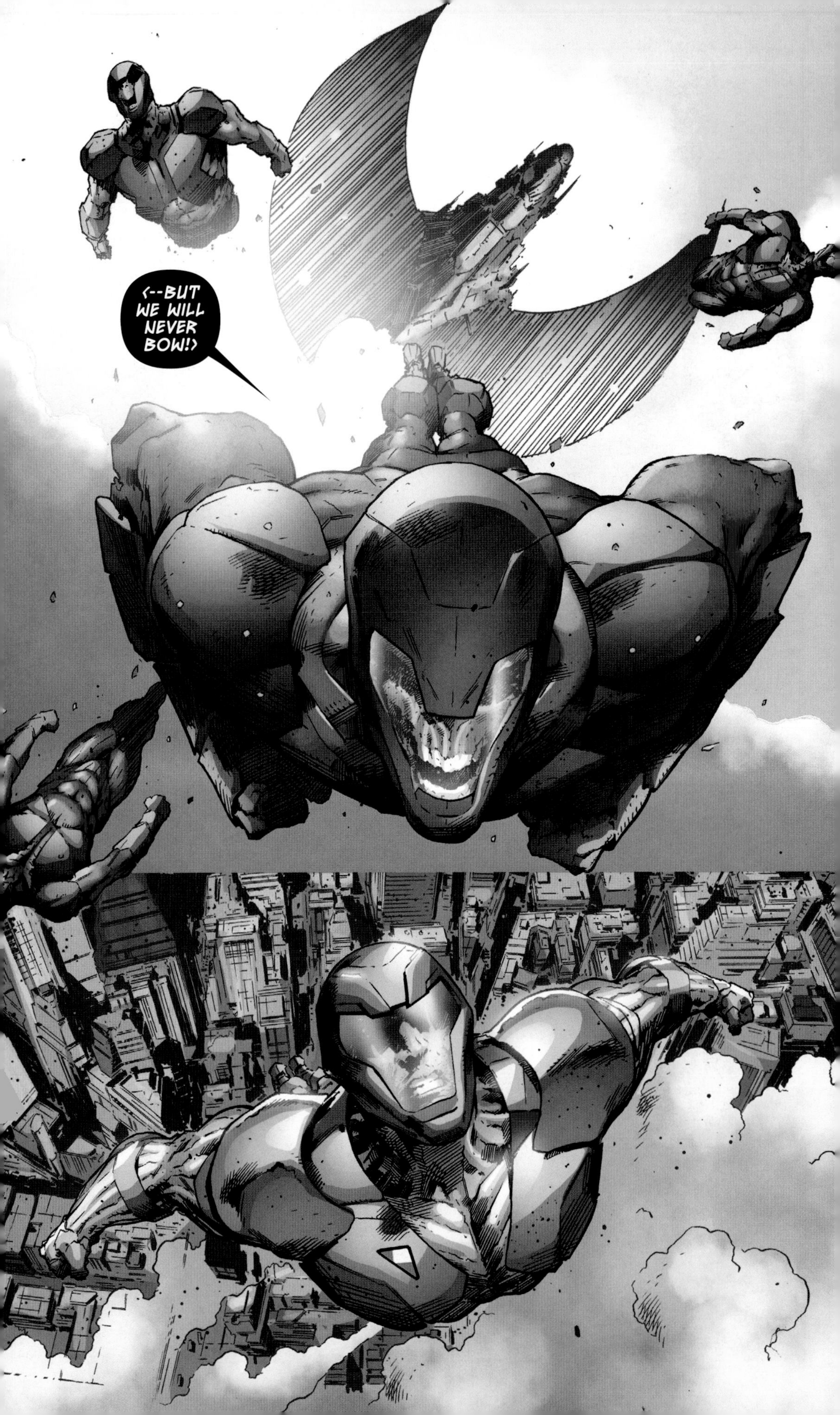
<--BUT WE WILL NEVER BOW!>

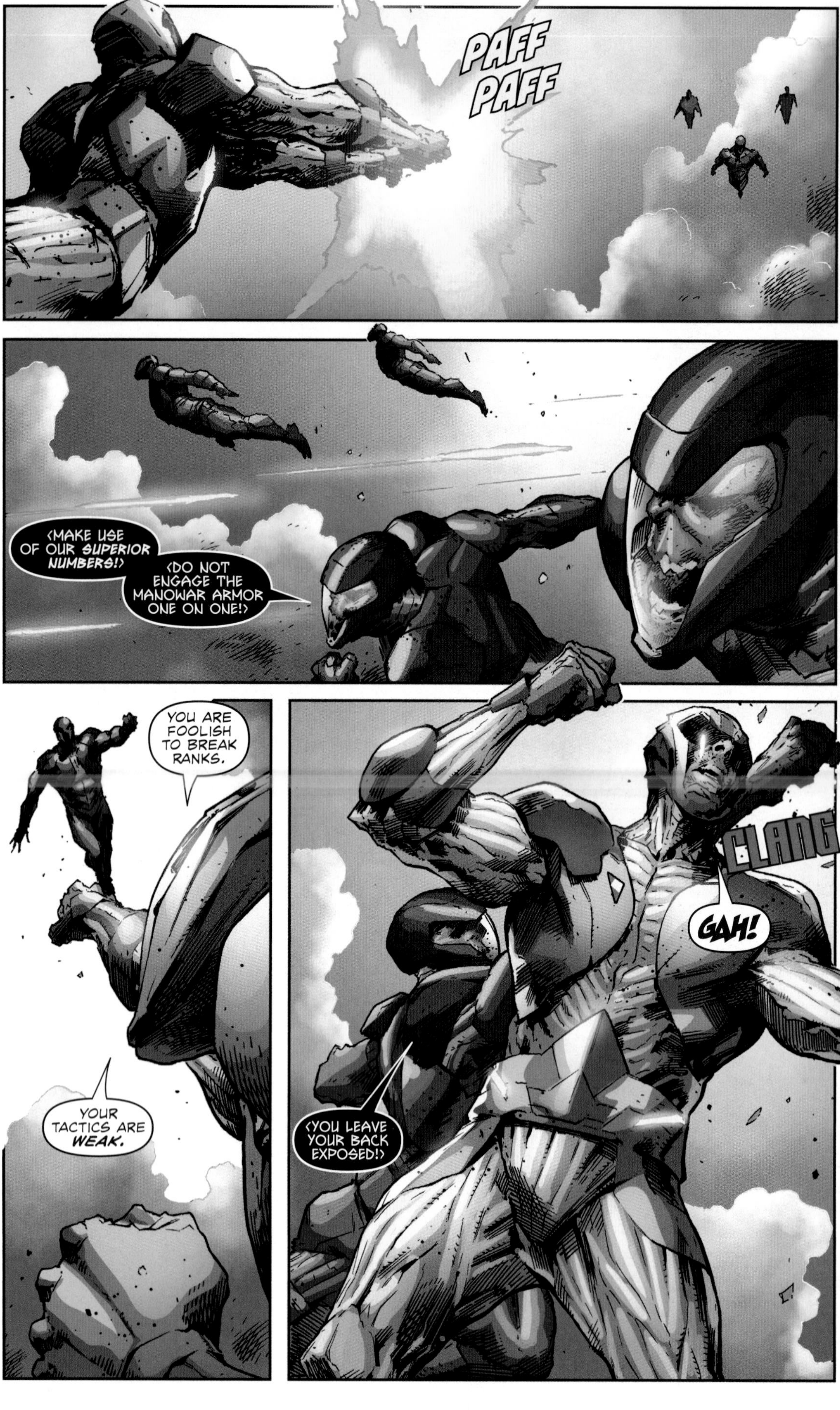
PAFF PAFF
<MAKE USE OF OUR SUPERIOR NUMBERS!>
<DO NOT ENGAGE THE MANOWAR ARMOR ONE ON ONE!>
YOU ARE FOOLISH TO BREAK RANKS.
YOUR TACTICS ARE WEAK.
CLANG
GAH!
<YOU LEAVE YOUR BACK EXPOSED!>

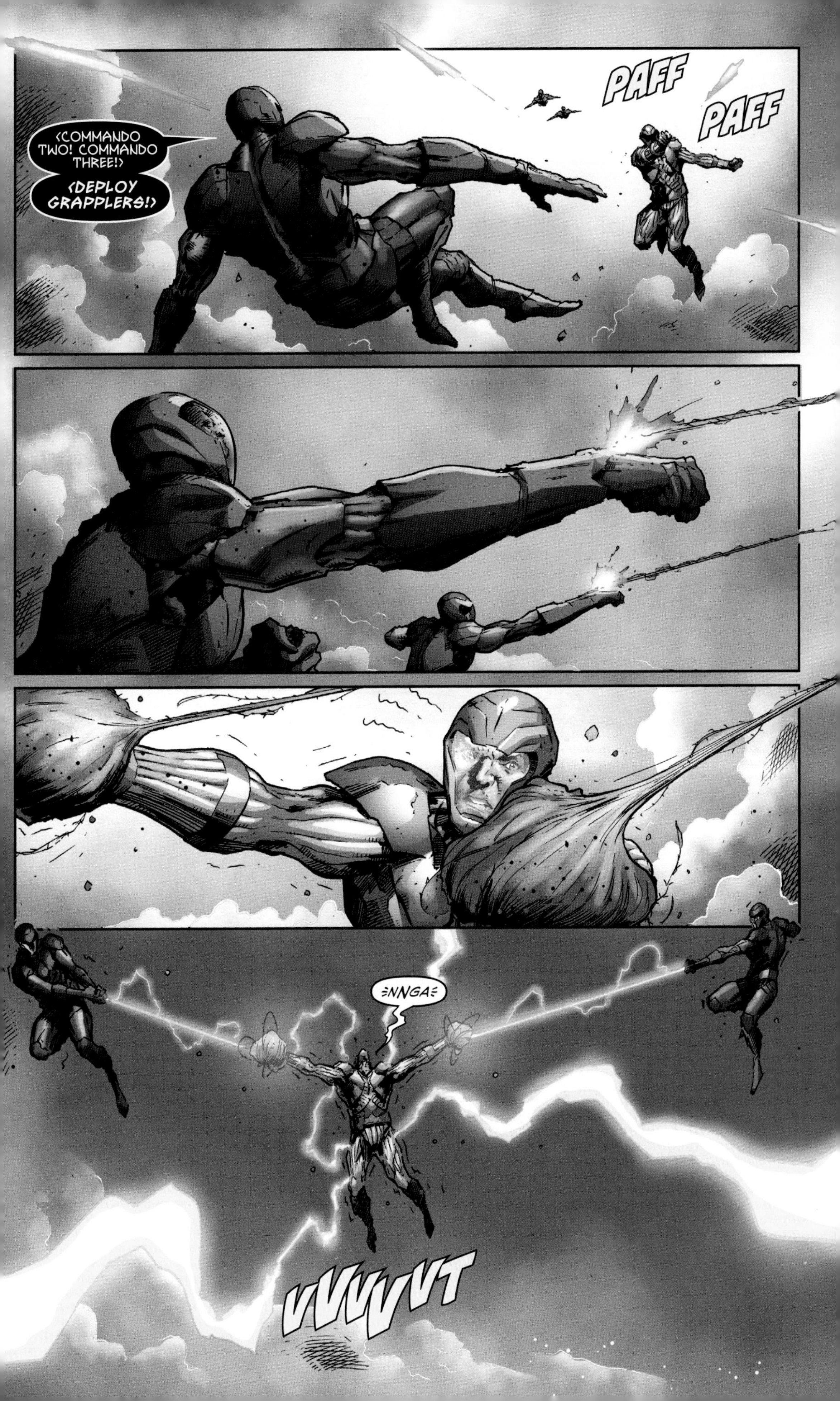

PAFF
PAFF
<COMMANDO TWO! COMMANDO THREE!>
<DEPLOY GRAPPLERS!>
NNGA
VVVVVT

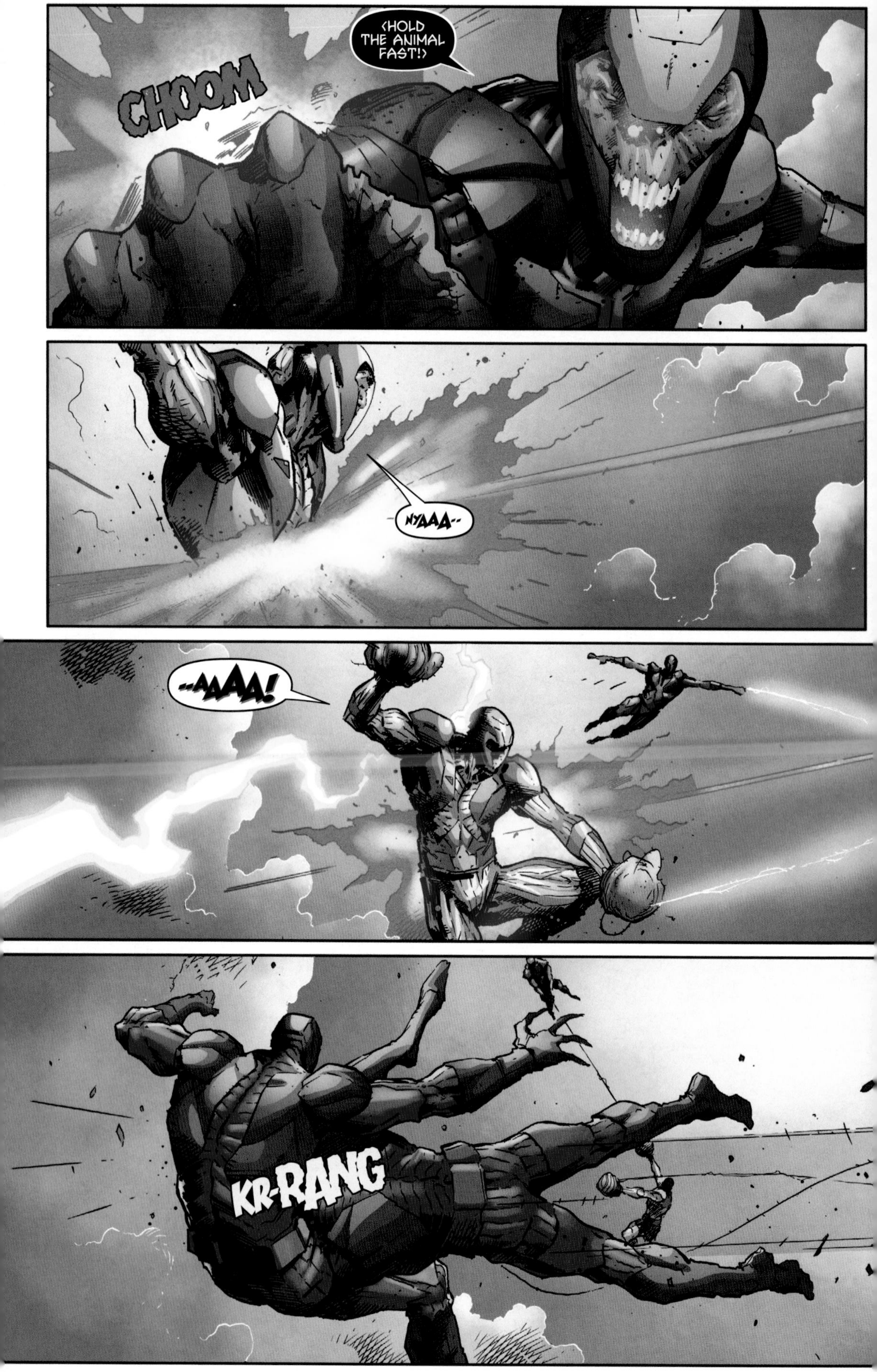
<HOLD THE ANIMAL FAST!>
CHOOM
NYAAA--
--AAAA!
KR-RANG

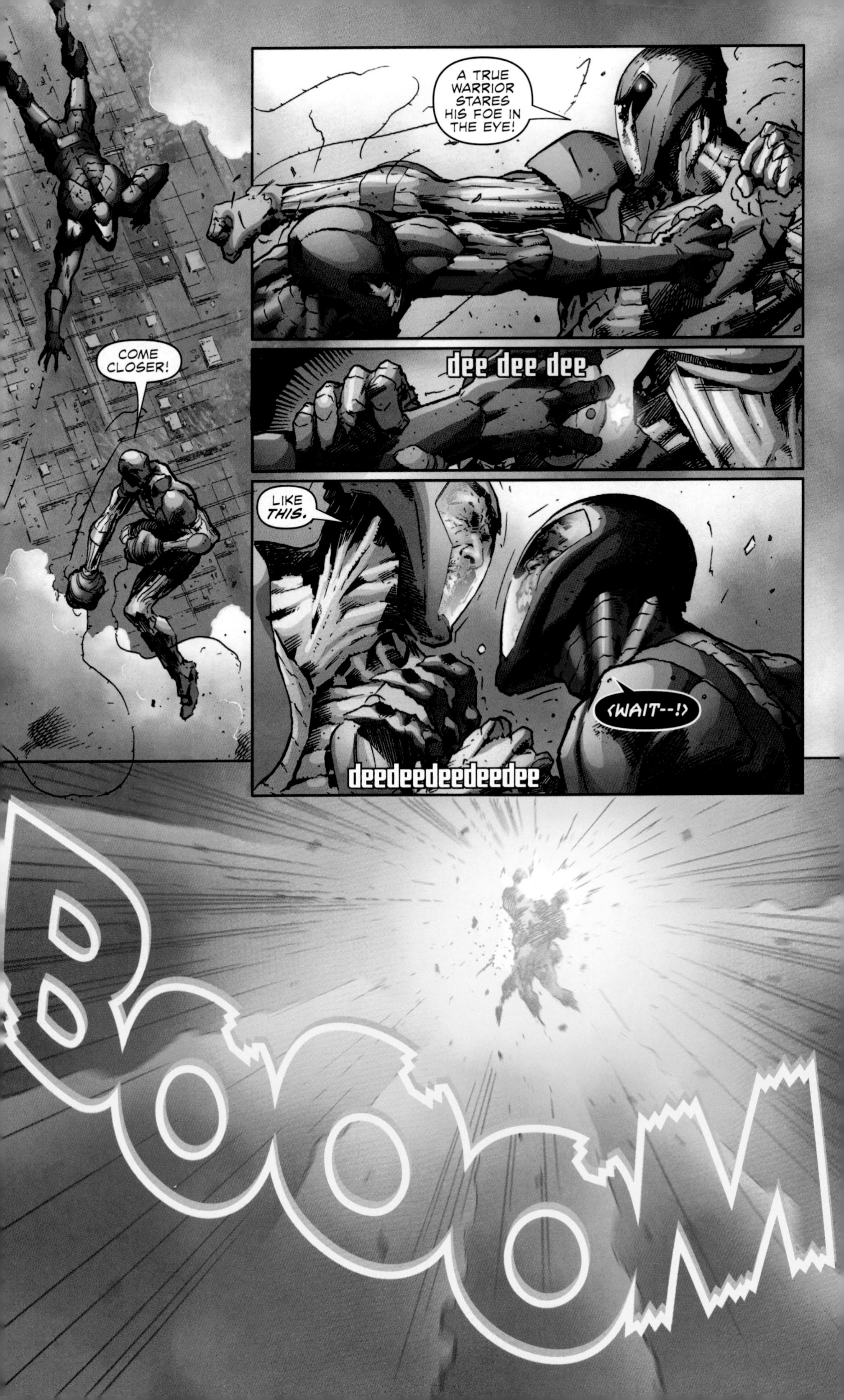
COME CLOSER!
A TRUE WARRIOR STARES HIS FOE IN THE EYE!
dee dee dee
LIKE THIS.
‹WAIT--!›
deedeedeedeedee
BOOOOM

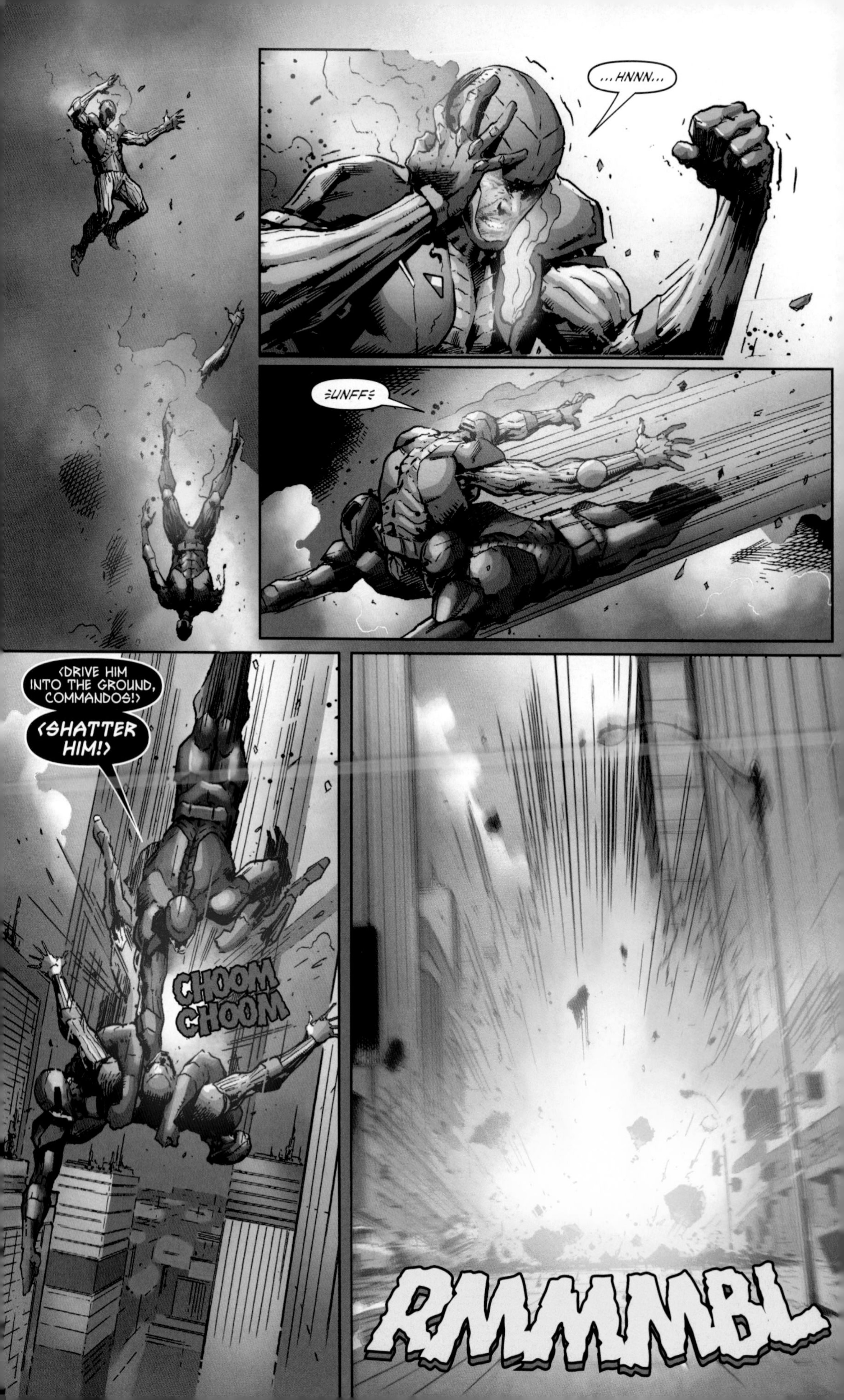
...HNNN...
UNFF
‹DRIVE HIM INTO THE GROUND, COMMANDOS!›
‹SHATTER HIM!›
CHOOM CHOOM
RMMMBL

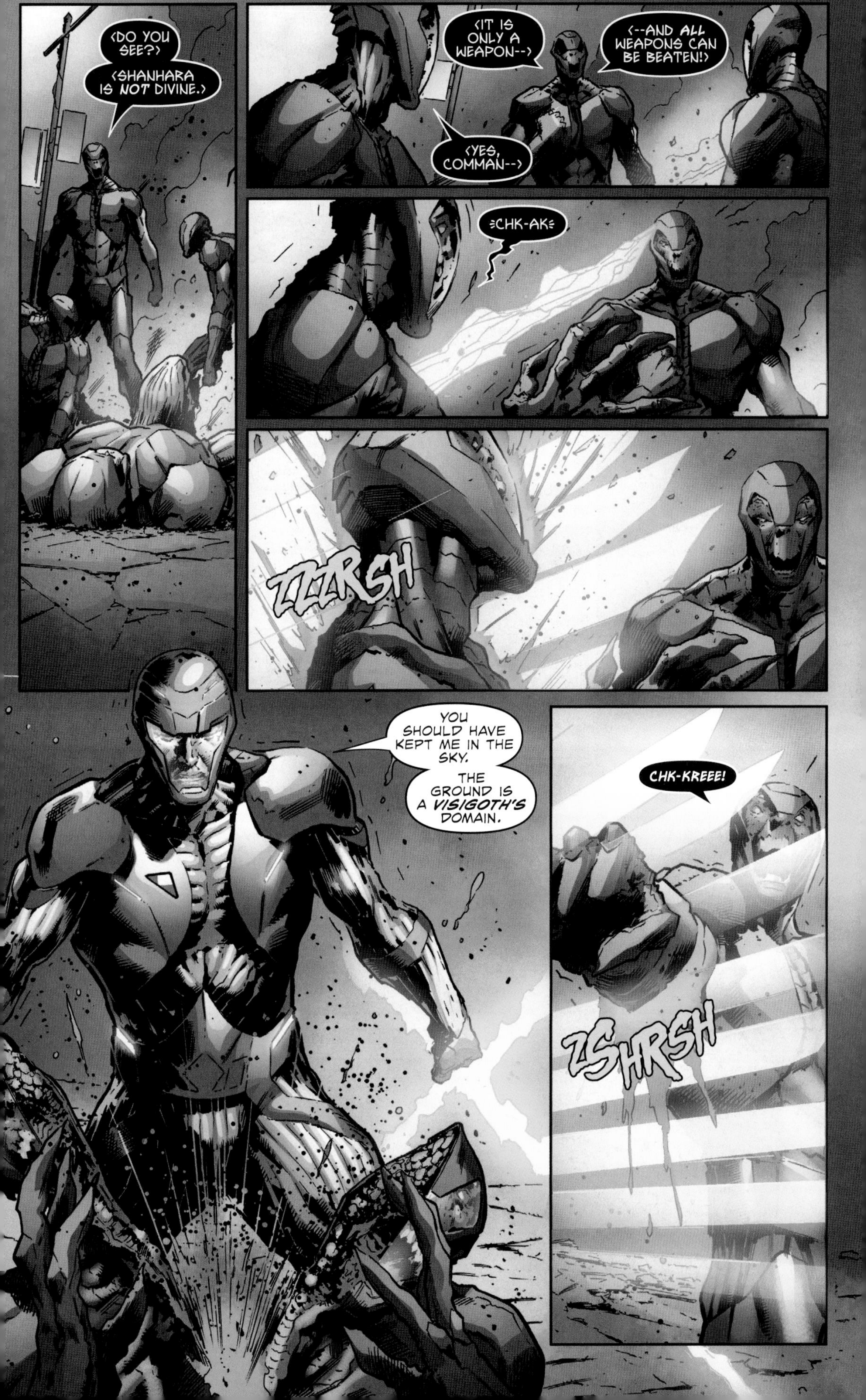

<DO YOU SEE?>
<SHANHARA IS *NOT* DIVINE.>
<IT IS ONLY A WEAPON-->
<YES, COMMAN-->
<--AND *ALL* WEAPONS CAN BE BEATEN!>
=CHK-AK=
ZZZRSH
YOU SHOULD HAVE KEPT ME IN THE SKY.
THE GROUND IS A *VISIGOTH'S* DOMAIN.
CHK-KREEE!
ZSHRSH

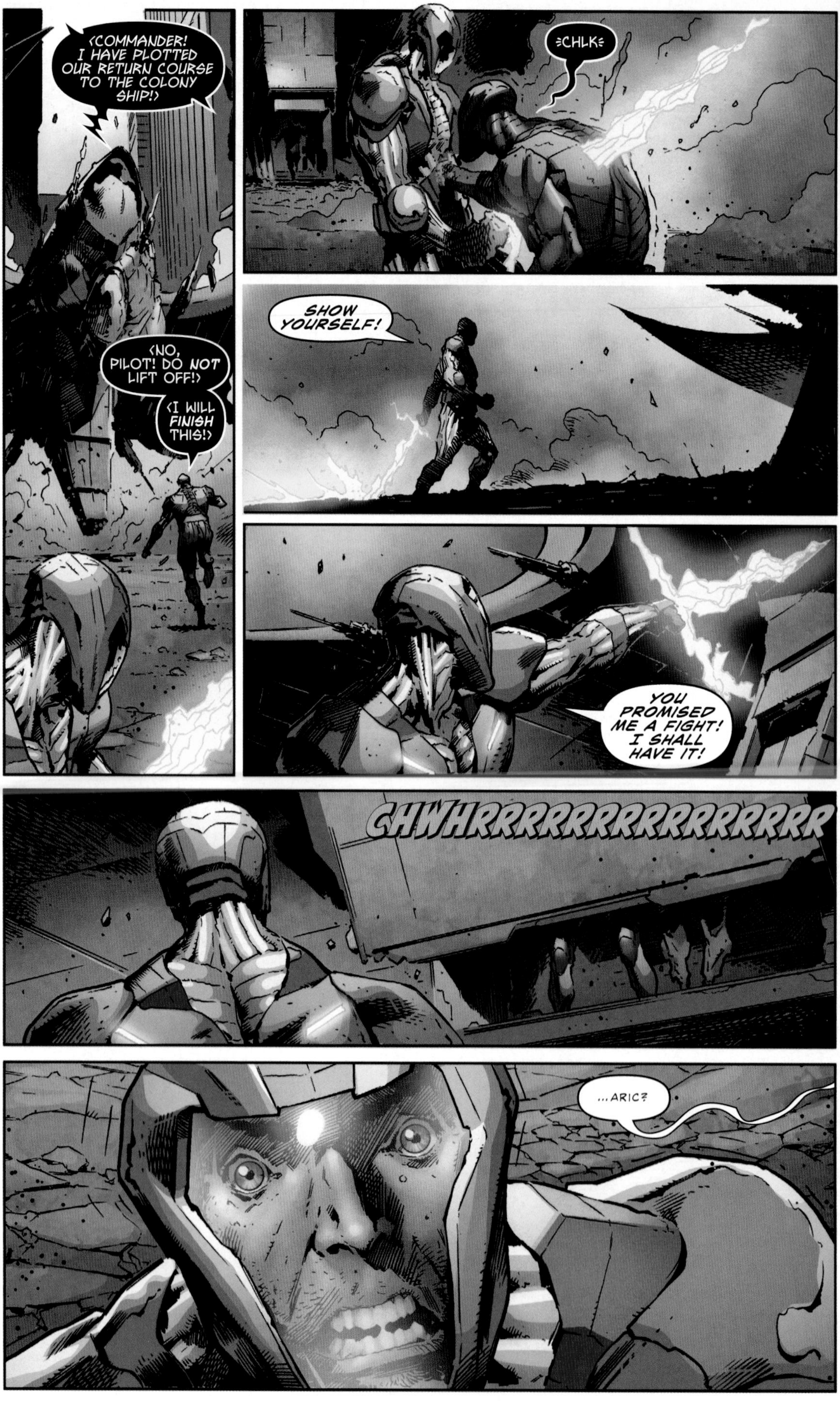
‹COMMANDER! I HAVE PLOTTED OUR RETURN COURSE TO THE COLONY SHIP!›
CHLK
SHOW YOURSELF!
‹NO, PILOT! DO NOT LIFT OFF!›
‹I WILL FINISH THIS!›
YOU PROMISED ME A FIGHT! I SHALL HAVE IT!
CHWHRRRRRRRRRRRRRRRR
...ARIC?

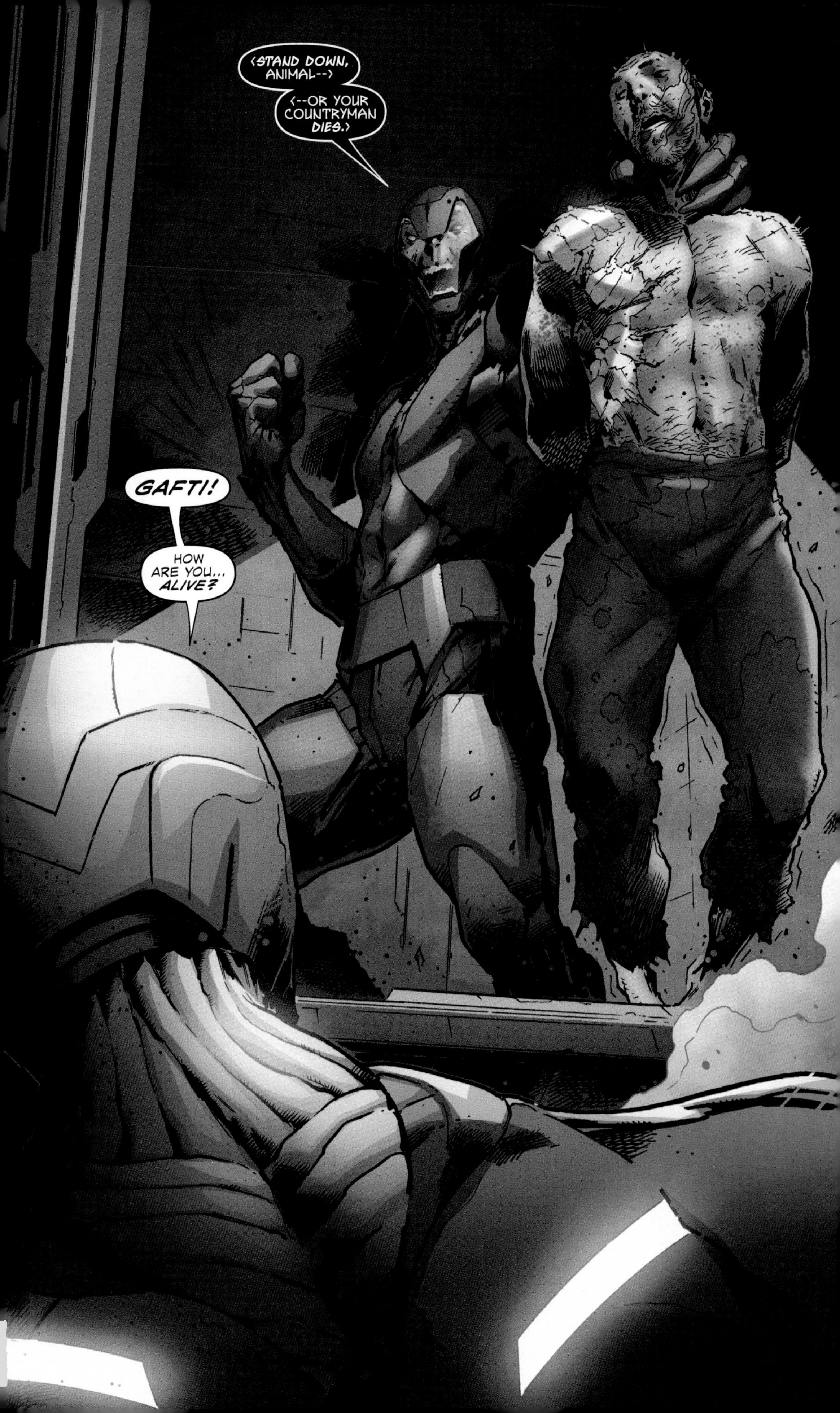
<STAND DOWN, ANIMAL-->
<--OR YOUR COUNTRYMAN DIES.>
GAFTI!
HOW ARE YOU... ALIVE?

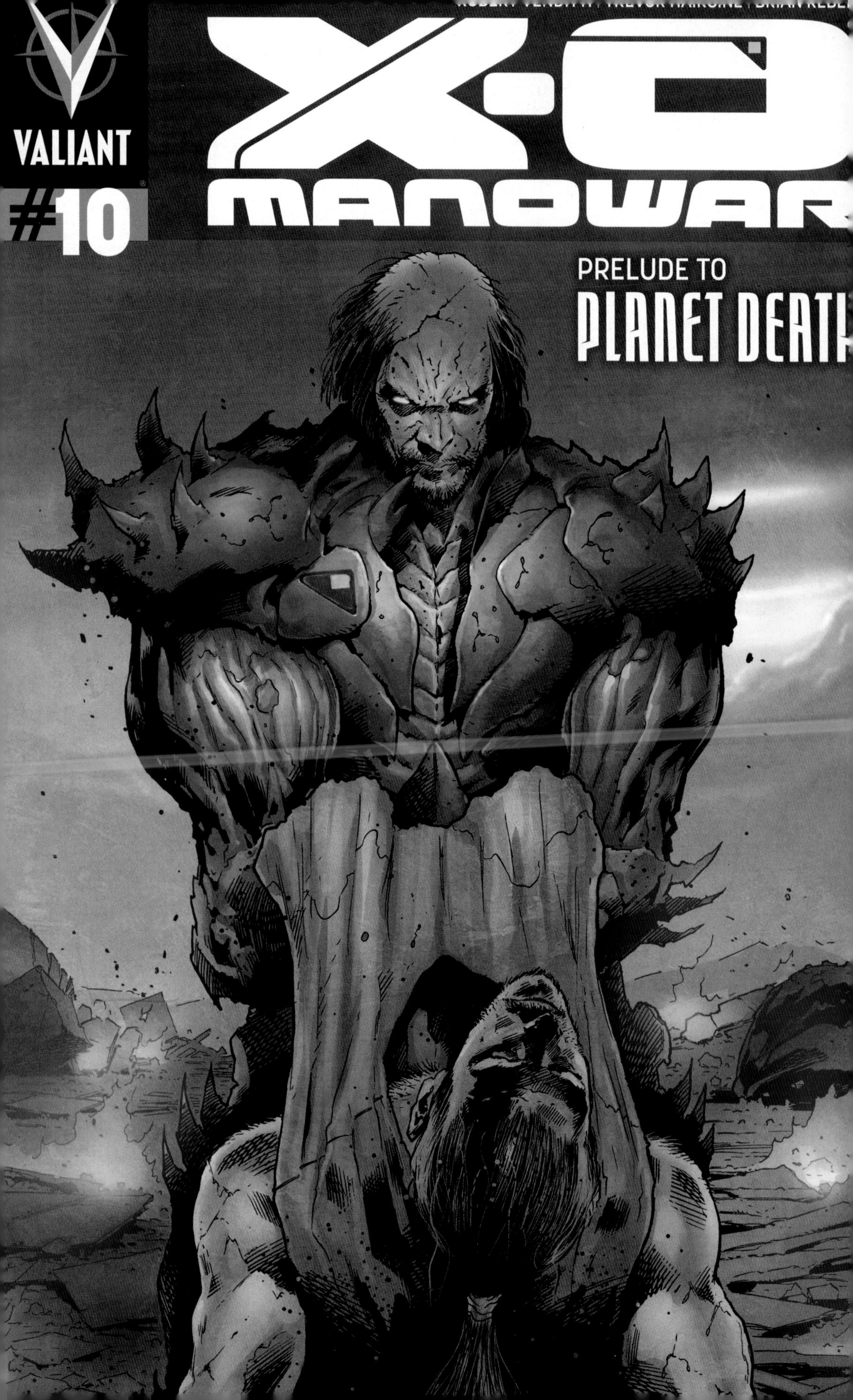
VALIANT
X-O MANOWAR
#10
PRELUDE TO
PLANET DEATH

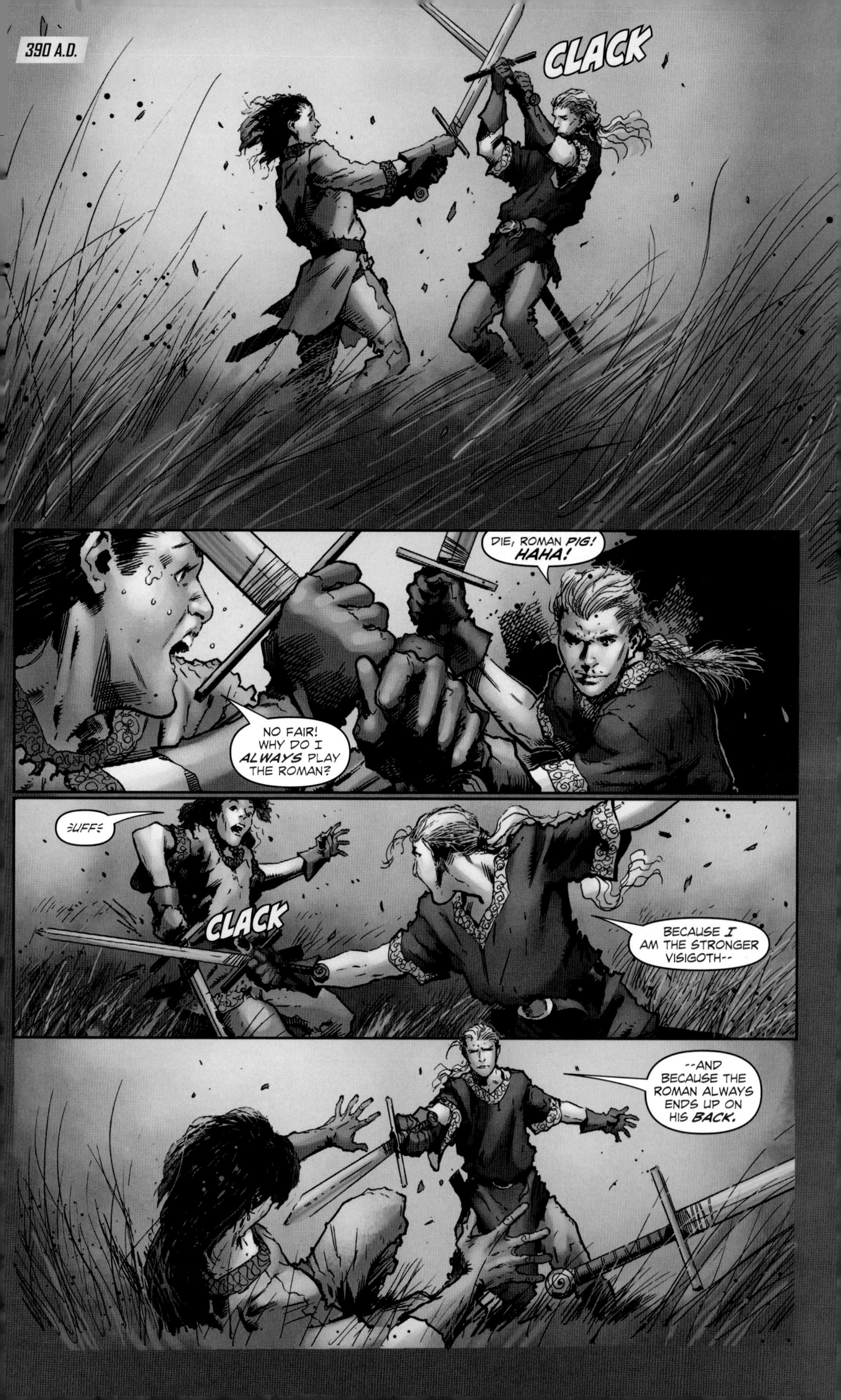
390 A.D.
CLACK
DIE, ROMAN PIG! HAHA!
NO FAIR! WHY DO I ALWAYS PLAY THE ROMAN?
UFF
CLACK
BECAUSE I AM THE STRONGER VISIGOTH--
--AND BECAUSE THE ROMAN ALWAYS ENDS UP ON HIS BACK.

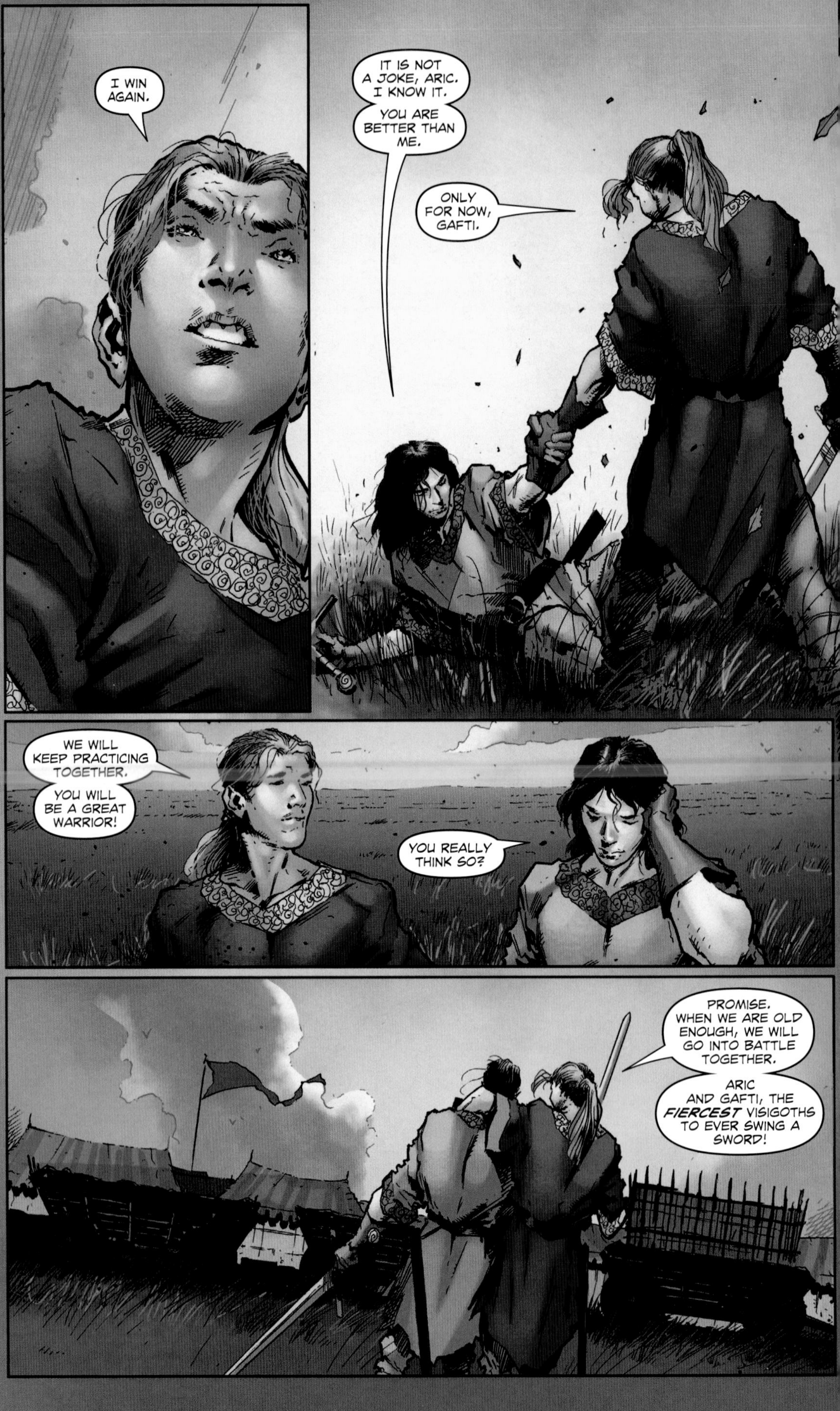
I WIN AGAIN.
IT IS NOT A JOKE, ARIC. I KNOW IT.
YOU ARE BETTER THAN ME.
ONLY FOR NOW, GAFTI.
WE WILL KEEP PRACTICING TOGETHER.
YOU WILL BE A GREAT WARRIOR!
YOU REALLY THINK SO?
PROMISE. WHEN WE ARE OLD ENOUGH, WE WILL GO INTO BATTLE TOGETHER.
ARIC AND GAFTI, THE *FIERCEST* VISIGOTHS TO EVER SWING A SWORD!

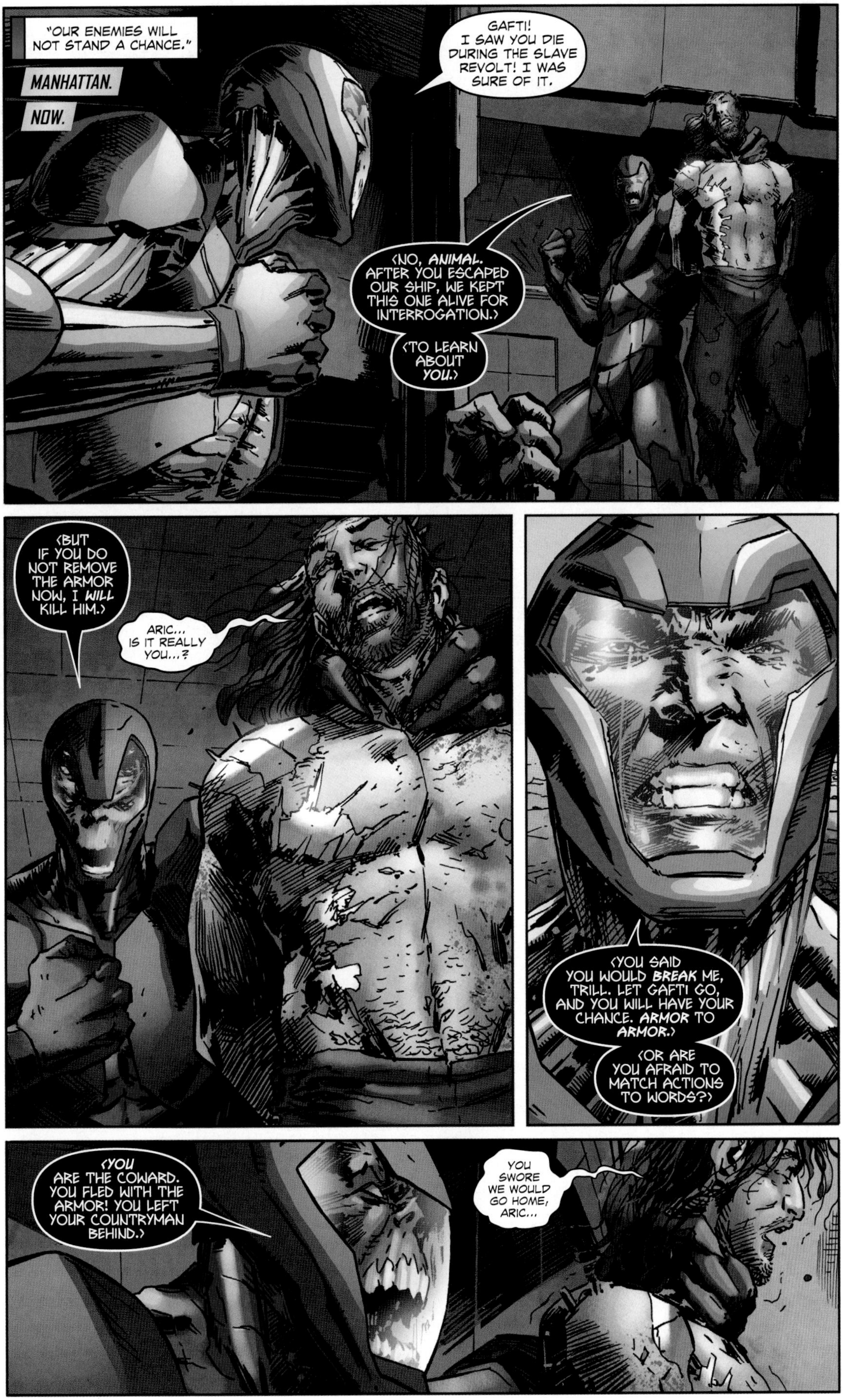
"OUR ENEMIES WILL NOT STAND A CHANCE."
MANHATTAN.
NOW.
GAFTI! I SAW YOU DIE DURING THE SLAVE REVOLT! I WAS SURE OF IT.
‹NO, ANIMAL. AFTER YOU ESCAPED OUR SHIP, WE KEPT THIS ONE ALIVE FOR INTERROGATION.›
‹TO LEARN ABOUT YOU.›
‹BUT IF YOU DO NOT REMOVE THE ARMOR NOW, I WILL KILL HIM.›
ARIC... IS IT REALLY YOU...?
‹YOU SAID YOU WOULD BREAK ME, TRILL. LET GAFTI GO, AND YOU WILL HAVE YOUR CHANCE. ARMOR TO ARMOR.›
‹OR ARE YOU AFRAID TO MATCH ACTIONS TO WORDS?›
‹YOU ARE THE COWARD. YOU FLED WITH THE ARMOR! YOU LEFT YOUR COUNTRYMAN BEHIND.›
YOU SWORE WE WOULD GO HOME, ARIC...

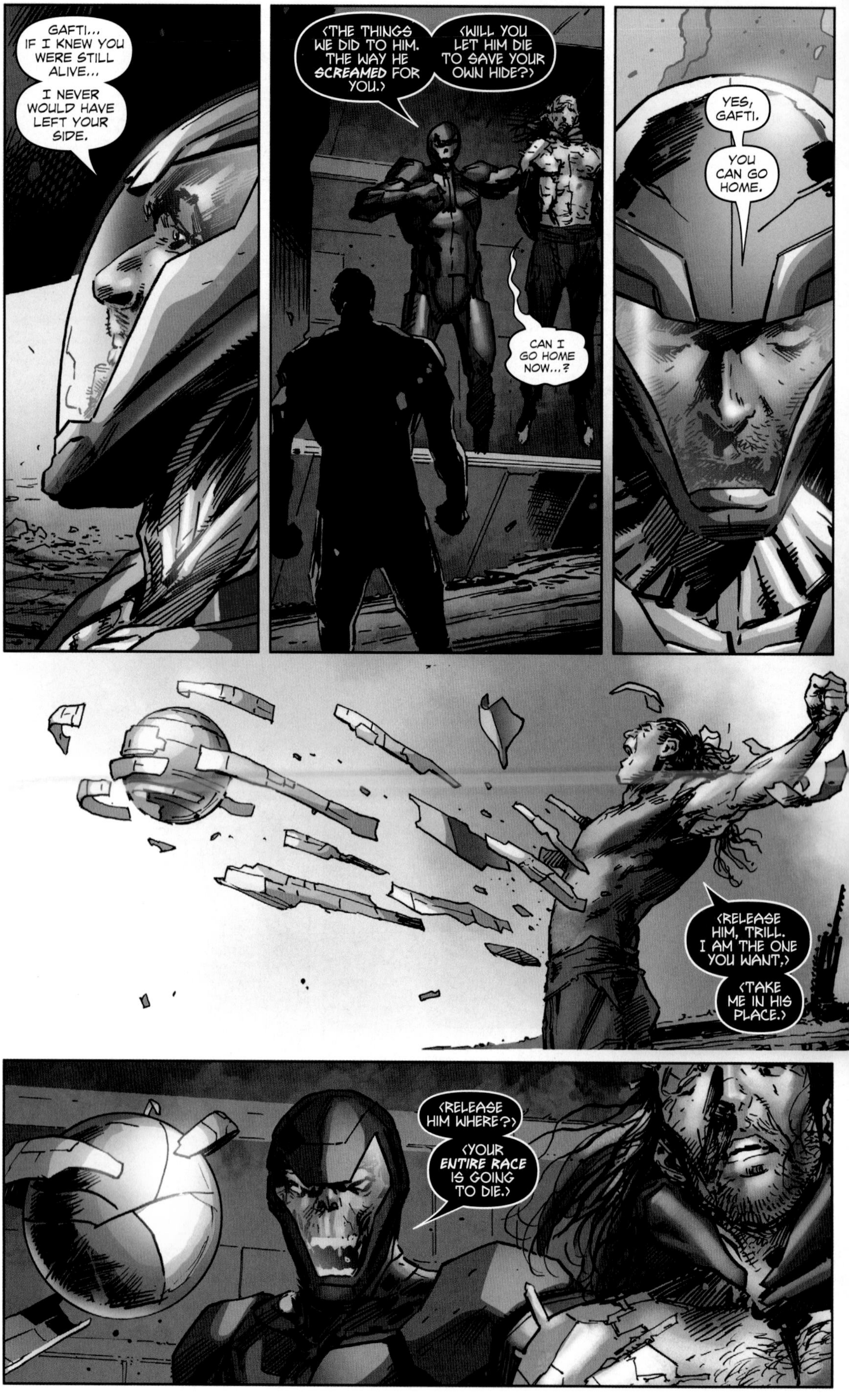

GAFTI... IF I KNEW YOU WERE STILL ALIVE...
I NEVER WOULD HAVE LEFT YOUR SIDE.
<THE THINGS WE DID TO HIM. THE WAY HE SCREAMED FOR YOU.>
<WILL YOU LET HIM DIE TO SAVE YOUR OWN HIDE?>
CAN I GO HOME NOW...?
YES, GAFTI.
YOU CAN GO HOME.
<RELEASE HIM, TRILL. I AM THE ONE YOU WANT.>
<TAKE ME IN HIS PLACE.>
<RELEASE HIM WHERE?>
<YOUR ENTIRE RACE IS GOING TO DIE.>

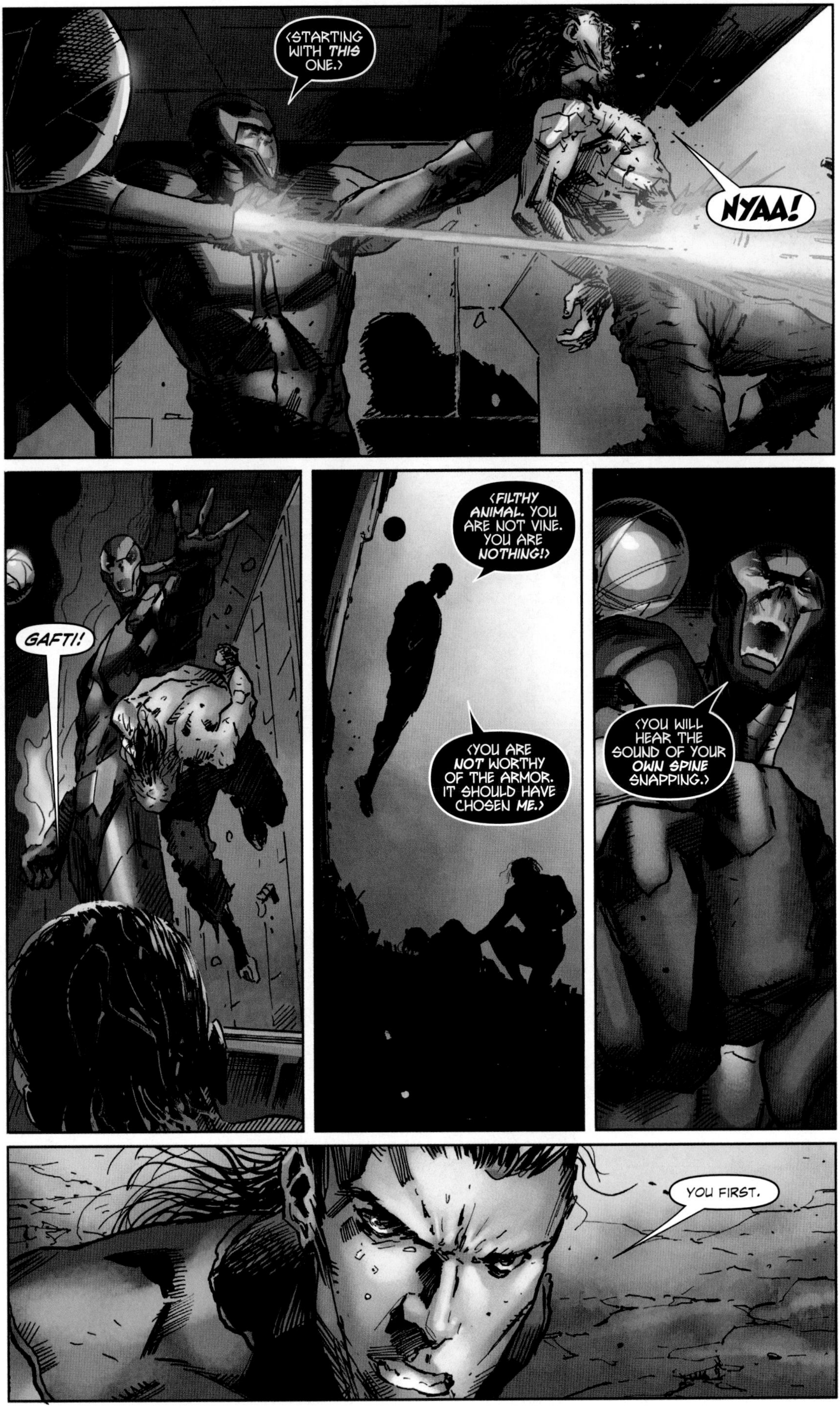

<STARTING WITH THIS ONE.>
NYAA!
GAFTI!
<FILTHY ANIMAL. YOU ARE NOT VINE. YOU ARE NOTHING!>
<YOU ARE NOT WORTHY OF THE ARMOR. IT SHOULD HAVE CHOSEN ME.>
<YOU WILL HEAR THE SOUND OF YOUR OWN SPINE SNAPPING.>
YOU FIRST.

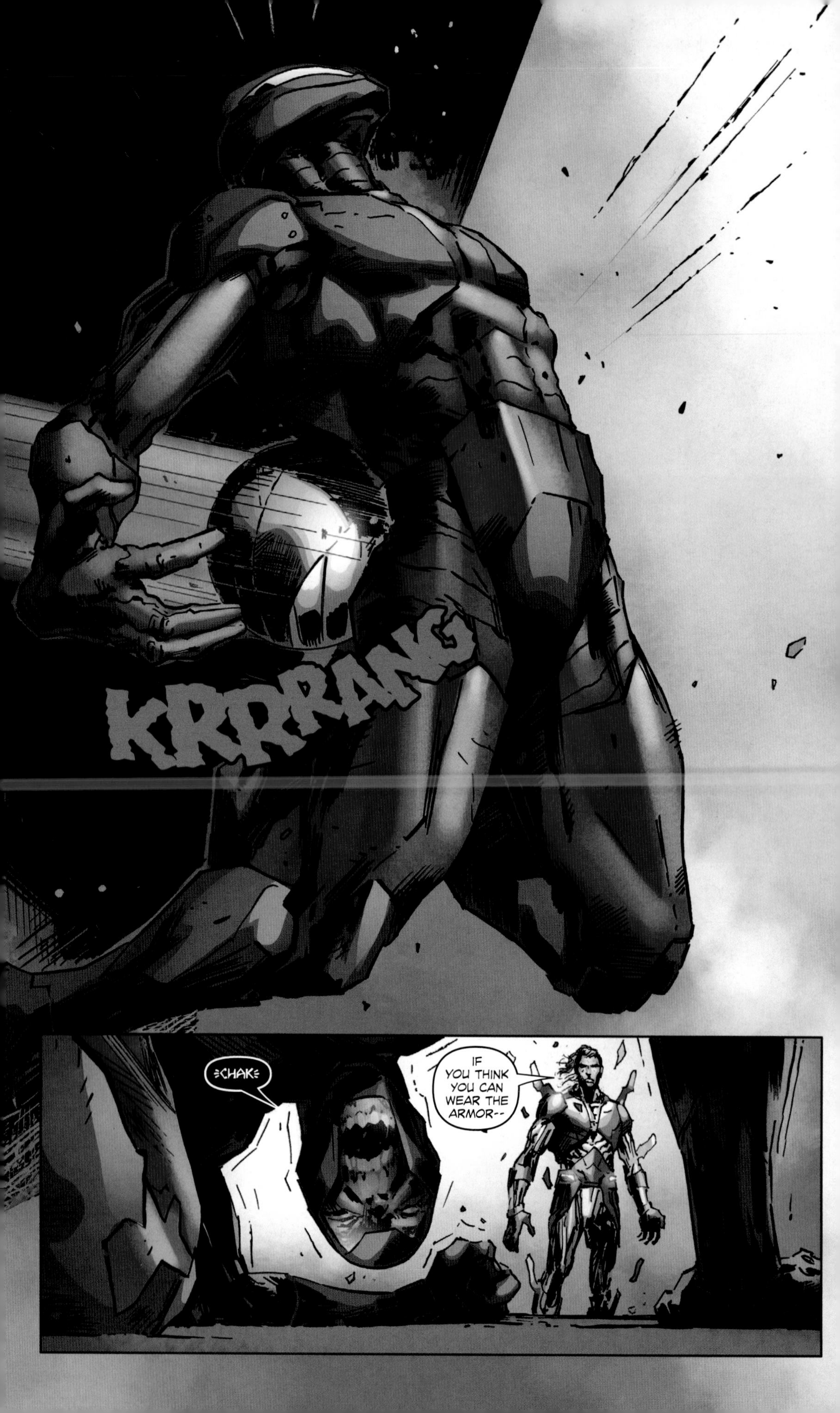
KRRRANG
CHAK
IF YOU THINK YOU CAN WEAR THE ARMOR--

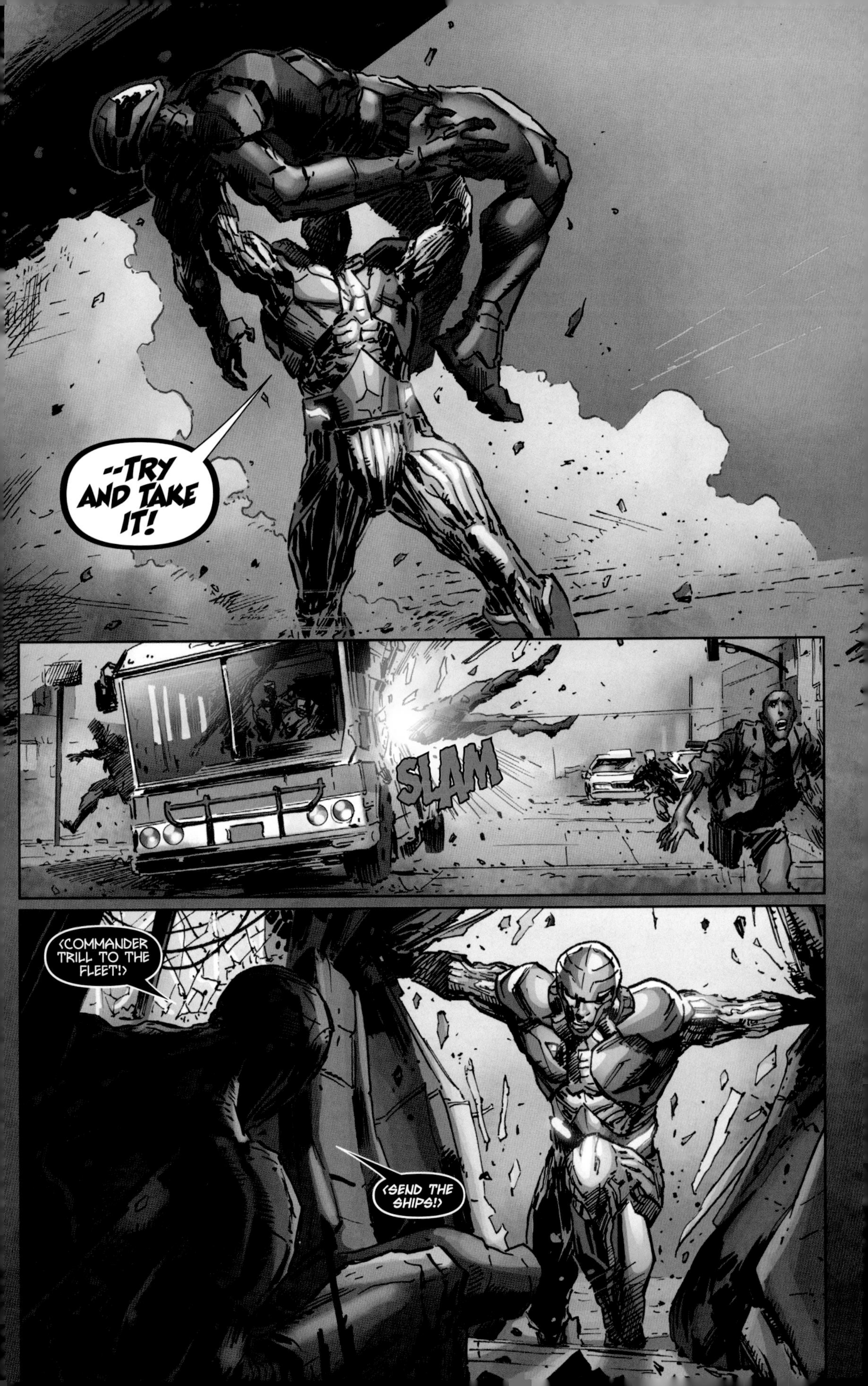
--TRY AND TAKE IT!
SLAM
‹COMMANDER TRILL TO THE FLEET!›
‹SEND THE SHIPS!›

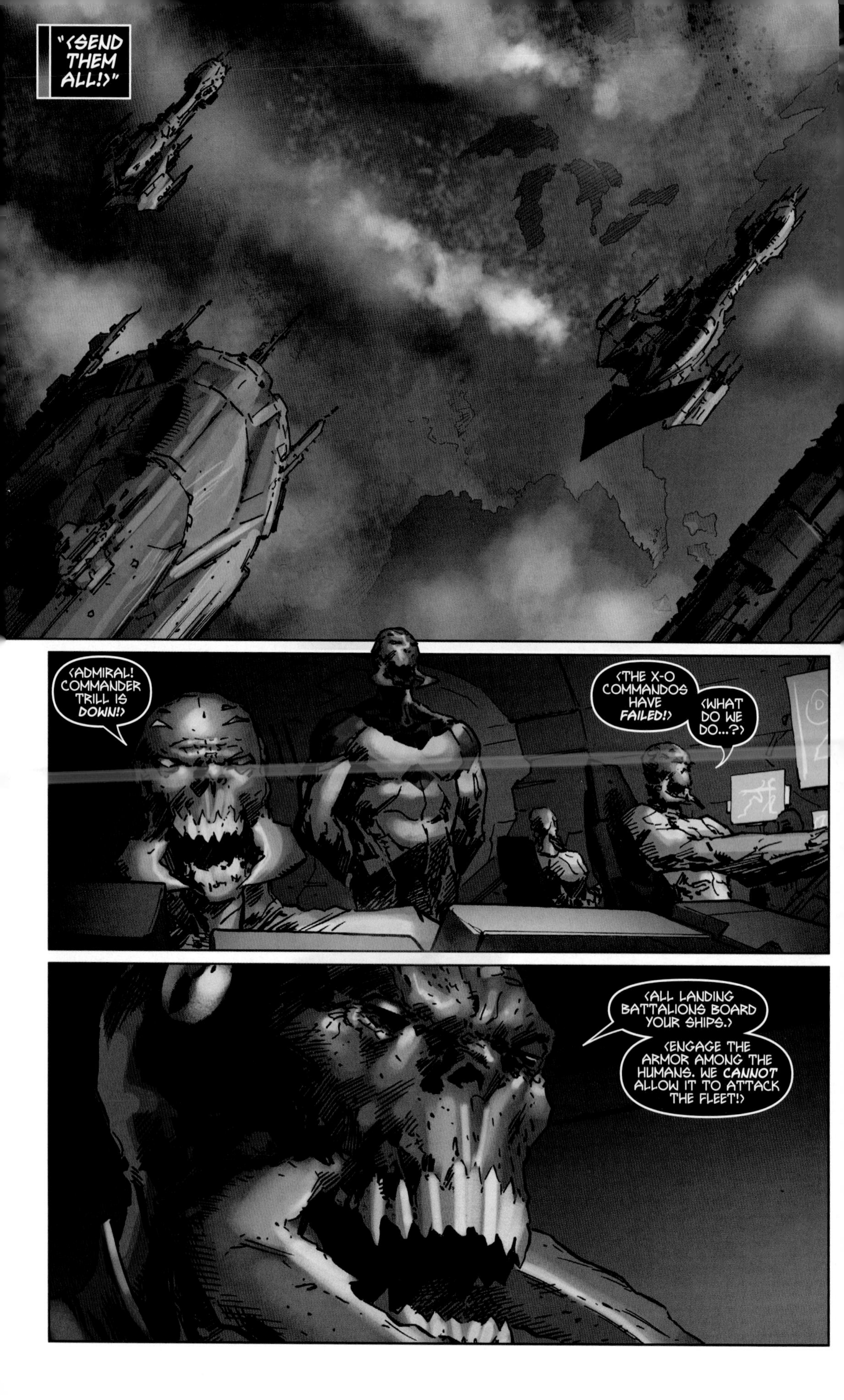
"<SEND THEM ALL!>"
<ADMIRAL! COMMANDER TRILL IS DOWN!>
<THE X-O COMMANDOS HAVE FAILED!>
<WHAT DO WE DO...?>
<ALL LANDING BATTALIONS BOARD YOUR SHIPS.>
<ENGAGE THE ARMOR AMONG THE HUMANS. WE CANNOT ALLOW IT TO ATTACK THE FLEET!>

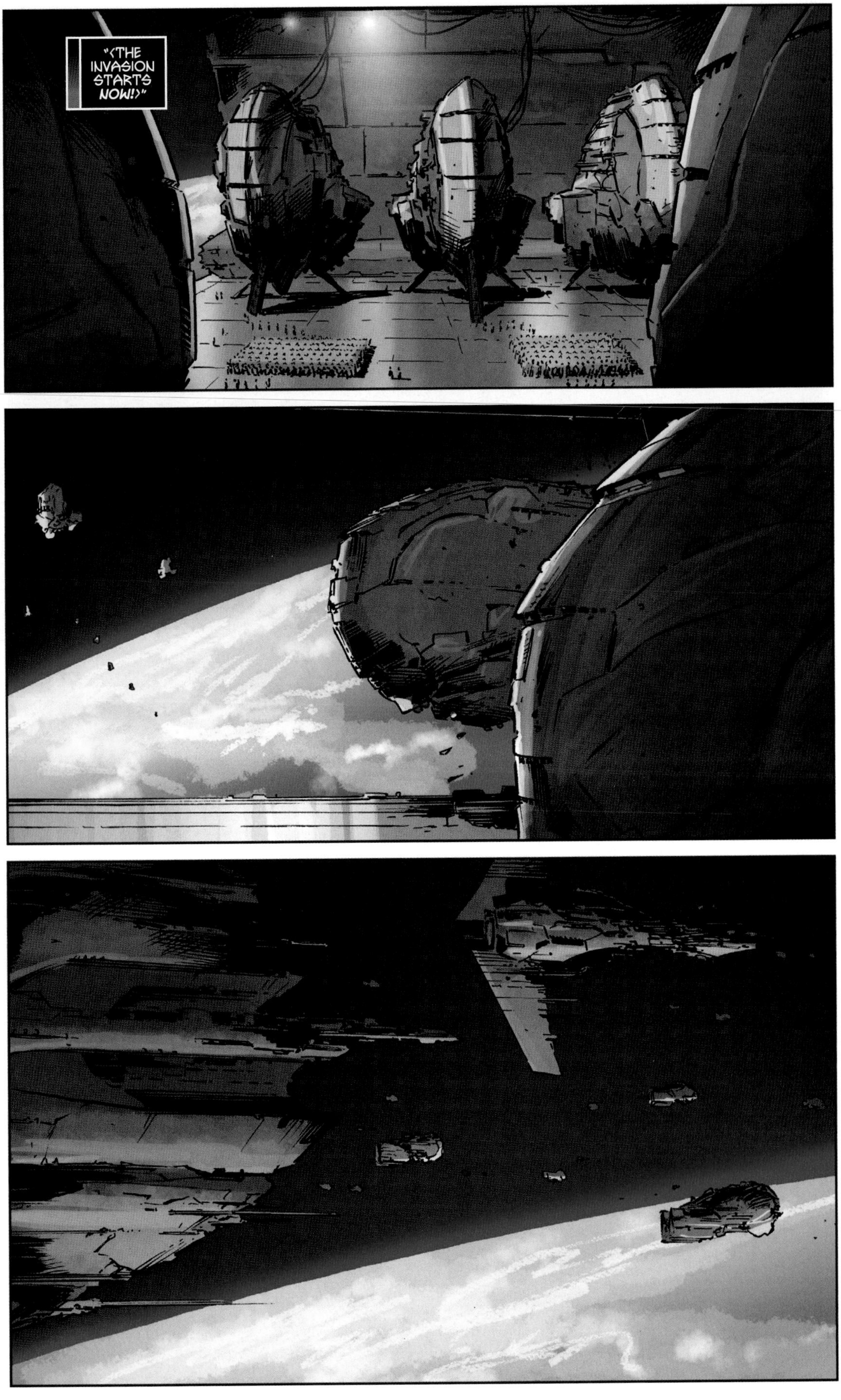
"‹THE INVASION STARTS NOW!›"

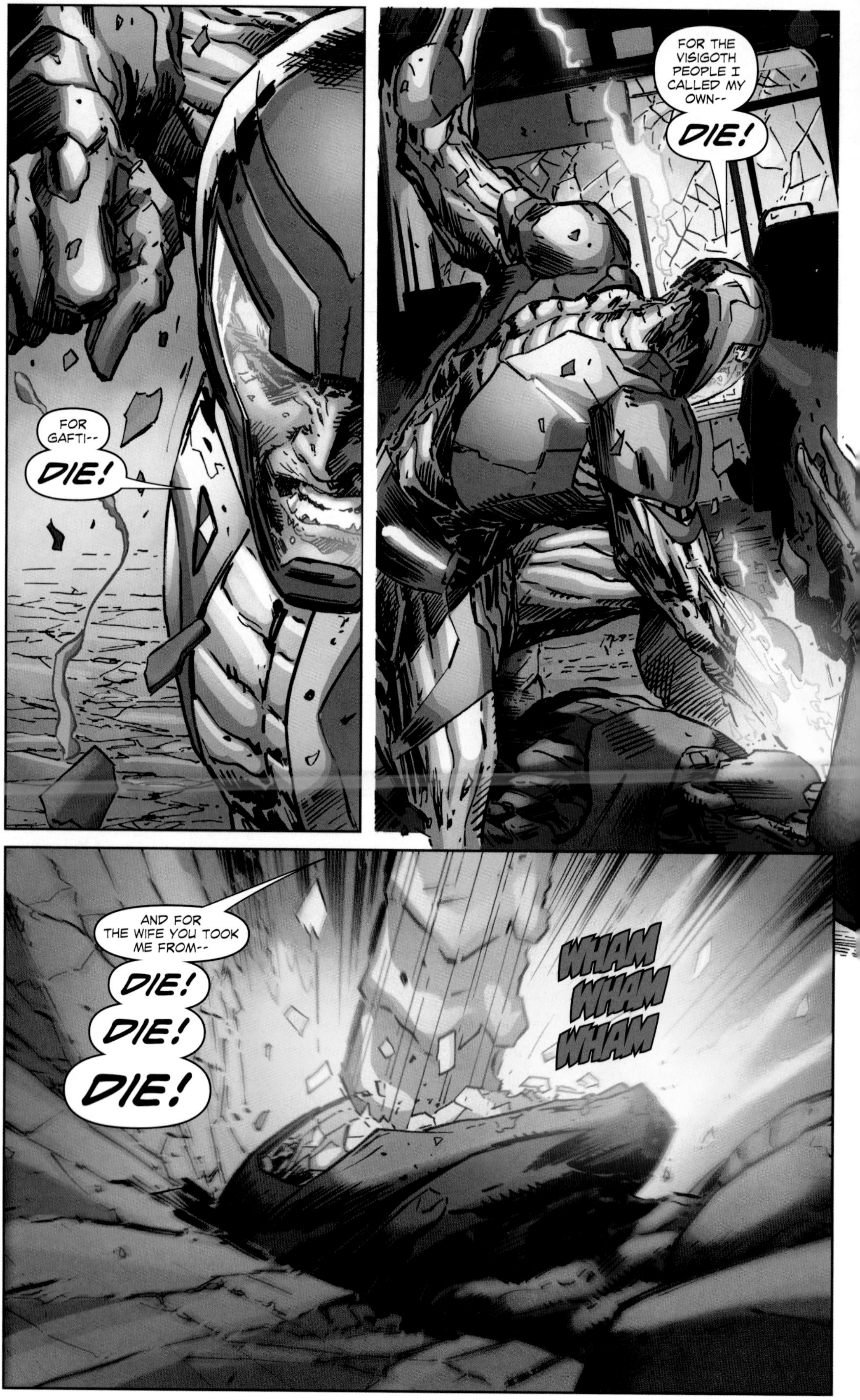
FOR GAFTI--
DIE!
FOR THE VISIGOTH PEOPLE I CALLED MY OWN--
DIE!
AND FOR THE WIFE YOU TOOK ME FROM--
DIE!
DIE!
DIE!
WHAM
WHAM
WHAM

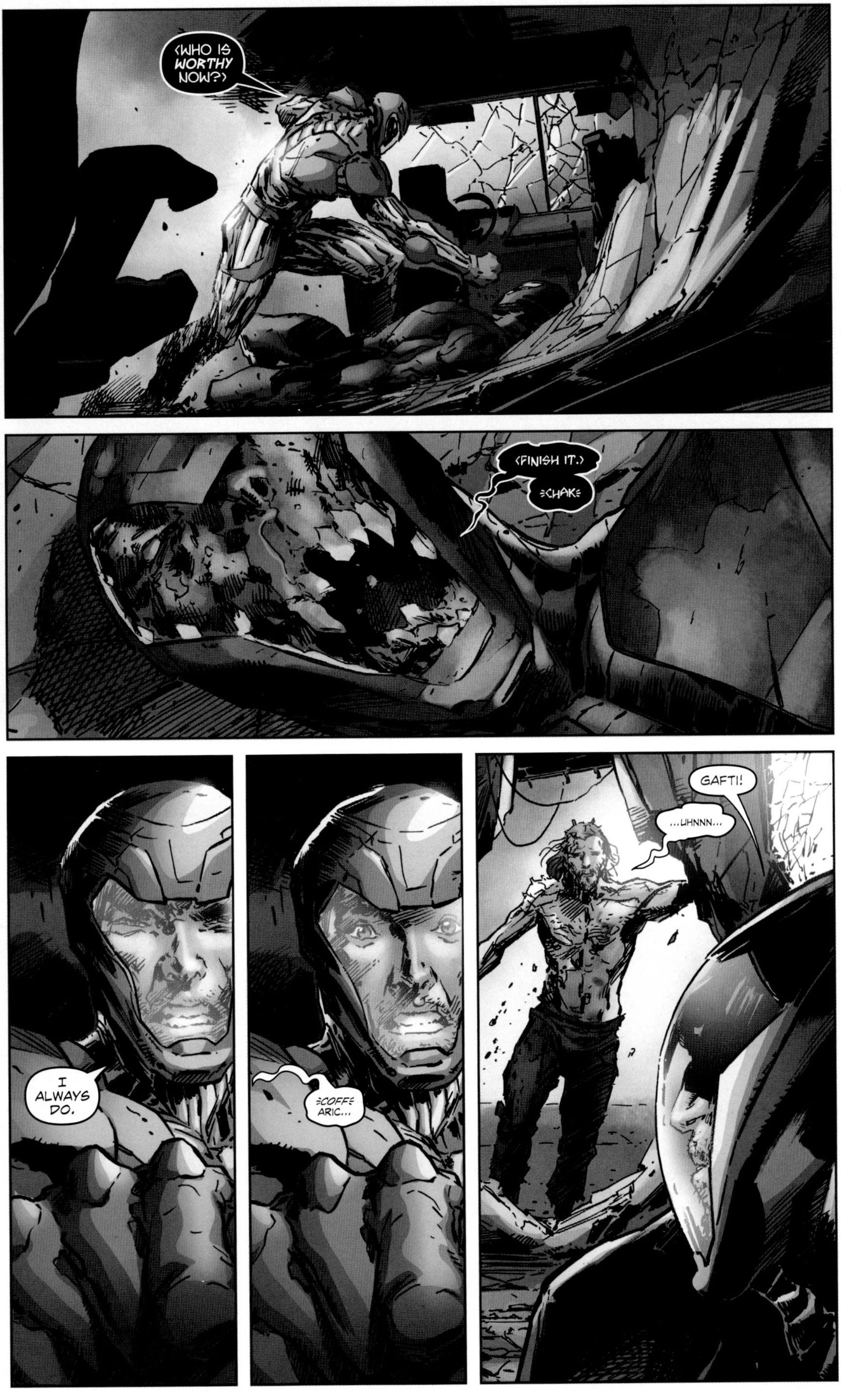
<WHO IS WORTHY NOW?>
<FINISH IT.>
CHAK
I ALWAYS DO.
COFF ARIC...
GAFTI!
...UHNNN...

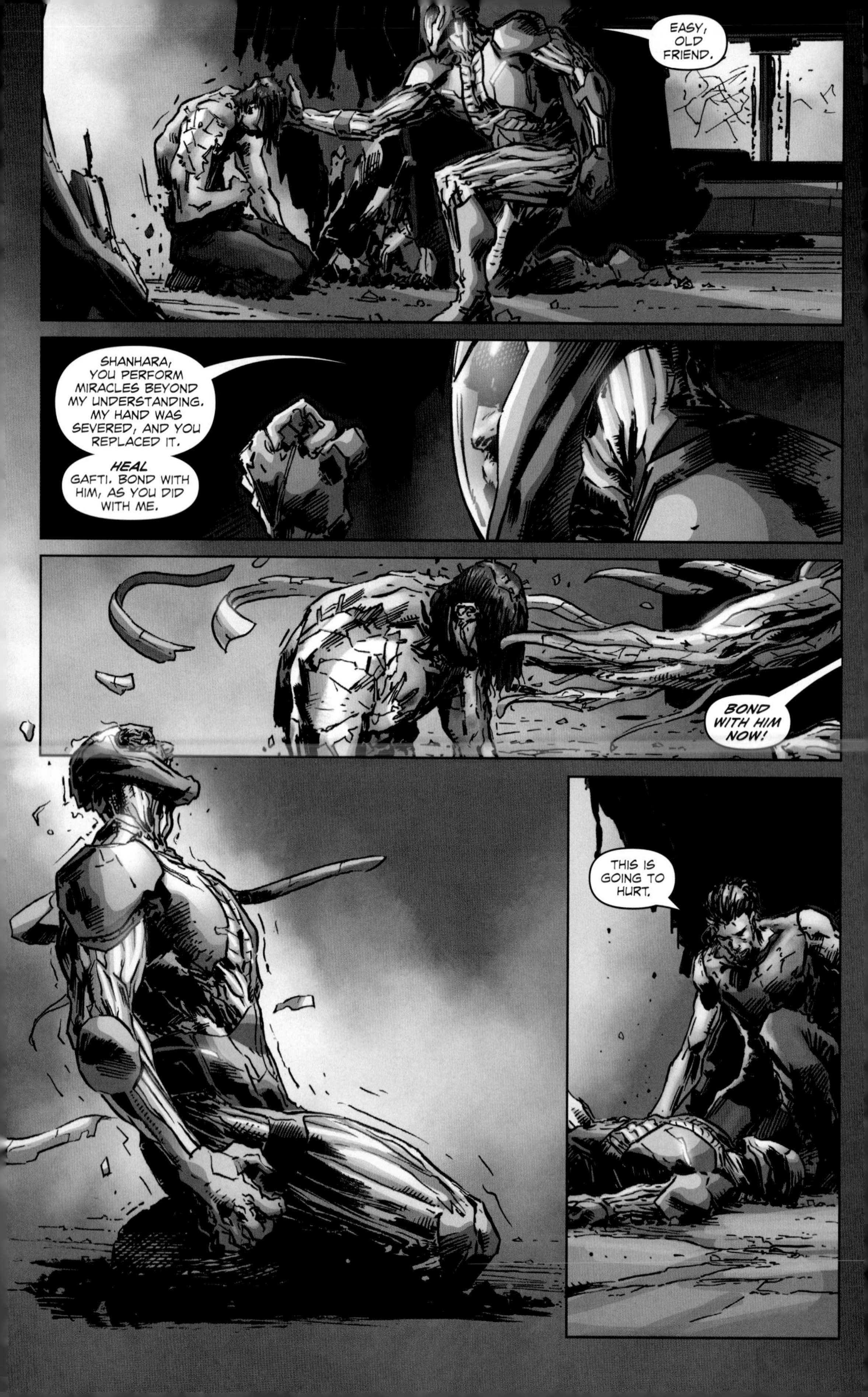
EASY, OLD FRIEND.
SHANHARA, YOU PERFORM MIRACLES BEYOND MY UNDERSTANDING. MY HAND WAS SEVERED, AND YOU REPLACED IT.
HEAL GAFTI. BOND WITH HIM, AS YOU DID WITH ME.
BOND WITH HIM NOW!
THIS IS GOING TO HURT.

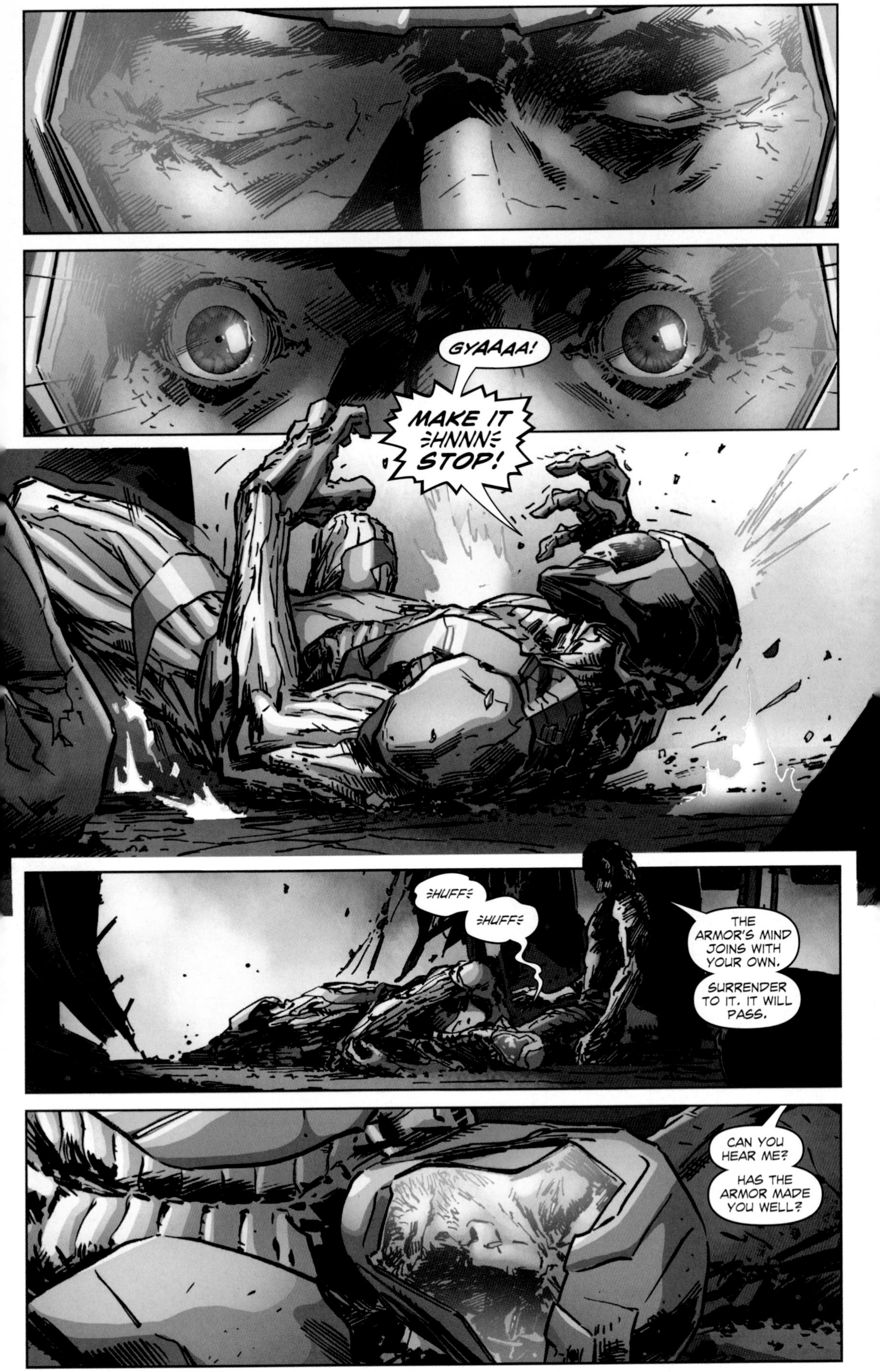
GYAAAA!
MAKE IT =HNNN= STOP!
=HUFF=
=HUFF=
THE ARMOR'S MIND JOINS WITH YOUR OWN.
SURRENDER TO IT. IT WILL PASS.
CAN YOU HEAR ME?
HAS THE ARMOR MADE YOU WELL?

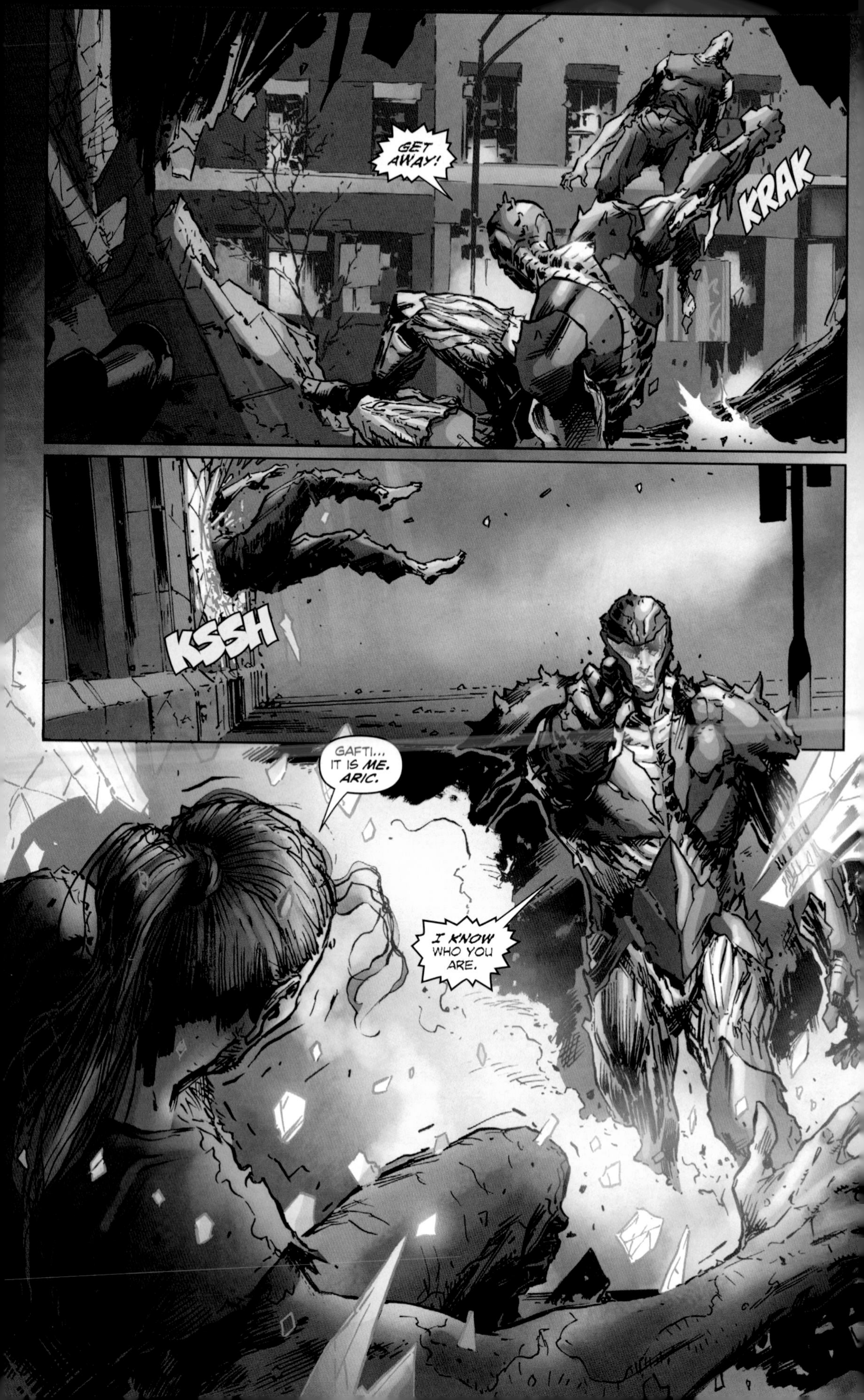
GET AWAY!
KRAK
KSSH
GAFTI... IT IS ME. ARIC.
I KNOW WHO YOU ARE.

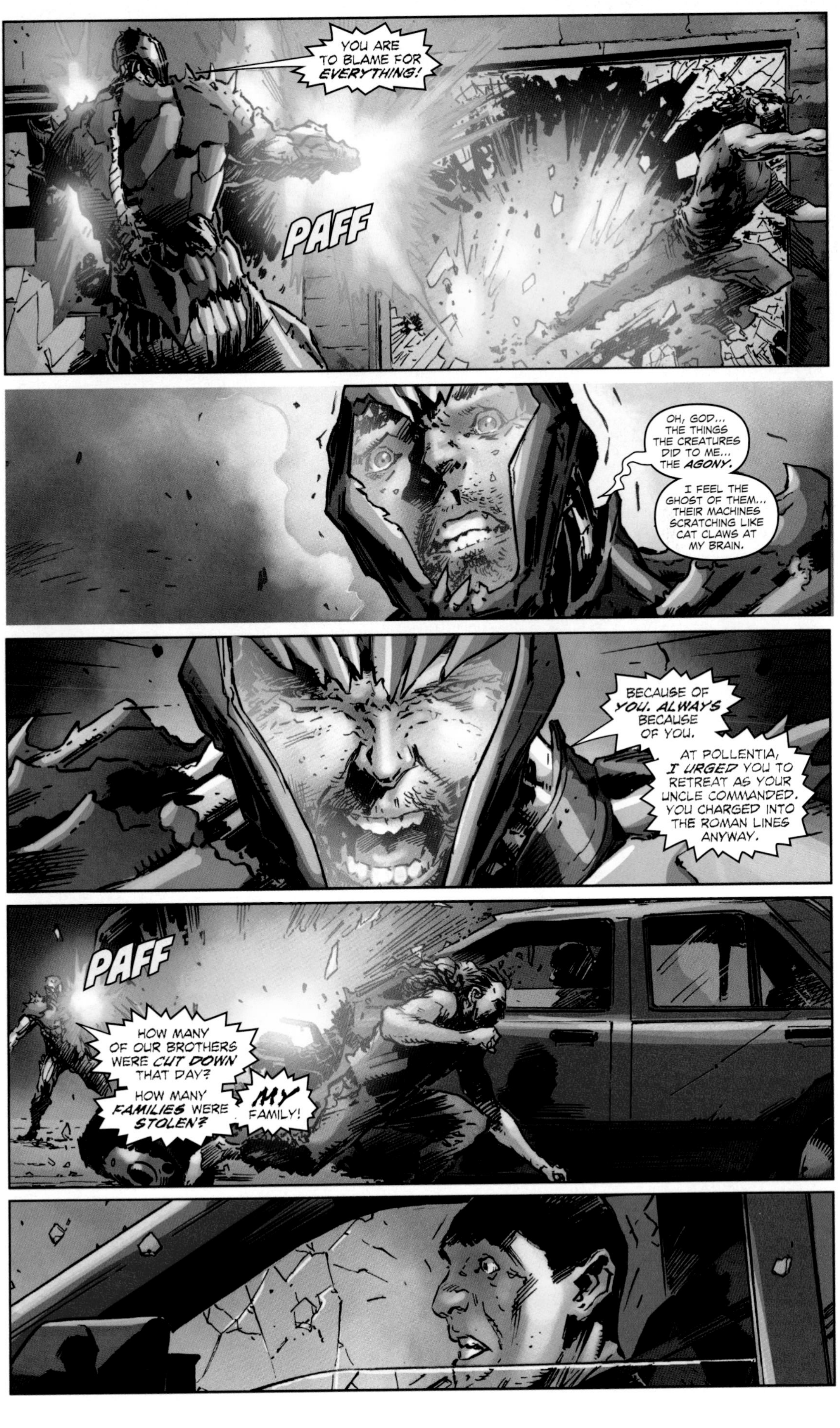
YOU ARE TO BLAME FOR EVERYTHING!
PAFF
OH, GOD... THE THINGS THE CREATURES DID TO ME... THE AGONY.
I FEEL THE GHOST OF THEM... THEIR MACHINES SCRATCHING LIKE CAT CLAWS AT MY BRAIN.
BECAUSE OF YOU. ALWAYS BECAUSE OF YOU.
AT POLLENTIA, I URGED YOU TO RETREAT AS YOUR UNCLE COMMANDED. YOU CHARGED INTO THE ROMAN LINES ANYWAY.
PAFF
HOW MANY OF OUR BROTHERS WERE CUT DOWN THAT DAY?
HOW MANY FAMILIES WERE STOLEN?
MY FAMILY!

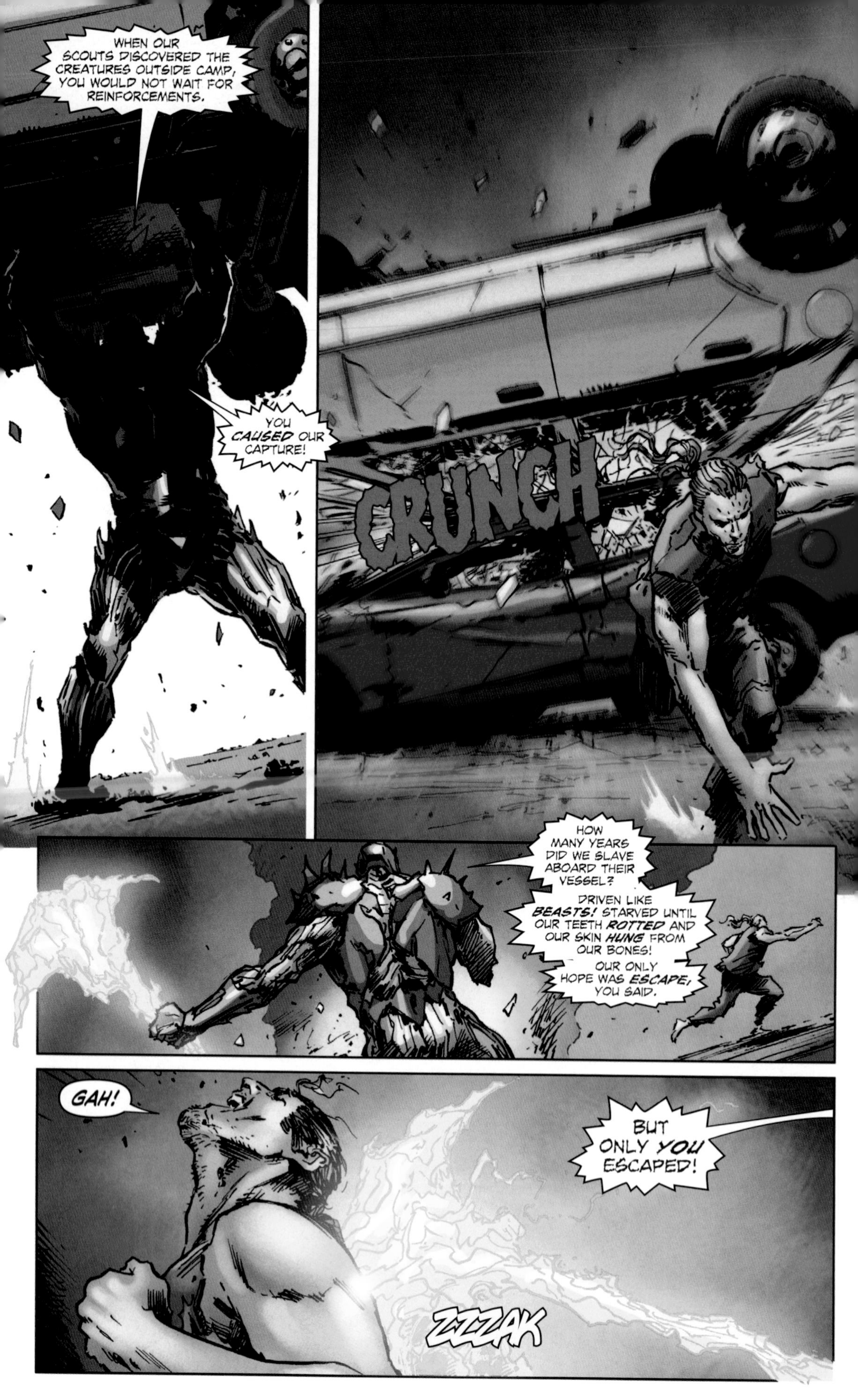
WHEN OUR SCOUTS DISCOVERED THE CREATURES OUTSIDE CAMP, YOU WOULD NOT WAIT FOR REINFORCEMENTS.
YOU CAUSED OUR CAPTURE!
CRUNCH
HOW MANY YEARS DID WE SLAVE ABOARD THEIR VESSEL?
DRIVEN LIKE BEASTS! STARVED UNTIL OUR TEETH ROTTED AND OUR SKIN HUNG FROM OUR BONES!
OUR ONLY HOPE WAS ESCAPE, YOU SAID.
GAH!
BUT ONLY YOU ESCAPED!
ZZZAK

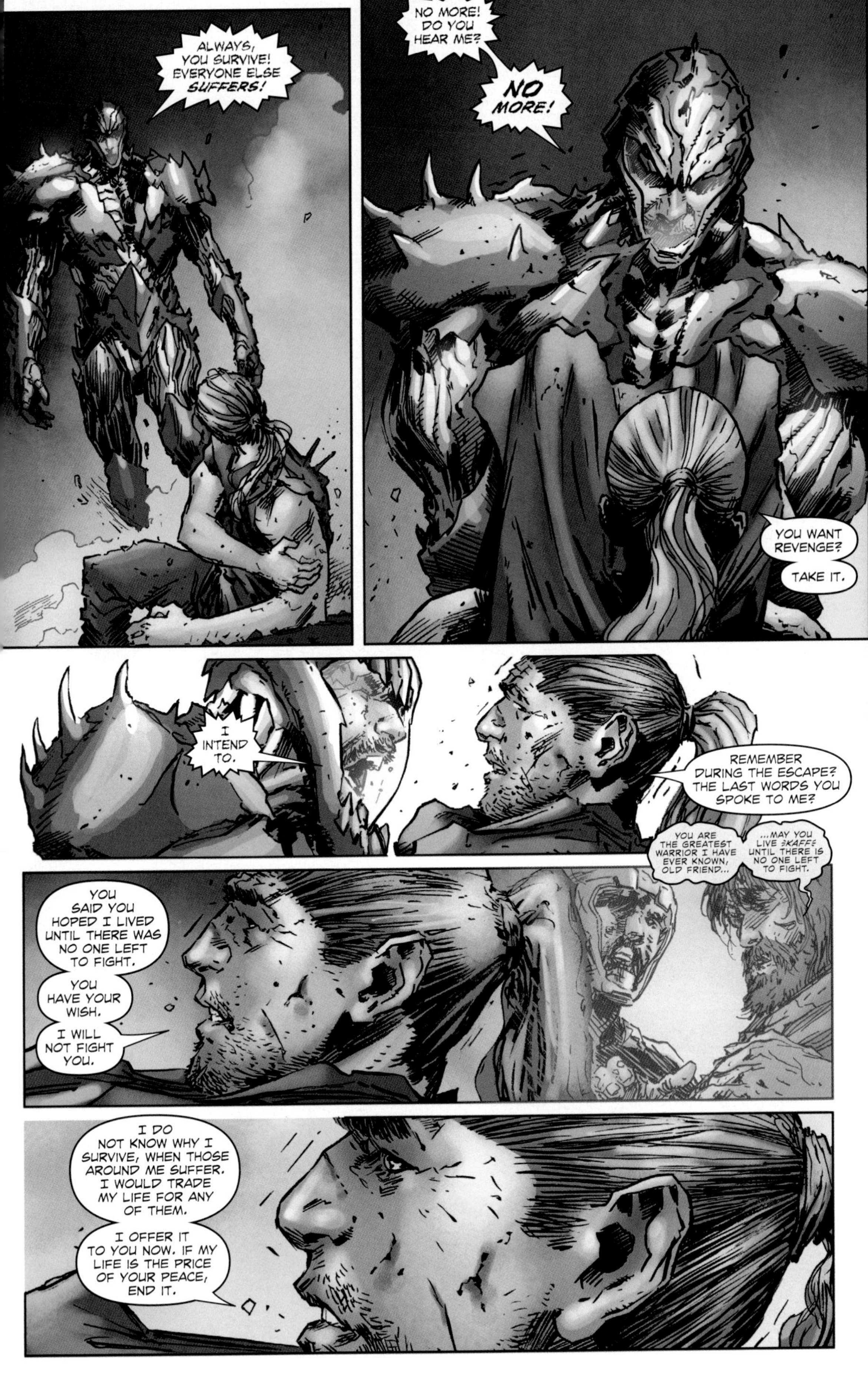
ALWAYS, YOU SURVIVE! EVERYONE ELSE SUFFERS!
NO MORE! DO YOU HEAR ME?
NO MORE!
YOU WANT REVENGE?
TAKE IT.
I INTEND TO.
REMEMBER DURING THE ESCAPE? THE LAST WORDS YOU SPOKE TO ME?
YOU ARE THE GREATEST WARRIOR I HAVE EVER KNOWN, OLD FRIEND...
...MAY YOU LIVE =KAFF= UNTIL THERE IS NO ONE LEFT TO FIGHT.
YOU SAID YOU HOPED I LIVED UNTIL THERE WAS NO ONE LEFT TO FIGHT.
YOU HAVE YOUR WISH.
I WILL NOT FIGHT YOU.
I DO NOT KNOW WHY I SURVIVE, WHEN THOSE AROUND ME SUFFER. I WOULD TRADE MY LIFE FOR ANY OF THEM.
I OFFER IT TO YOU NOW. IF MY LIFE IS THE PRICE OF YOUR PEACE, END IT.

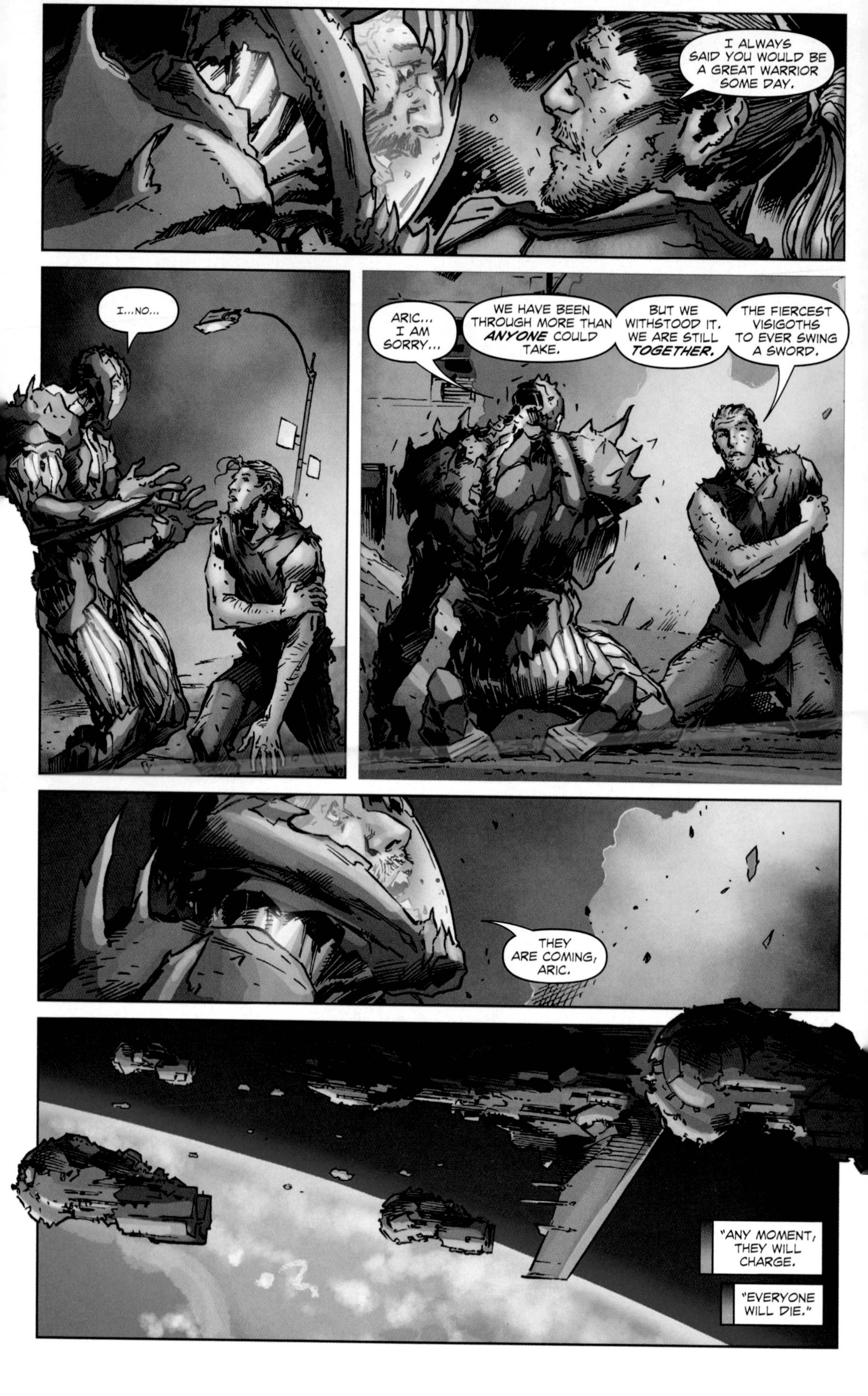
I ALWAYS SAID YOU WOULD BE A GREAT WARRIOR SOME DAY.
I...NO...
ARIC... I AM SORRY...
WE HAVE BEEN THROUGH MORE THAN ANYONE COULD TAKE.
BUT WE WITHSTOOD IT. WE ARE STILL TOGETHER.
THE FIERCEST VISIGOTHS TO EVER SWING A SWORD.
THEY ARE COMING, ARIC.
"ANY MOMENT, THEY WILL CHARGE.
"EVERYONE WILL DIE."

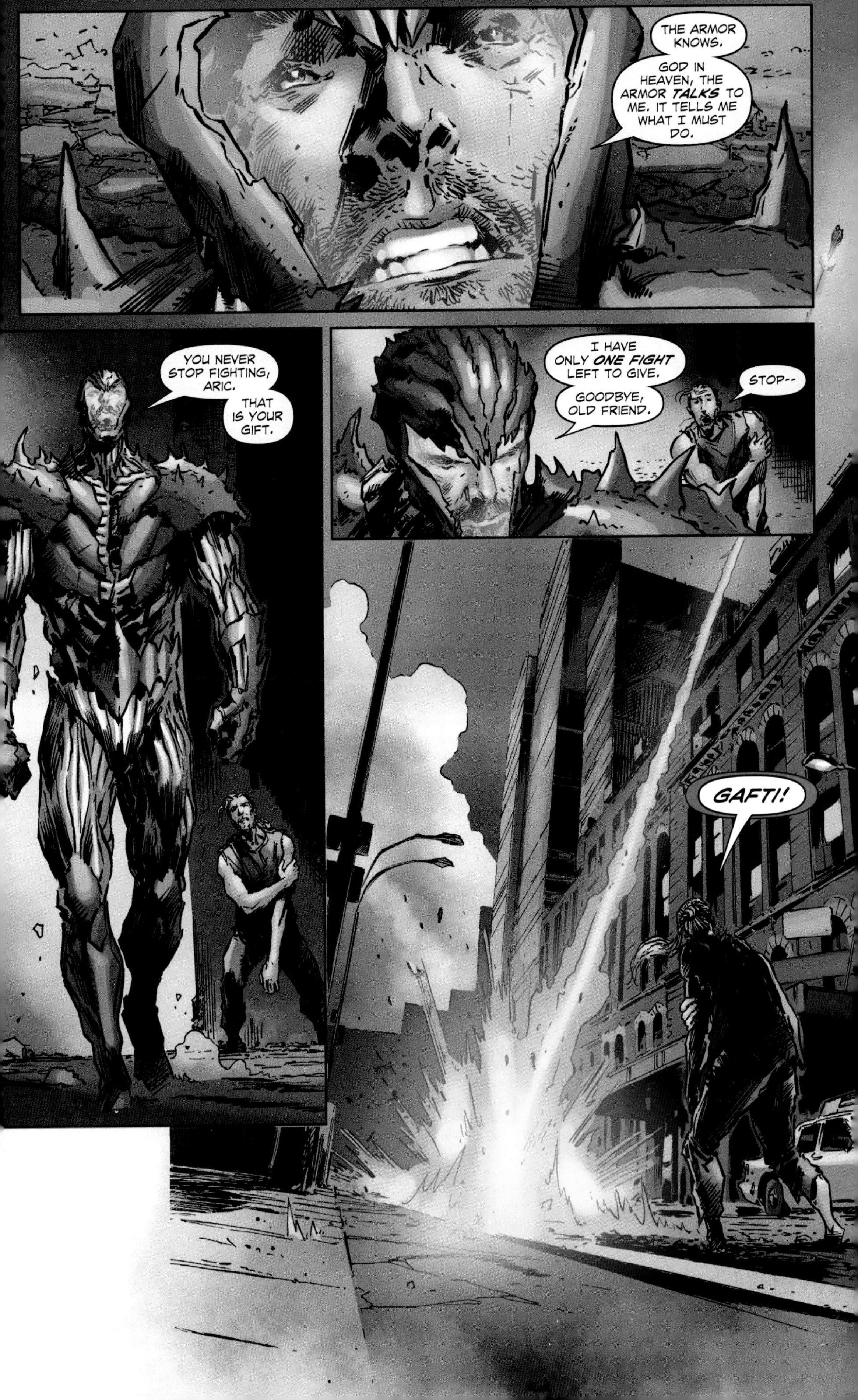
THE ARMOR KNOWS.
GOD IN HEAVEN, THE ARMOR TALKS TO ME. IT TELLS ME WHAT I MUST DO.
YOU NEVER STOP FIGHTING, ARIC.
THAT IS YOUR GIFT.
I HAVE ONLY ONE FIGHT LEFT TO GIVE.
GOODBYE, OLD FRIEND.
STOP--
GAFTI!

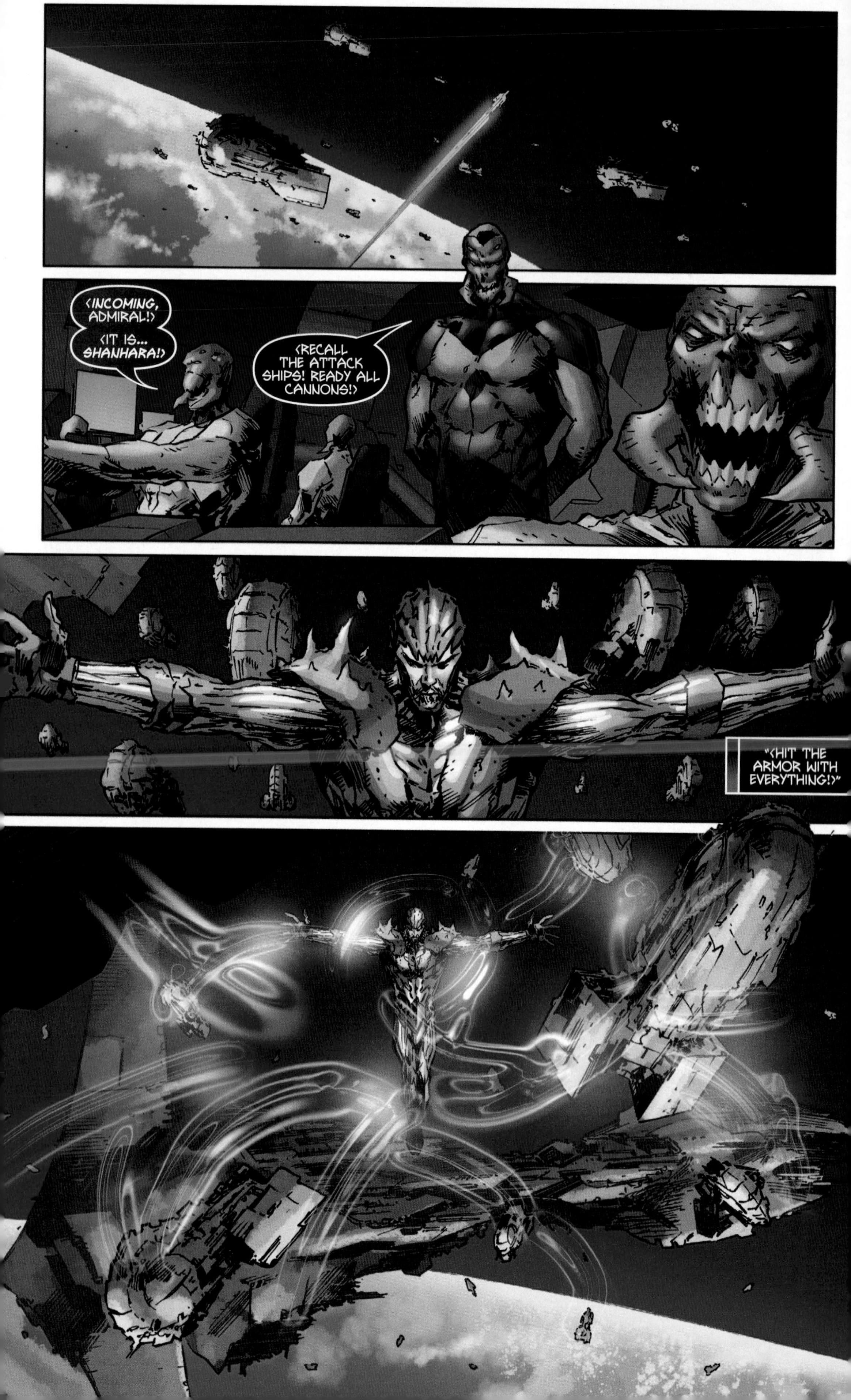

<INCOMING, ADMIRAL!>
<IT IS... SHANHARA!>
<RECALL THE ATTACK SHIPS! READY ALL CANNONS!>
"<HIT THE ARMOR WITH EVERYTHING!>"

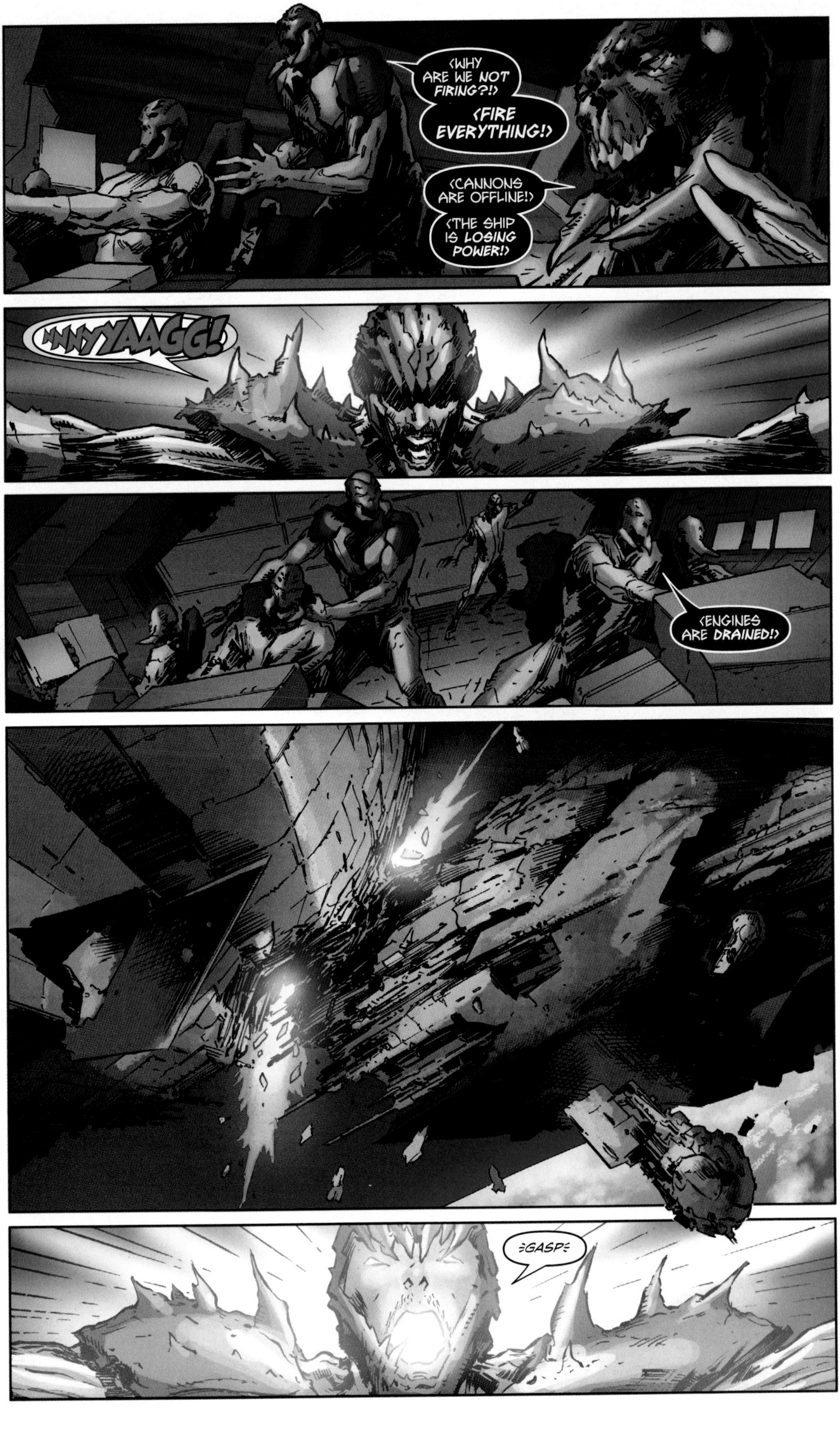

<WHY ARE WE NOT FIRING?!>
<FIRE EVERYTHING!>
<CANNONS ARE OFFLINE!>
<THE SHIP IS LOSING POWER!>
NNNYYAAGG!
<ENGINES ARE DRAINED!>
GASP

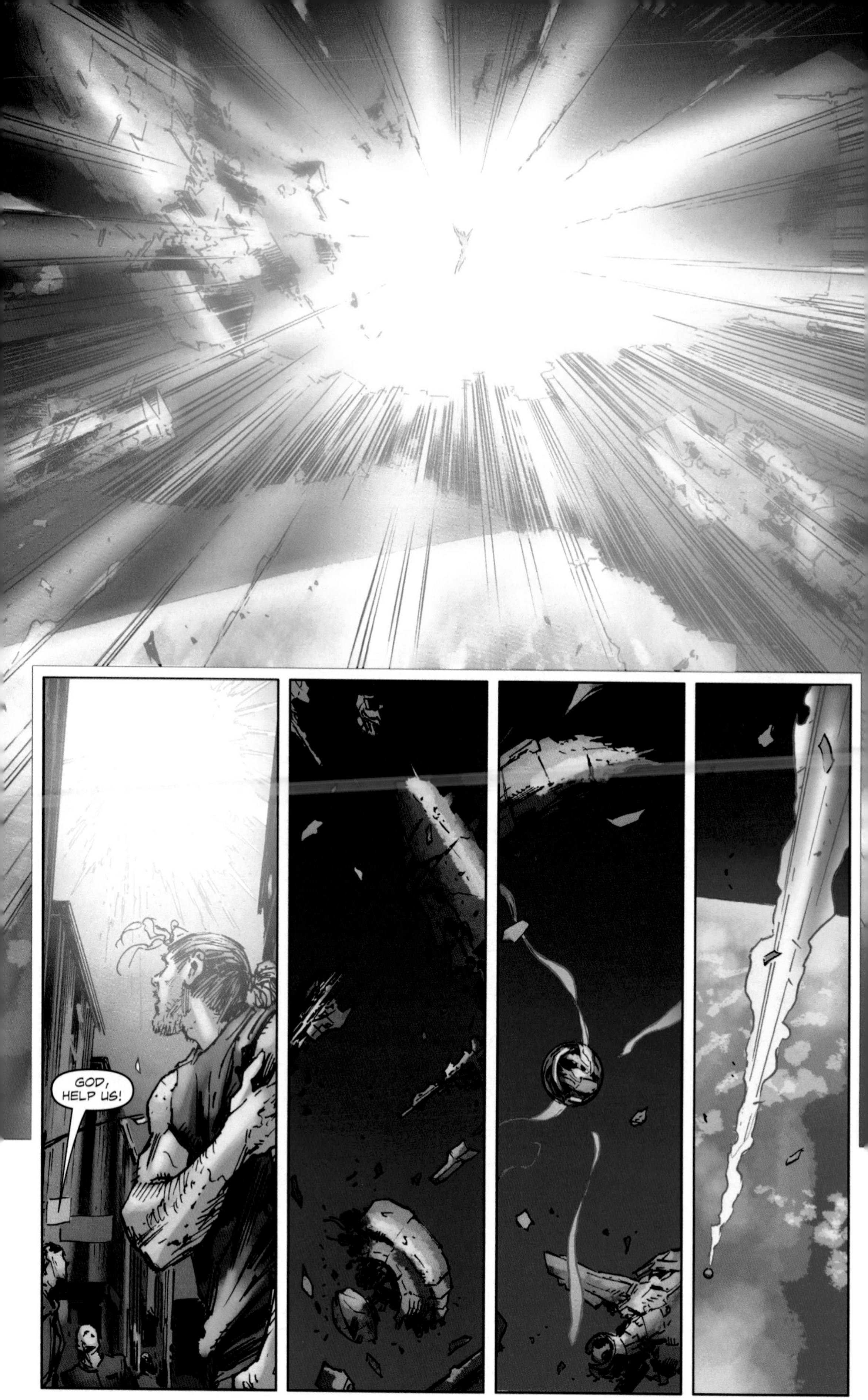
GOD, HELP US!

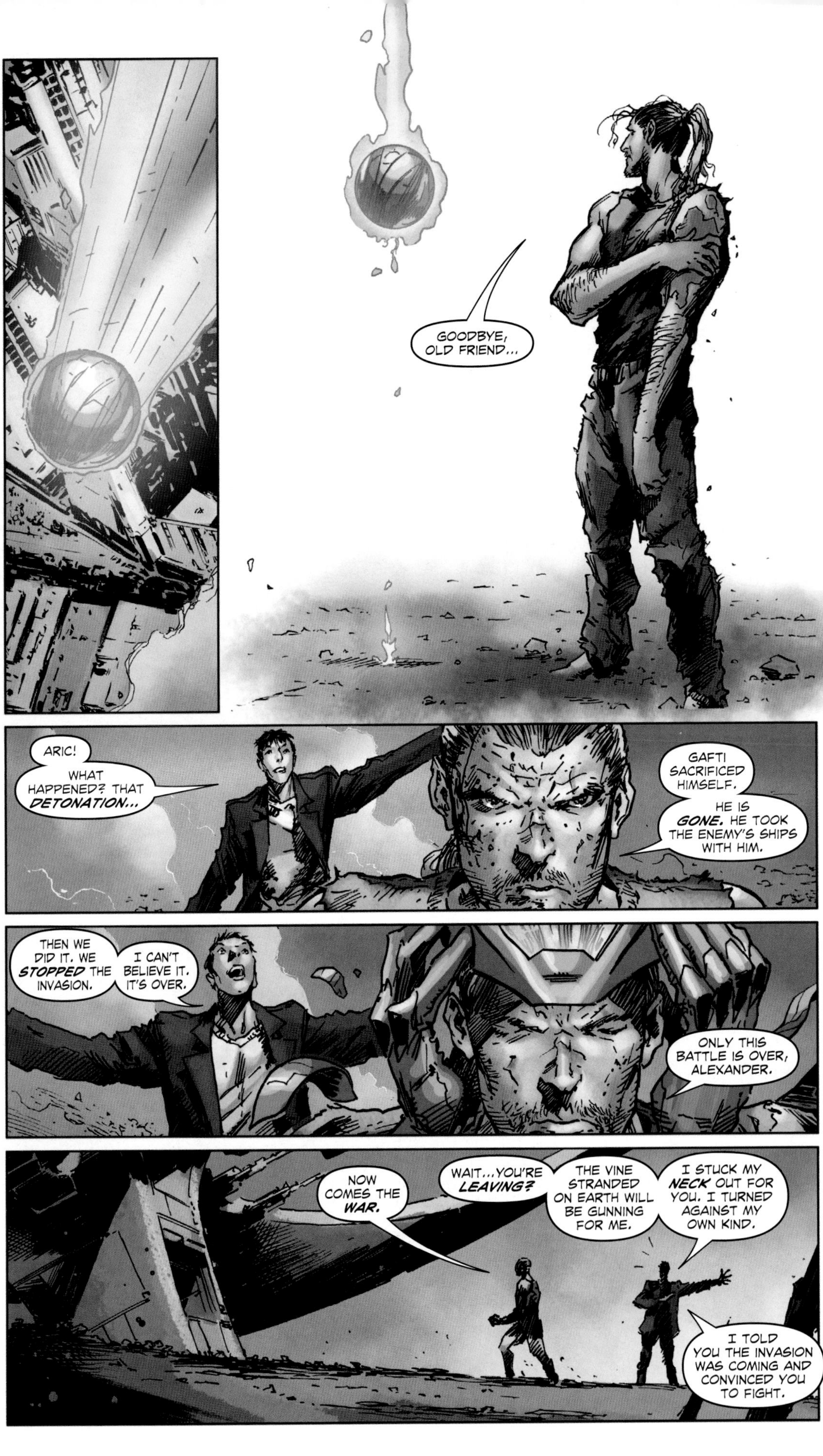

GOODBYE, OLD FRIEND...
ARIC!
WHAT HAPPENED? THAT DETONATION...
GAFTI SACRIFICED HIMSELF.
HE IS GONE. HE TOOK THE ENEMY'S SHIPS WITH HIM.
THEN WE DID IT. WE STOPPED THE INVASION.
I CAN'T BELIEVE IT. IT'S OVER.
ONLY THIS BATTLE IS OVER, ALEXANDER.
NOW COMES THE WAR.
WAIT...YOU'RE LEAVING?
THE VINE STRANDED ON EARTH WILL BE GUNNING FOR ME.
I STUCK MY NECK OUT FOR YOU. I TURNED AGAINST MY OWN KIND.
I TOLD YOU THE INVASION WAS COMING AND CONVINCED YOU TO FIGHT.

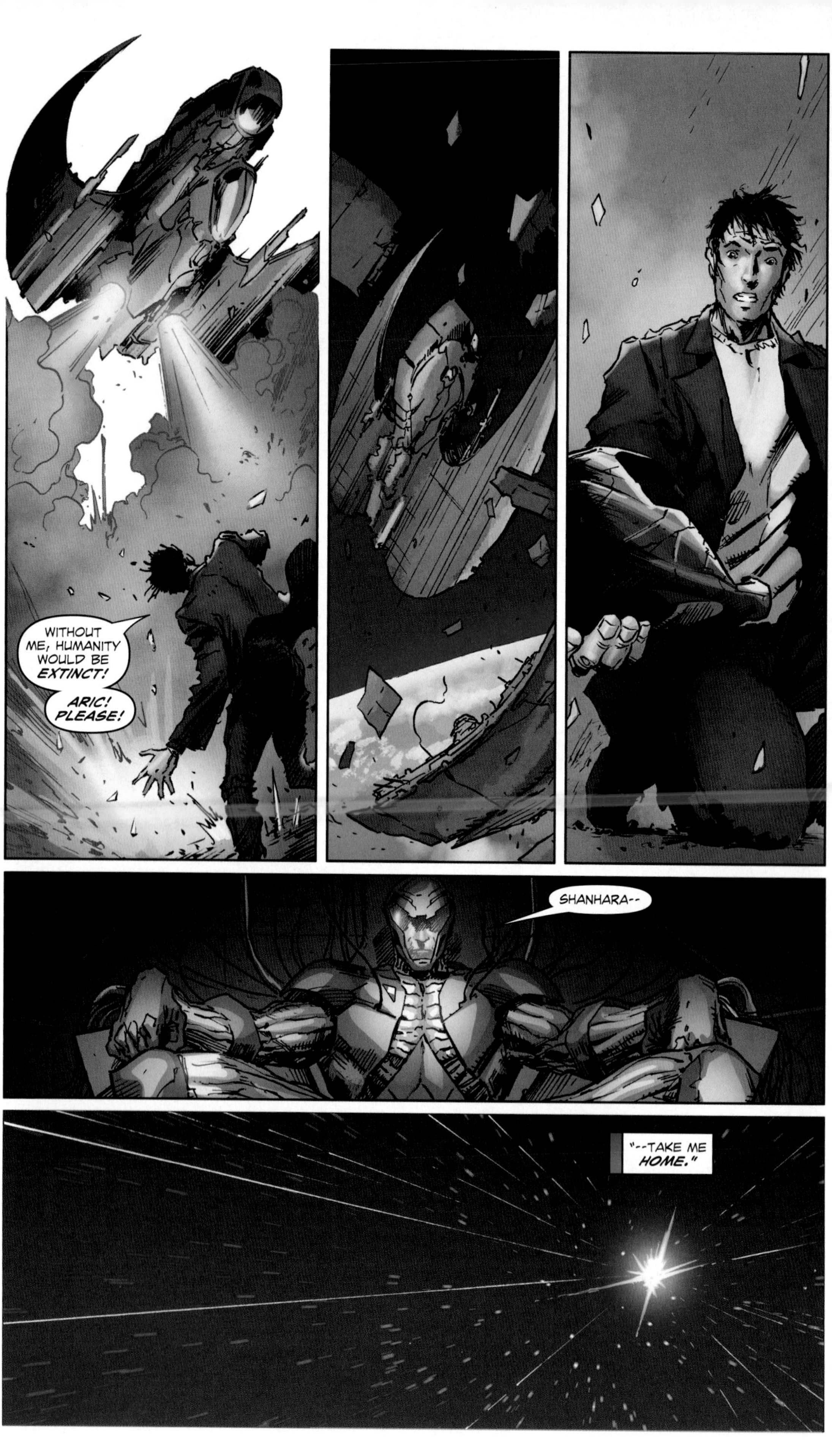
WITHOUT ME, HUMANITY WOULD BE EXTINCT!
ARIC! PLEASE!
SHANHARA--
"--TAKE ME HOME."

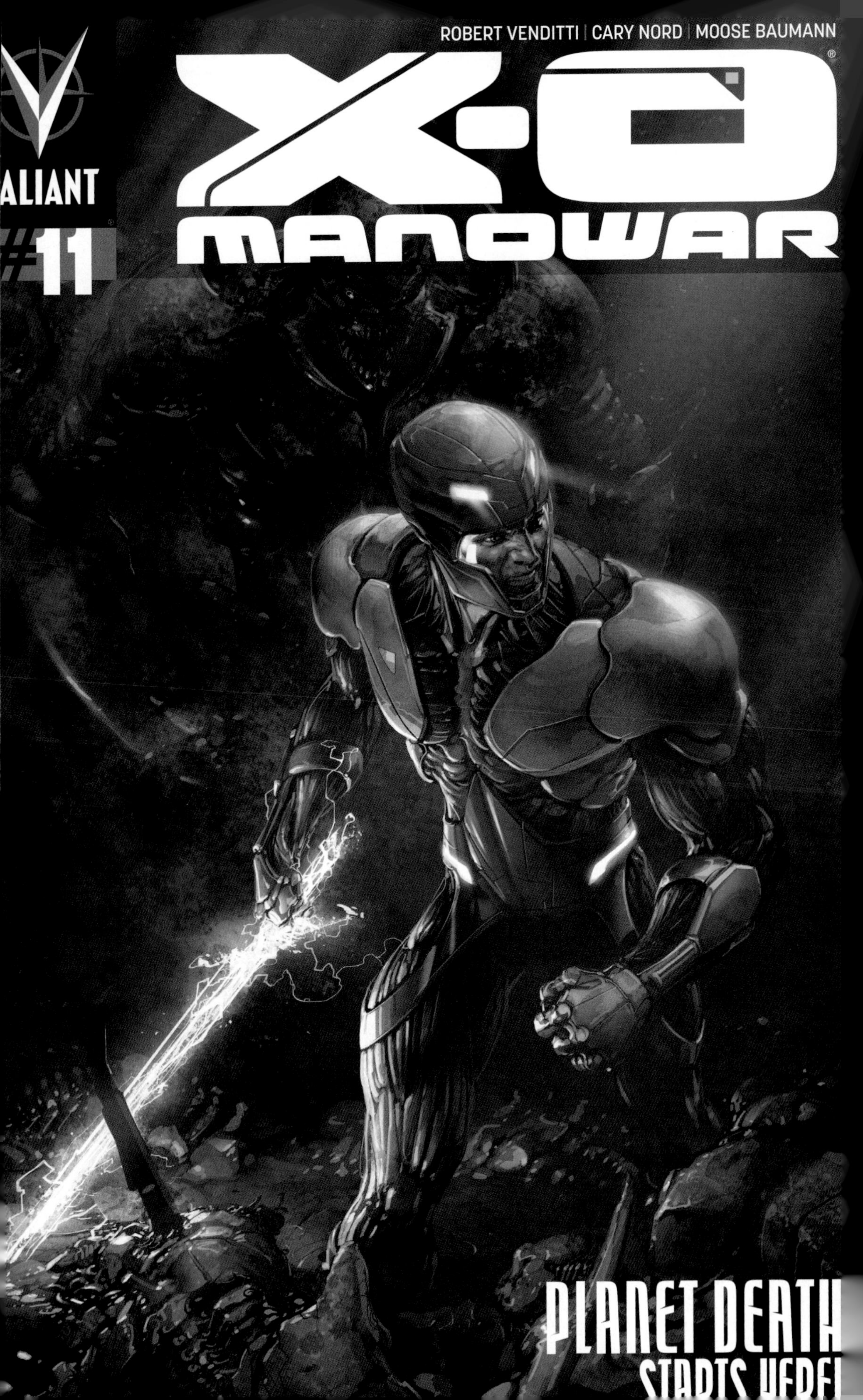
ROBERT VENDITTI | CARY NORD | MOOSE BAUMANN
VALIANT
X-O MANOWAR
#11
PLANET DEATH
STARTS HERE!

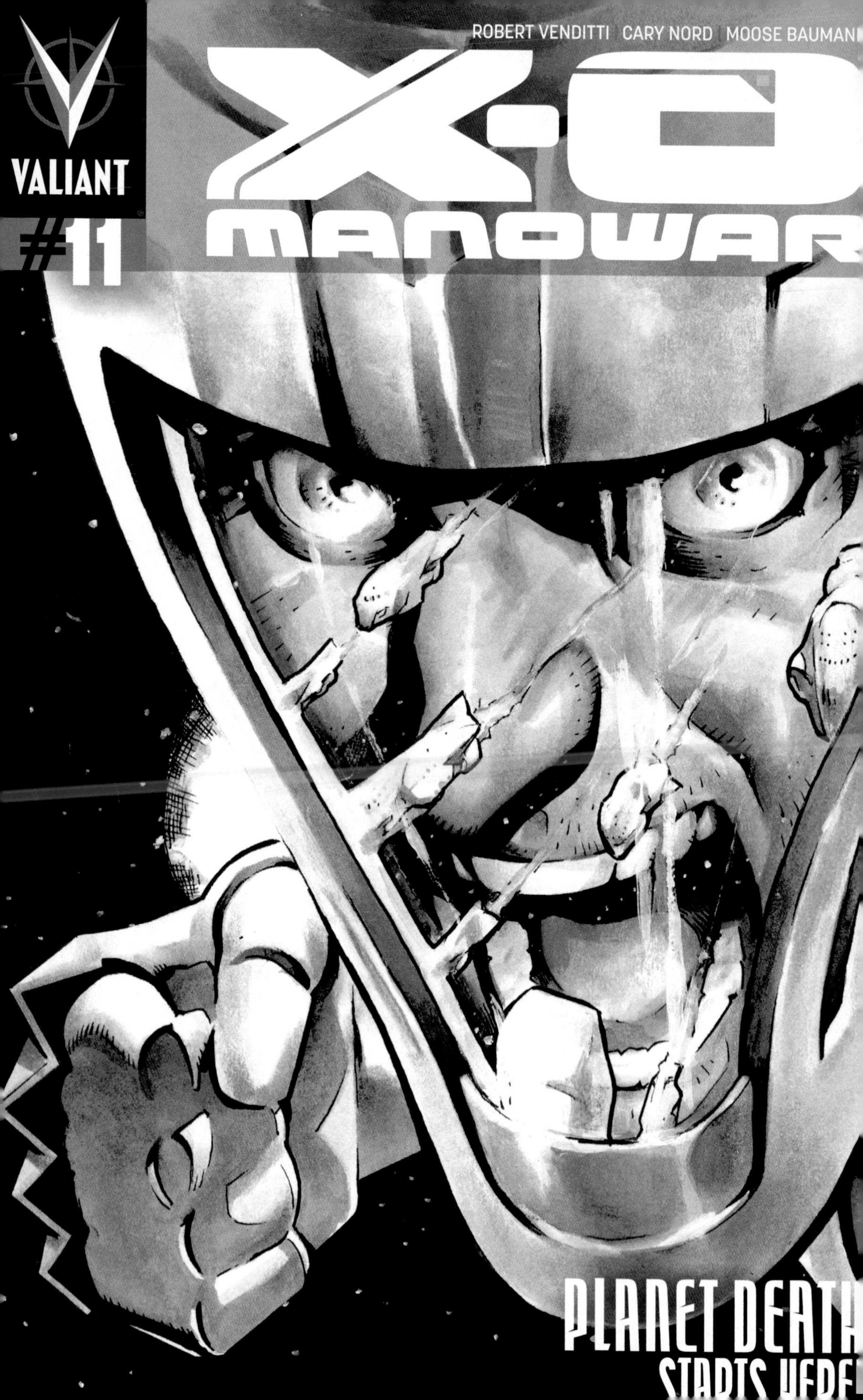
VALIANT
#11
ROBERT VENDITTI | CARY NORD | MOOSE BAUMAN
X-O
MANOWAR
PLANET DEATH
STARTS HERE

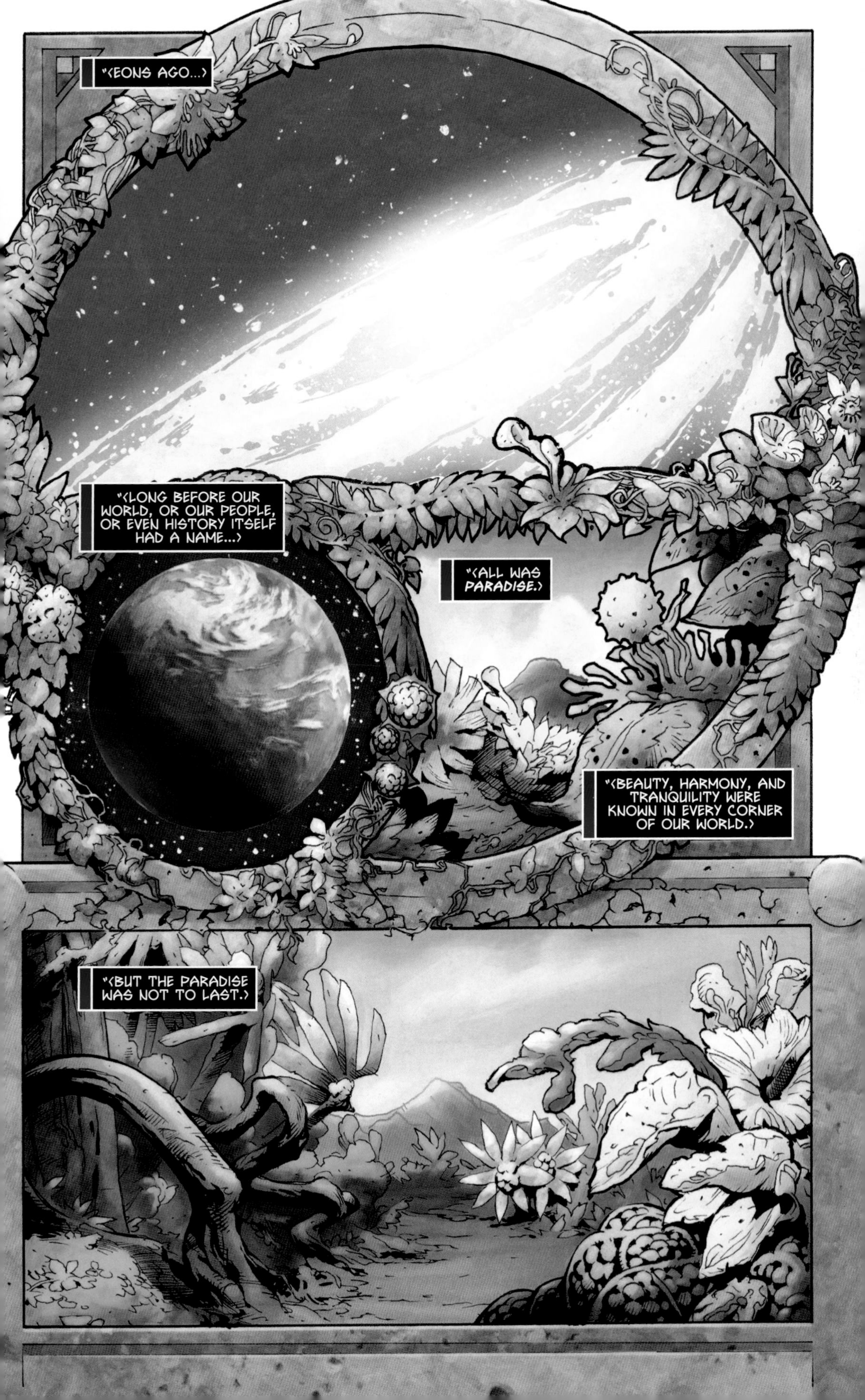
"<EONS AGO...>
"<LONG BEFORE OUR WORLD, OR OUR PEOPLE, OR EVEN HISTORY ITSELF HAD A NAME...>
"<ALL WAS *PARADISE.*>
"<BEAUTY, HARMONY, AND TRANQUILITY WERE KNOWN IN EVERY CORNER OF OUR WORLD.>
"<BUT THE PARADISE WAS NOT TO LAST.>

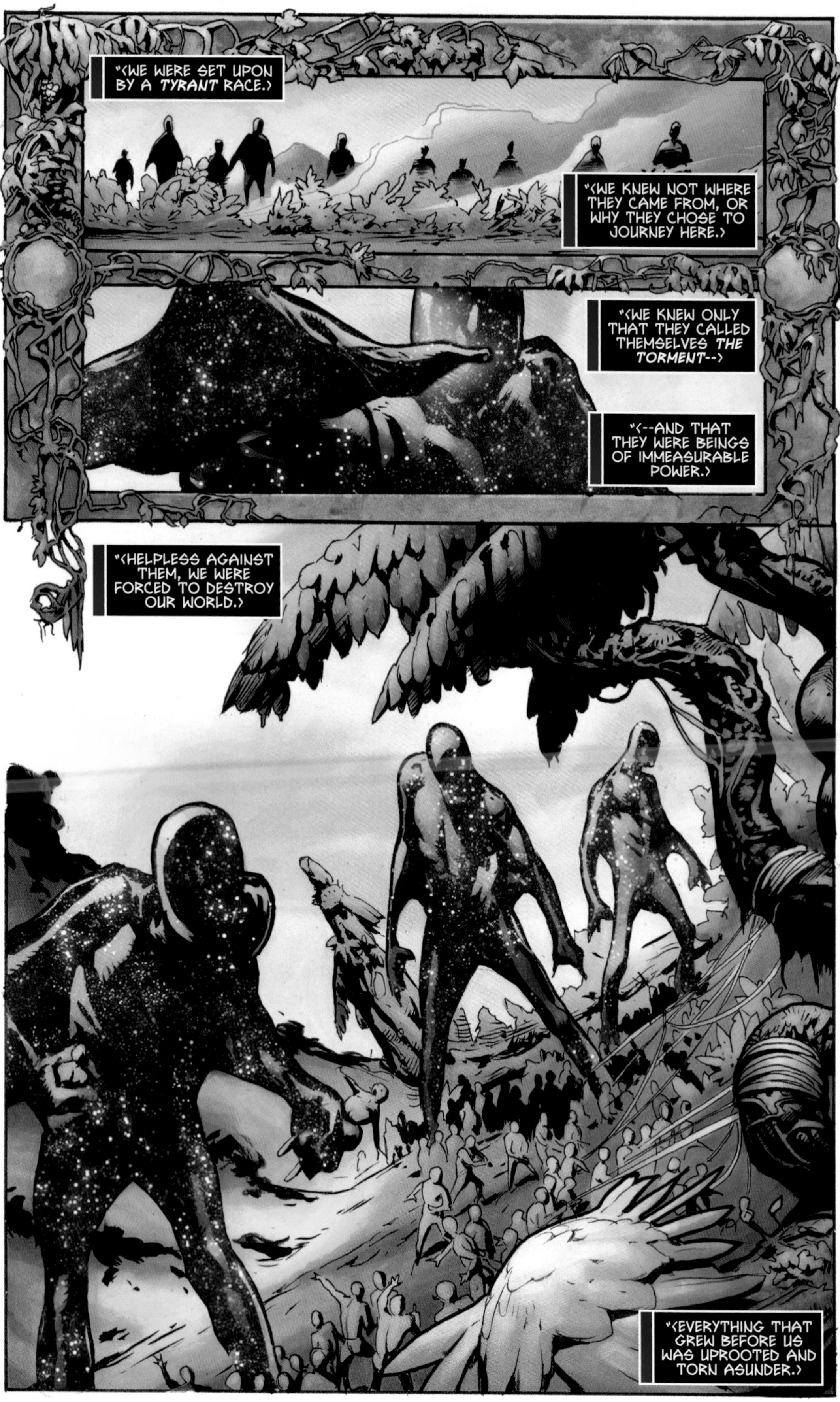
"<WE WERE SET UPON BY A *TYRANT* RACE.>
"<WE KNEW NOT WHERE THEY CAME FROM, OR WHY THEY CHOSE TO JOURNEY HERE.>
"<WE KNEW ONLY THAT THEY CALLED THEMSELVES *THE TORMENT*-->
"<--AND THAT THEY WERE BEINGS OF IMMEASURABLE POWER.>
"<HELPLESS AGAINST THEM, WE WERE FORCED TO DESTROY OUR WORLD.>
"<EVERYTHING THAT GREW BEFORE US WAS UPROOTED AND TORN ASUNDER.>

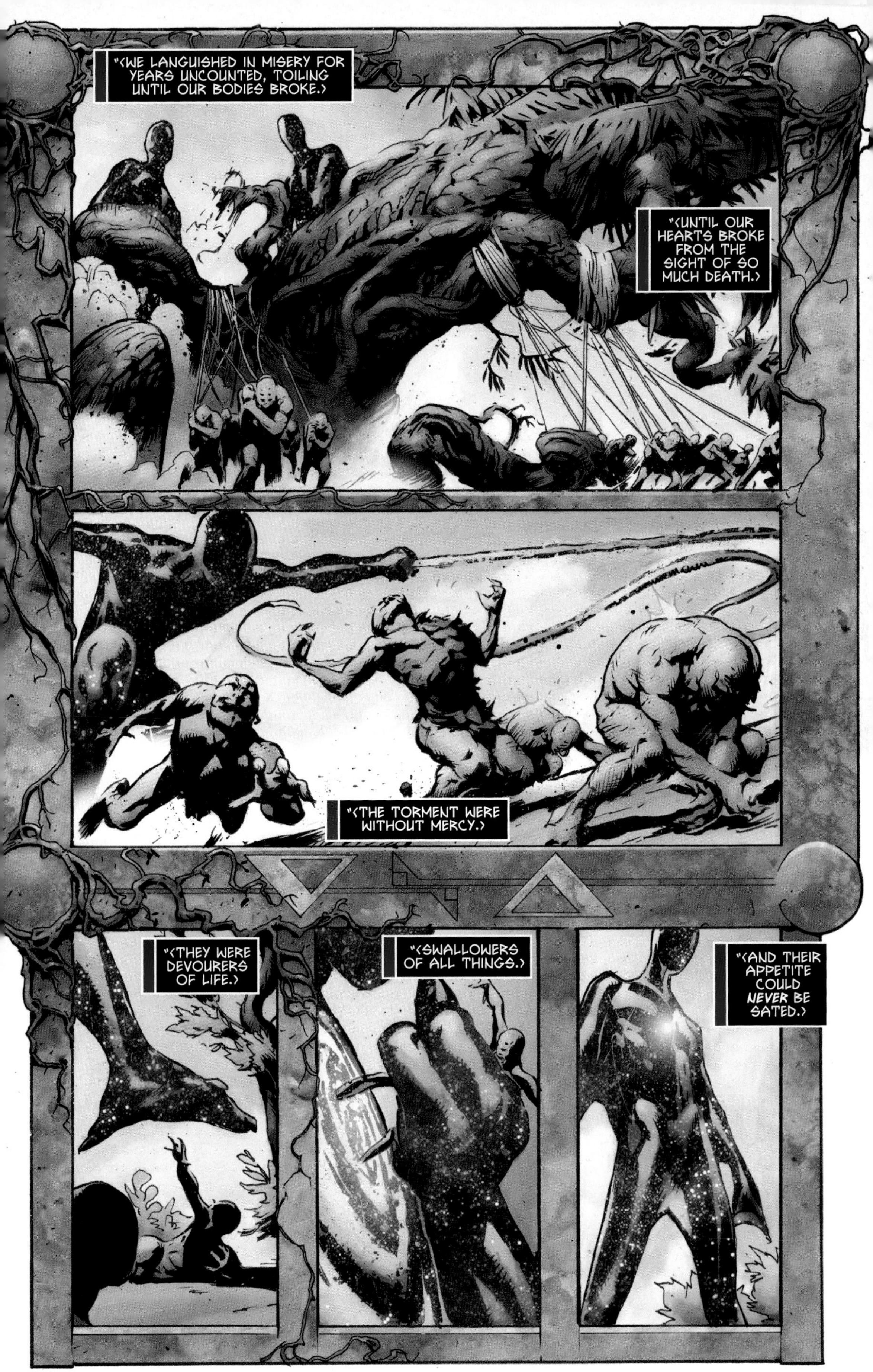
"<WE LANGUISHED IN MISERY FOR YEARS UNCOUNTED, TOILING UNTIL OUR BODIES BROKE.>
"<UNTIL OUR HEARTS BROKE FROM THE SIGHT OF SO MUCH DEATH.>
"<THE TORMENT WERE WITHOUT MERCY.>
"<THEY WERE DEVOURERS OF LIFE.>
"<SWALLOWERS OF ALL THINGS.>
"<AND THEIR APPETITE COULD ***NEVER*** BE SATED.>

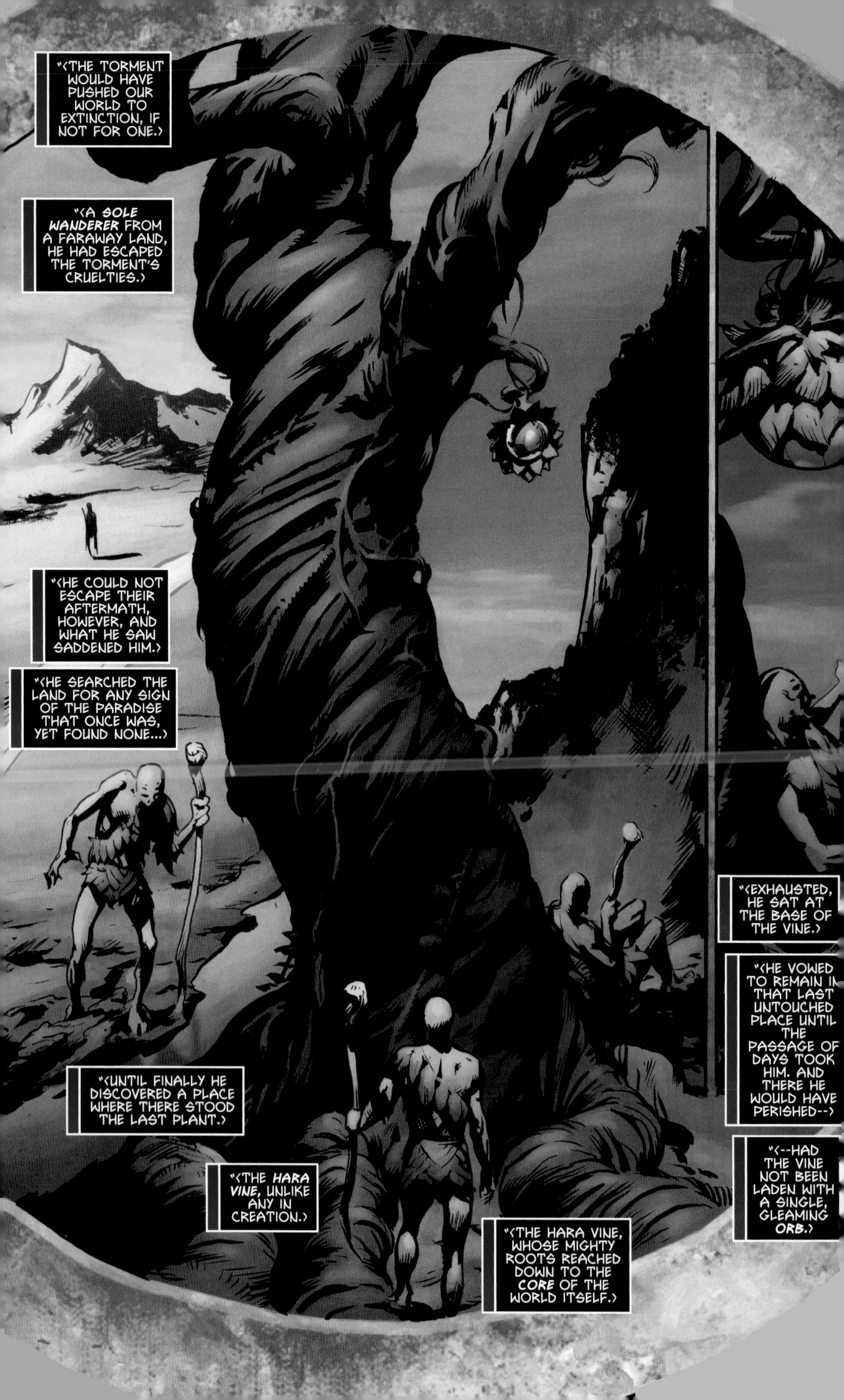
"<THE TORMENT WOULD HAVE PUSHED OUR WORLD TO EXTINCTION, IF NOT FOR ONE.>
"<A SOLE WANDERER FROM A FARAWAY LAND, HE HAD ESCAPED THE TORMENT'S CRUELTIES.>
"<HE COULD NOT ESCAPE THEIR AFTERMATH, HOWEVER, AND WHAT HE SAW SADDENED HIM.>
"<HE SEARCHED THE LAND FOR ANY SIGN OF THE PARADISE THAT ONCE WAS, YET FOUND NONE...>
"<UNTIL FINALLY HE DISCOVERED A PLACE WHERE THERE STOOD THE LAST PLANT.>
"<THE HARA VINE, UNLIKE ANY IN CREATION.>
"<THE HARA VINE, WHOSE MIGHTY ROOTS REACHED DOWN TO THE CORE OF THE WORLD ITSELF.>
"<EXHAUSTED, HE SAT AT THE BASE OF THE VINE.>
"<HE VOWED TO REMAIN IN THAT LAST UNTOUCHED PLACE UNTIL THE PASSAGE OF DAYS TOOK HIM. AND THERE HE WOULD HAVE PERISHED-->
"<--HAD THE VINE NOT BEEN LADEN WITH A SINGLE, GLEAMING ORB.>

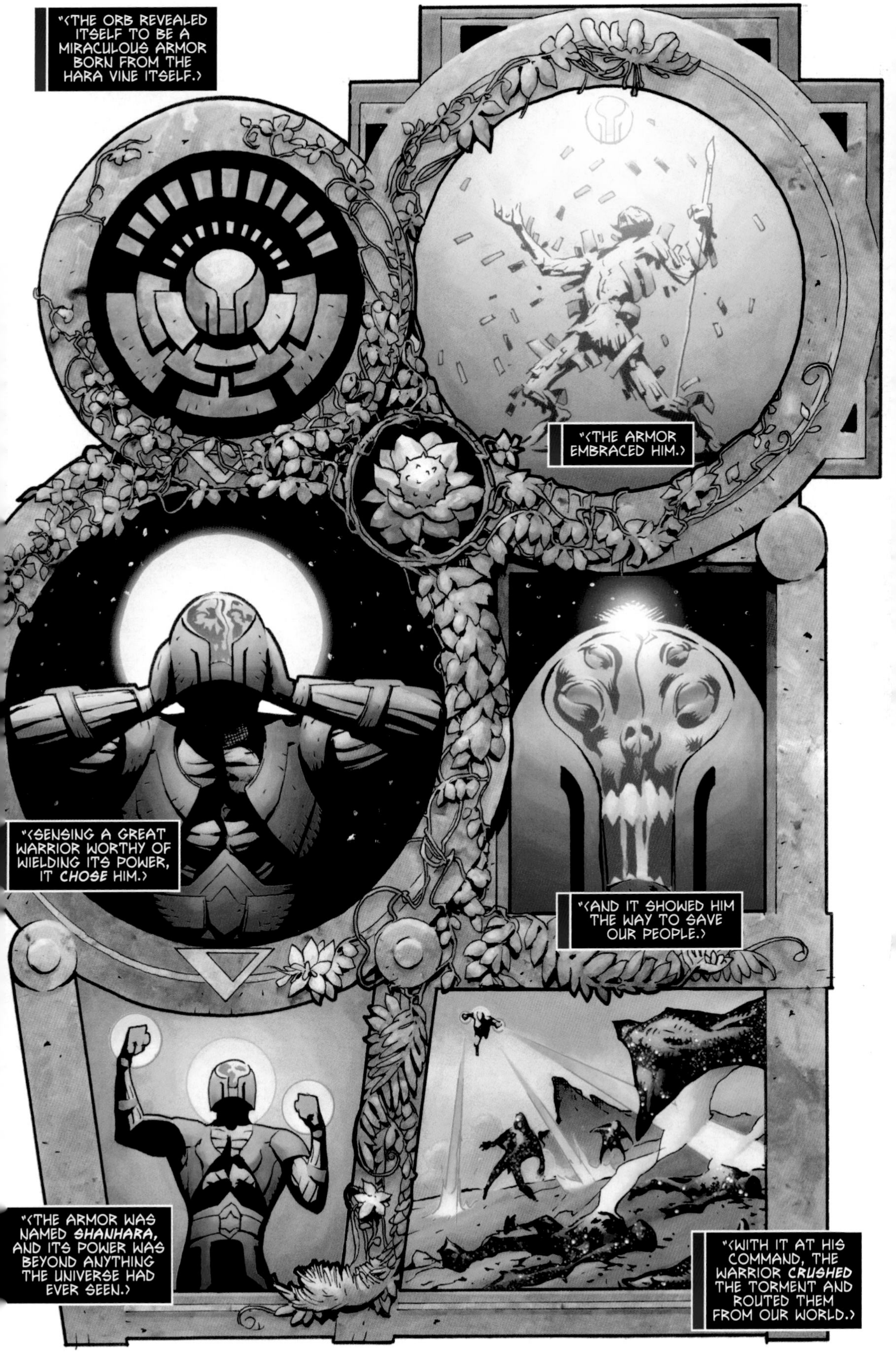
"<THE ORB REVEALED ITSELF TO BE A MIRACULOUS ARMOR BORN FROM THE HARA VINE ITSELF.>
"<THE ARMOR EMBRACED HIM.>
"<SENSING A GREAT WARRIOR WORTHY OF WIELDING ITS POWER, IT CHOSE HIM.>
"<AND IT SHOWED HIM THE WAY TO SAVE OUR PEOPLE.>
"<THE ARMOR WAS NAMED SHANHARA, AND ITS POWER WAS BEYOND ANYTHING THE UNIVERSE HAD EVER SEEN.>
"<WITH IT AT HIS COMMAND, THE WARRIOR CRUSHED THE TORMENT AND ROUTED THEM FROM OUR WORLD.>

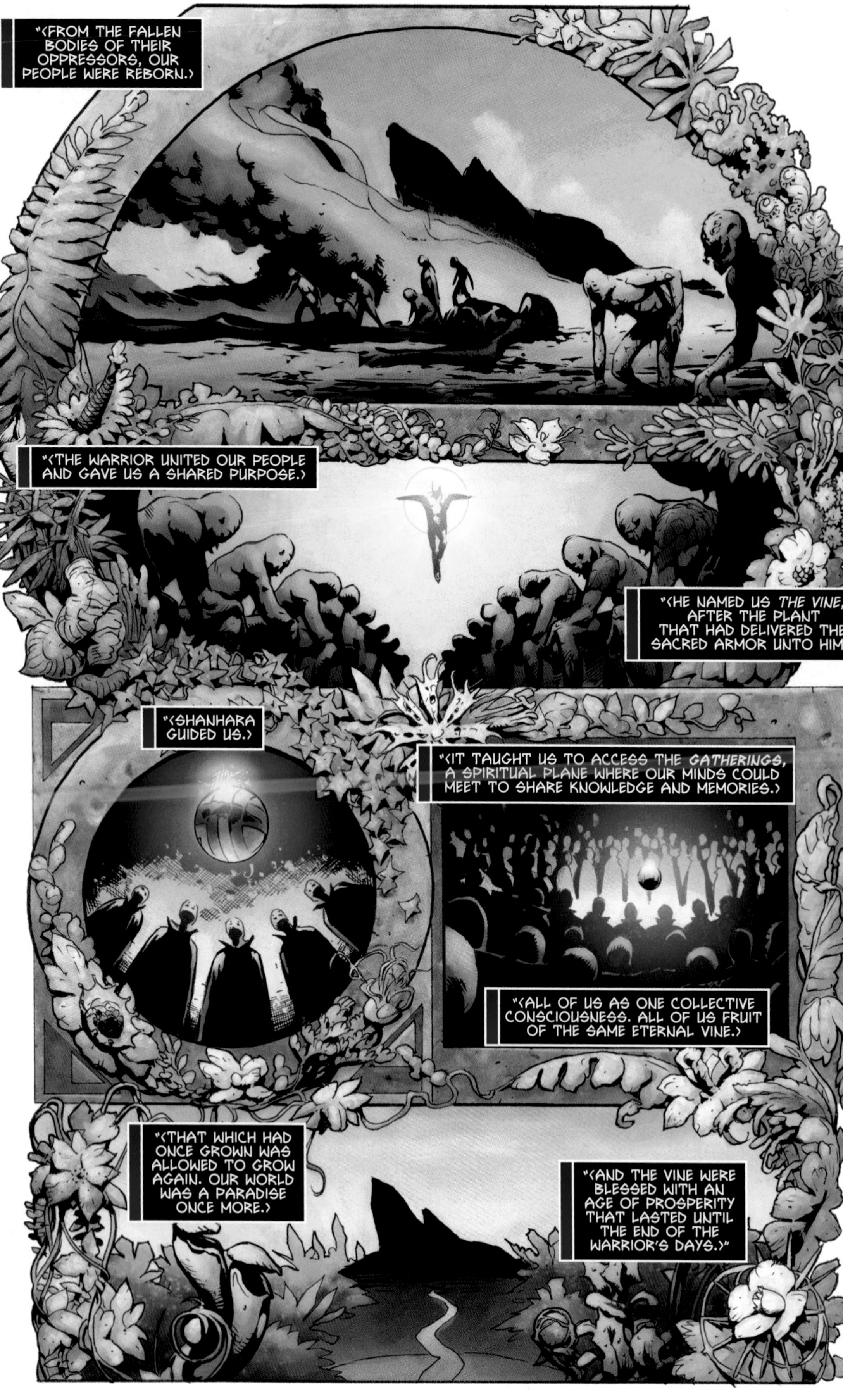
"<FROM THE FALLEN BODIES OF THEIR OPPRESSORS, OUR PEOPLE WERE REBORN.>
"<THE WARRIOR UNITED OUR PEOPLE AND GAVE US A SHARED PURPOSE.>
"<HE NAMED US THE VINE, AFTER THE PLANT THAT HAD DELIVERED THE SACRED ARMOR UNTO HIM.>
"<SHANHARA GUIDED US.>
"<IT TAUGHT US TO ACCESS THE GATHERINGS, A SPIRITUAL PLANE WHERE OUR MINDS COULD MEET TO SHARE KNOWLEDGE AND MEMORIES.>
"<ALL OF US AS ONE COLLECTIVE CONSCIOUSNESS. ALL OF US FRUIT OF THE SAME ETERNAL VINE.>
"<THAT WHICH HAD ONCE GROWN WAS ALLOWED TO GROW AGAIN. OUR WORLD WAS A PARADISE ONCE MORE.>
"<AND THE VINE WERE BLESSED WITH AN AGE OF PROSPERITY THAT LASTED UNTIL THE END OF THE WARRIOR'S DAYS.>"

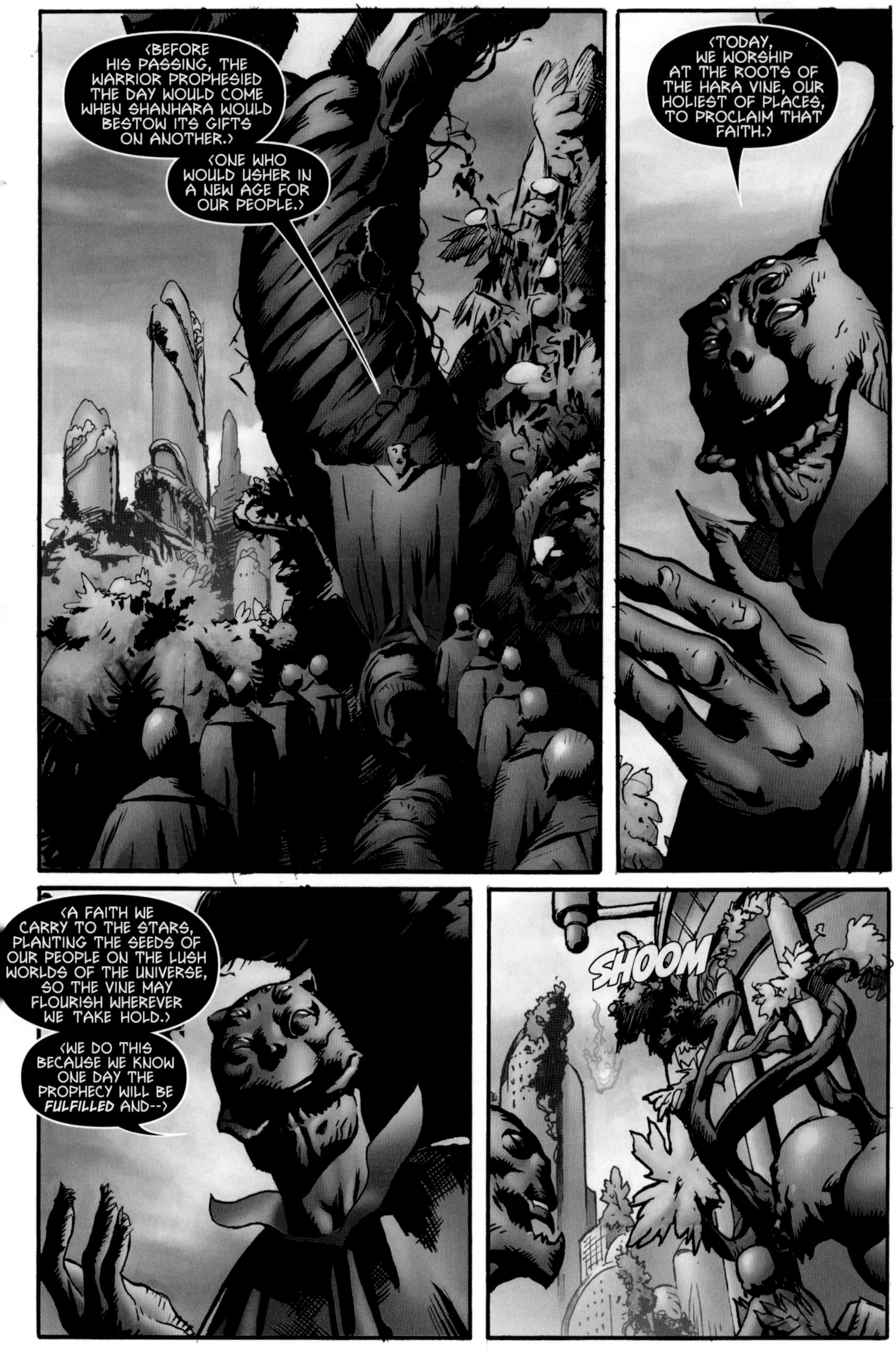

‹BEFORE HIS PASSING, THE WARRIOR PROPHESIED THE DAY WOULD COME WHEN SHANHARA WOULD BESTOW ITS GIFTS ON ANOTHER.›
‹ONE WHO WOULD USHER IN A NEW AGE FOR OUR PEOPLE.›
‹TODAY, WE WORSHIP AT THE ROOTS OF THE HARA VINE, OUR HOLIEST OF PLACES, TO PROCLAIM THAT FAITH.›
‹A FAITH WE CARRY TO THE STARS, PLANTING THE SEEDS OF OUR PEOPLE ON THE LUSH WORLDS OF THE UNIVERSE, SO THE VINE MAY FLOURISH WHEREVER WE TAKE HOLD.›
‹WE DO THIS BECAUSE WE KNOW ONE DAY THE PROPHECY WILL BE ***FULFILLED*** AND--›
SHOOM

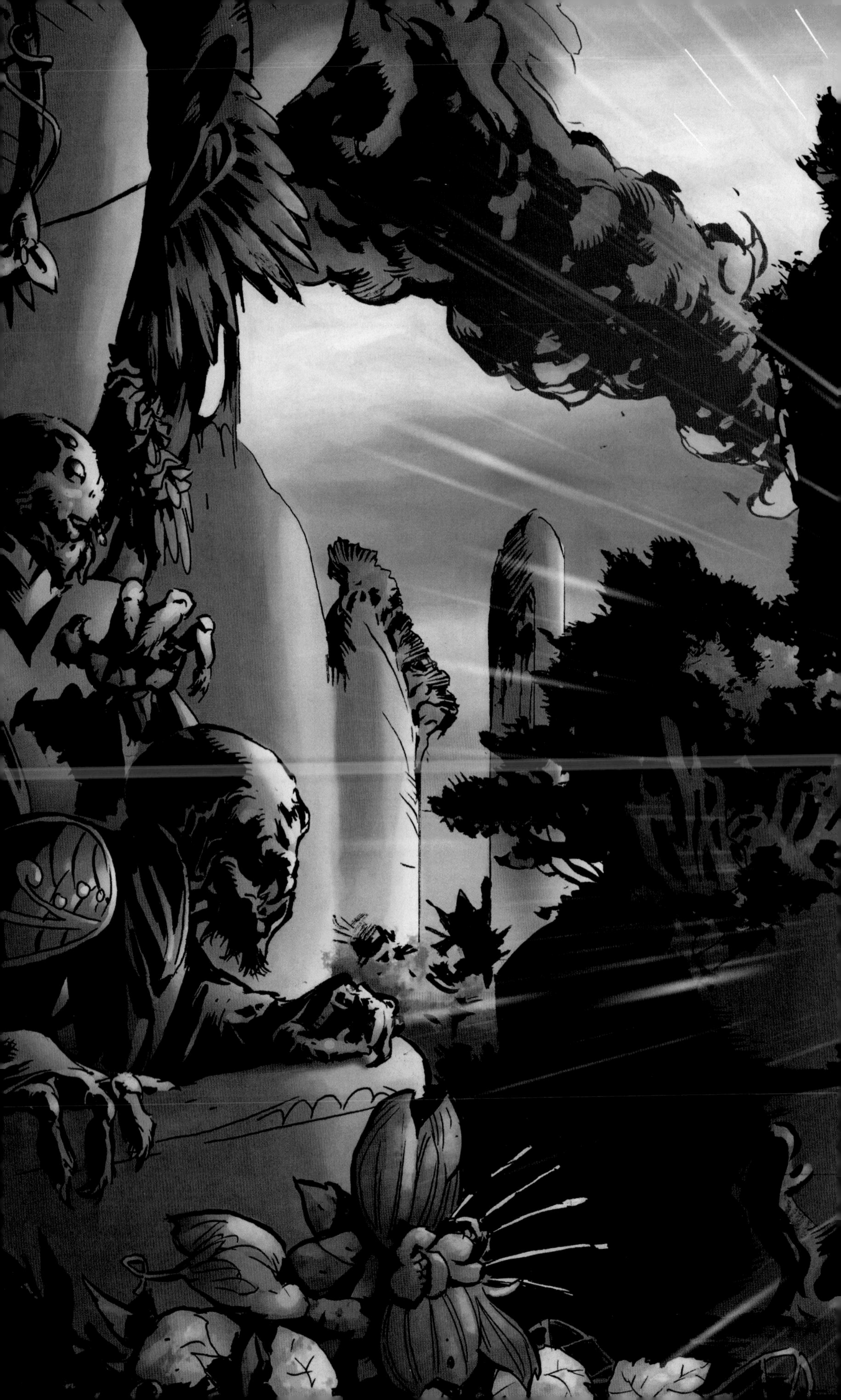

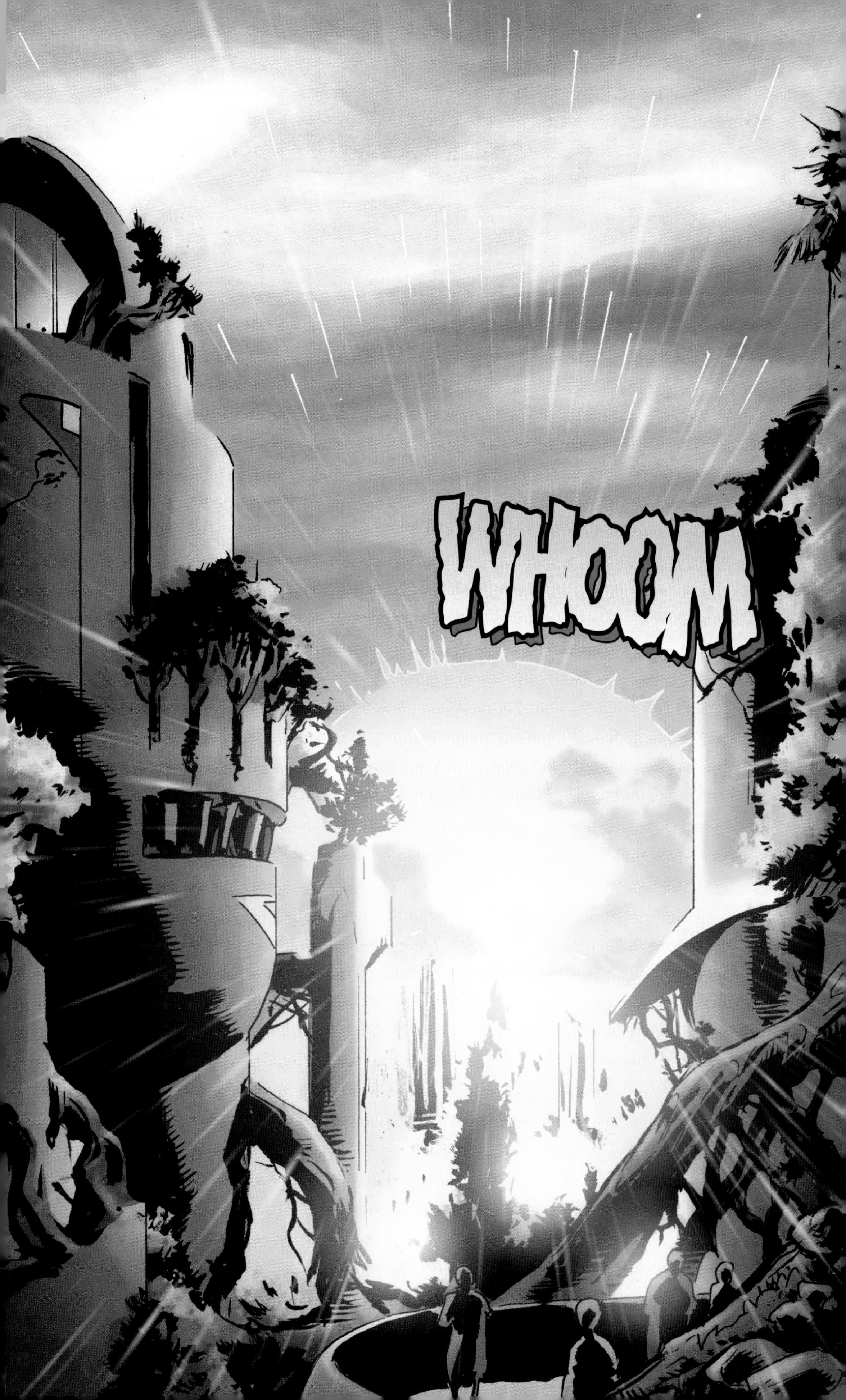
WHOOM

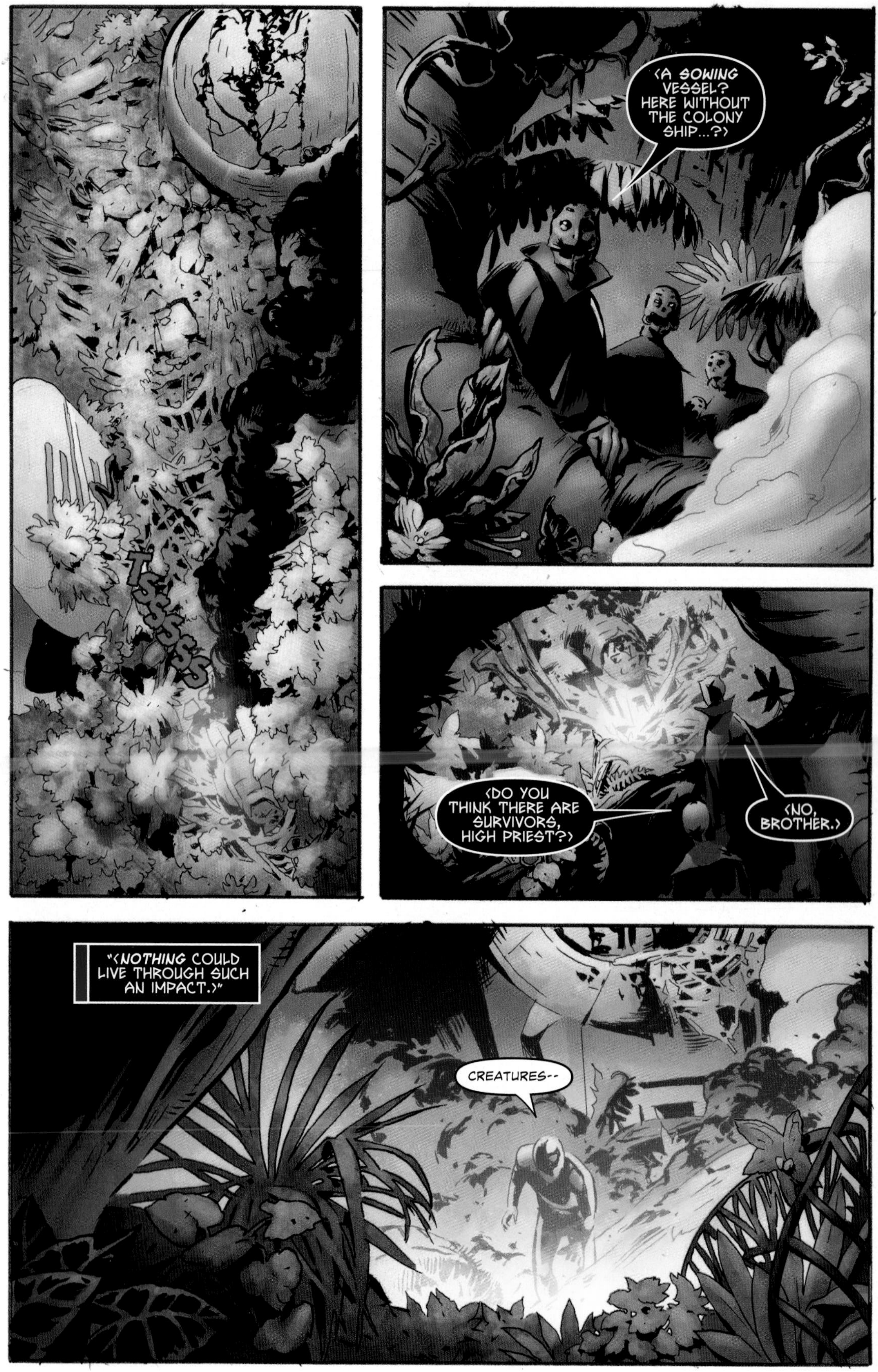

TSSSSS
<A SOWING VESSEL? HERE WITHOUT THE COLONY SHIP...?>
<DO YOU THINK THERE ARE SURVIVORS, HIGH PRIEST?>
<NO, BROTHER.>
"<NOTHING COULD LIVE THROUGH SUCH AN IMPACT.>"
CREATURES--

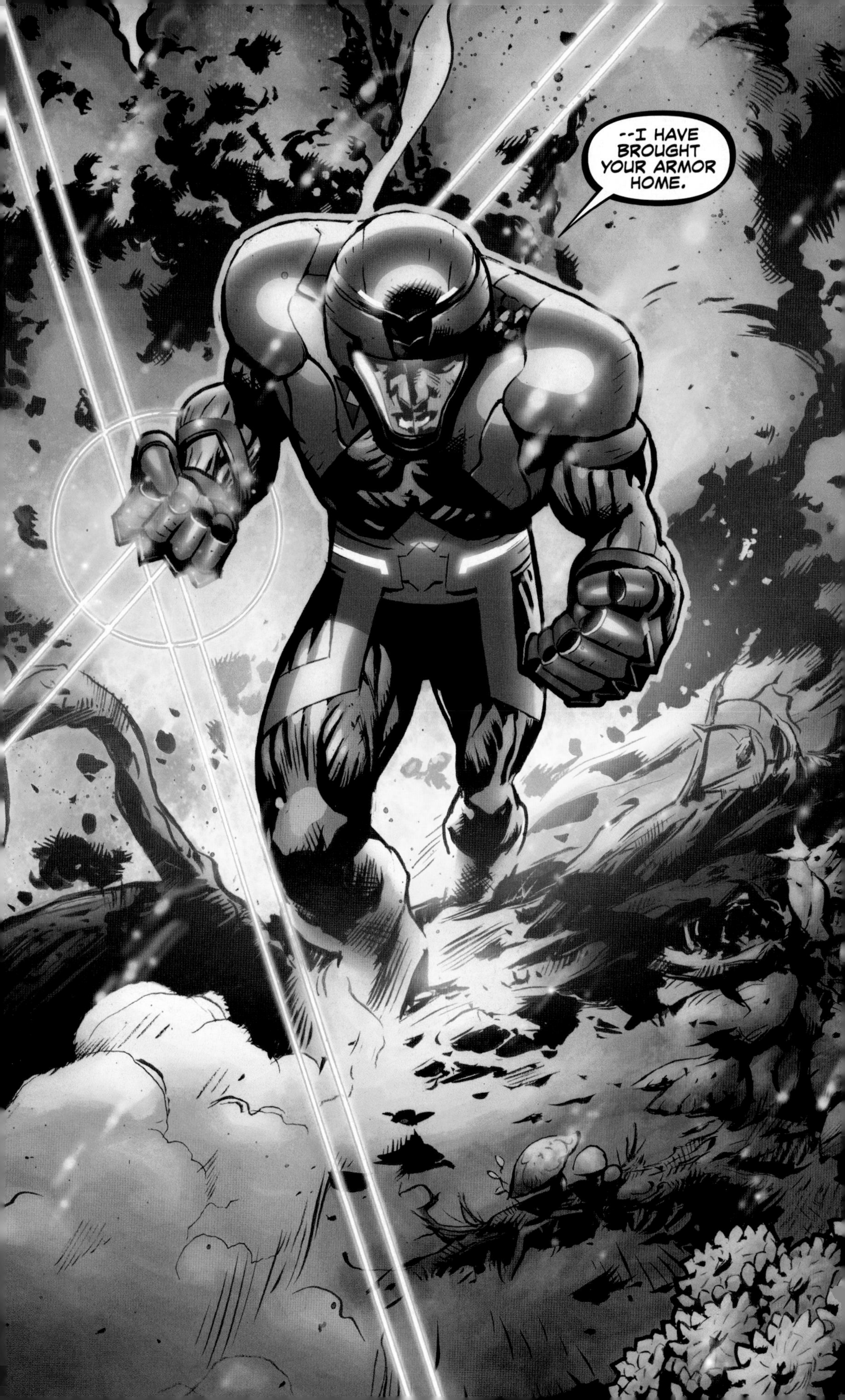
--I HAVE BROUGHT YOUR ARMOR HOME.

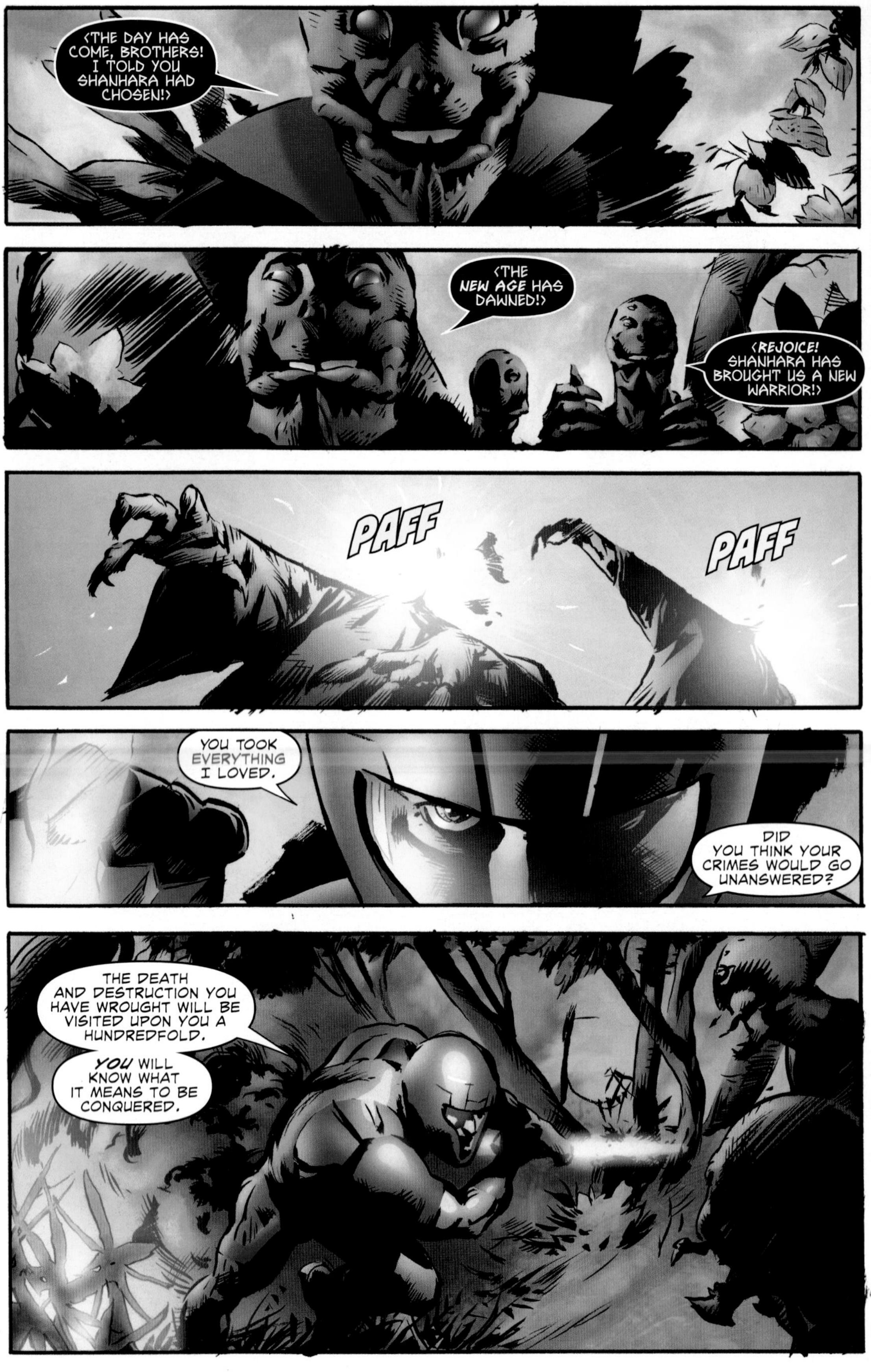
‹THE DAY HAS COME, BROTHERS! I TOLD YOU SHANHARA HAD CHOSEN!›
‹THE NEW AGE HAS DAWNED!›
‹REJOICE! SHANHARA HAS BROUGHT US A NEW WARRIOR!›
PAFF
PAFF
YOU TOOK EVERYTHING I LOVED.
DID YOU THINK YOUR CRIMES WOULD GO UNANSWERED?
THE DEATH AND DESTRUCTION YOU HAVE WROUGHT WILL BE VISITED UPON YOU A HUNDREDFOLD.
YOU WILL KNOW WHAT IT MEANS TO BE CONQUERED.

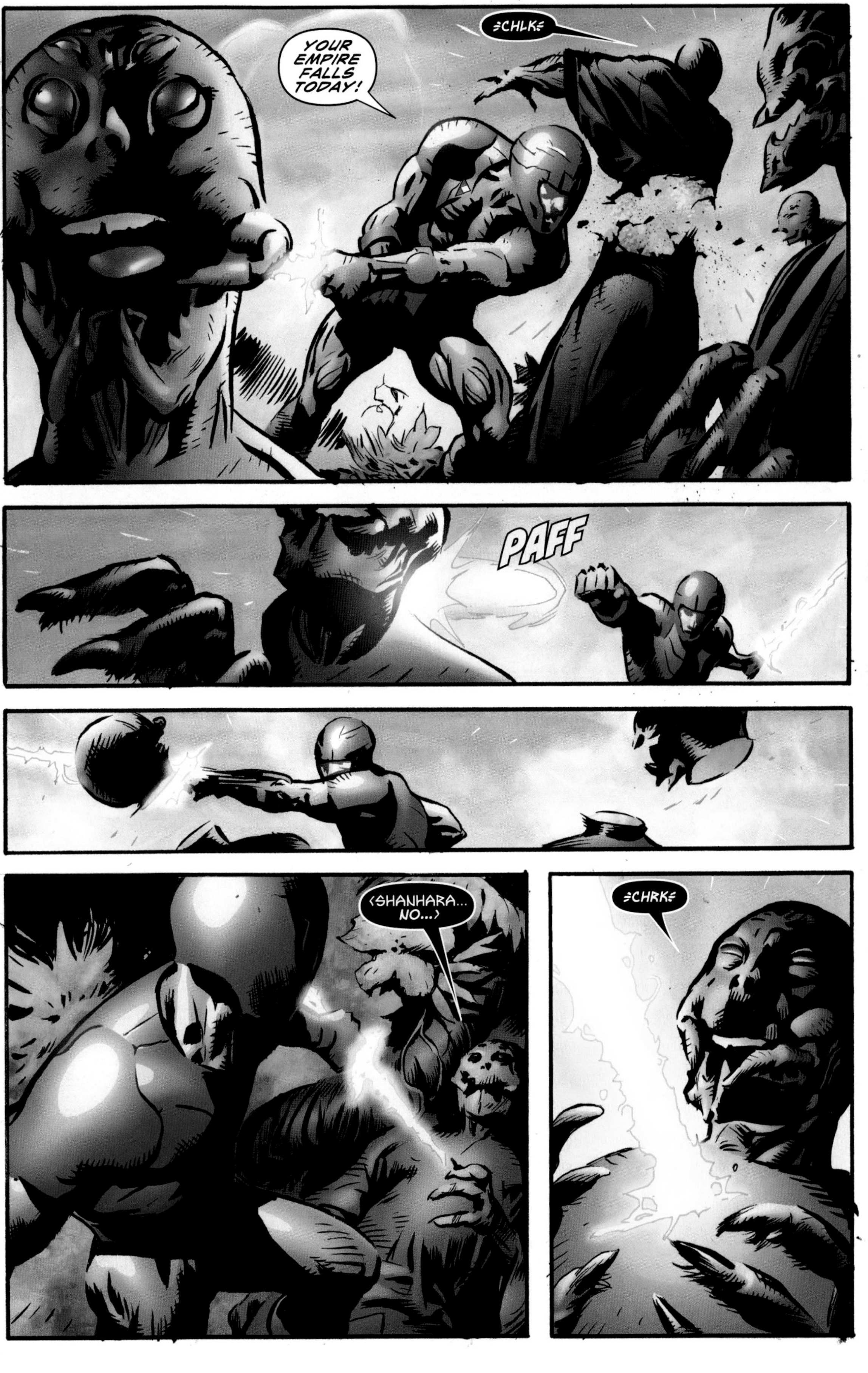
YOUR EMPIRE FALLS TODAY!
=CHLK=
PAFF
‹SHANHARA... NO...›
=CHRK=

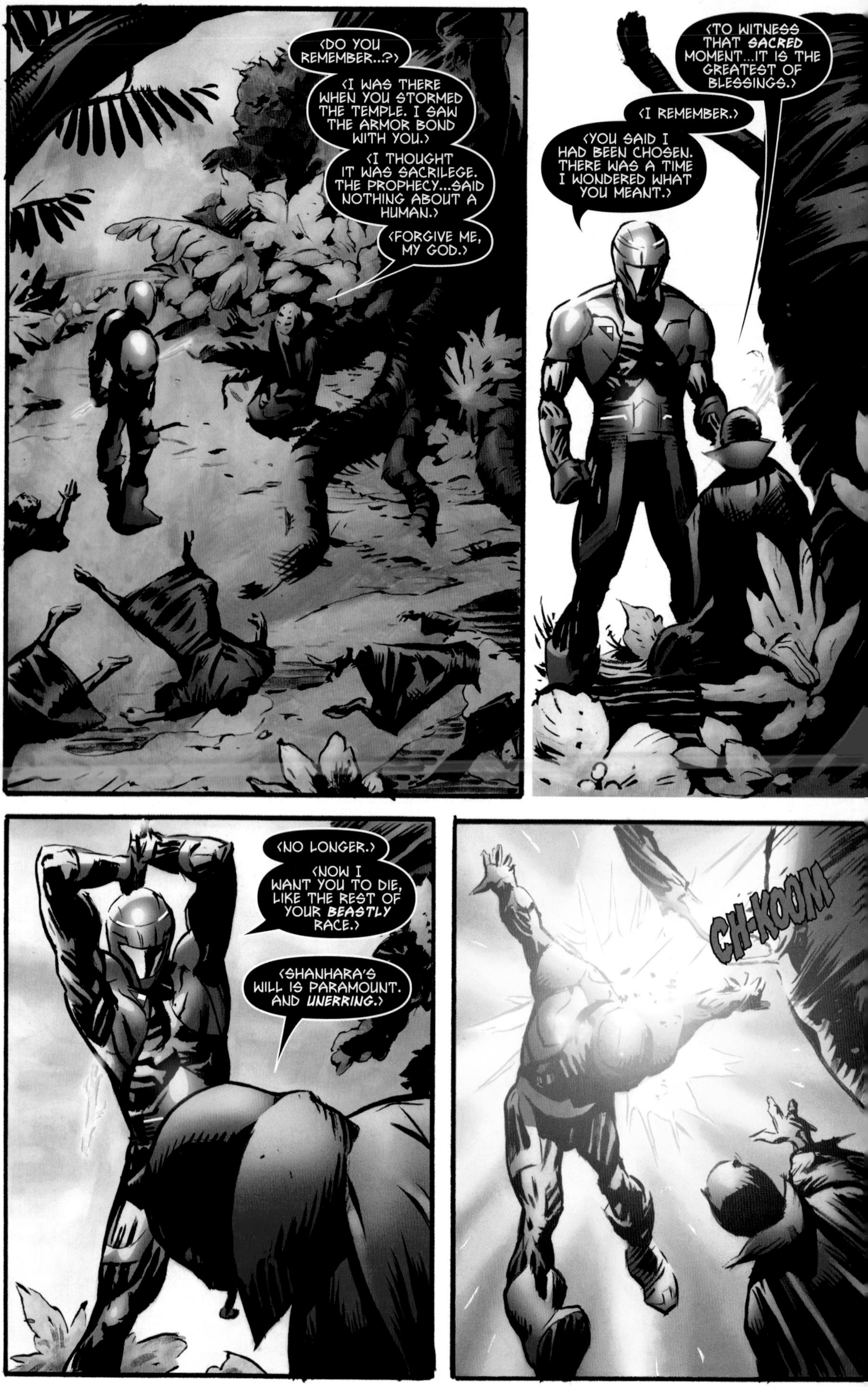
‹DO YOU REMEMBER...?›
‹I WAS THERE WHEN YOU STORMED THE TEMPLE. I SAW THE ARMOR BOND WITH YOU.›
‹I THOUGHT IT WAS SACRILEGE. THE PROPHECY...SAID NOTHING ABOUT A HUMAN.›
‹FORGIVE ME, MY GOD.›
‹TO WITNESS THAT SACRED MOMENT...IT IS THE GREATEST OF BLESSINGS.›
‹I REMEMBER.›
‹YOU SAID I HAD BEEN CHOSEN. THERE WAS A TIME I WONDERED WHAT YOU MEANT.›
‹NO LONGER.›
‹NOW I WANT YOU TO DIE, LIKE THE REST OF YOUR BEASTLY RACE.›
‹SHANHARA'S WILL IS PARAMOUNT. AND UNERRING.›
CH-KOOM

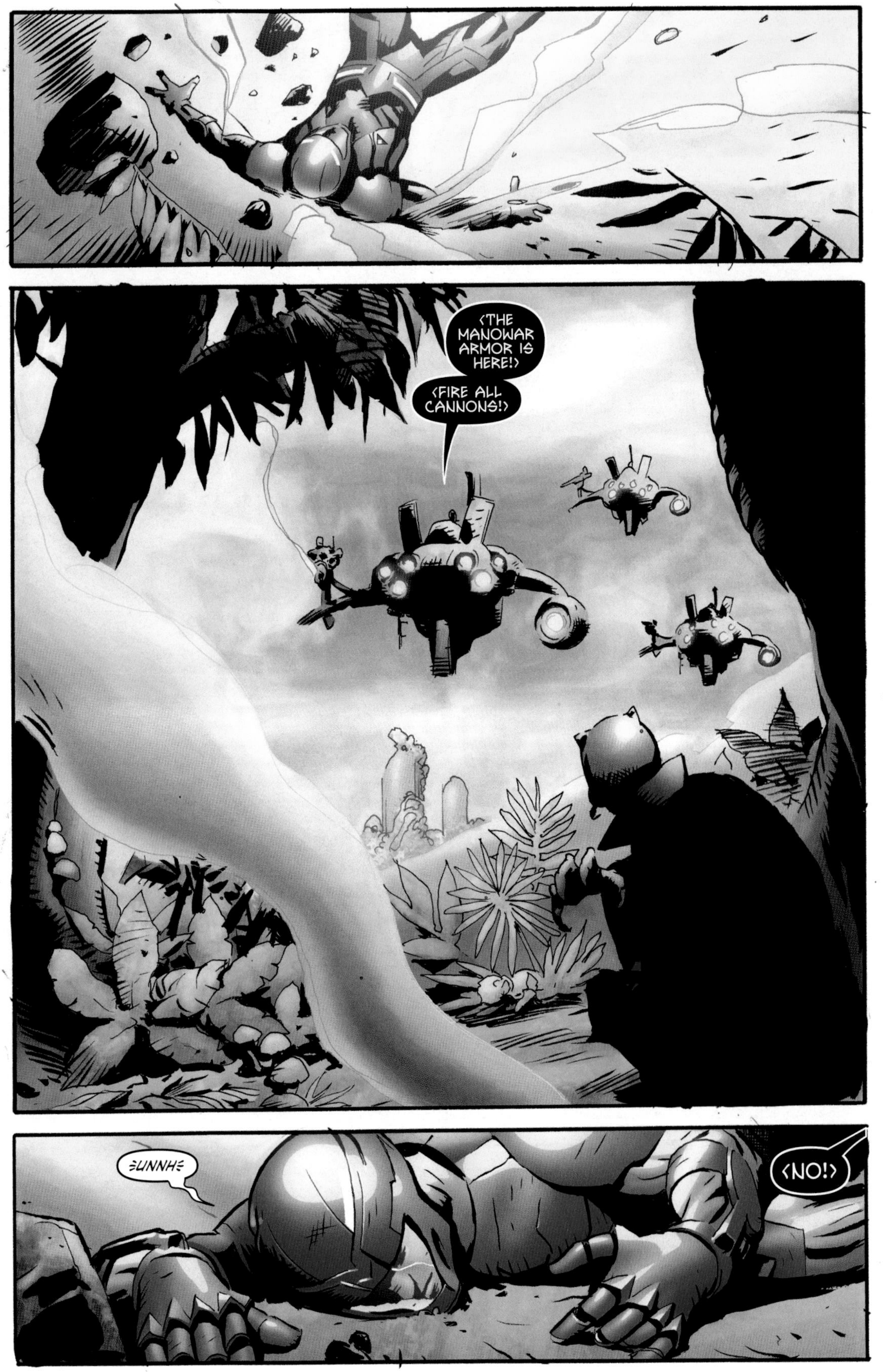
‹THE MANOWAR ARMOR IS HERE!›
‹FIRE ALL CANNONS!›
UNNH
‹NO!›

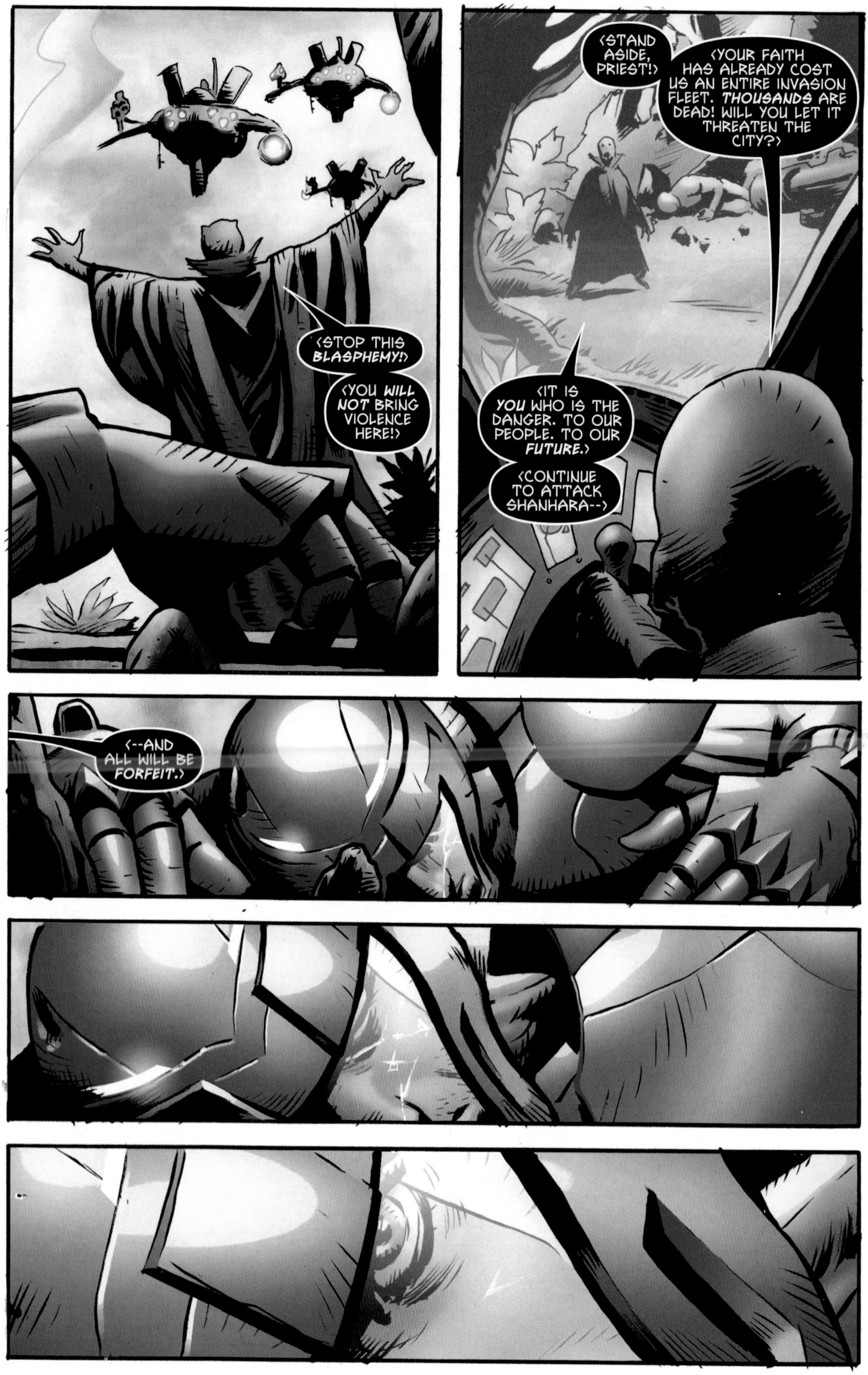

<STOP THIS BLASPHEMY!>
<YOU WILL NOT BRING VIOLENCE HERE!>
<STAND ASIDE, PRIEST!>
<YOUR FAITH HAS ALREADY COST US AN ENTIRE INVASION FLEET. THOUSANDS ARE DEAD! WILL YOU LET IT THREATEN THE CITY?>
<IT IS YOU WHO IS THE DANGER. TO OUR PEOPLE. TO OUR FUTURE.>
<CONTINUE TO ATTACK SHANHARA-->
<--AND ALL WILL BE FORFEIT.>

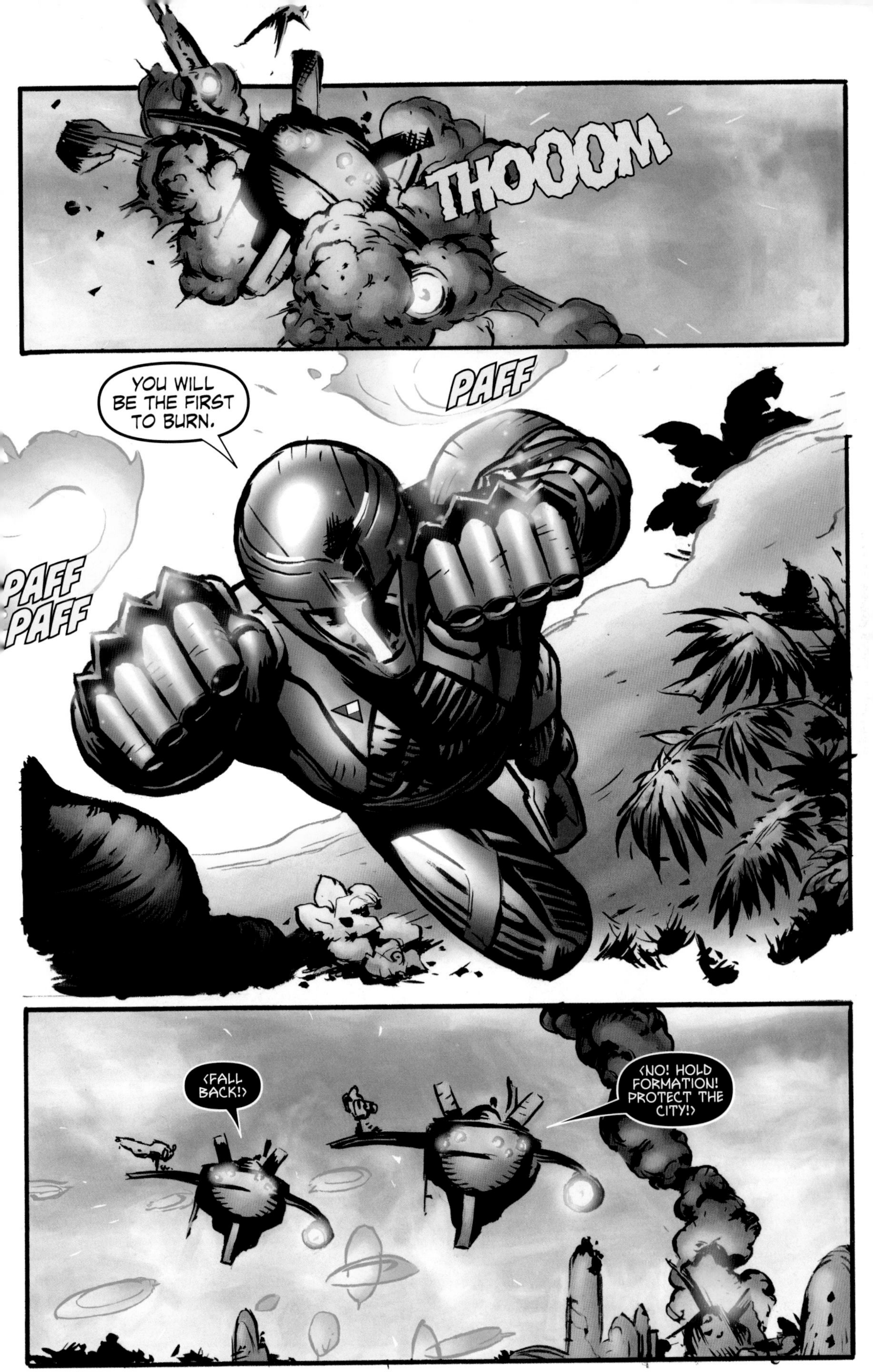
THOOOM
YOU WILL BE THE FIRST TO BURN.
PAFF
PAFF PAFF
<FALL BACK!>
<NO! HOLD FORMATION! PROTECT THE CITY!>

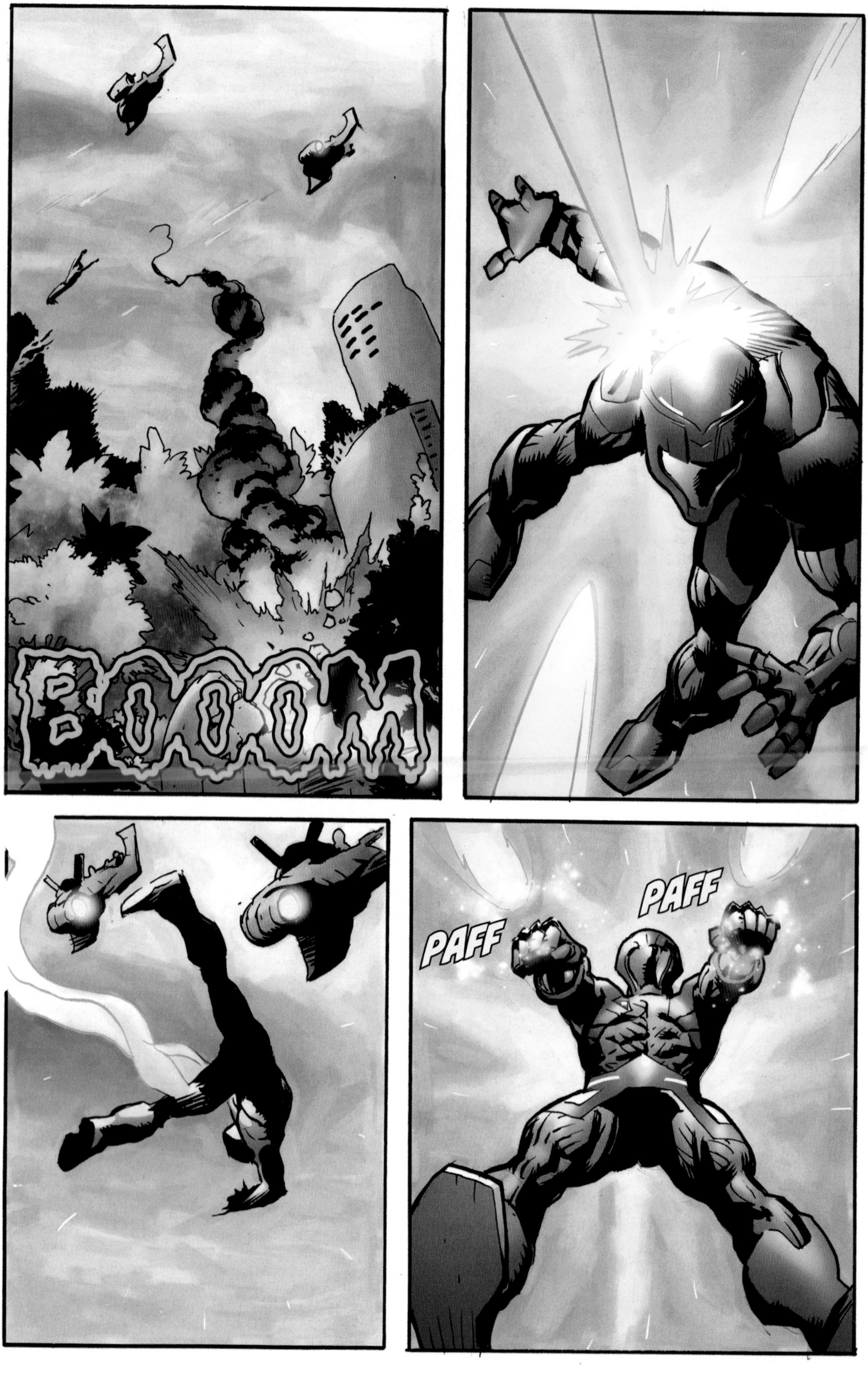
BOOOM
PAFF
PAFF

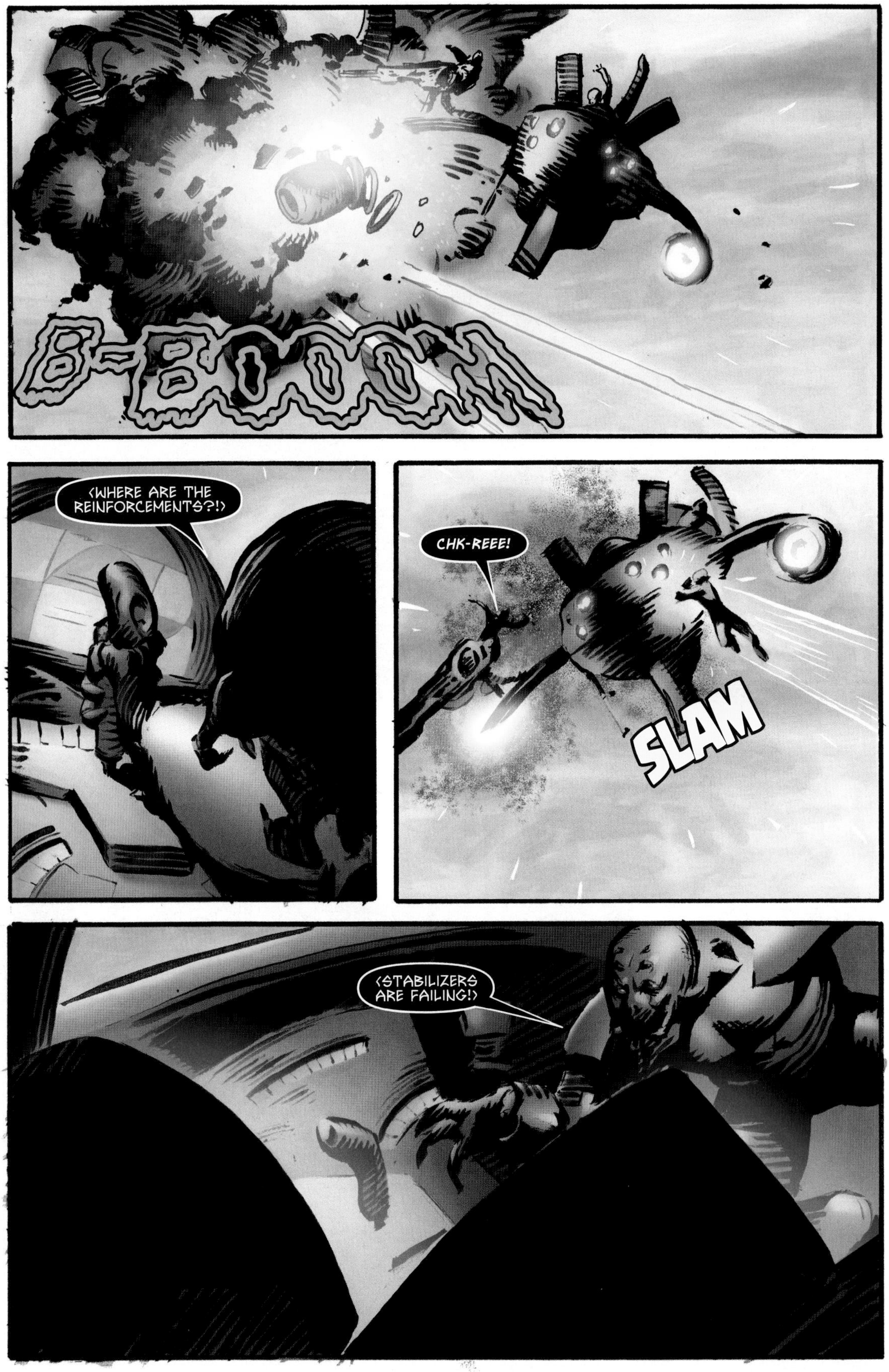
B-BOOOM
<WHERE ARE THE REINFORCEMENTS?!>
CHK-REEE!
SLAM
<STABILIZERS ARE FAILING!>

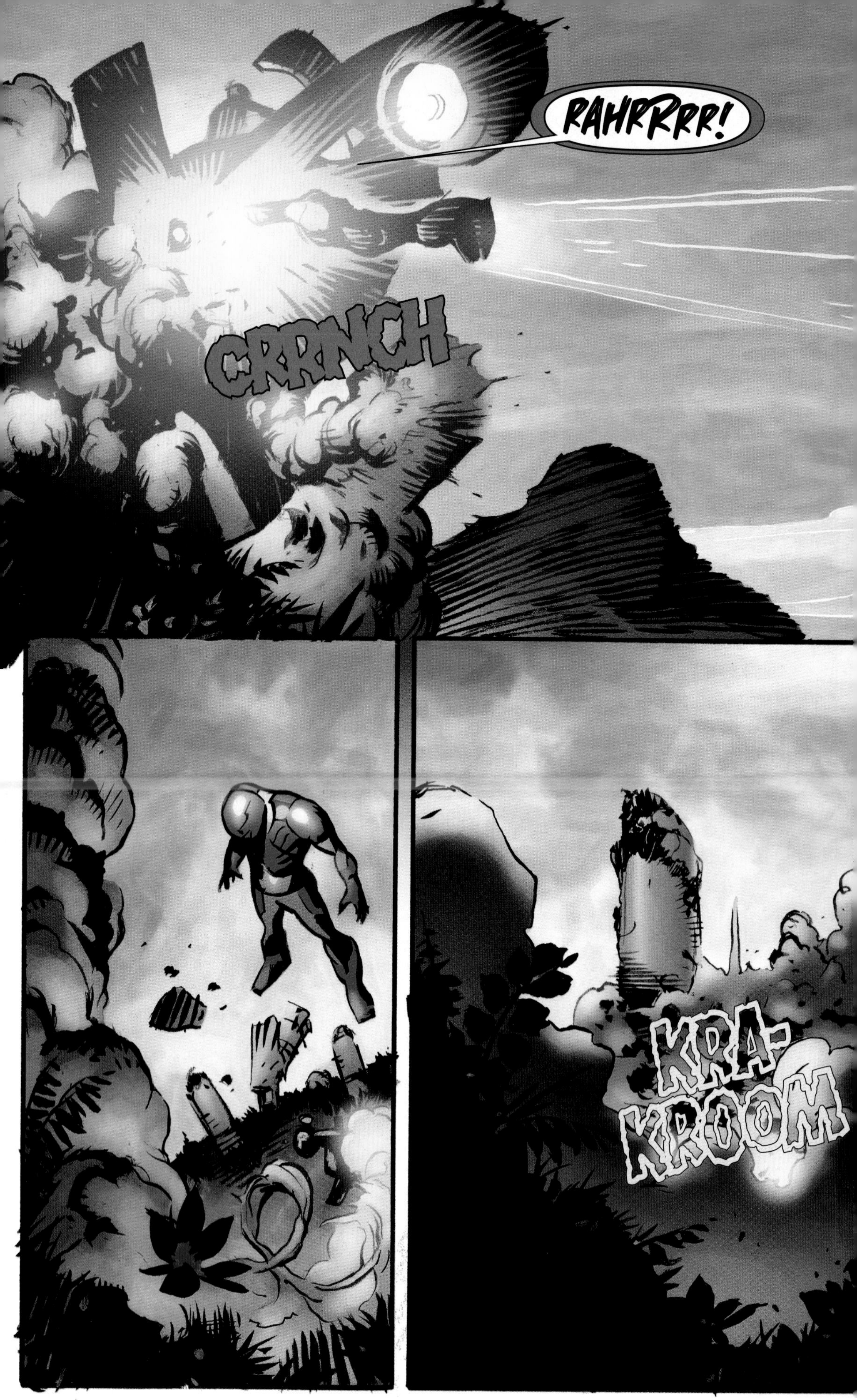
RAHRRRR!
CRRNCH
KRA-KROOM

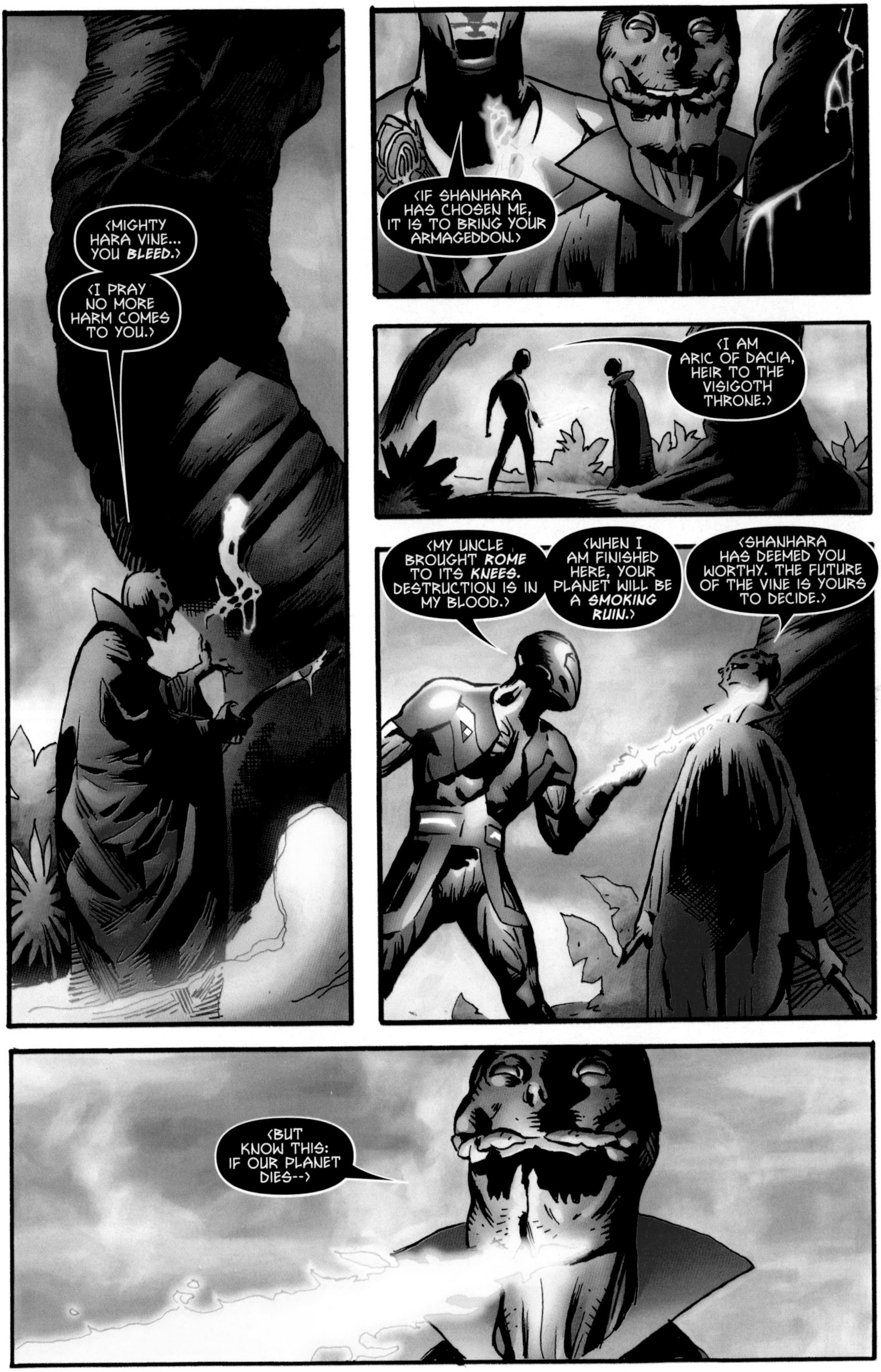

‹MIGHTY HARA VINE... YOU BLEED.›
‹I PRAY NO MORE HARM COMES TO YOU.›
‹IF SHANHARA HAS CHOSEN ME, IT IS TO BRING YOUR ARMAGEDDON.›
‹I AM ARIC OF DACIA, HEIR TO THE VISIGOTH THRONE.›
‹MY UNCLE BROUGHT ROME TO ITS KNEES. DESTRUCTION IS IN MY BLOOD.›
‹WHEN I AM FINISHED HERE, YOUR PLANET WILL BE A SMOKING RUIN.›
‹SHANHARA HAS DEEMED YOU WORTHY. THE FUTURE OF THE VINE IS YOURS TO DECIDE.›
‹BUT KNOW THIS: IF OUR PLANET DIES--›

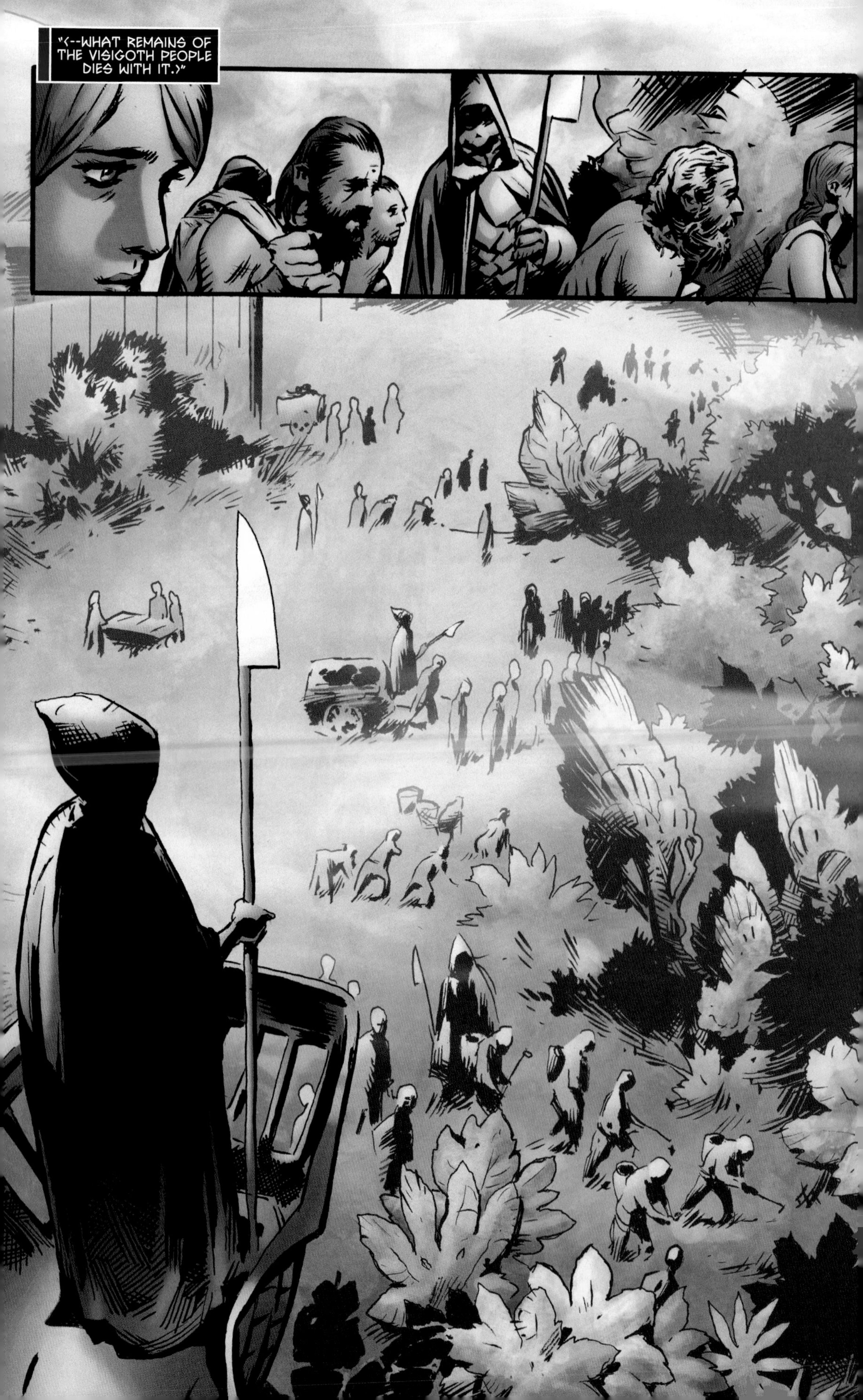
"<--WHAT REMAINS OF THE VISIGOTH PEOPLE DIES WITH IT.>"

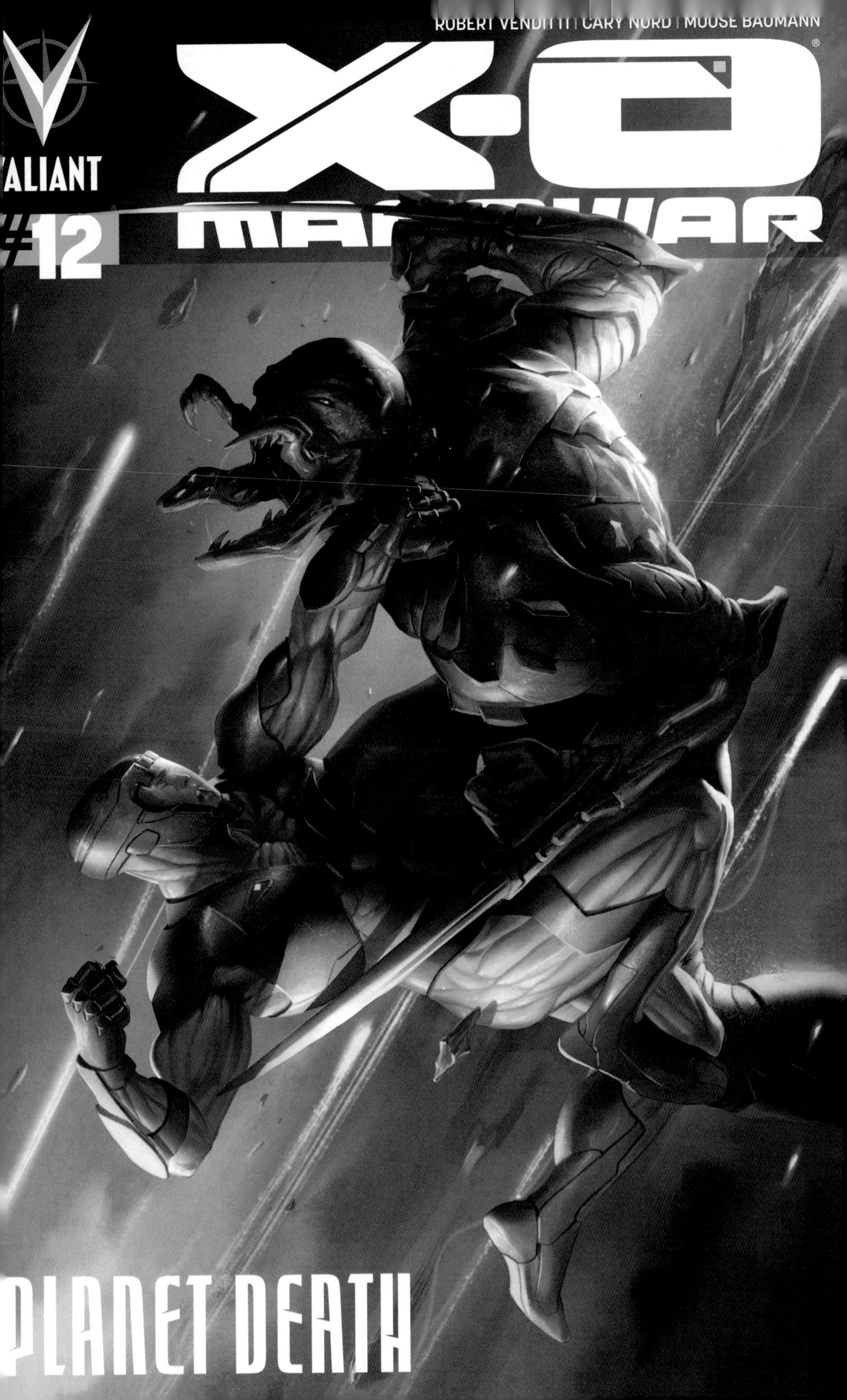
ROBERT VENDITTI | CARY NORD | MOOSE BAUMANN
VALIANT
X-O
#12
PLANET DEATH

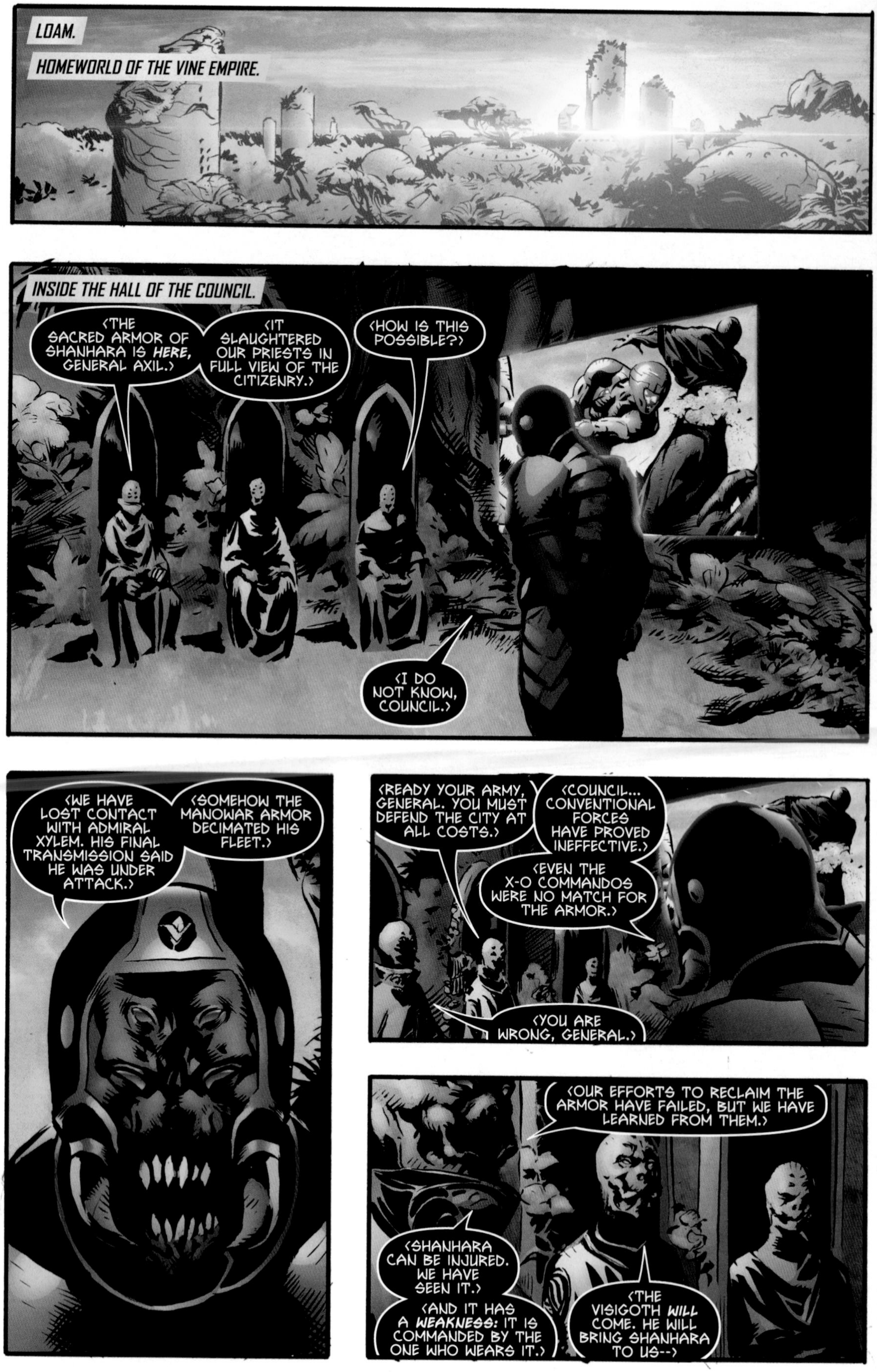
LOAM.
HOMEWORLD OF THE VINE EMPIRE.
INSIDE THE HALL OF THE COUNCIL.
‹THE SACRED ARMOR OF SHANHARA IS *HERE*, GENERAL AXIL.›
‹IT SLAUGHTERED OUR PRIESTS IN FULL VIEW OF THE CITIZENRY.›
‹HOW IS THIS POSSIBLE?›
‹I DO NOT KNOW, COUNCIL.›
‹WE HAVE LOST CONTACT WITH ADMIRAL XYLEM. HIS FINAL TRANSMISSION SAID HE WAS UNDER ATTACK.›
‹SOMEHOW THE MANOWAR ARMOR DECIMATED HIS FLEET.›
‹READY YOUR ARMY, GENERAL. YOU MUST DEFEND THE CITY AT ALL COSTS.›
‹COUNCIL... CONVENTIONAL FORCES HAVE PROVED INEFFECTIVE.›
‹EVEN THE X-O COMMANDOS WERE NO MATCH FOR THE ARMOR.›
‹YOU ARE WRONG, GENERAL.›
‹OUR EFFORTS TO RECLAIM THE ARMOR HAVE FAILED, BUT WE HAVE LEARNED FROM THEM.›
‹SHANHARA CAN BE INJURED. WE HAVE SEEN IT.›
‹AND IT HAS A *WEAKNESS*: IT IS COMMANDED BY THE ONE WHO WEARS IT.›
‹THE VISIGOTH *WILL* COME. HE WILL BRING SHANHARA TO US--›

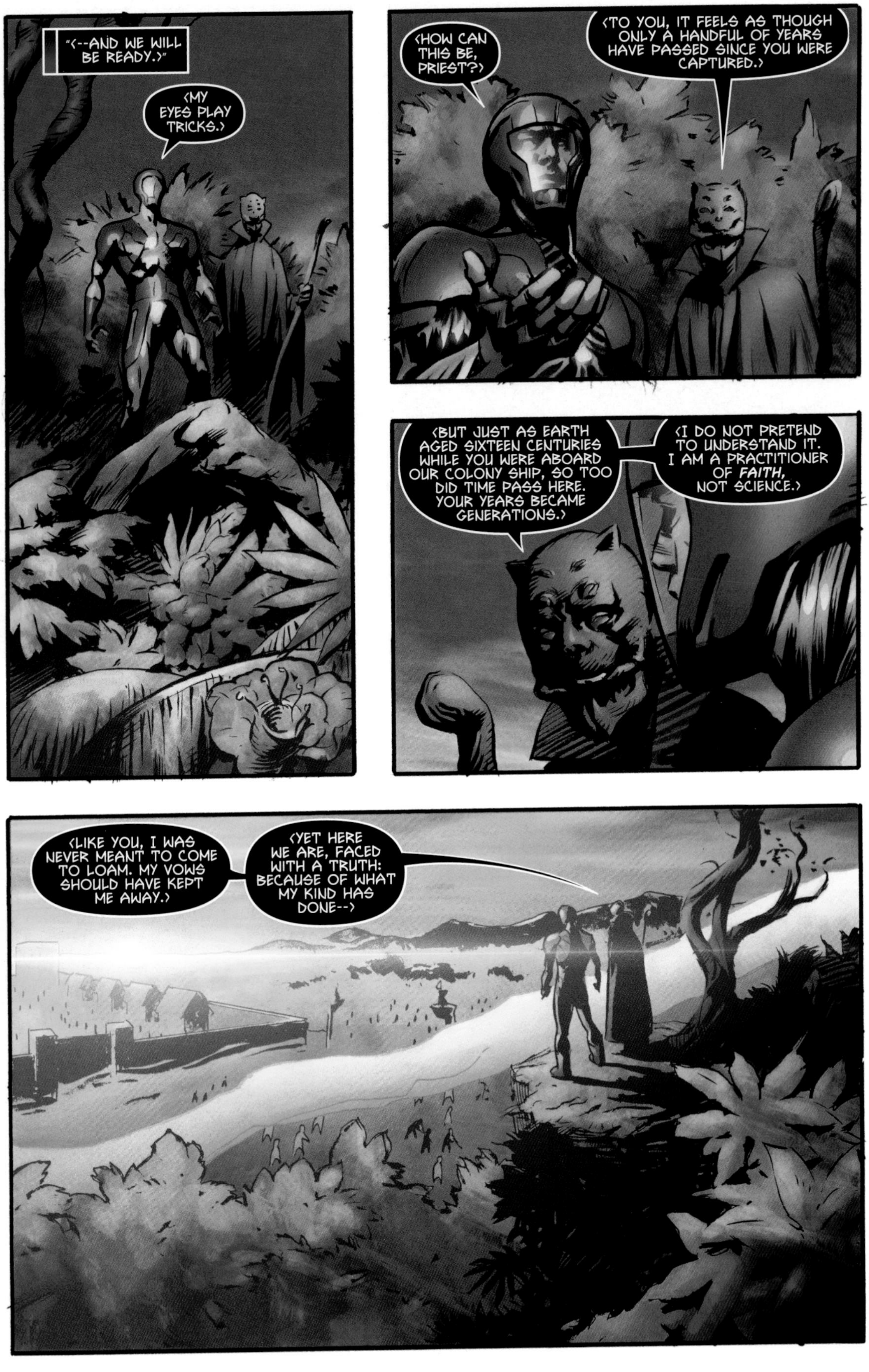
"<--AND WE WILL BE READY.>"
<MY EYES PLAY TRICKS.>
<HOW CAN THIS BE, PRIEST?>
<TO YOU, IT FEELS AS THOUGH ONLY A HANDFUL OF YEARS HAVE PASSED SINCE YOU WERE CAPTURED.>
<BUT JUST AS EARTH AGED SIXTEEN CENTURIES WHILE YOU WERE ABOARD OUR COLONY SHIP, SO TOO DID TIME PASS HERE. YOUR YEARS BECAME GENERATIONS.>
<I DO NOT PRETEND TO UNDERSTAND IT. I AM A PRACTITIONER OF *FAITH*, NOT SCIENCE.>
<LIKE YOU, I WAS NEVER MEANT TO COME TO LOAM. MY VOWS SHOULD HAVE KEPT ME AWAY.>
<YET HERE WE ARE, FACED WITH A TRUTH: BECAUSE OF WHAT MY KIND HAS DONE-->

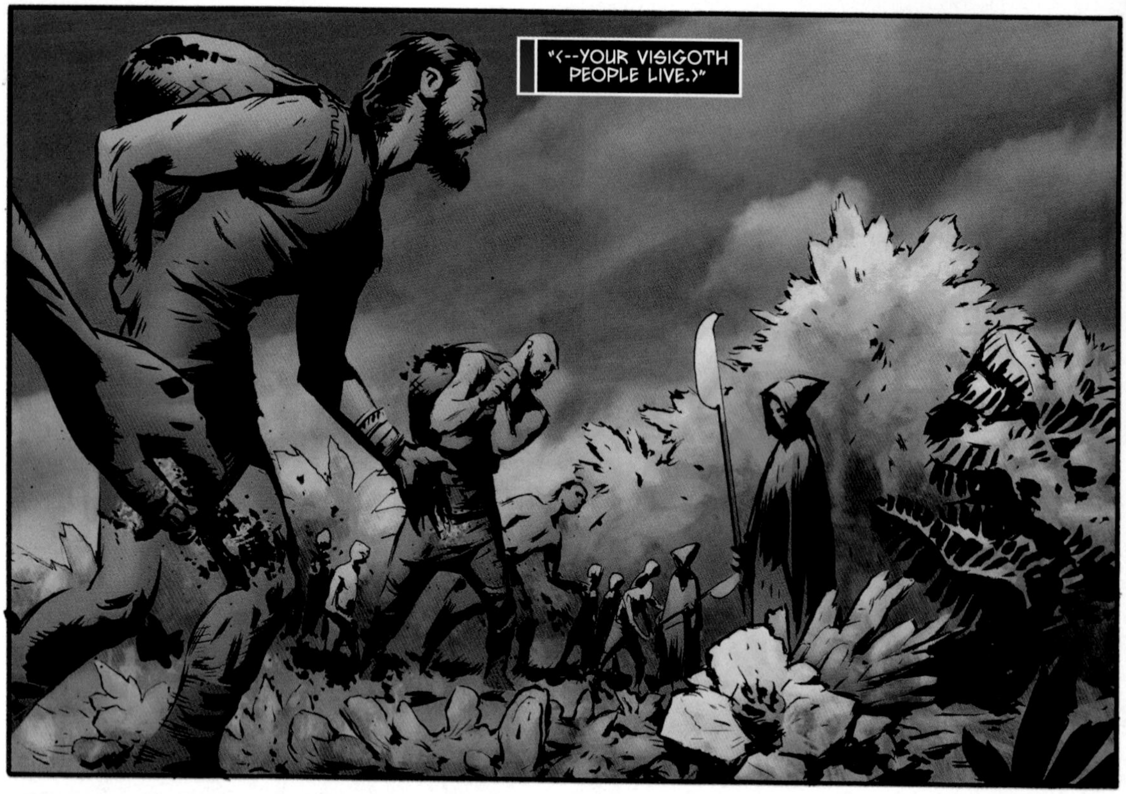
"<--YOUR VISIGOTH PEOPLE LIVE.>"

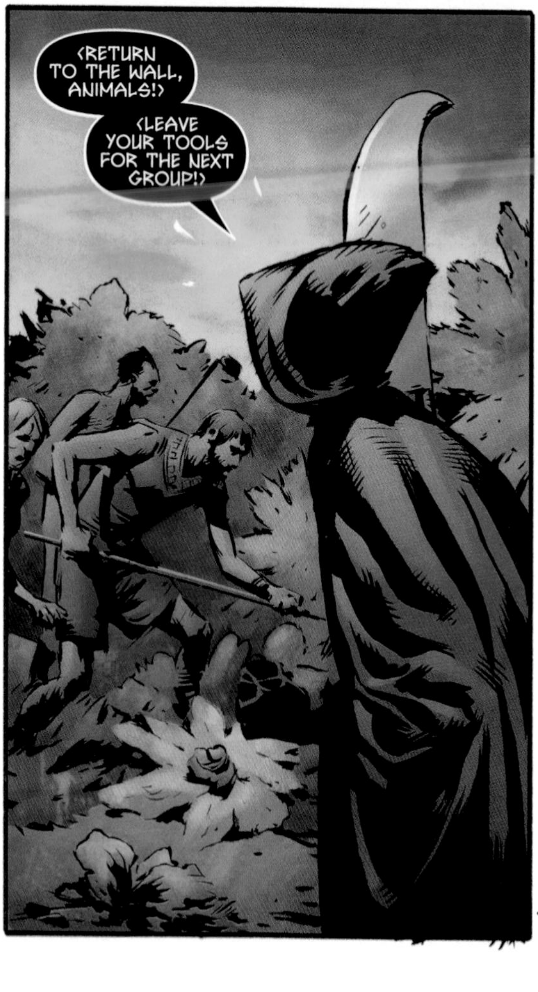
<RETURN TO THE WALL, ANIMALS!>
<LEAVE YOUR TOOLS FOR THE NEXT GROUP!>

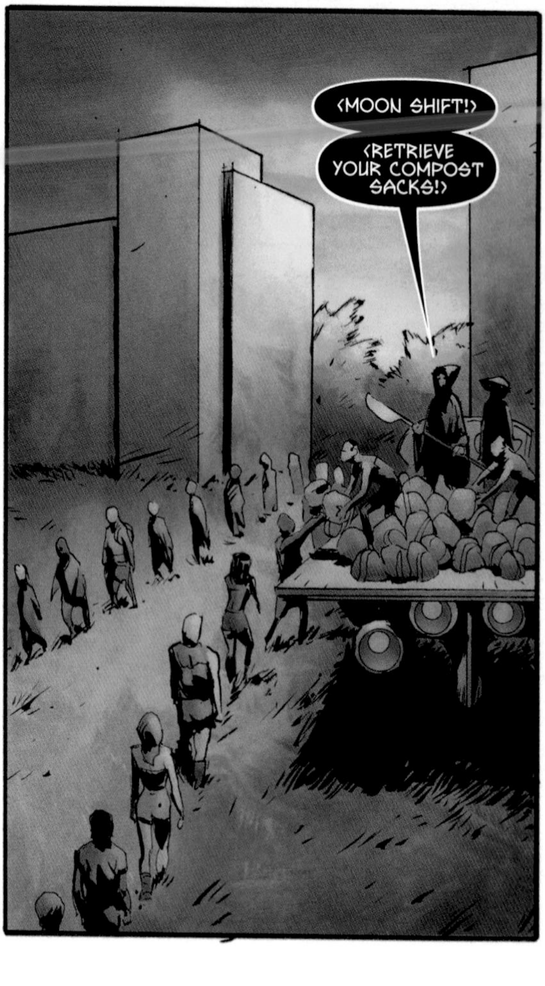
<MOON SHIFT!>
<RETRIEVE YOUR COMPOST SACKS!>

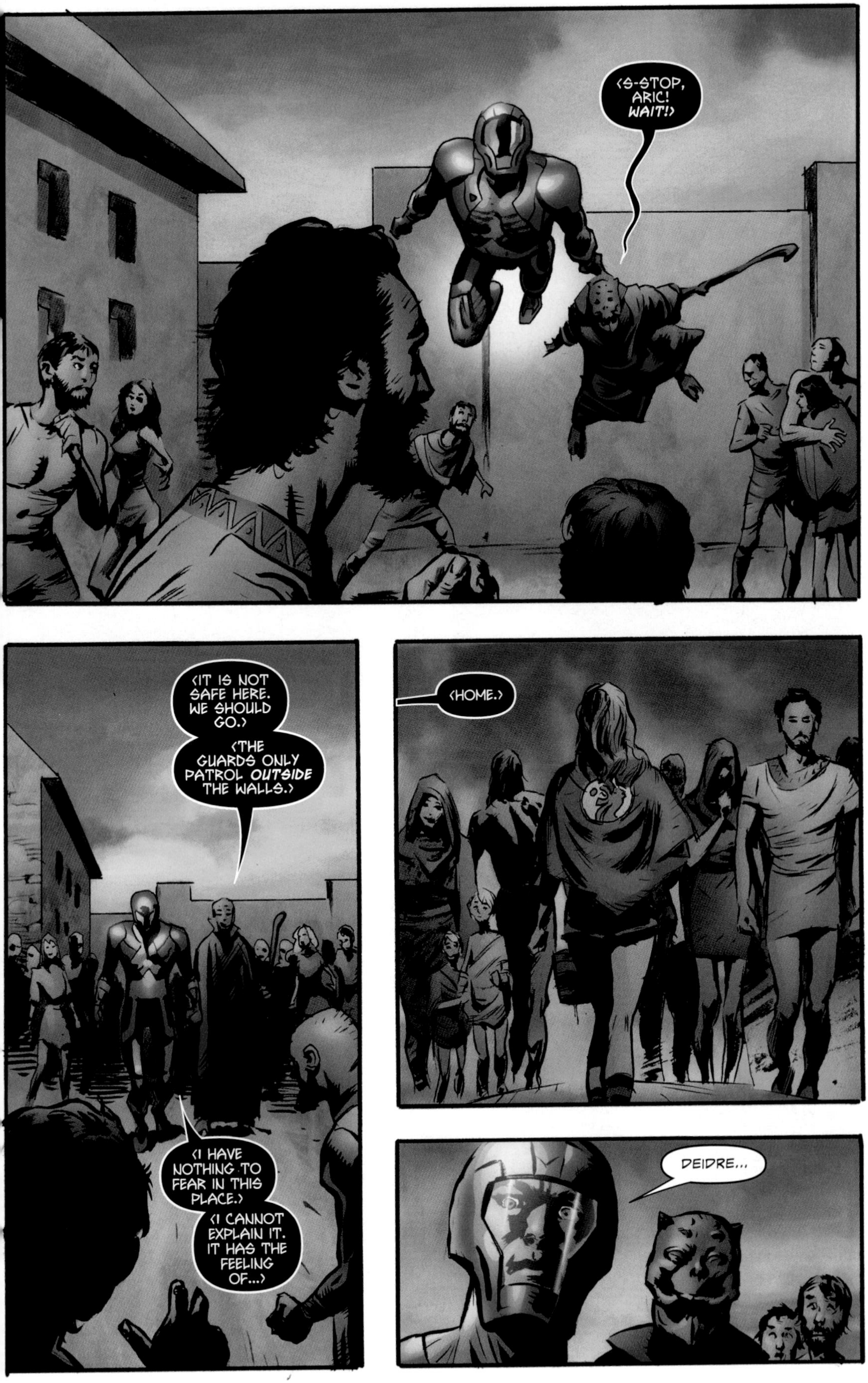

‹S-STOP, ARIC! WAIT!›
‹IT IS NOT SAFE HERE. WE SHOULD GO.›
‹THE GUARDS ONLY PATROL OUTSIDE THE WALLS.›
‹I HAVE NOTHING TO FEAR IN THIS PLACE.›
‹I CANNOT EXPLAIN IT. IT HAS THE FEELING OF...›
‹HOME.›
DEIDRE...

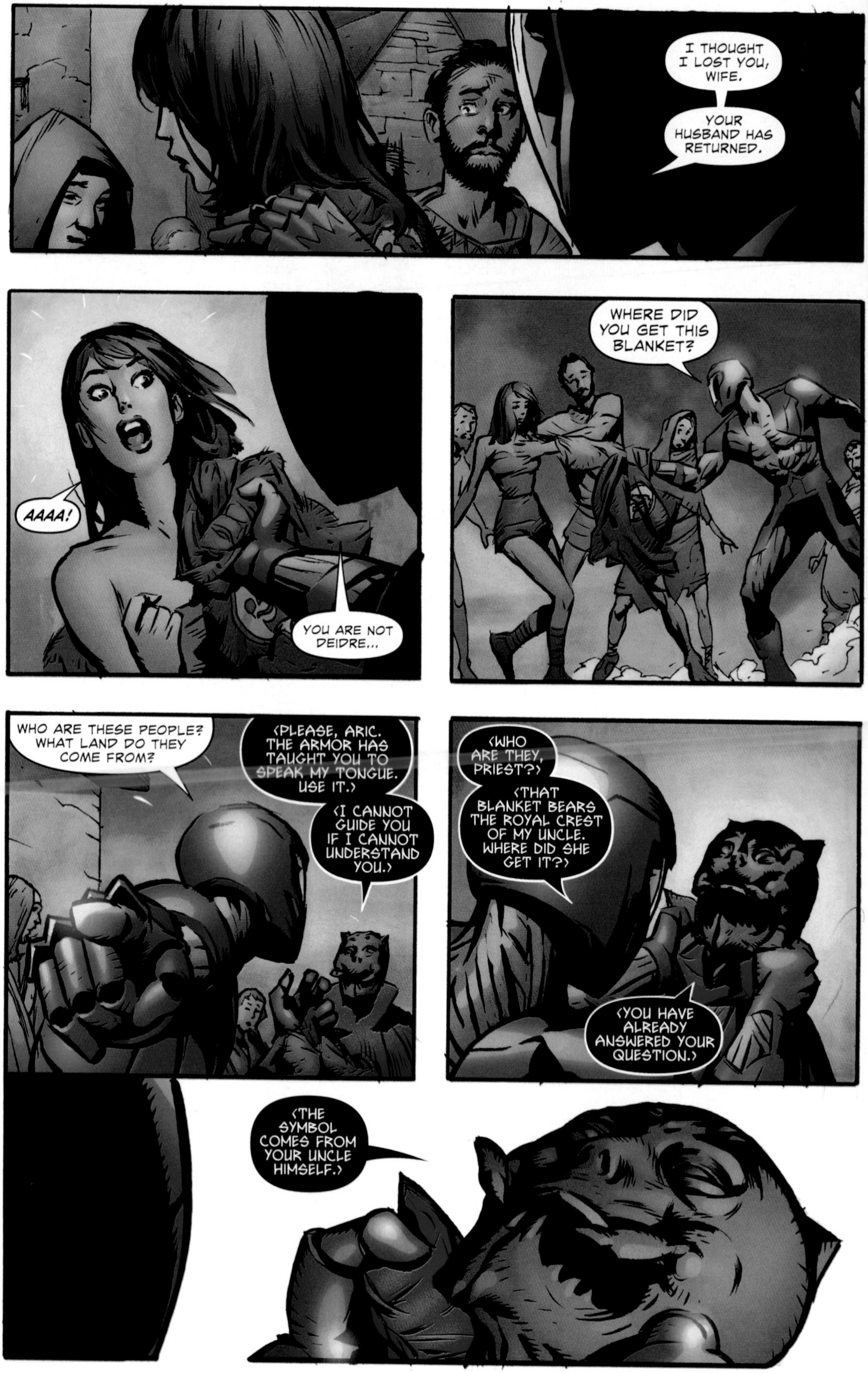
I THOUGHT I LOST YOU, WIFE.
YOUR HUSBAND HAS RETURNED.
AAAA!
YOU ARE NOT DEIDRE...
WHERE DID YOU GET THIS BLANKET?
WHO ARE THESE PEOPLE? WHAT LAND DO THEY COME FROM?
<PLEASE, ARIC. THE ARMOR HAS TAUGHT YOU TO SPEAK MY TONGUE. USE IT.>
<I CANNOT GUIDE YOU IF I CANNOT UNDERSTAND YOU.>
<WHO ARE THEY, PRIEST?>
<THAT BLANKET BEARS THE ROYAL CREST OF MY UNCLE. WHERE DID SHE GET IT?>
<YOU HAVE ALREADY ANSWERED YOUR QUESTION.>
<THE SYMBOL COMES FROM YOUR UNCLE HIMSELF.>

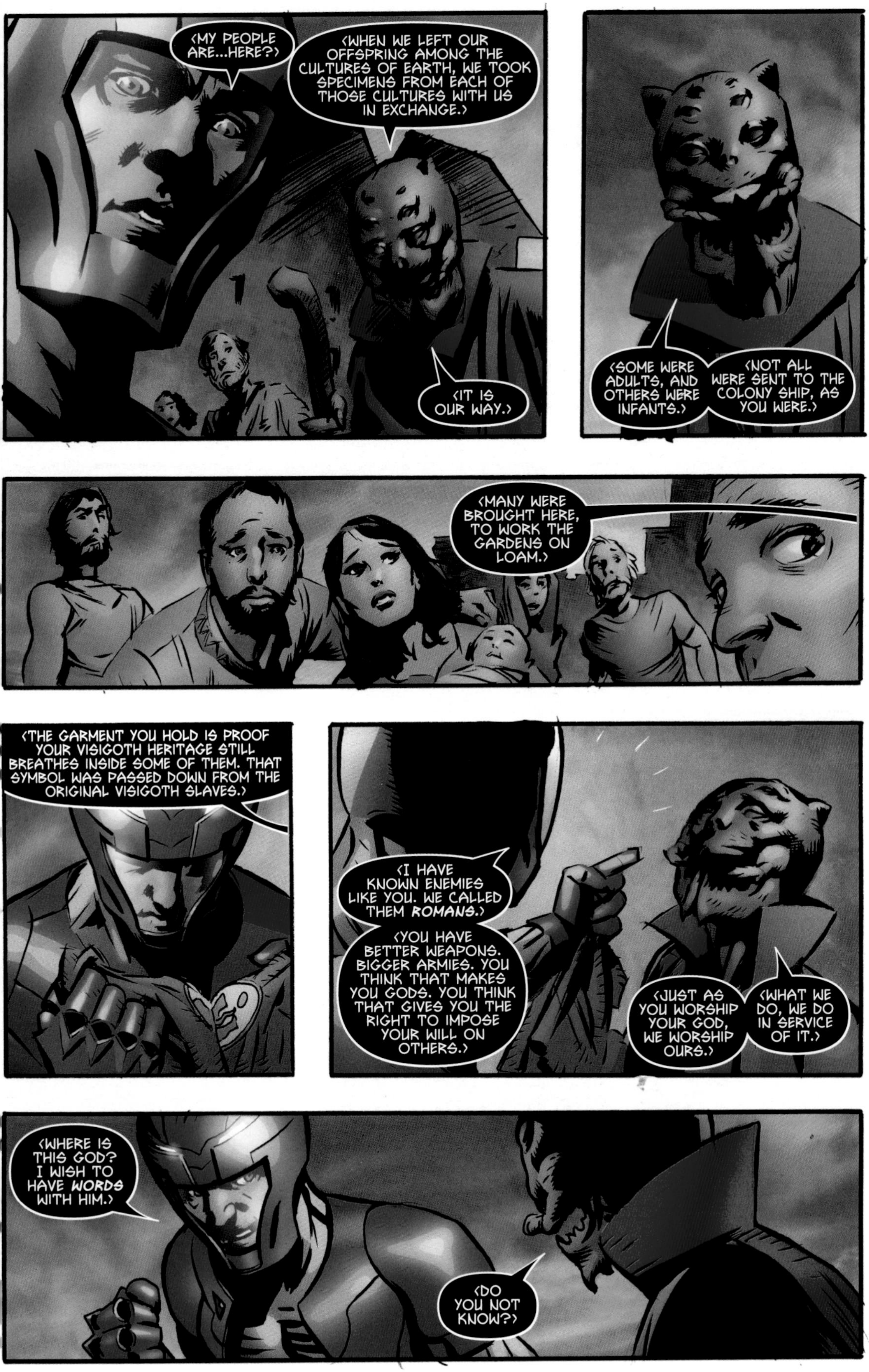

<MY PEOPLE ARE...HERE?>
<WHEN WE LEFT OUR OFFSPRING AMONG THE CULTURES OF EARTH, WE TOOK SPECIMENS FROM EACH OF THOSE CULTURES WITH US IN EXCHANGE.>
<IT IS OUR WAY.>
<SOME WERE ADULTS, AND OTHERS WERE INFANTS.>
<NOT ALL WERE SENT TO THE COLONY SHIP, AS YOU WERE.>
<MANY WERE BROUGHT HERE, TO WORK THE GARDENS ON LOAM.>
<THE GARMENT YOU HOLD IS PROOF YOUR VISIGOTH HERITAGE STILL BREATHES INSIDE SOME OF THEM. THAT SYMBOL WAS PASSED DOWN FROM THE ORIGINAL VISIGOTH SLAVES.>
<I HAVE KNOWN ENEMIES LIKE YOU. WE CALLED THEM **ROMANS**.>
<YOU HAVE BETTER WEAPONS. BIGGER ARMIES. YOU THINK THAT MAKES YOU GODS. YOU THINK THAT GIVES YOU THE RIGHT TO IMPOSE YOUR WILL ON OTHERS.>
<JUST AS YOU WORSHIP YOUR GOD, WE WORSHIP OURS.>
<WHAT WE DO, WE DO IN SERVICE OF IT.>
<WHERE IS THIS GOD? I WISH TO HAVE **WORDS** WITH HIM.>
<DO YOU NOT KNOW?>

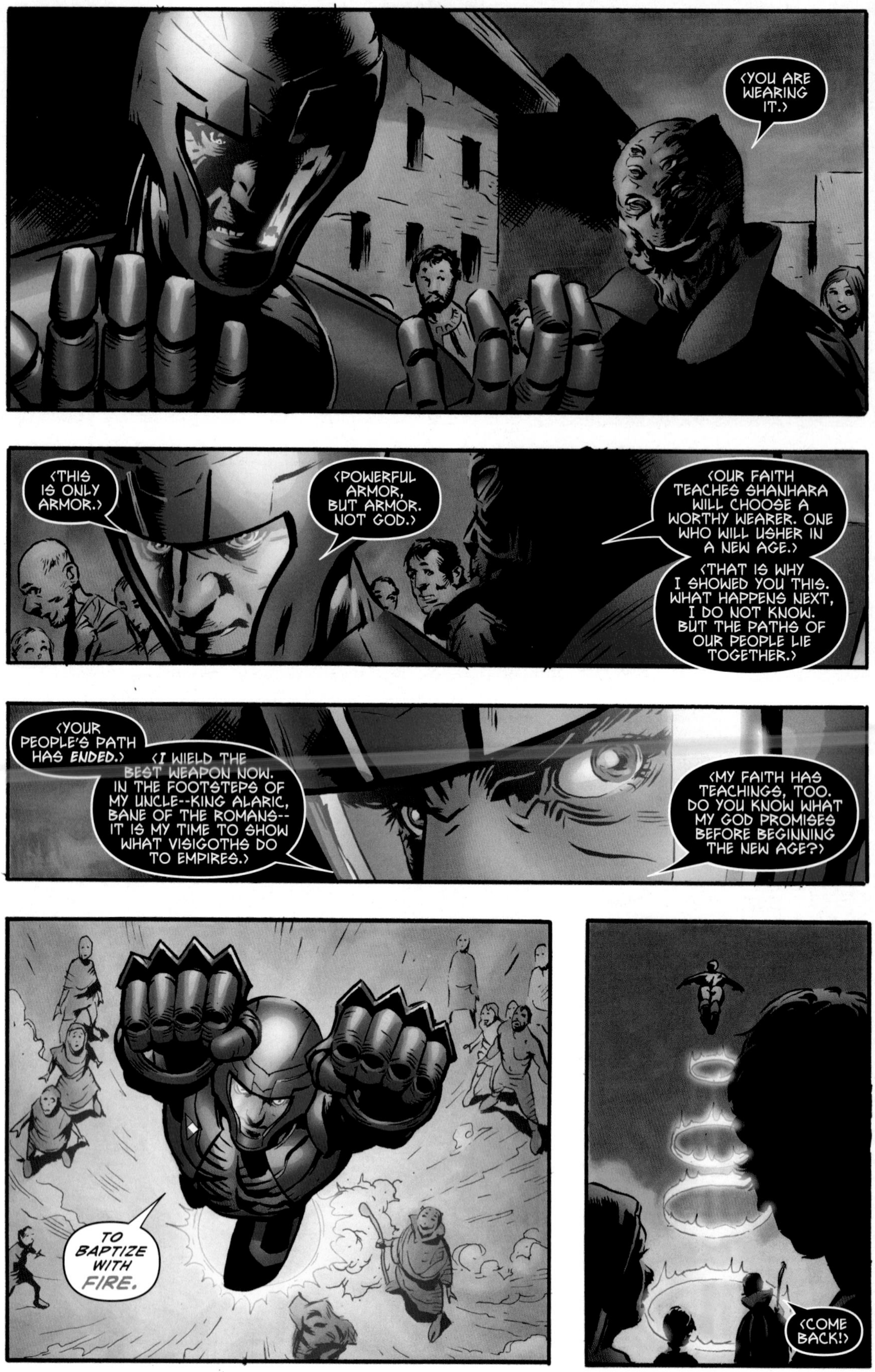

‹YOU ARE WEARING IT.›
‹THIS IS ONLY ARMOR.›
‹POWERFUL ARMOR, BUT ARMOR. NOT GOD.›
‹OUR FAITH TEACHES SHANHARA WILL CHOOSE A WORTHY WEARER. ONE WHO WILL USHER IN A NEW AGE.›
‹THAT IS WHY I SHOWED YOU THIS. WHAT HAPPENS NEXT, I DO NOT KNOW. BUT THE PATHS OF OUR PEOPLE LIE TOGETHER.›
‹YOUR PEOPLE'S PATH HAS ENDED.›
‹I WIELD THE BEST WEAPON NOW. IN THE FOOTSTEPS OF MY UNCLE--KING ALARIC, BANE OF THE ROMANS--IT IS MY TIME TO SHOW WHAT VISIGOTHS DO TO EMPIRES.›
‹MY FAITH HAS TEACHINGS, TOO. DO YOU KNOW WHAT MY GOD PROMISES BEFORE BEGINNING THE NEW AGE?›
TO BAPTIZE WITH FIRE.
‹COME BACK!›

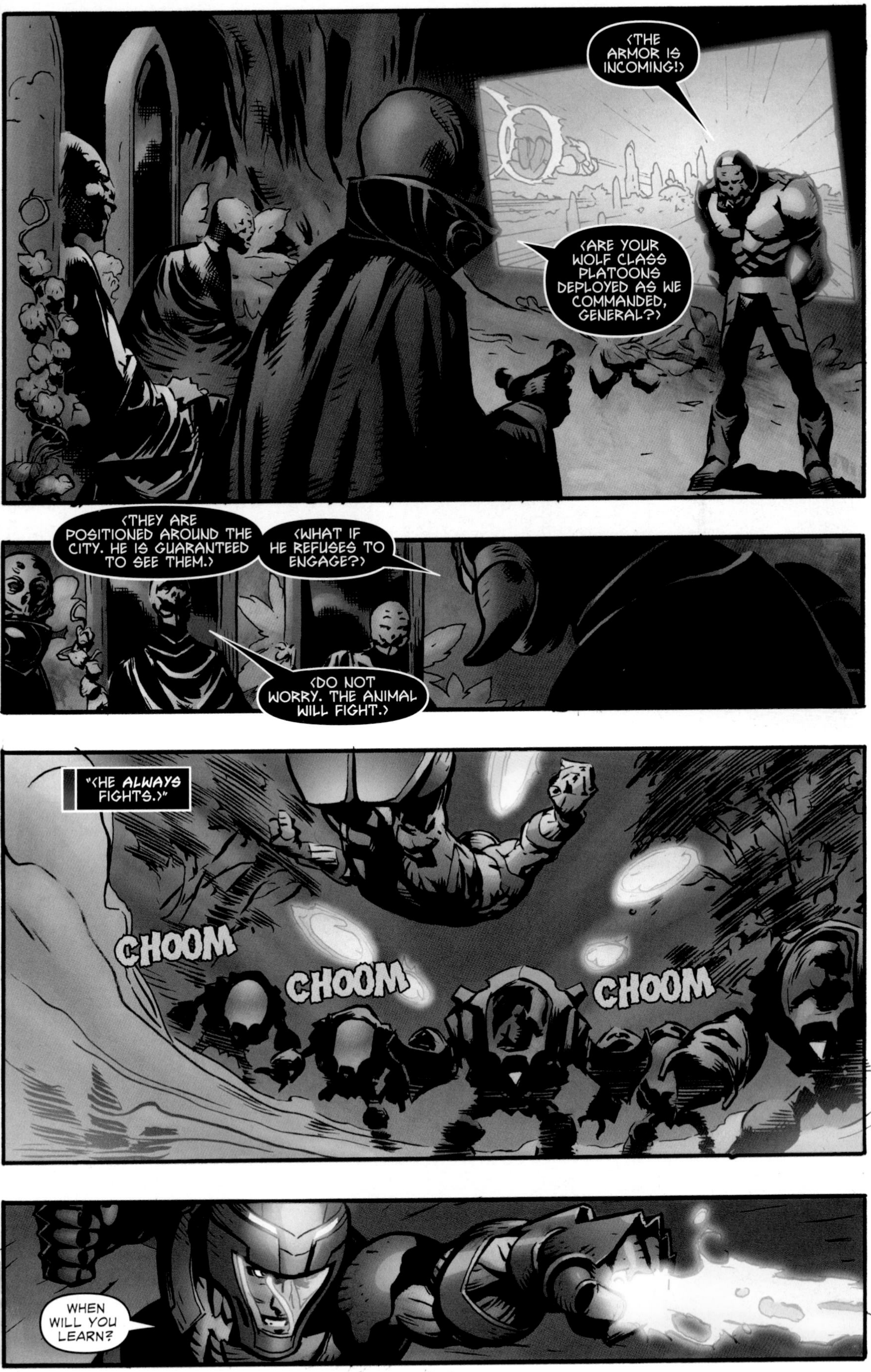

<THE ARMOR IS INCOMING!>
<ARE YOUR WOLF CLASS PLATOONS DEPLOYED AS WE COMMANDED, GENERAL?>
<THEY ARE POSITIONED AROUND THE CITY. HE IS GUARANTEED TO SEE THEM.>
<WHAT IF HE REFUSES TO ENGAGE?>
<DO NOT WORRY. THE ANIMAL WILL FIGHT.>
"<HE ALWAYS FIGHTS.>"
CHOOM
CHOOM
CHOOM
WHEN WILL YOU LEARN?

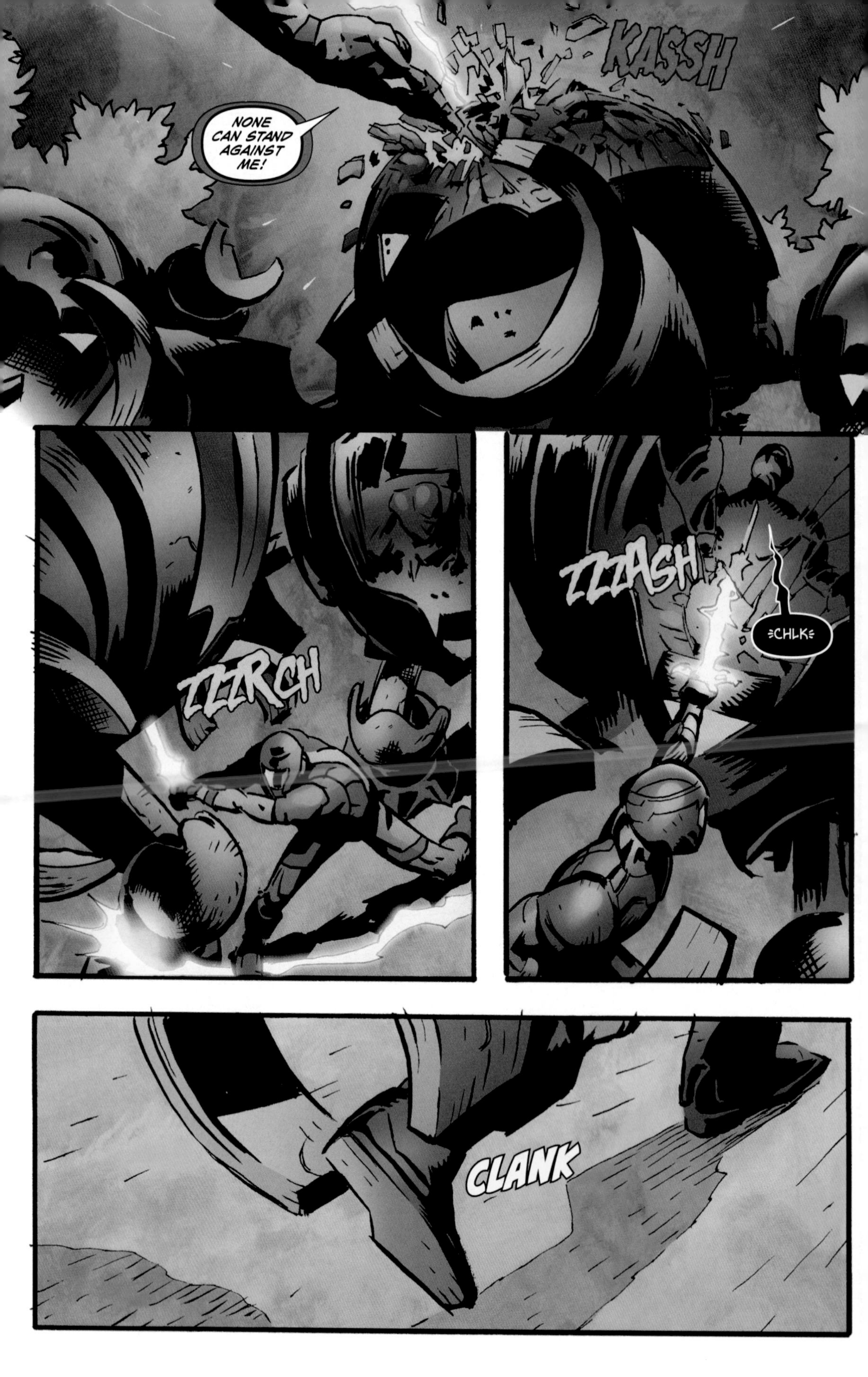
KASSH
NONE CAN STAND AGAINST ME!
ZZZRCH
ZZZASH
CHLK
CLANK

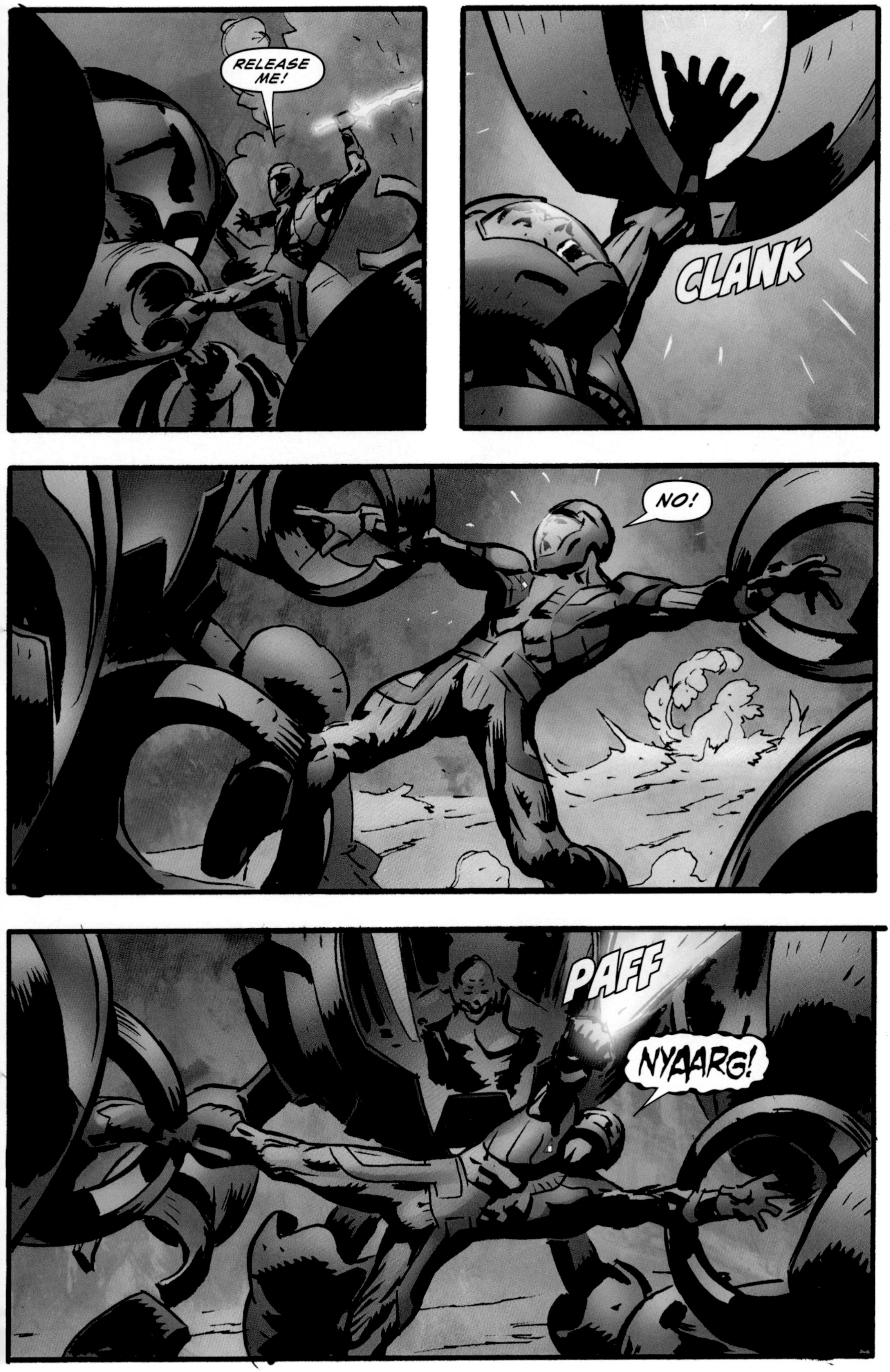
RELEASE ME!
CLANK
NO!
PAFF
NYAARG!

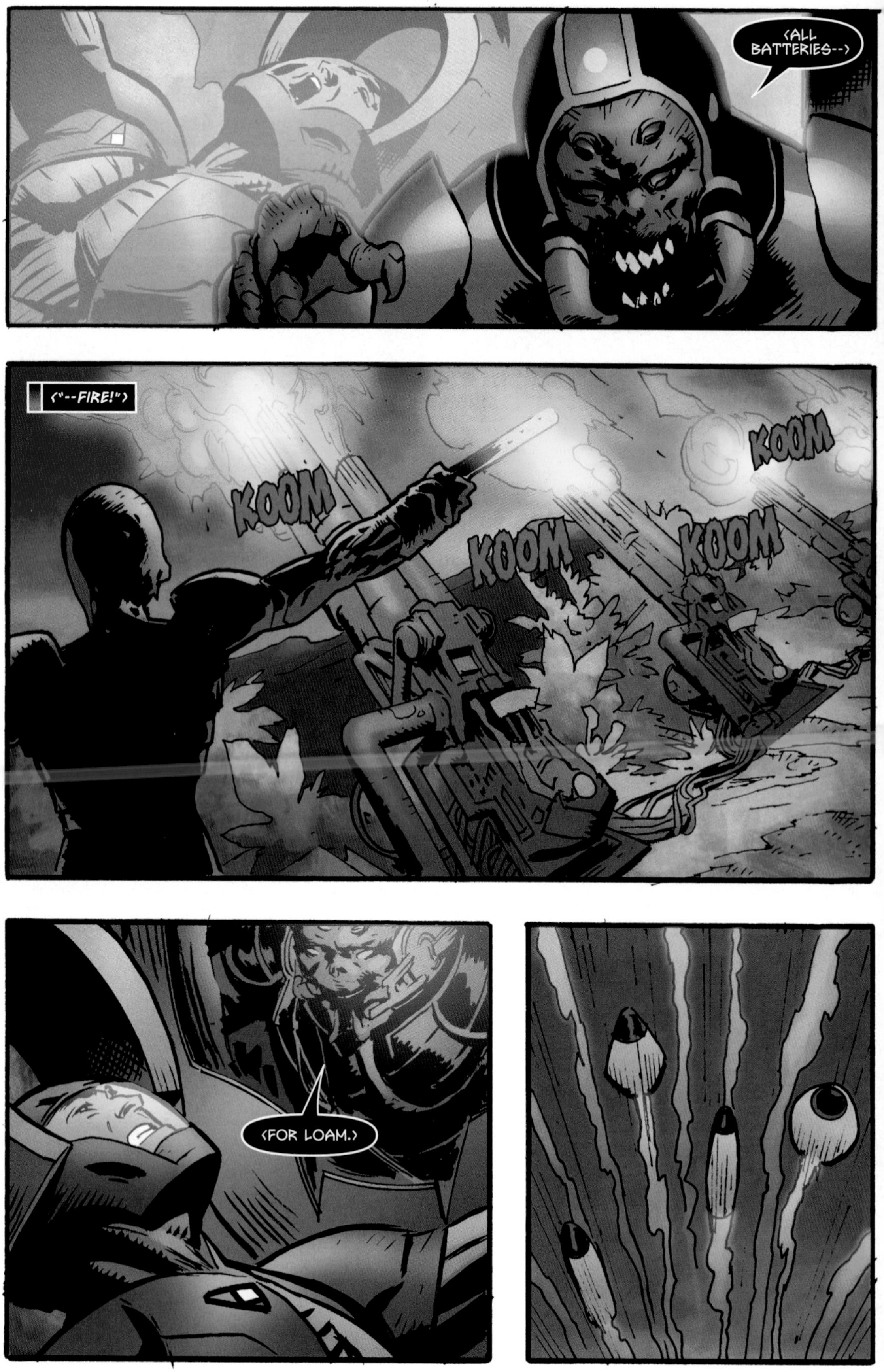

‹ALL BATTERIES--›
‹"--FIRE!"›
KOOM
KOOM
KOOM
KOOM
‹FOR LOAM.›

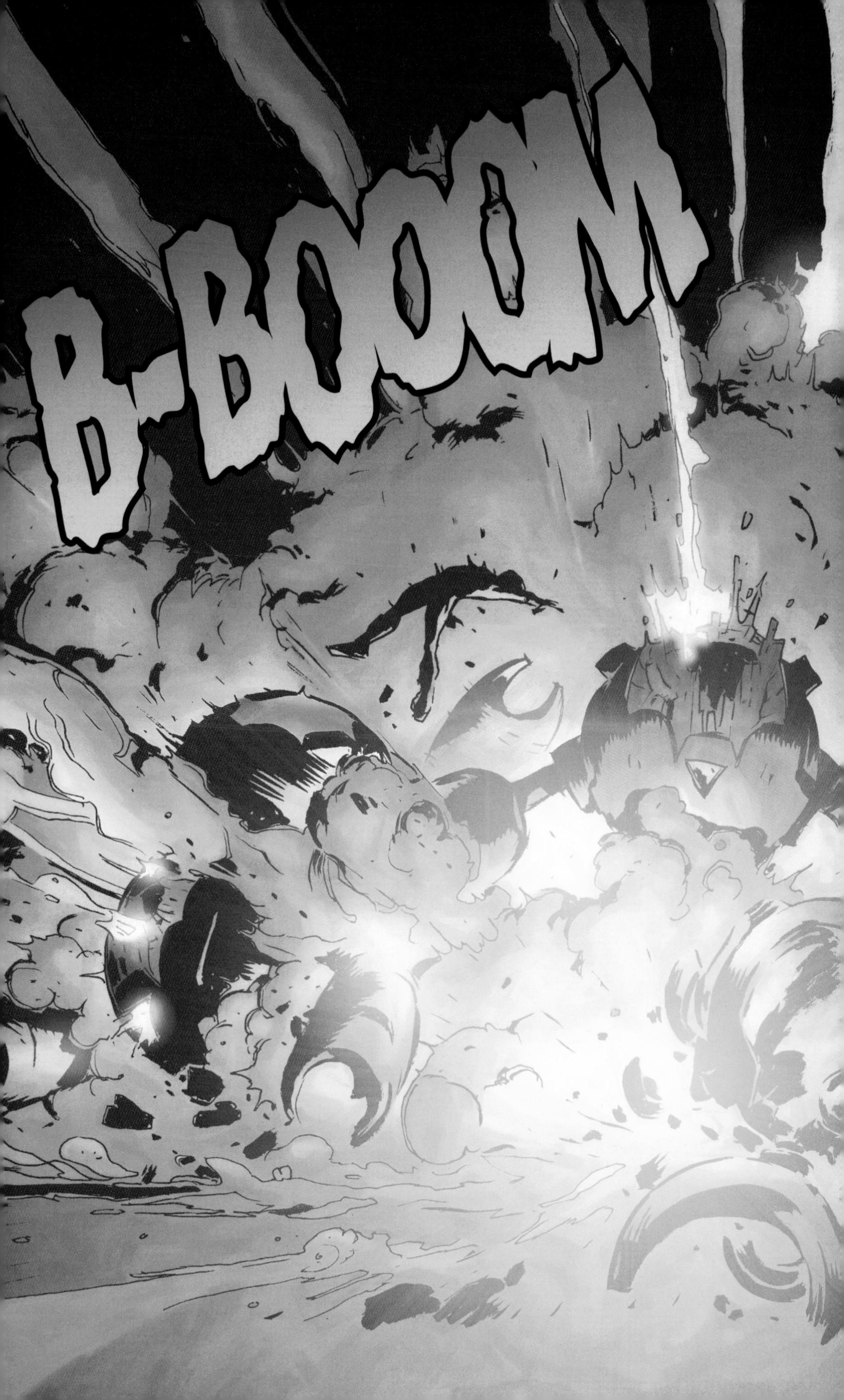
B-BOOM

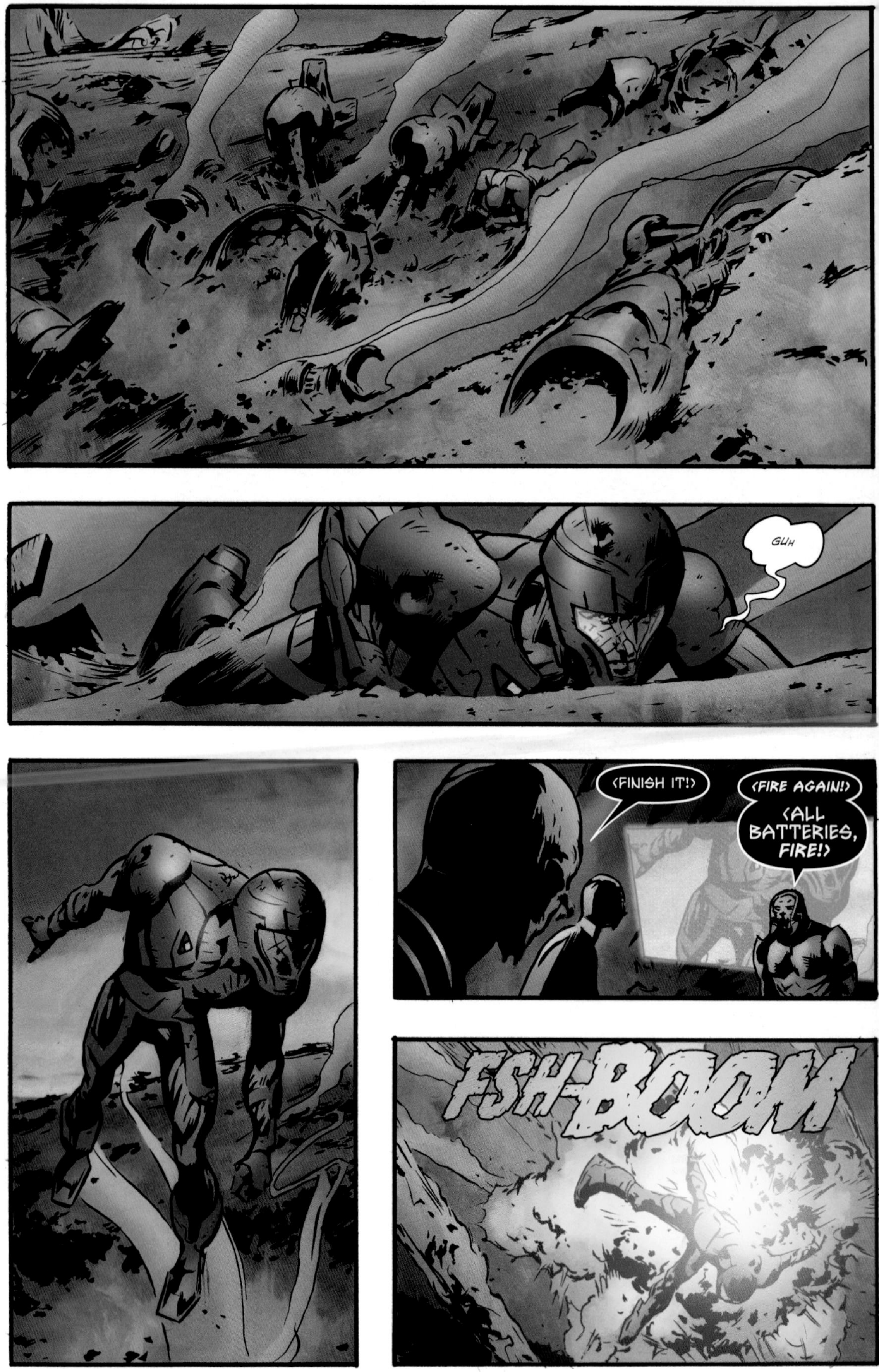
GUH
‹FINISH IT!›
‹FIRE AGAIN!›
‹ALL BATTERIES, FIRE!›
FSH-BOOM

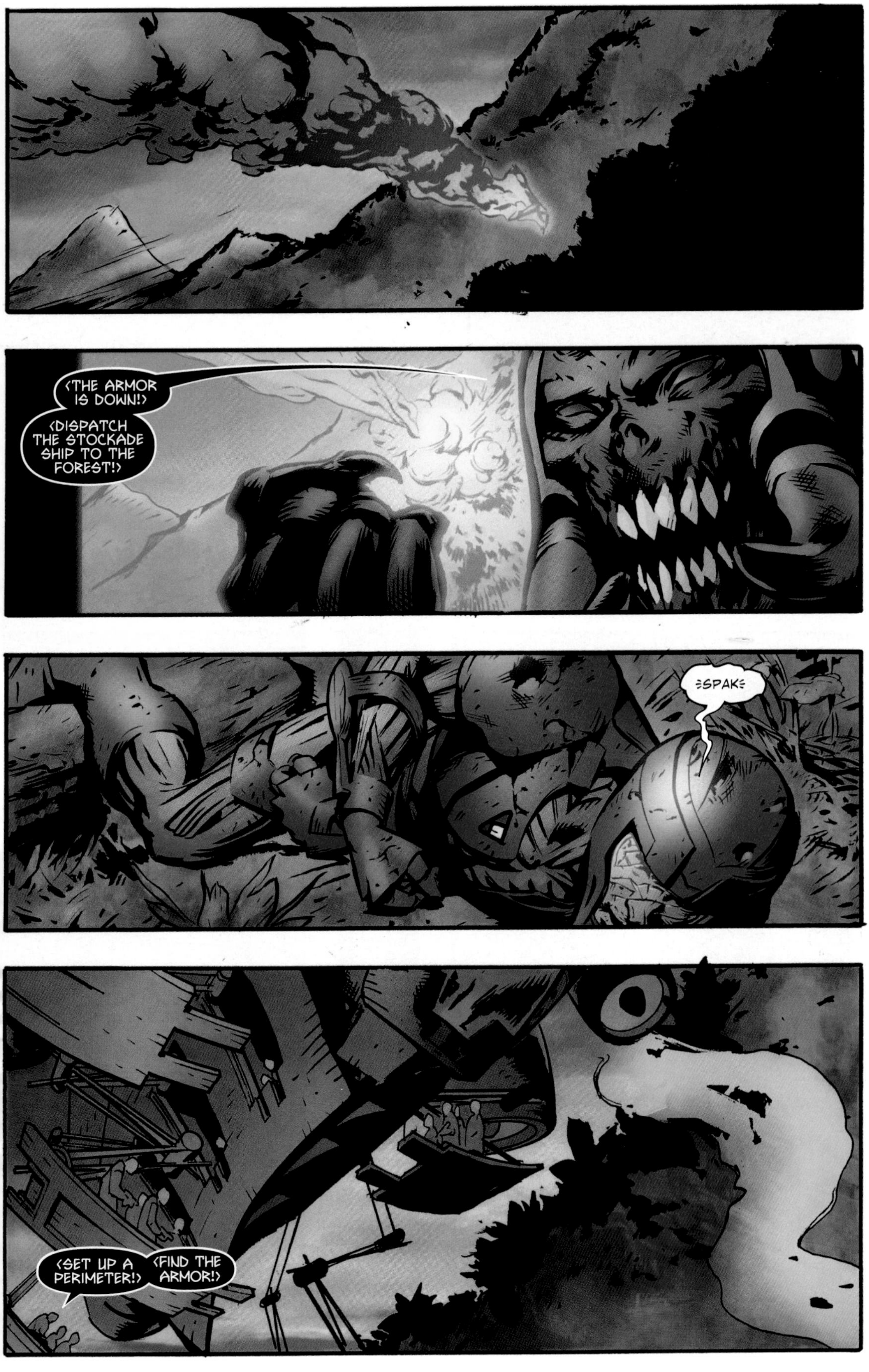
‹THE ARMOR IS DOWN!›
‹DISPATCH THE STOCKADE SHIP TO THE FOREST!›
=SPAK=
‹SET UP A PERIMETER!›
‹FIND THE ARMOR!›

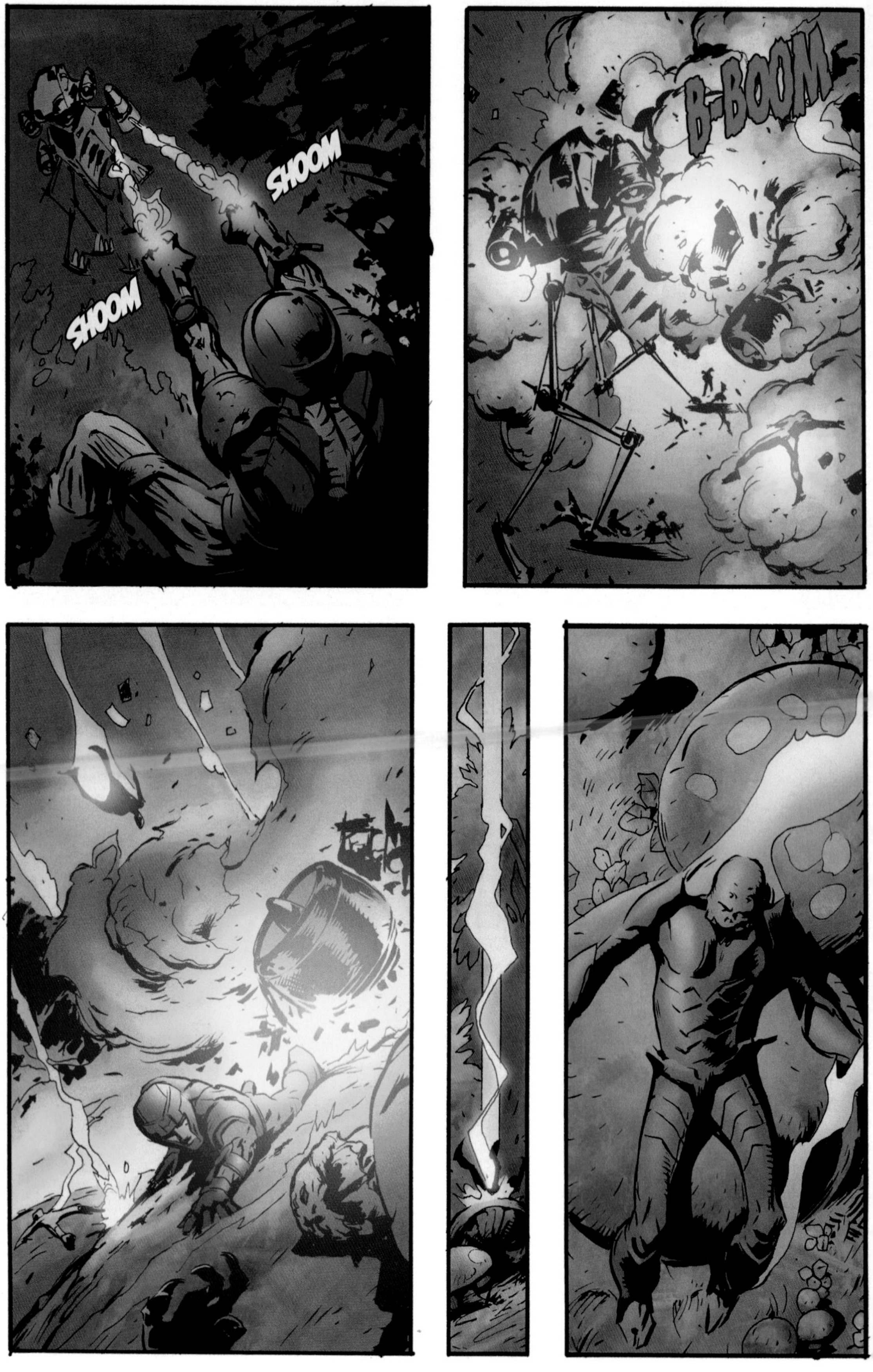
SHOOM
SHOOM
B-BOOM

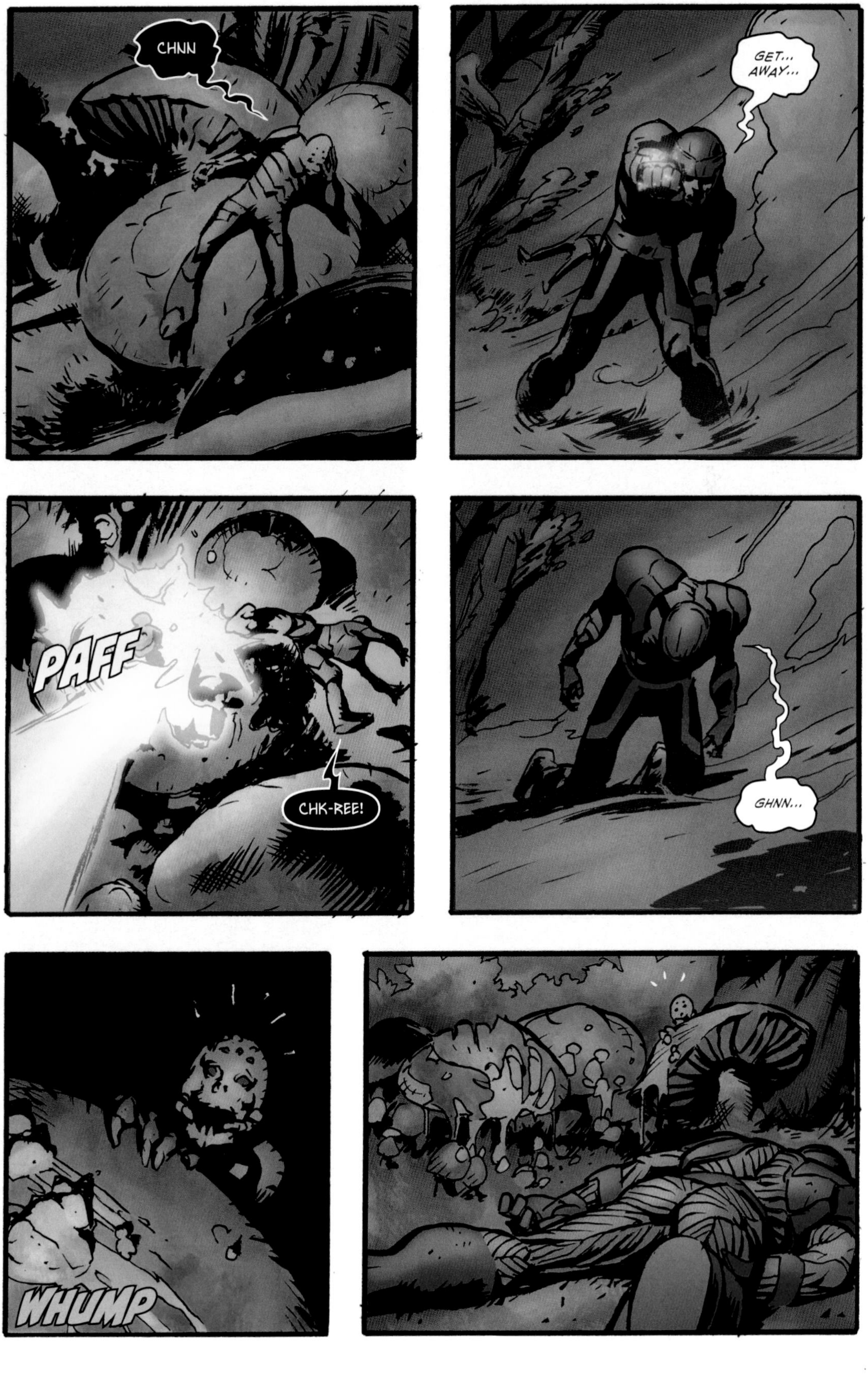
CHNN
GET... AWAY...
PAFF
CHK-REE!
GHNN...
WHUMP

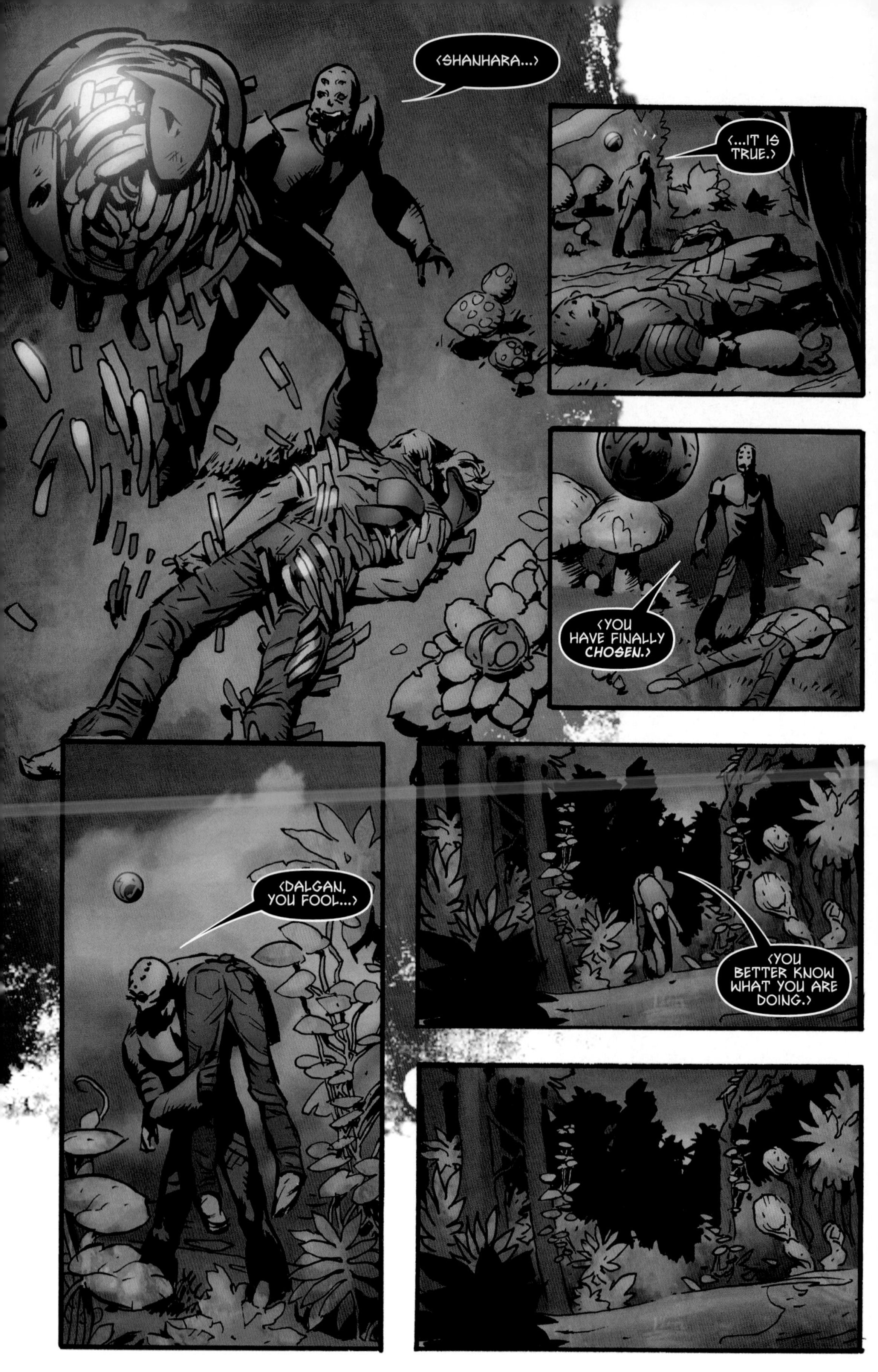
‹SHANHARA...›
‹...IT IS TRUE.›
‹YOU HAVE FINALLY CHOSEN.›
‹DALGAN, YOU FOOL...›
‹YOU BETTER KNOW WHAT YOU ARE DOING.›

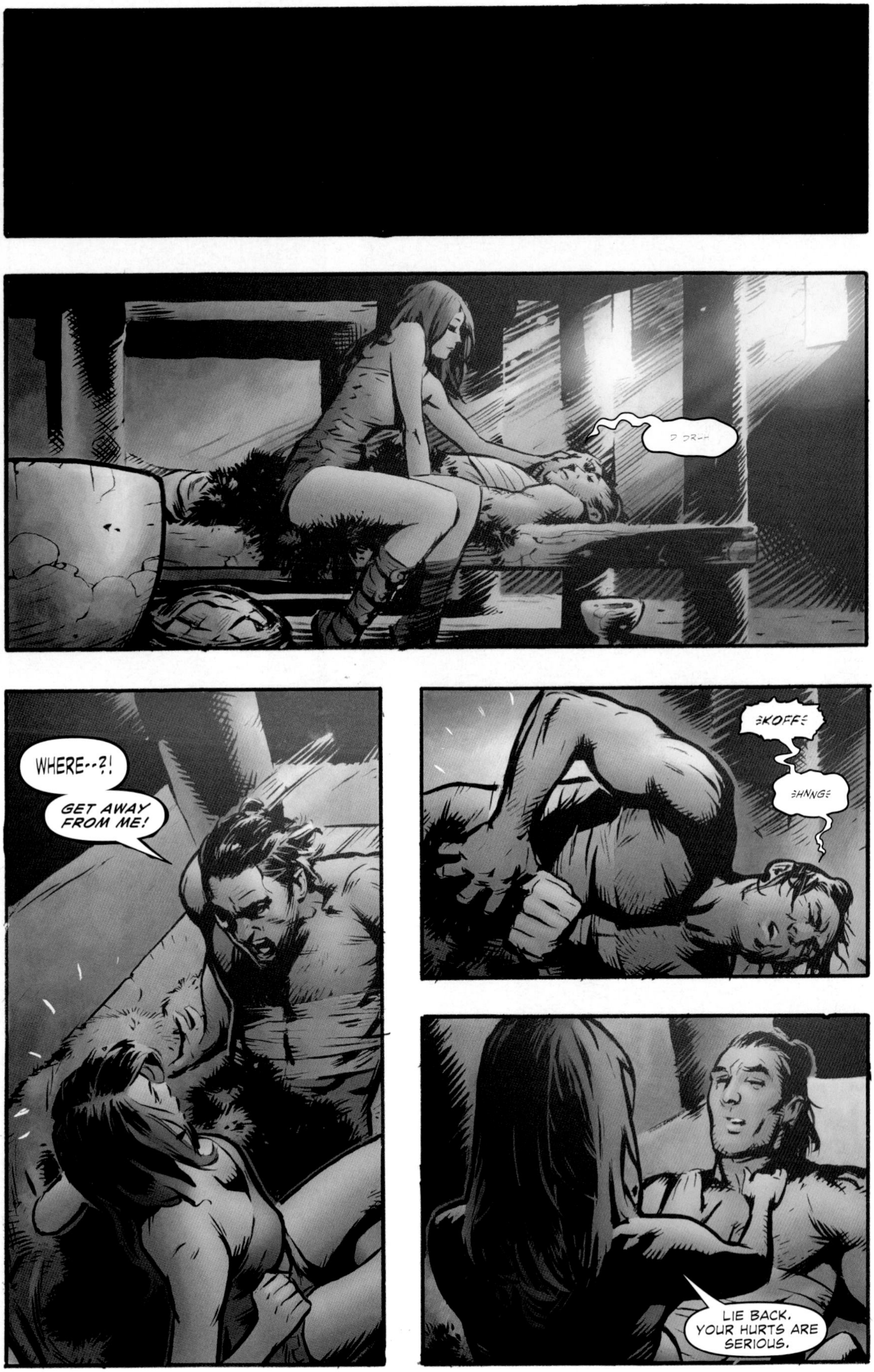
D DR-H
WHERE--?!
GET AWAY FROM ME!
KOFF
HNNG
LIE BACK. YOUR HURTS ARE SERIOUS.

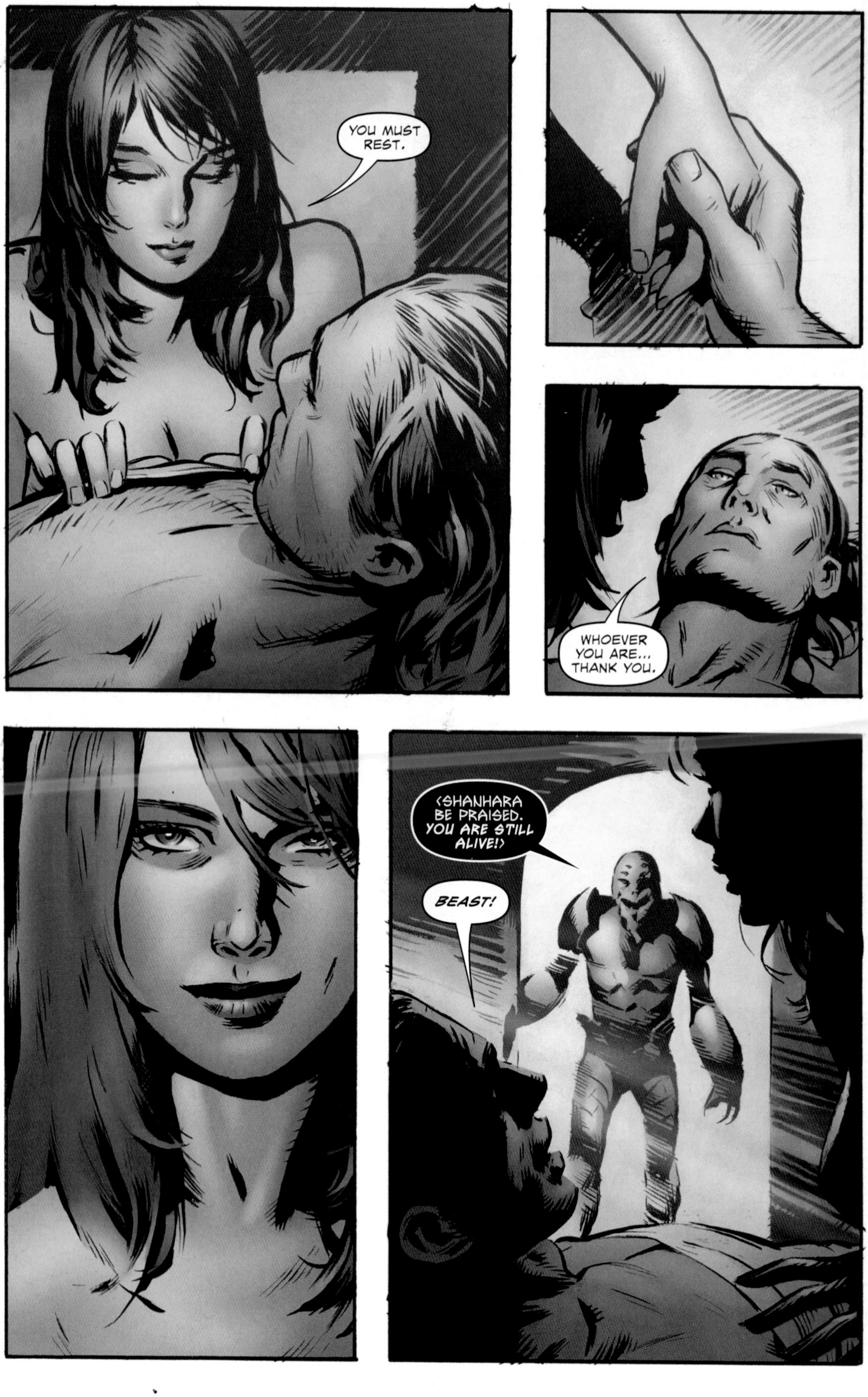
YOU MUST REST.
WHOEVER YOU ARE... THANK YOU.
<SHANHARA BE PRAISED. YOU ARE STILL ALIVE!>
BEAST!

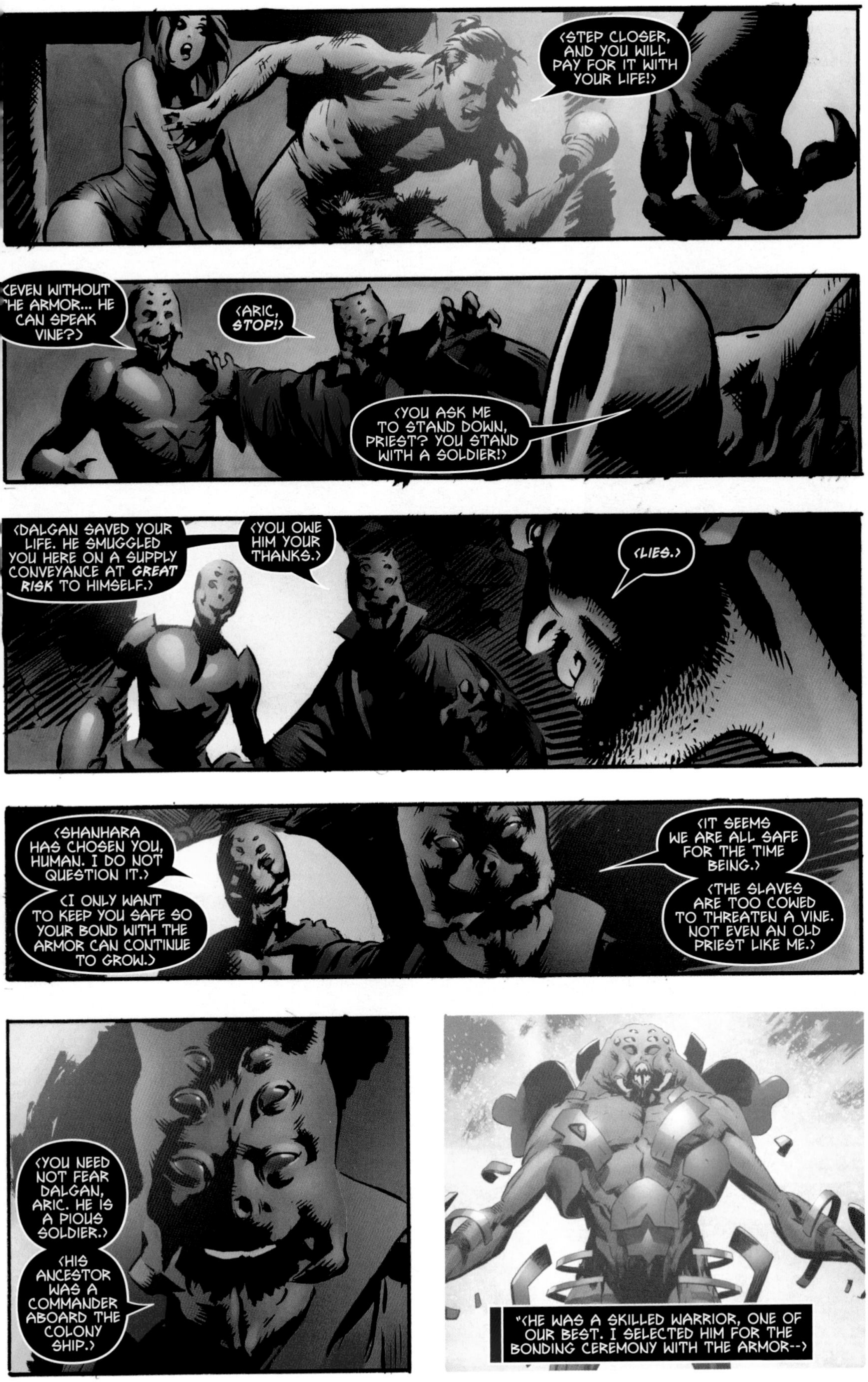
‹STEP CLOSER, AND YOU WILL PAY FOR IT WITH YOUR LIFE!›
‹EVEN WITHOUT THE ARMOR... HE CAN SPEAK VINE?›
‹ARIC, STOP!›
‹YOU ASK ME TO STAND DOWN, PRIEST? YOU STAND WITH A SOLDIER!›
‹DALGAN SAVED YOUR LIFE. HE SMUGGLED YOU HERE ON A SUPPLY CONVEYANCE AT GREAT RISK TO HIMSELF.›
‹YOU OWE HIM YOUR THANKS.›
‹LIES.›
‹SHANHARA HAS CHOSEN YOU, HUMAN. I DO NOT QUESTION IT.›
‹I ONLY WANT TO KEEP YOU SAFE SO YOUR BOND WITH THE ARMOR CAN CONTINUE TO GROW.›
‹IT SEEMS WE ARE ALL SAFE FOR THE TIME BEING.›
‹THE SLAVES ARE TOO COWED TO THREATEN A VINE. NOT EVEN AN OLD PRIEST LIKE ME.›
‹YOU NEED NOT FEAR DALGAN, ARIC. HE IS A PIOUS SOLDIER.›
‹HIS ANCESTOR WAS A COMMANDER ABOARD THE COLONY SHIP.›
"‹HE WAS A SKILLED WARRIOR, ONE OF OUR BEST. I SELECTED HIM FOR THE BONDING CEREMONY WITH THE ARMOR--›

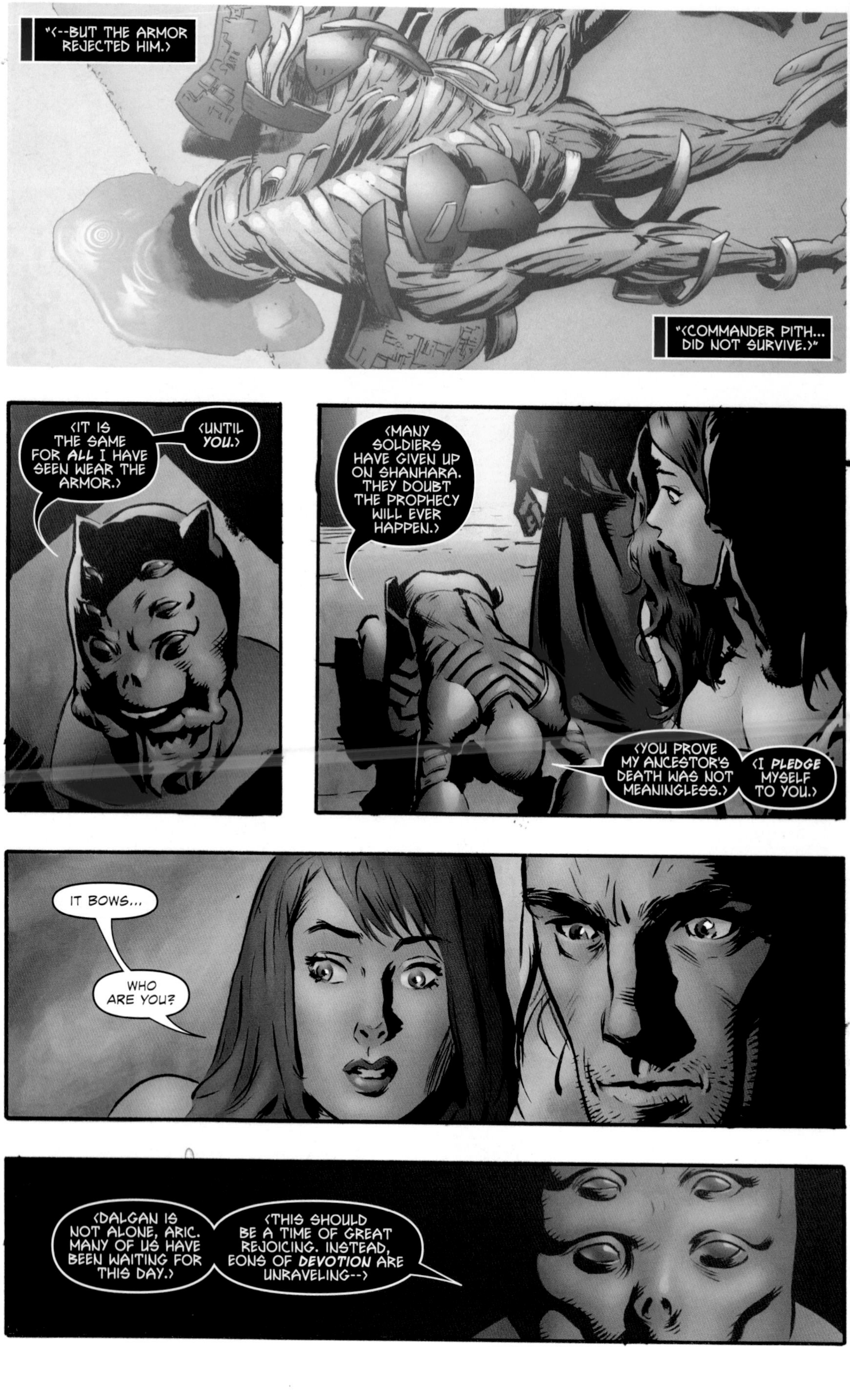
"<--BUT THE ARMOR REJECTED HIM.>
"<COMMANDER PITH... DID NOT SURVIVE.>"
<IT IS THE SAME FOR ALL I HAVE SEEN WEAR THE ARMOR.>
<UNTIL YOU.>
<MANY SOLDIERS HAVE GIVEN UP ON SHANHARA. THEY DOUBT THE PROPHECY WILL EVER HAPPEN.>
<YOU PROVE MY ANCESTOR'S DEATH WAS NOT MEANINGLESS.>
<I PLEDGE MYSELF TO YOU.>
IT BOWS...
WHO ARE YOU?
<DALGAN IS NOT ALONE, ARIC. MANY OF US HAVE BEEN WAITING FOR THIS DAY.>
<THIS SHOULD BE A TIME OF GREAT REJOICING. INSTEAD, EONS OF DEVOTION ARE UNRAVELING-->

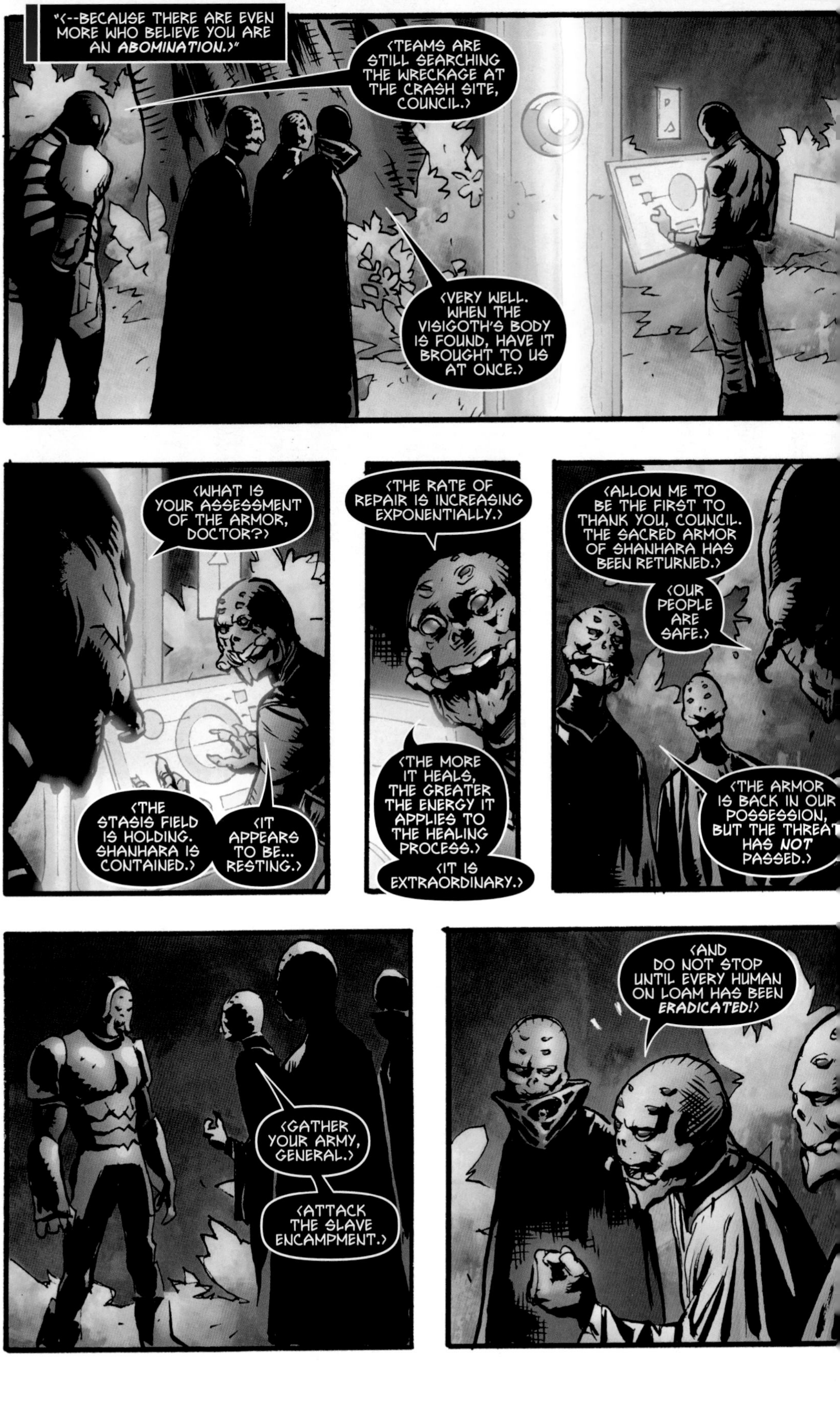
"<--BECAUSE THERE ARE EVEN MORE WHO BELIEVE YOU ARE AN *ABOMINATION.*>"
<TEAMS ARE STILL SEARCHING THE WRECKAGE AT THE CRASH SITE, COUNCIL.>
<VERY WELL. WHEN THE VISIGOTH'S BODY IS FOUND, HAVE IT BROUGHT TO US AT ONCE.>
<WHAT IS YOUR ASSESSMENT OF THE ARMOR, DOCTOR?>
<THE STASIS FIELD IS HOLDING. SHANHARA IS CONTAINED.>
<IT APPEARS TO BE... RESTING.>
<THE RATE OF REPAIR IS INCREASING EXPONENTIALLY.>
<THE MORE IT HEALS, THE GREATER THE ENERGY IT APPLIES TO THE HEALING PROCESS.>
<IT IS EXTRAORDINARY.>
<ALLOW ME TO BE THE FIRST TO THANK YOU, COUNCIL. THE SACRED ARMOR OF SHANHARA HAS BEEN RETURNED.>
<OUR PEOPLE ARE SAFE.>
<THE ARMOR IS BACK IN OUR POSSESSION, BUT THE THREAT HAS *NOT* PASSED.>
<GATHER YOUR ARMY, GENERAL.>
<ATTACK THE SLAVE ENCAMPMENT.>
<AND DO NOT STOP UNTIL EVERY HUMAN ON LOAM HAS BEEN *ERADICATED!*>

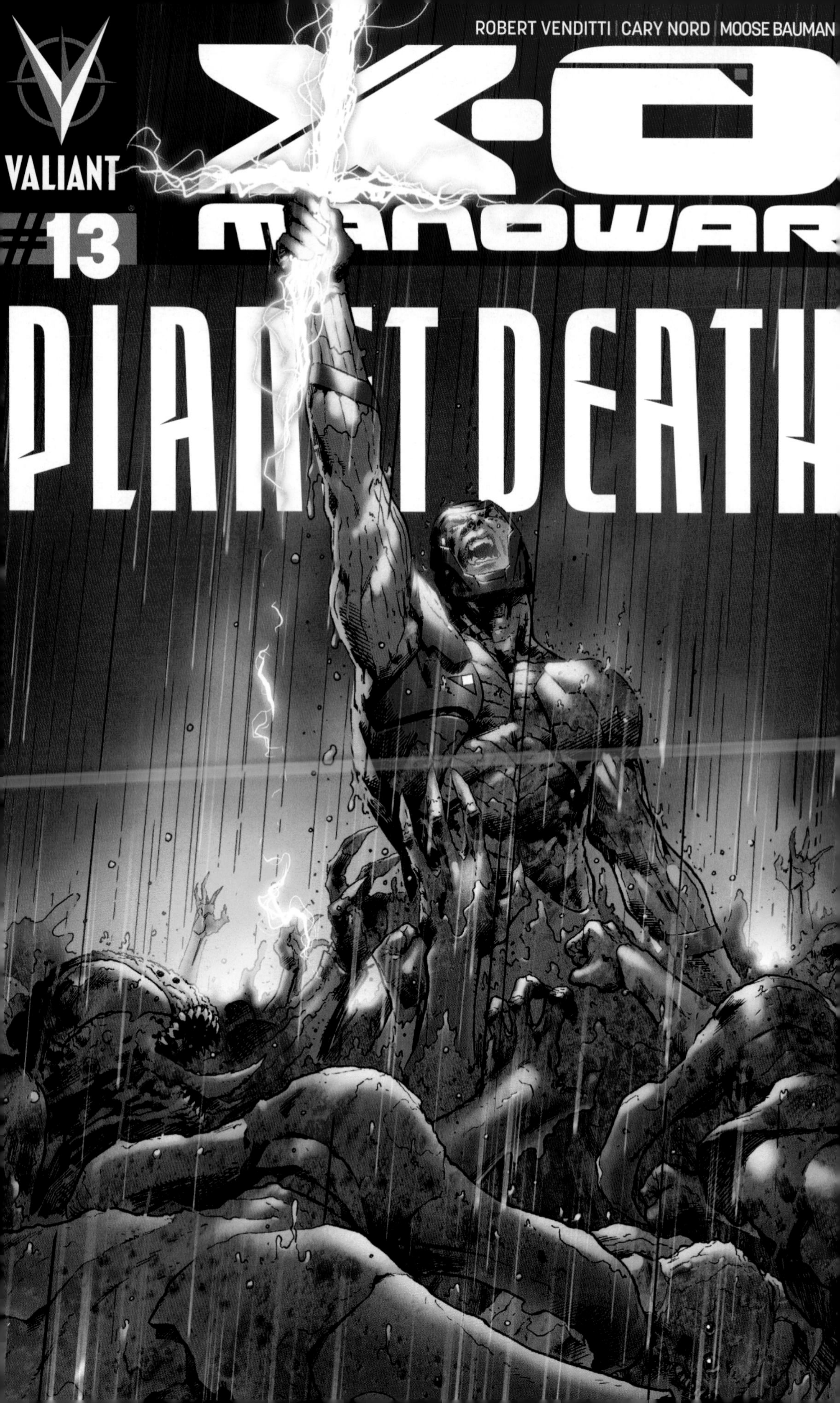

VALIANT
ROBERT VENDITTI | CARY NORD | MOOSE BAUMAN
X-O MANOWAR
#13
PLANET DEATH

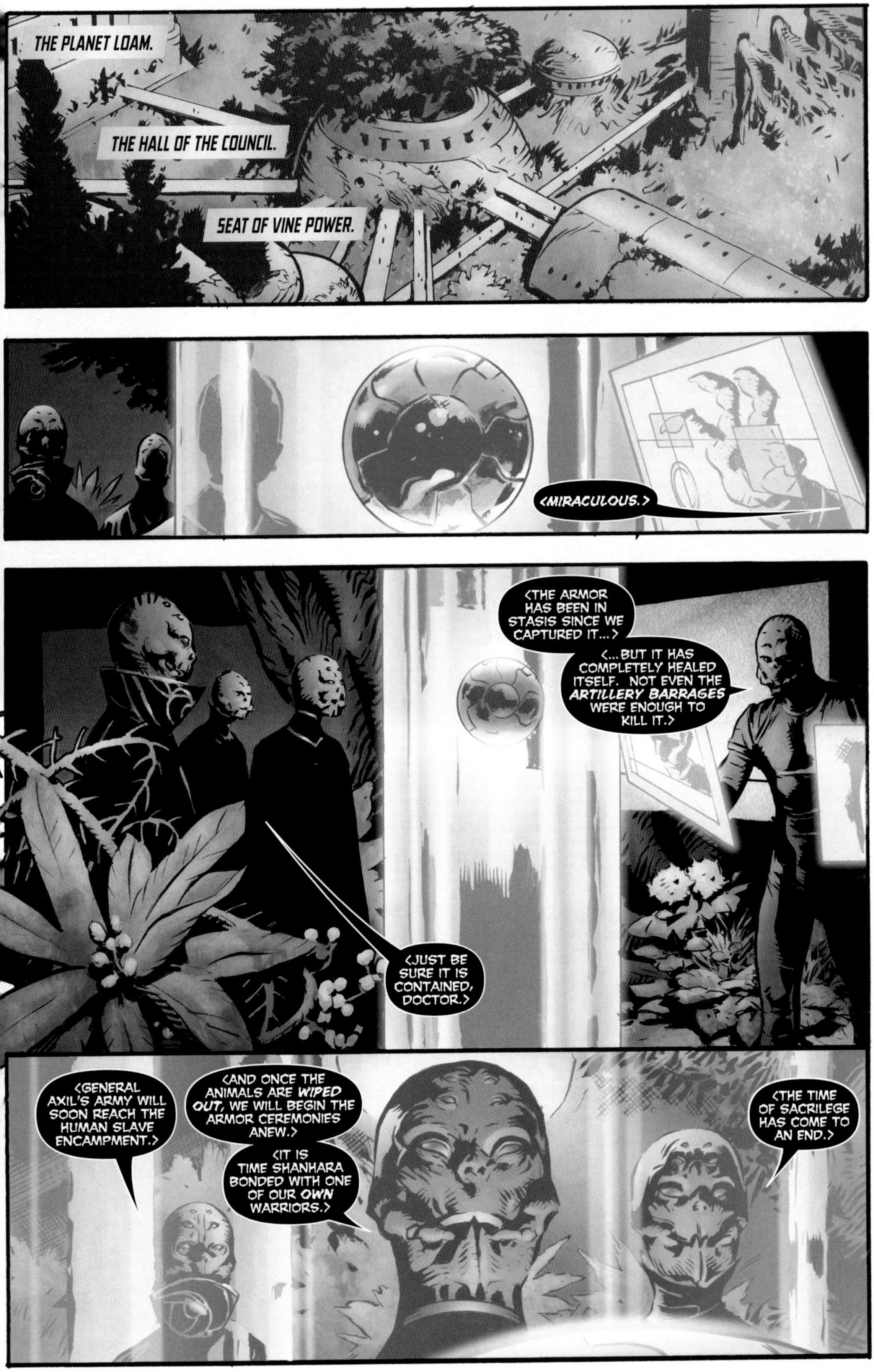
THE PLANET LOAM.
THE HALL OF THE COUNCIL.
SEAT OF VINE POWER.
<MIRACULOUS.>
<THE ARMOR HAS BEEN IN STASIS SINCE WE CAPTURED IT...>
<...BUT IT HAS COMPLETELY HEALED ITSELF. NOT EVEN THE ARTILLERY BARRAGES WERE ENOUGH TO KILL IT.>
<JUST BE SURE IT IS CONTAINED, DOCTOR.>
<GENERAL AXIL'S ARMY WILL SOON REACH THE HUMAN SLAVE ENCAMPMENT.>
<AND ONCE THE ANIMALS ARE WIPED OUT, WE WILL BEGIN THE ARMOR CEREMONIES ANEW.>
<IT IS TIME SHANHARA BONDED WITH ONE OF OUR OWN WARRIORS.>
<THE TIME OF SACRILEGE HAS COME TO AN END.>

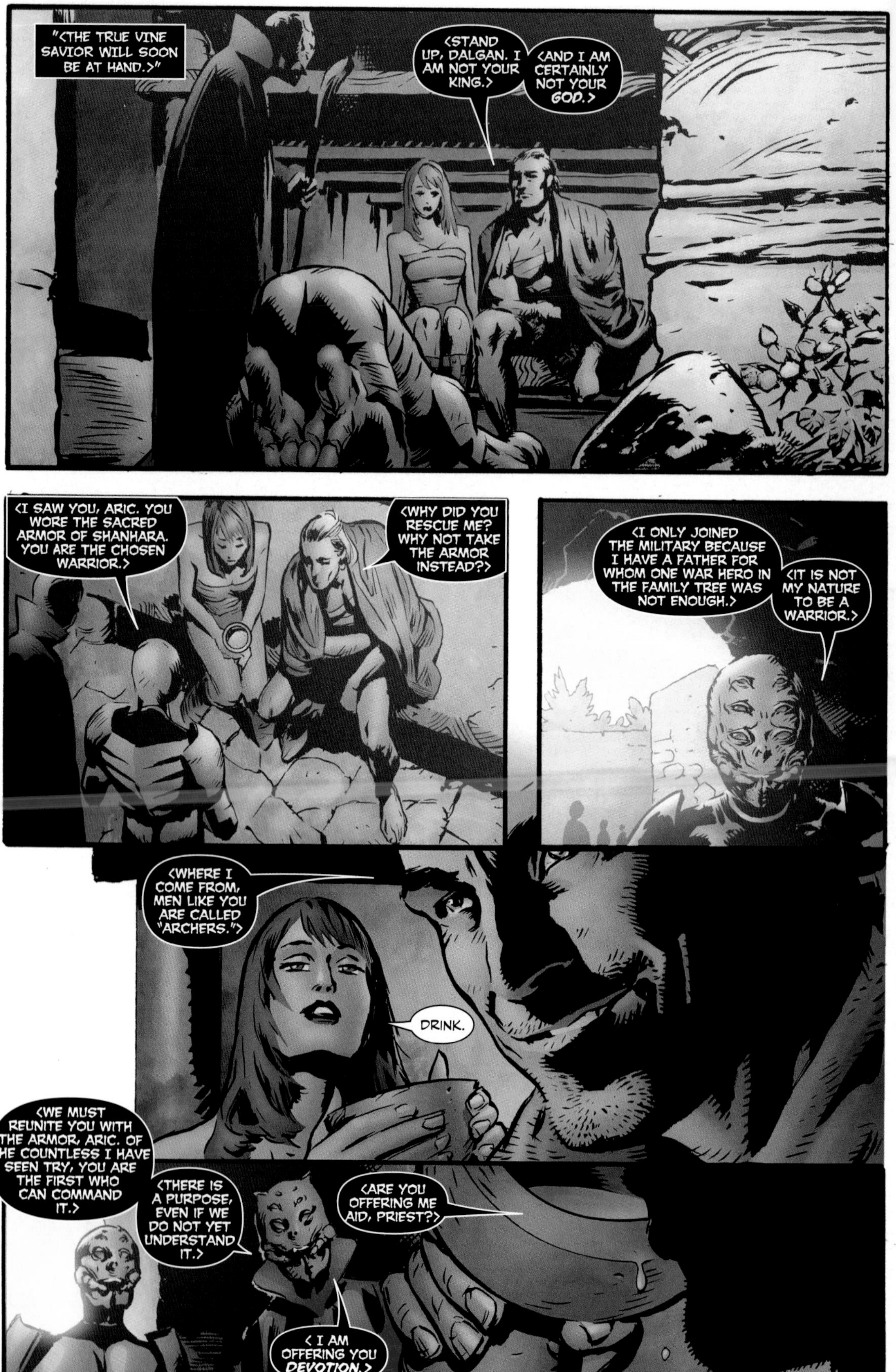
"<THE TRUE VINE SAVIOR WILL SOON BE AT HAND.>"
<STAND UP, DALGAN. I AM NOT YOUR KING.>
<AND I AM CERTAINLY NOT YOUR GOD.>
<I SAW YOU, ARIC. YOU WORE THE SACRED ARMOR OF SHANHARA. YOU ARE THE CHOSEN WARRIOR.>
<WHY DID YOU RESCUE ME? WHY NOT TAKE THE ARMOR INSTEAD?>
<I ONLY JOINED THE MILITARY BECAUSE I HAVE A FATHER FOR WHOM ONE WAR HERO IN THE FAMILY TREE WAS NOT ENOUGH.>
<IT IS NOT MY NATURE TO BE A WARRIOR.>
<WHERE I COME FROM, MEN LIKE YOU ARE CALLED "ARCHERS.">
DRINK.
<WE MUST REUNITE YOU WITH THE ARMOR, ARIC. OF THE COUNTLESS I HAVE SEEN TRY, YOU ARE THE FIRST WHO CAN COMMAND IT.>
<THERE IS A PURPOSE, EVEN IF WE DO NOT YET UNDERSTAND IT.>
<ARE YOU OFFERING ME AID, PRIEST?>
<I AM OFFERING YOU *DEVOTION.*>

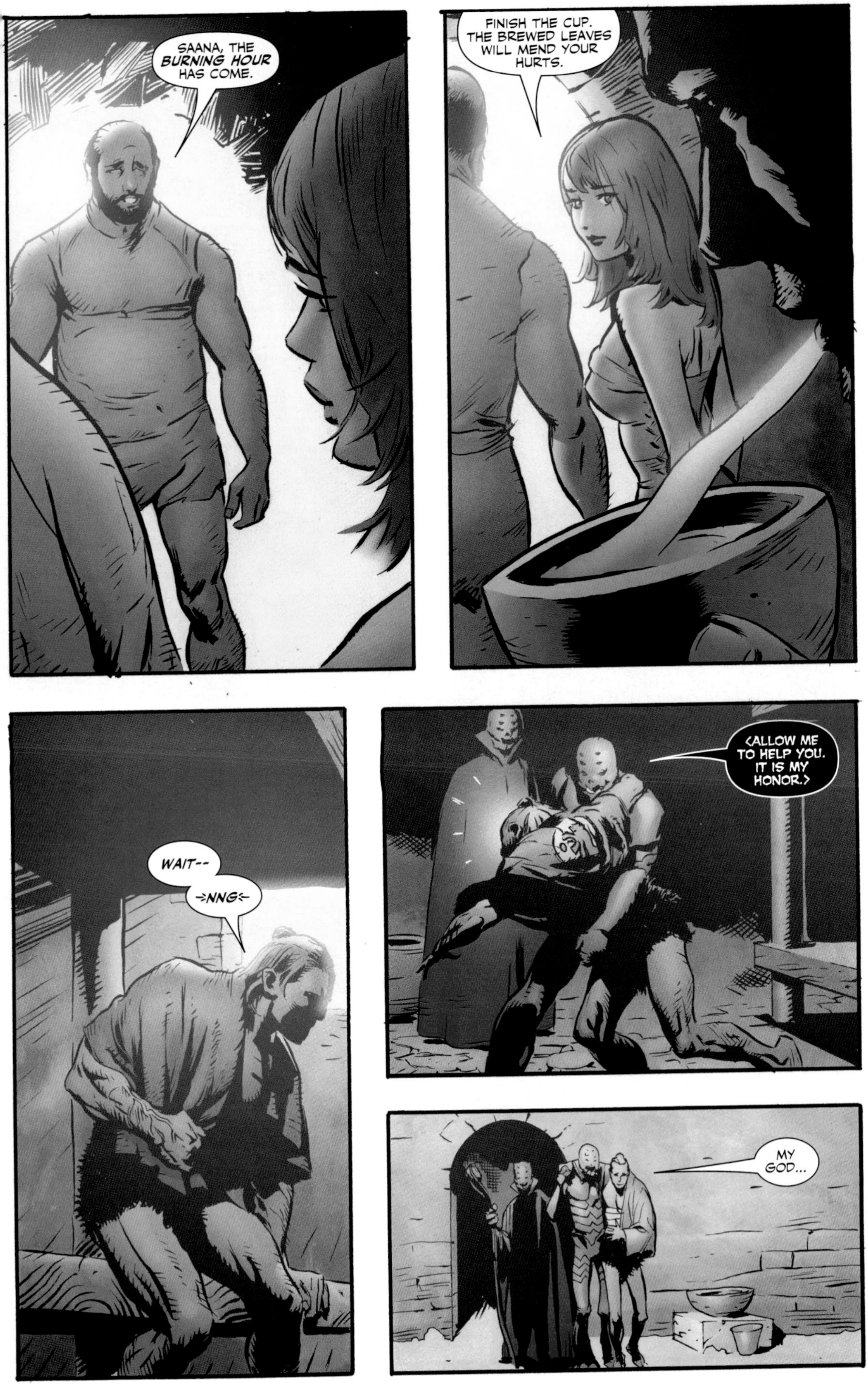
SAANA, THE BURNING HOUR HAS COME.
FINISH THE CUP. THE BREWED LEAVES WILL MEND YOUR HURTS.
WAIT--
-NNG-
<ALLOW ME TO HELP YOU. IT IS MY HONOR.>
MY GOD...

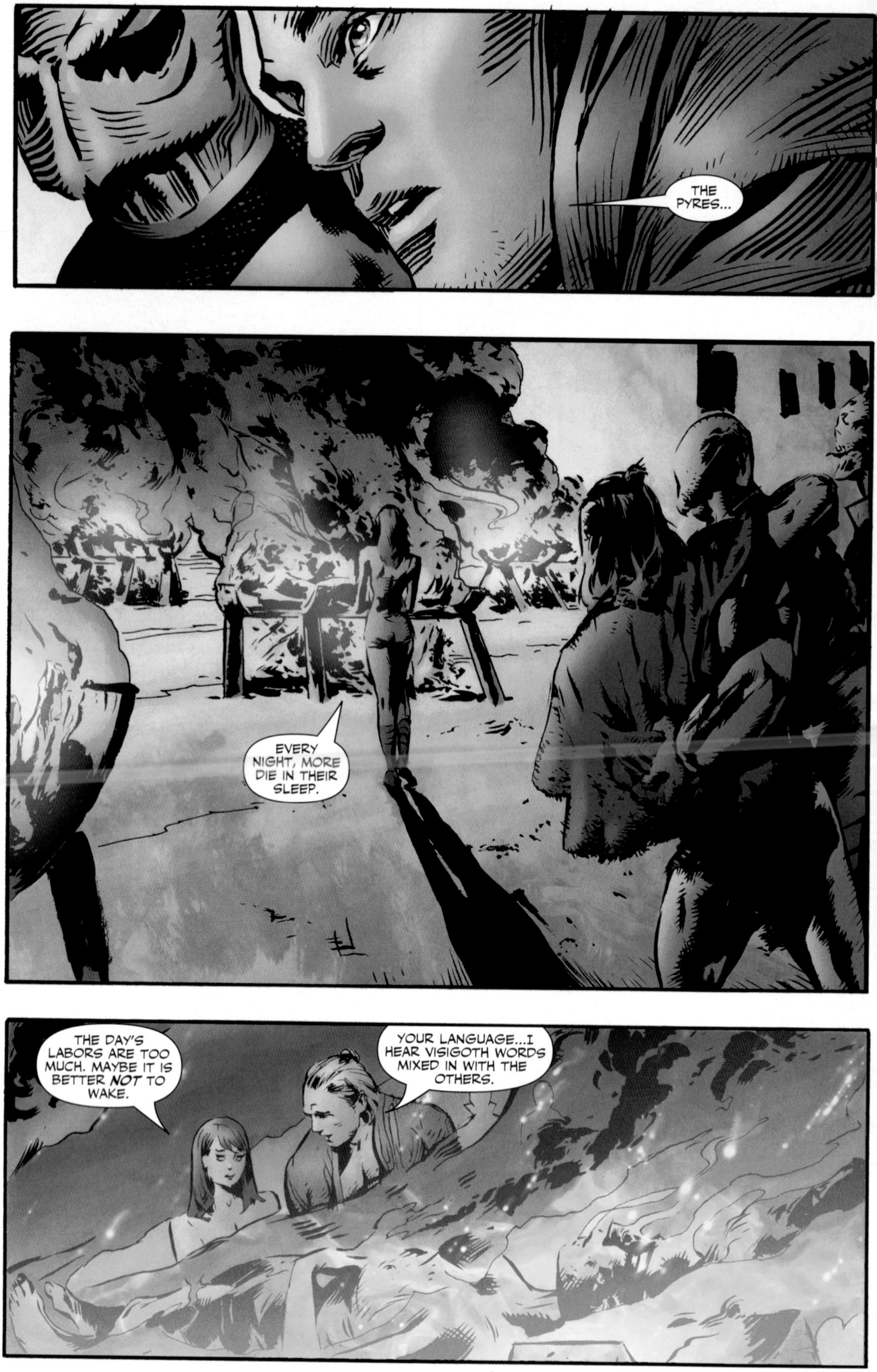
THE PYRES...
EVERY NIGHT, MORE DIE IN THEIR SLEEP.
THE DAY'S LABORS ARE TOO MUCH. MAYBE IT IS BETTER **NOT** TO WAKE.
YOUR LANGUAGE...I HEAR VISIGOTH WORDS MIXED IN WITH THE OTHERS.

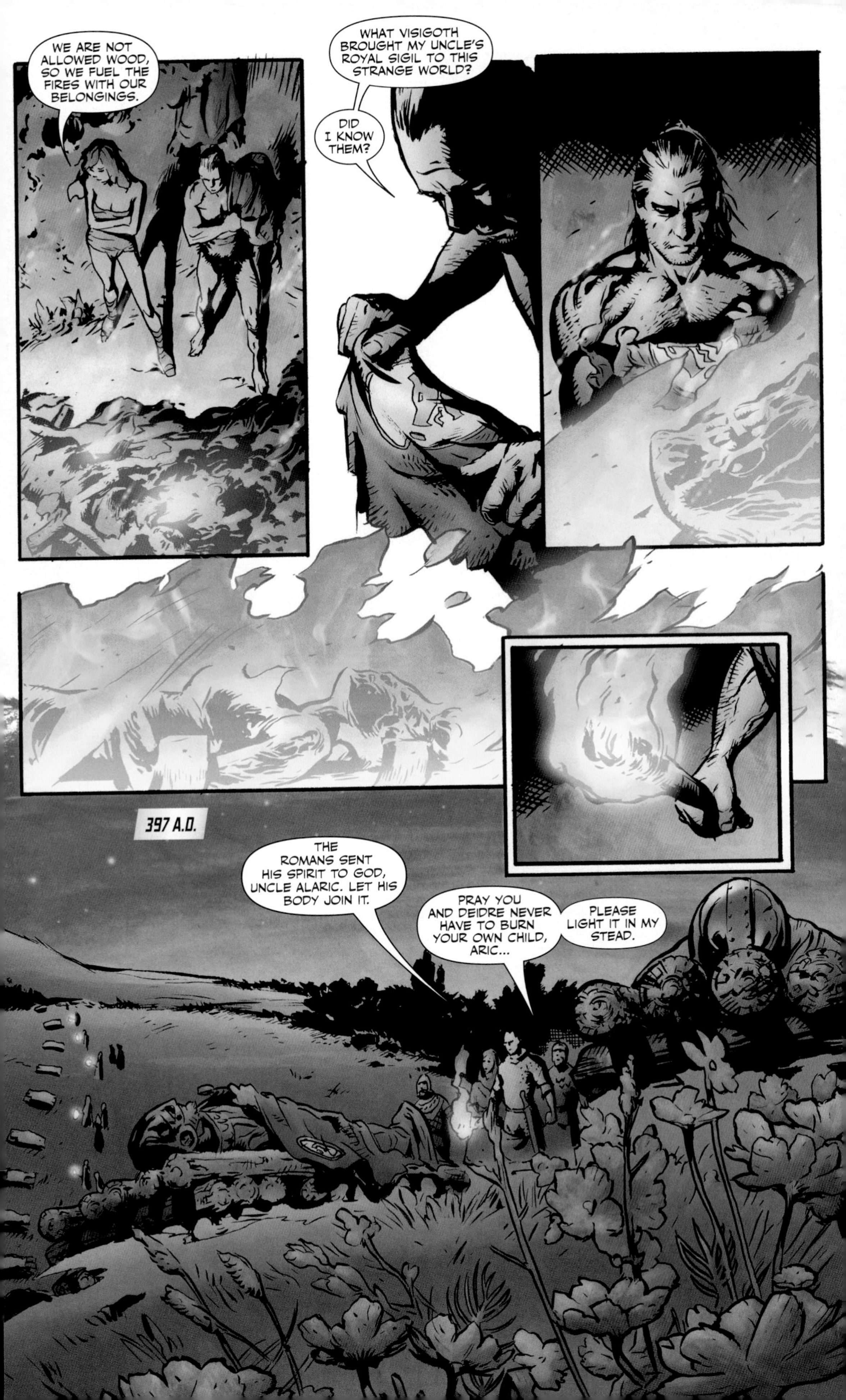
WE ARE NOT ALLOWED WOOD, SO WE FUEL THE FIRES WITH OUR BELONGINGS.
WHAT VISIGOTH BROUGHT MY UNCLE'S ROYAL SIGIL TO THIS STRANGE WORLD?
DID I KNOW THEM?
397 A.D.
THE ROMANS SENT HIS SPIRIT TO GOD, UNCLE ALARIC. LET HIS BODY JOIN IT.
PRAY YOU AND DEIDRE NEVER HAVE TO BURN YOUR OWN CHILD, ARIC...
PLEASE LIGHT IT IN MY STEAD.

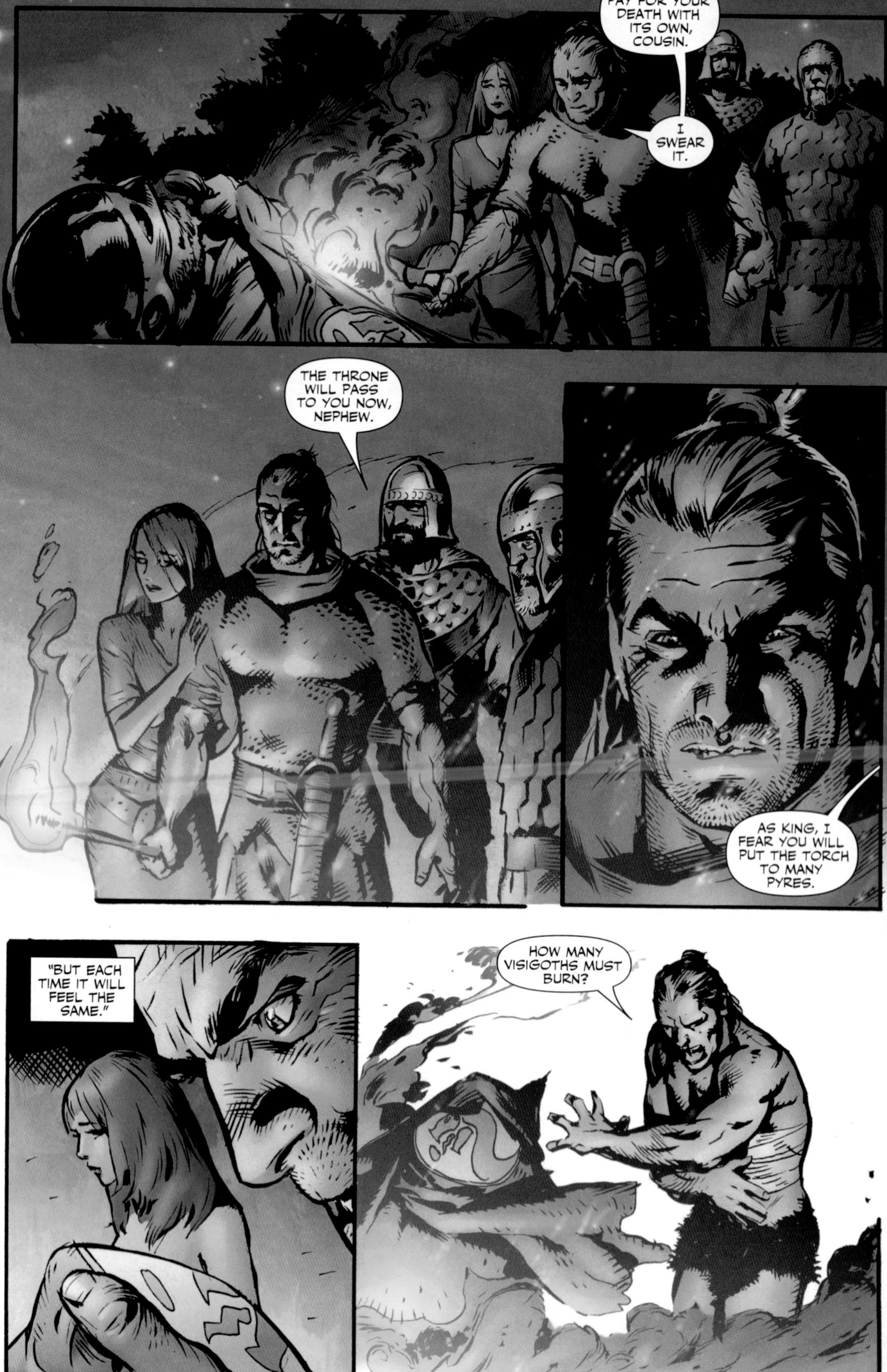
ROME WILL PAY FOR YOUR DEATH WITH ITS OWN, COUSIN.
I SWEAR IT.
THE THRONE WILL PASS TO YOU NOW, NEPHEW.
AS KING, I FEAR YOU WILL PUT THE TORCH TO MANY PYRES.
"BUT EACH TIME IT WILL FEEL THE SAME."
HOW MANY VISIGOTHS MUST BURN?

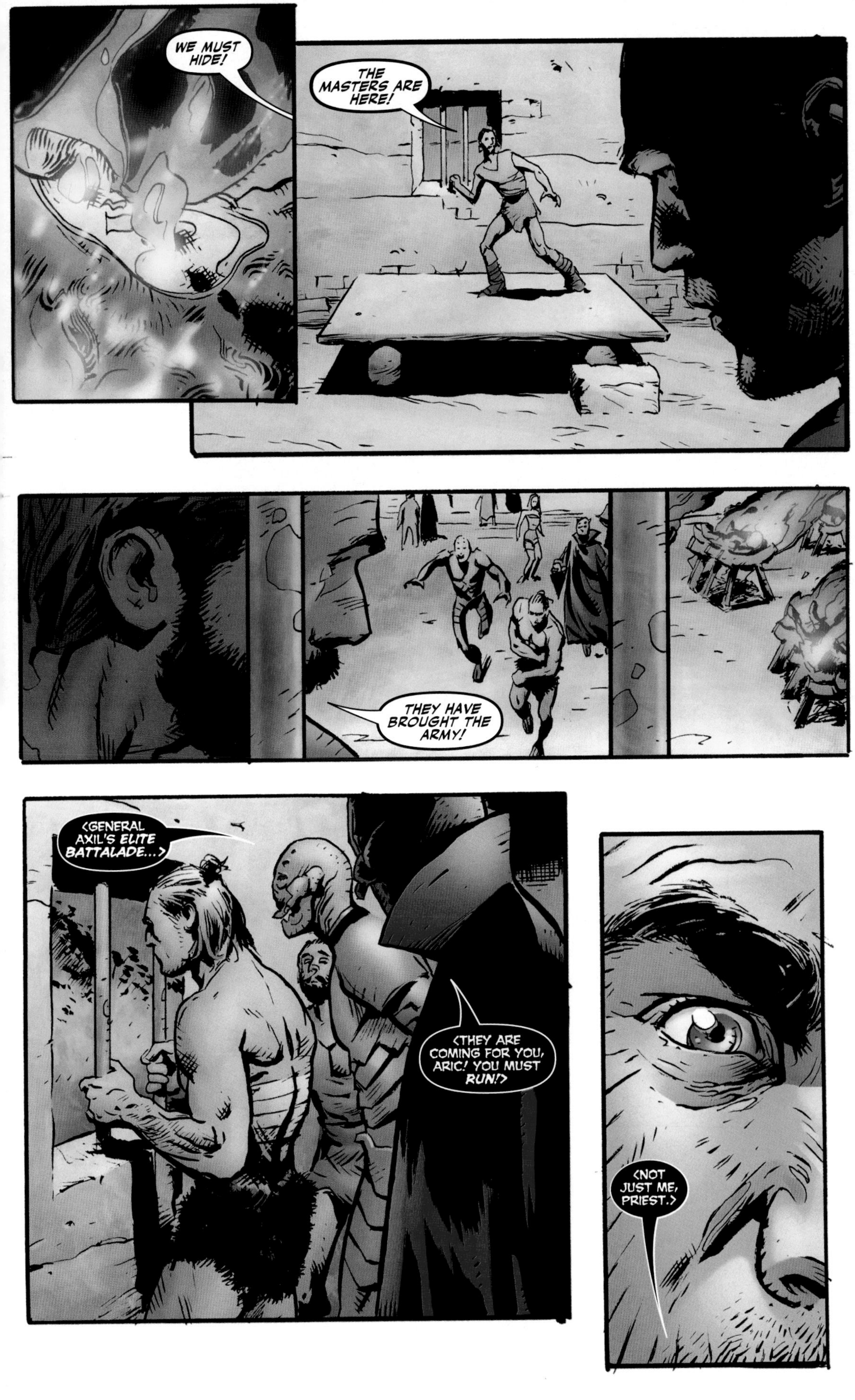
WE MUST HIDE!
THE MASTERS ARE HERE!
THEY HAVE BROUGHT THE ARMY!
<GENERAL AXIL'S ELITE BATTALADE...>
<THEY ARE COMING FOR YOU, ARIC! YOU MUST RUN!>
<NOT JUST ME, PRIEST.>

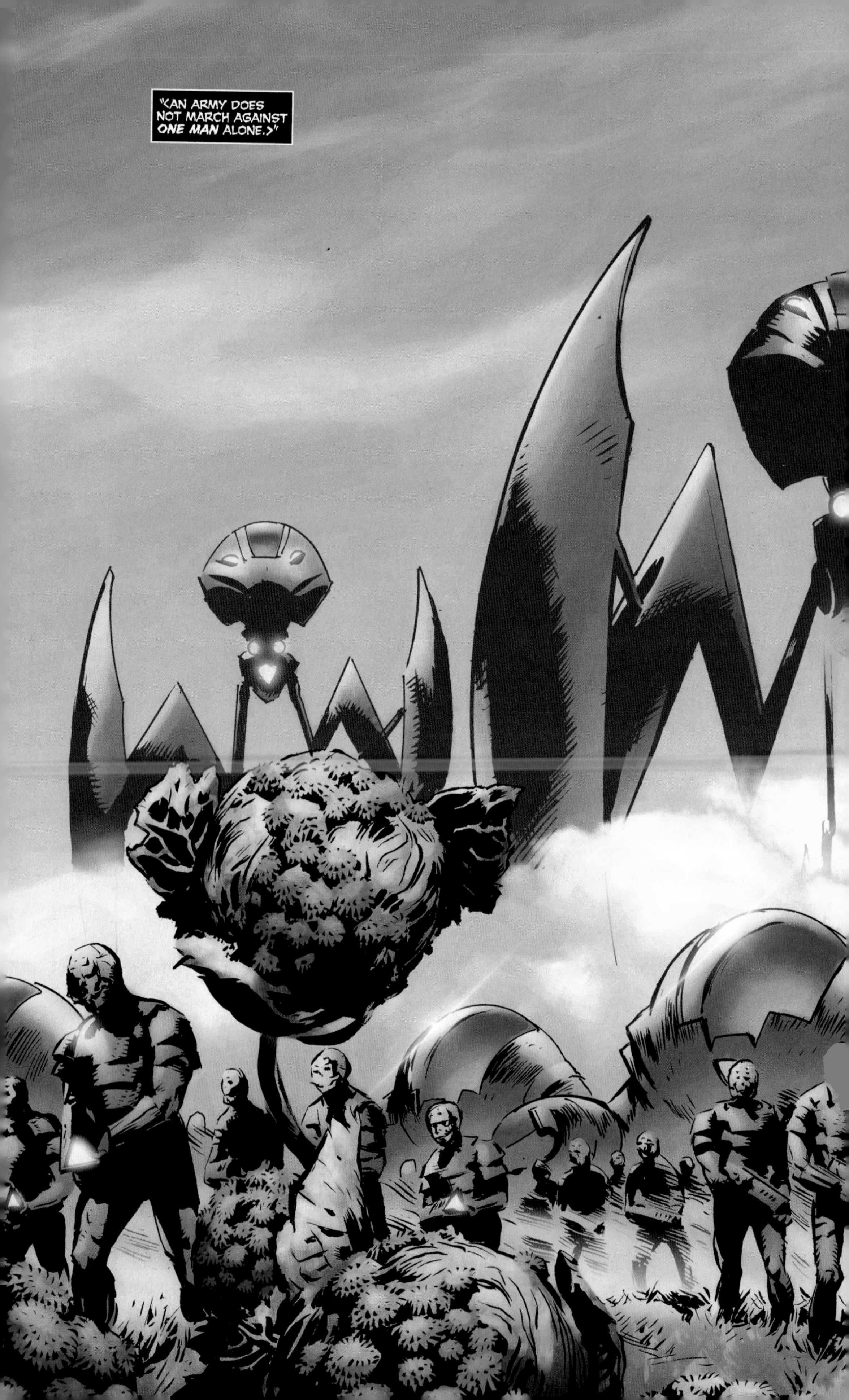
"<AN ARMY DOES NOT MARCH AGAINST ONE MAN ALONE.>"

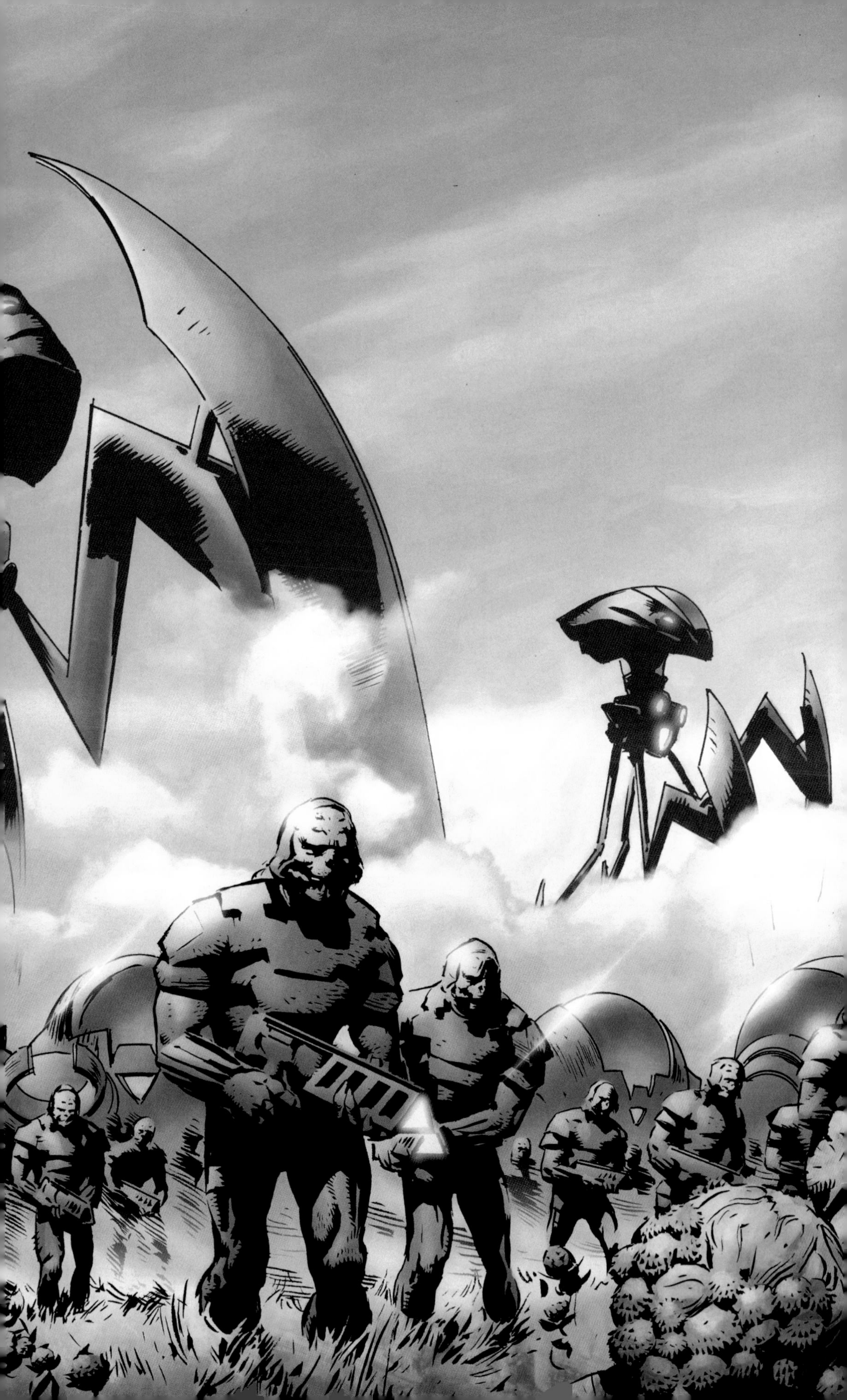

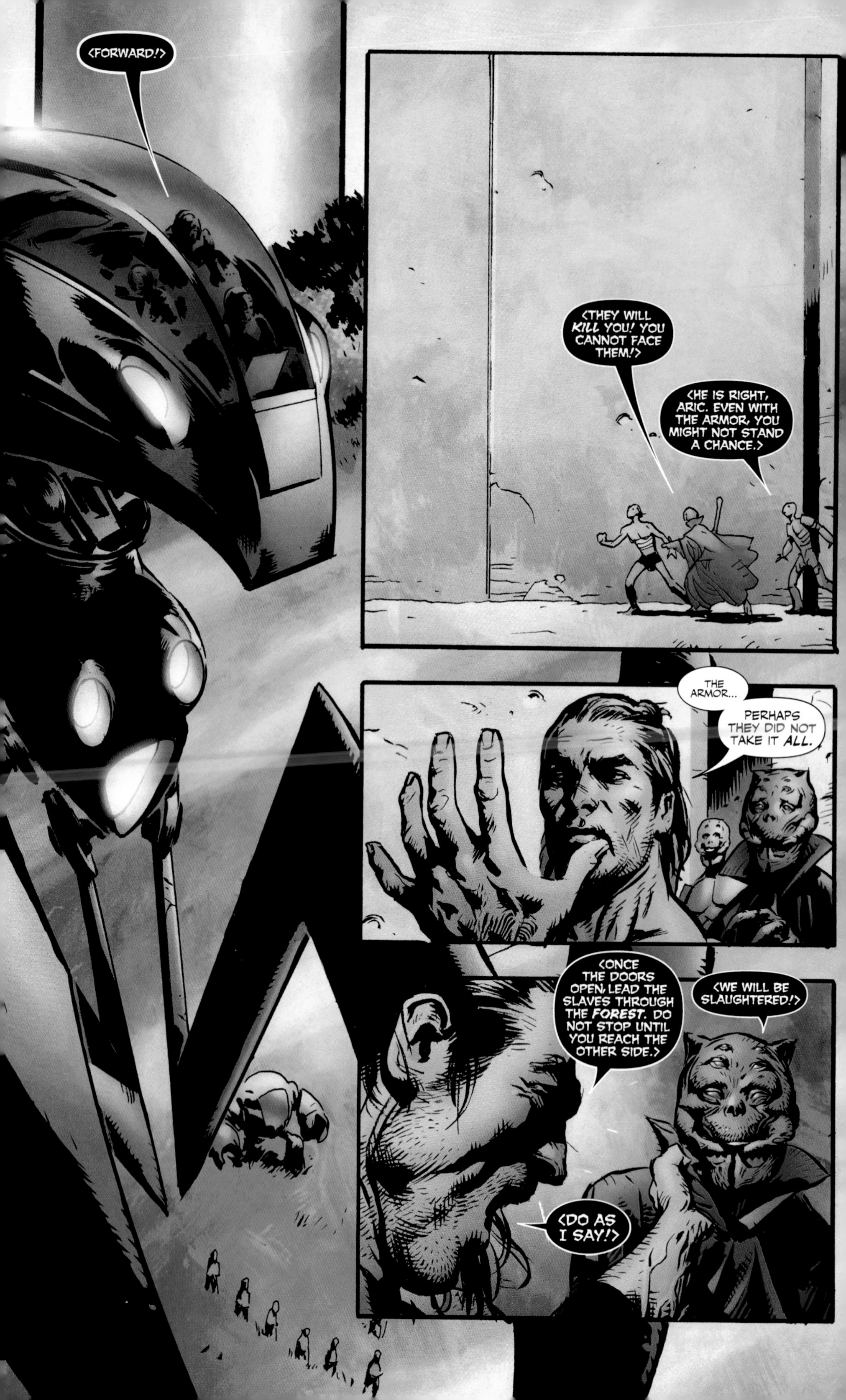

<FORWARD!>
<THEY WILL KILL YOU! YOU CANNOT FACE THEM!>
<HE IS RIGHT, ARIC. EVEN WITH THE ARMOR, YOU MIGHT NOT STAND A CHANCE.>
THE ARMOR...
PERHAPS THEY DID NOT TAKE IT ALL.
<ONCE THE DOORS OPEN, LEAD THE SLAVES THROUGH THE FOREST. DO NOT STOP UNTIL YOU REACH THE OTHER SIDE.>
<WE WILL BE SLAUGHTERED!>
<DO AS I SAY!>

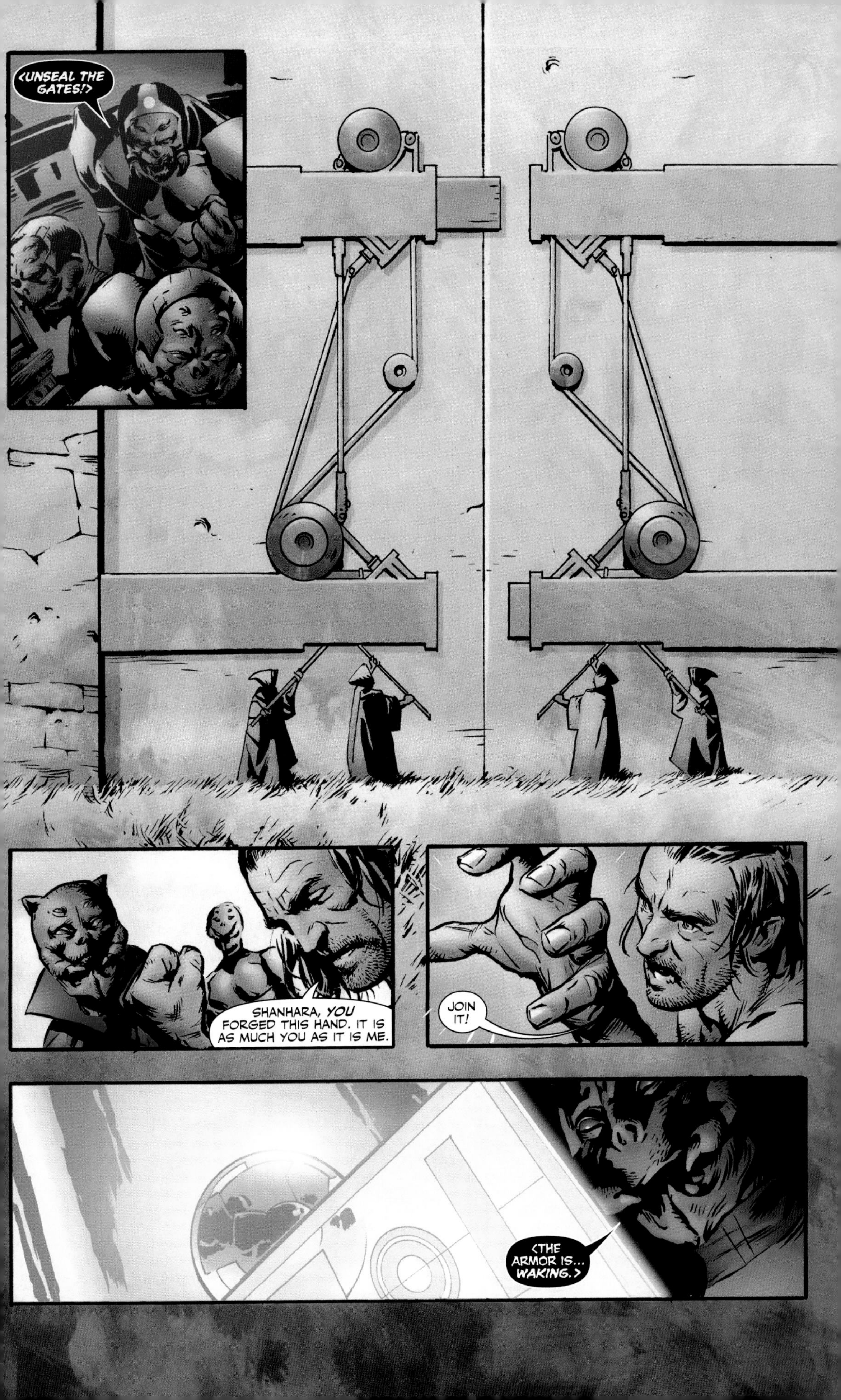
<UNSEAL THE GATES!>
SHANHARA, YOU FORGED THIS HAND. IT IS AS MUCH YOU AS IT IS ME.
JOIN IT!
<THE ARMOR IS... WAKING.>

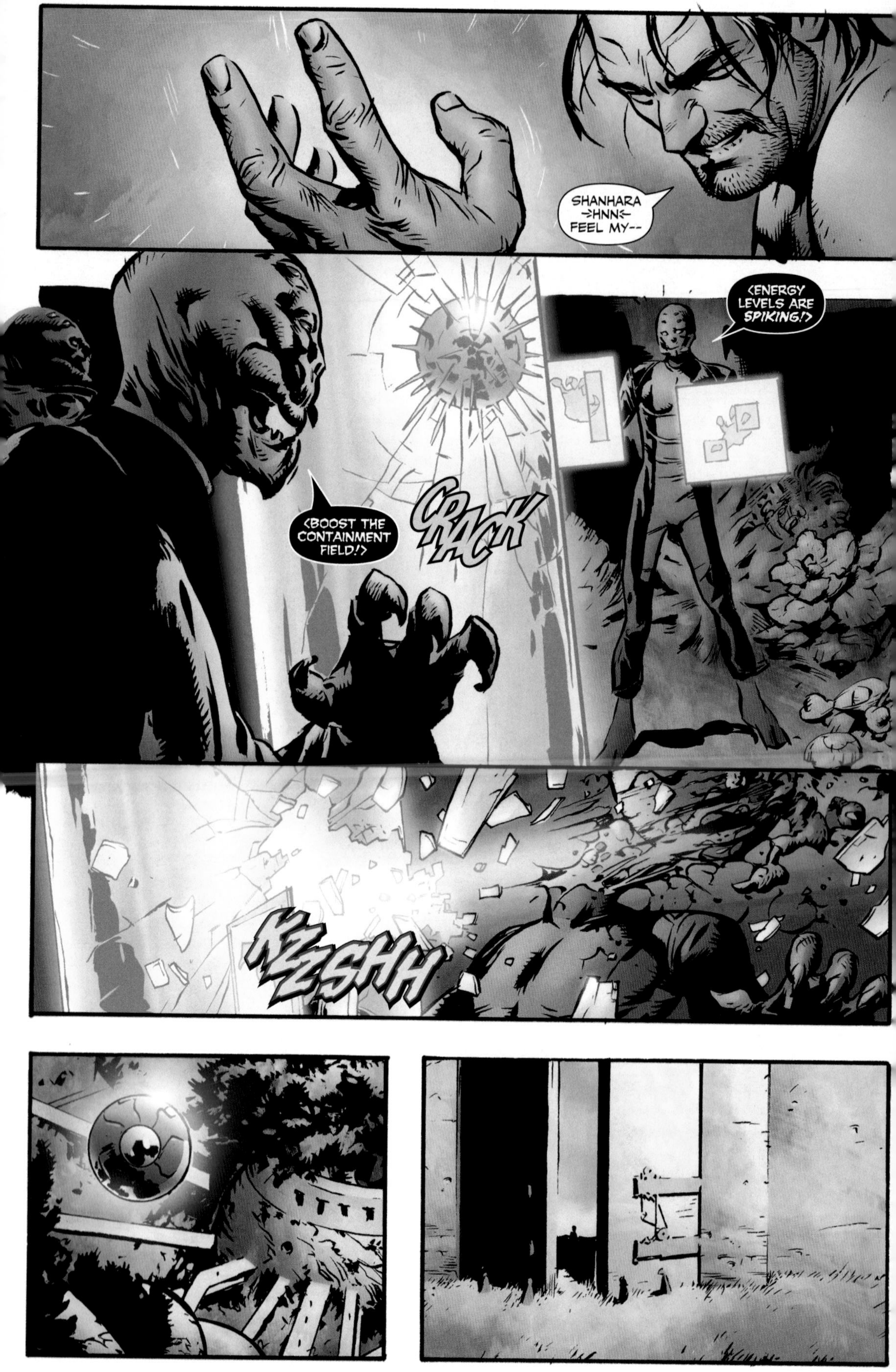
SHANHARA
-HNN-
FEEL MY--
<ENERGY LEVELS ARE SPIKING!>
<BOOST THE CONTAINMENT FIELD!>
CRACK
KZZSHH

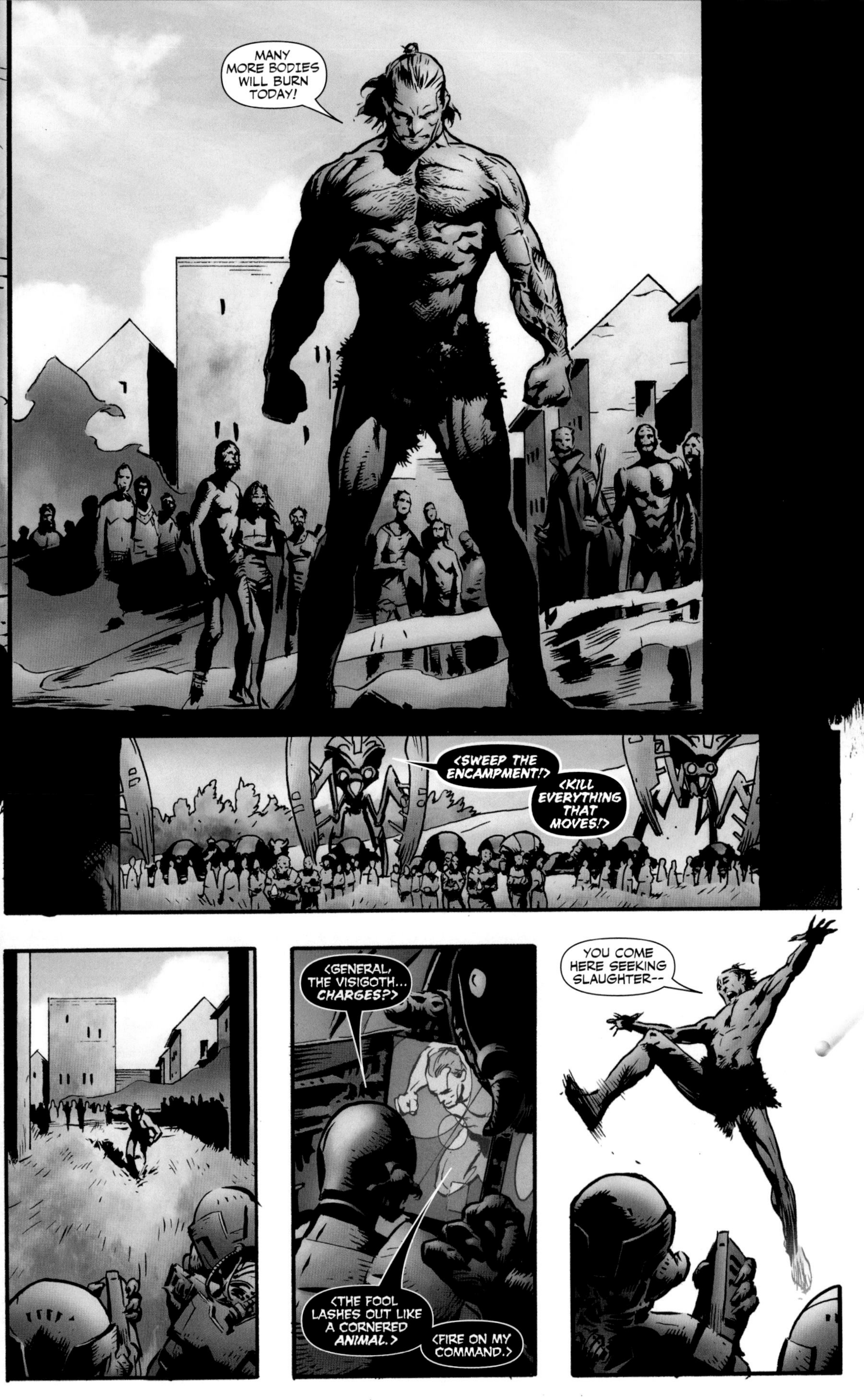
MANY MORE BODIES WILL BURN TODAY!
<SWEEP THE ENCAMPMENT!>
<KILL EVERYTHING THAT MOVES!>
<GENERAL, THE VISIGOTH... CHARGES?>
<THE FOOL LASHES OUT LIKE A CORNERED ANIMAL.>
<FIRE ON MY COMMAND.>
YOU COME HERE SEEKING SLAUGHTER--

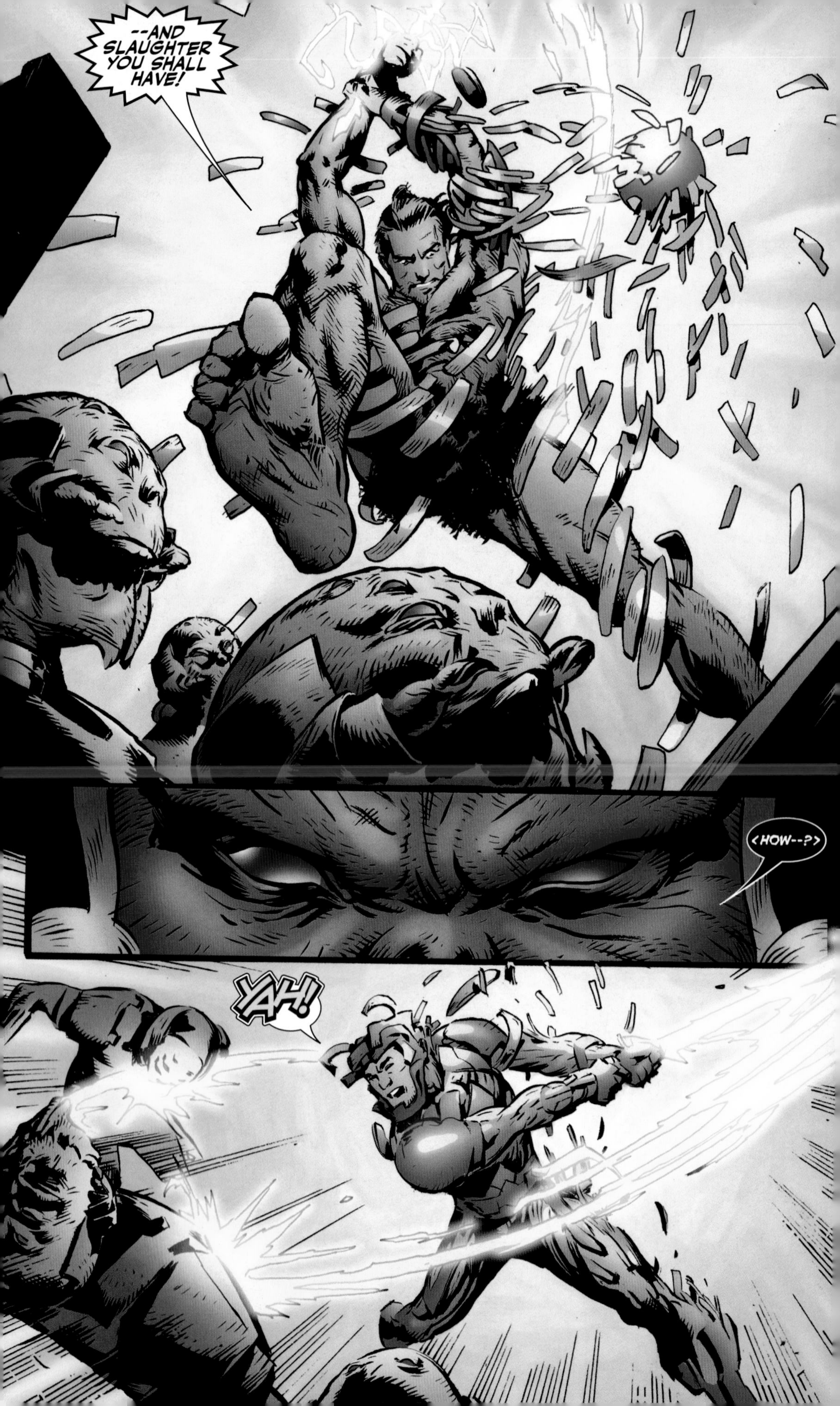
--AND SLAUGHTER YOU SHALL HAVE!
<HOW--?>
YAH!

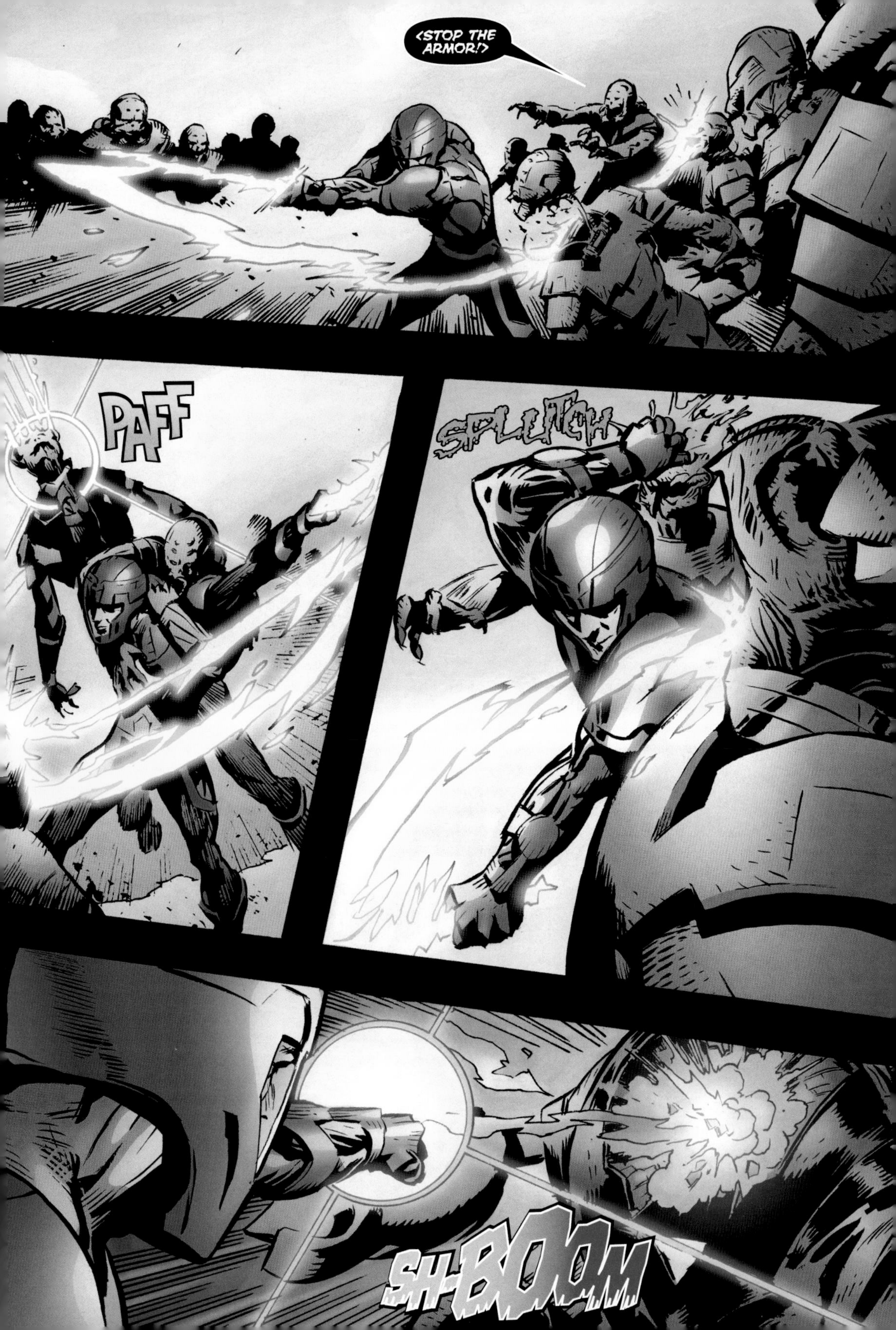
<STOP THE ARMOR!>
PAFF
SPLUTCH
SH-BOOM

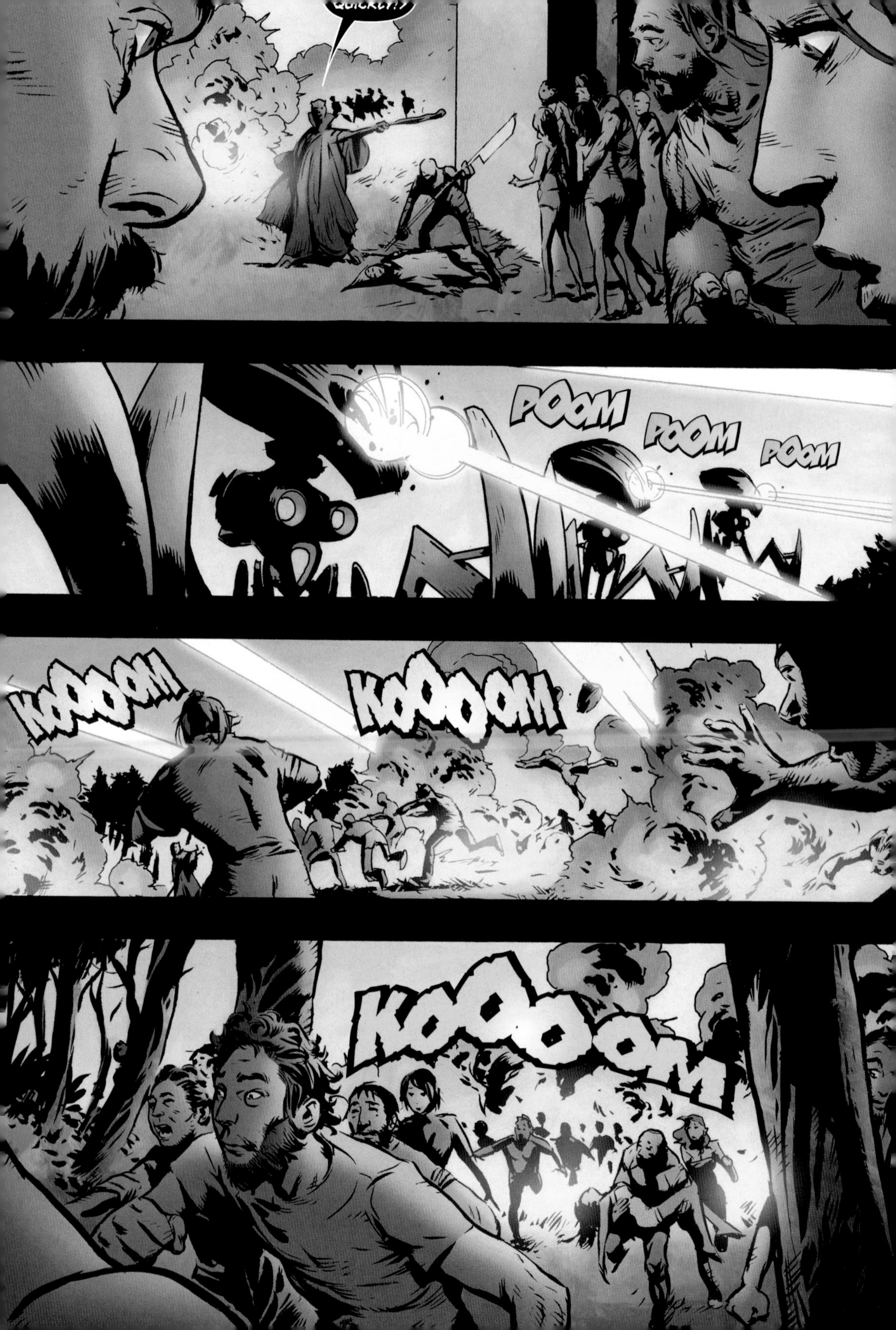
QUICKLY!?
POOM
POOM
POOM
KOOOOM
KOOOOM
KOOOOM

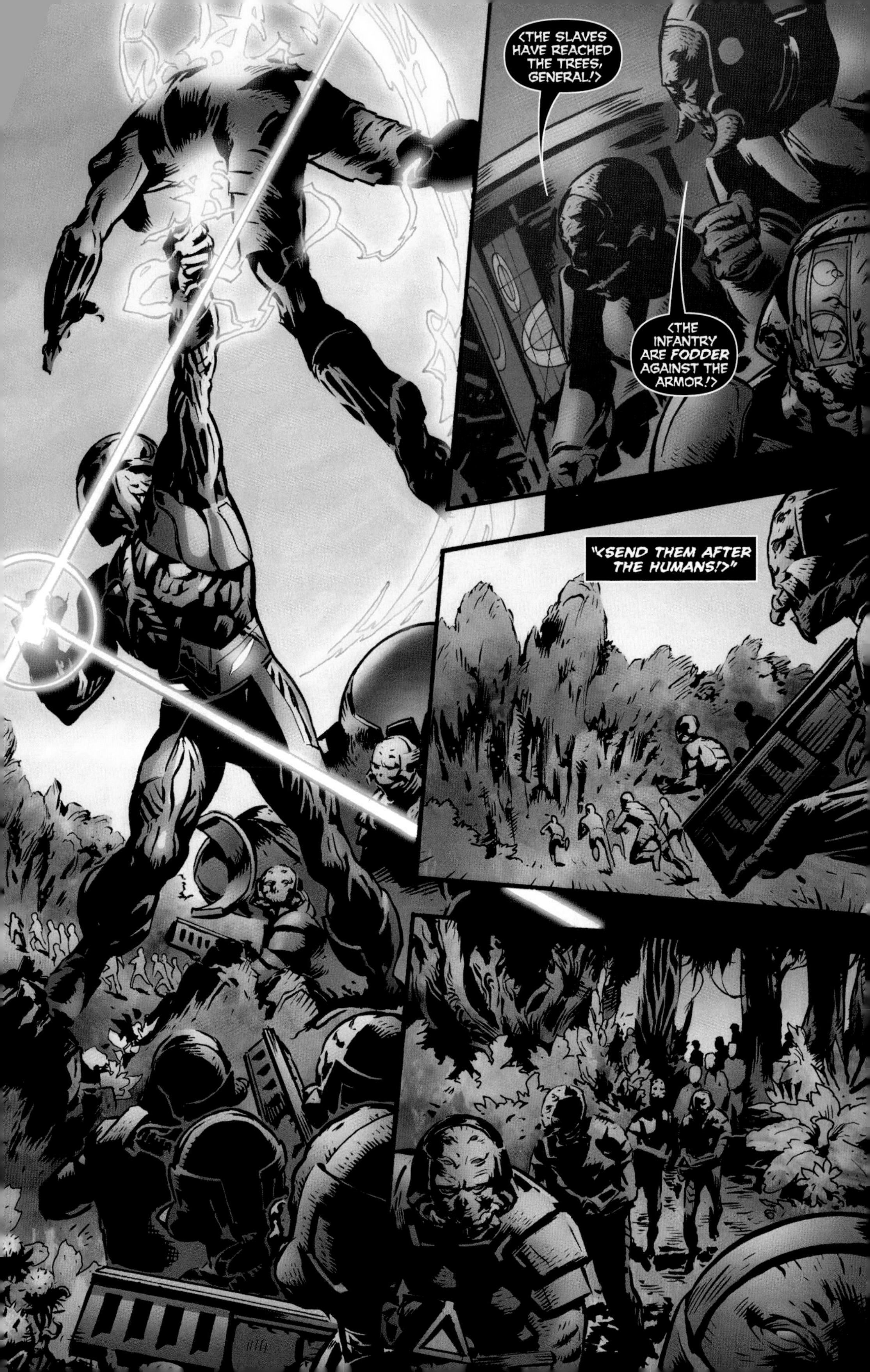

<THE SLAVES HAVE REACHED THE TREES, GENERAL!>
<THE INFANTRY ARE *FODDER* AGAINST THE ARMOR!>
"<SEND THEM AFTER THE HUMANS!>"

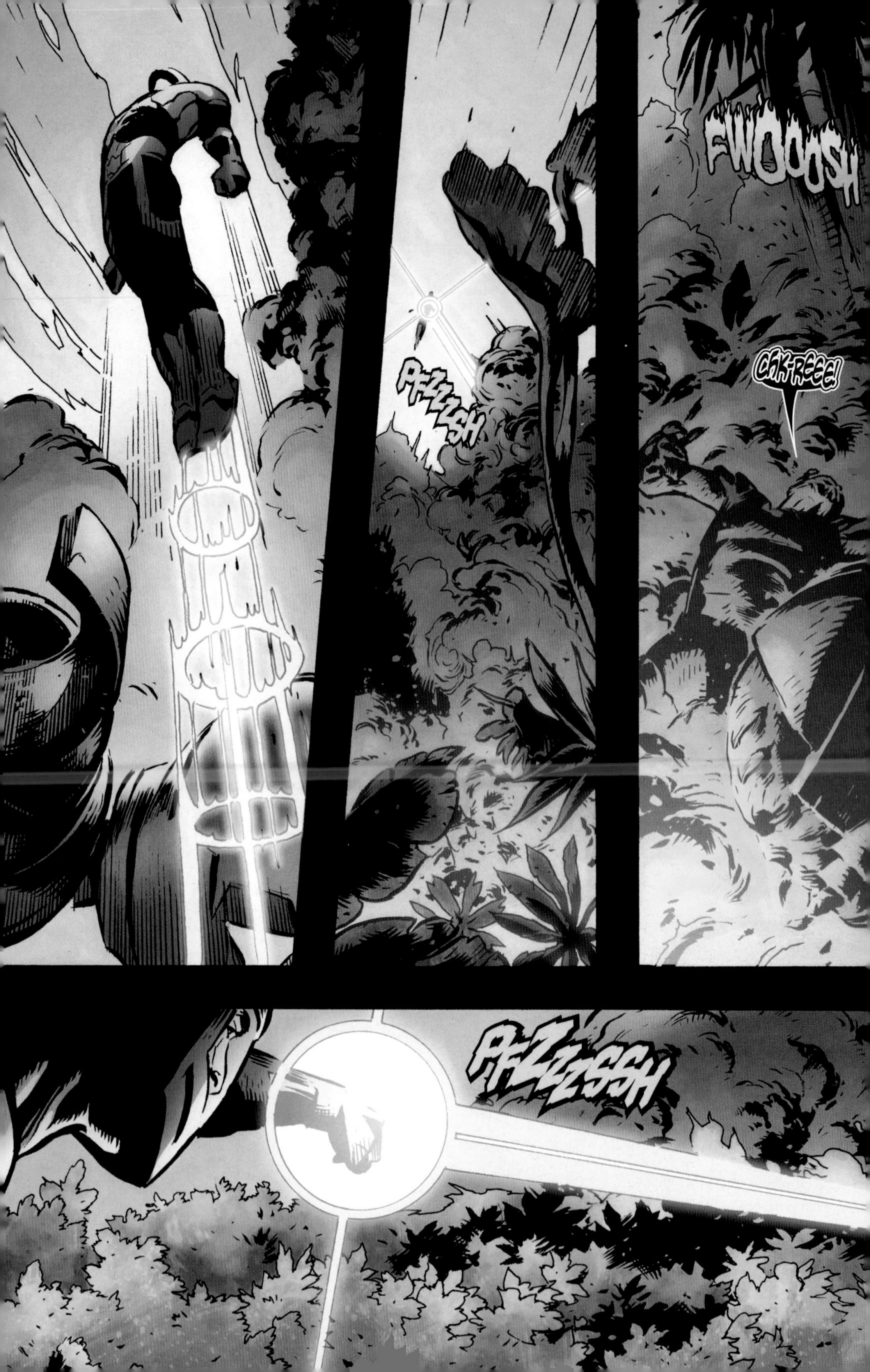
PFZZZSH
FWOOOSH
CHK-REEE!
PFZZZSSH

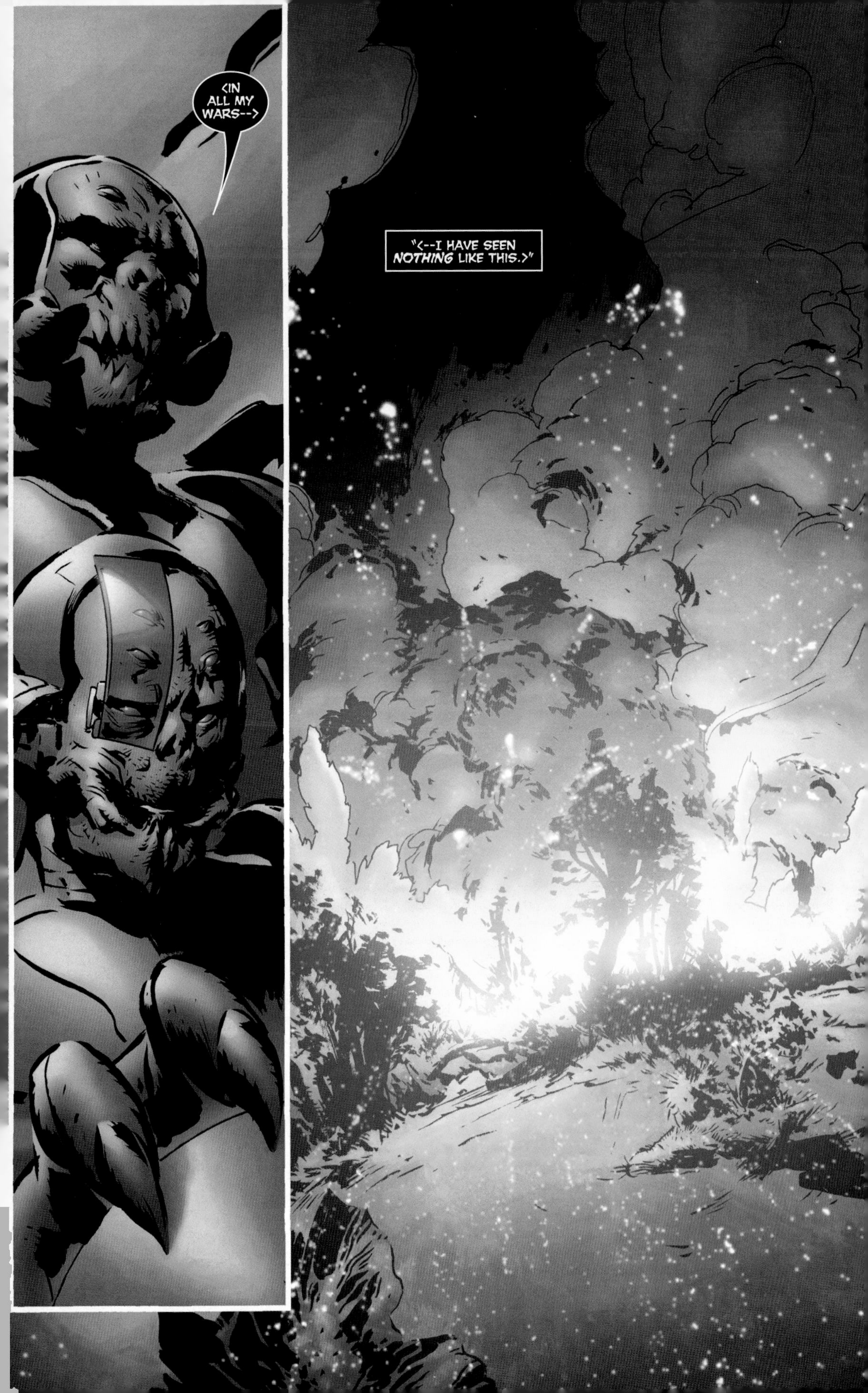
<IN ALL MY WARS-->
"<--I HAVE SEEN NOTHING LIKE THIS.>"

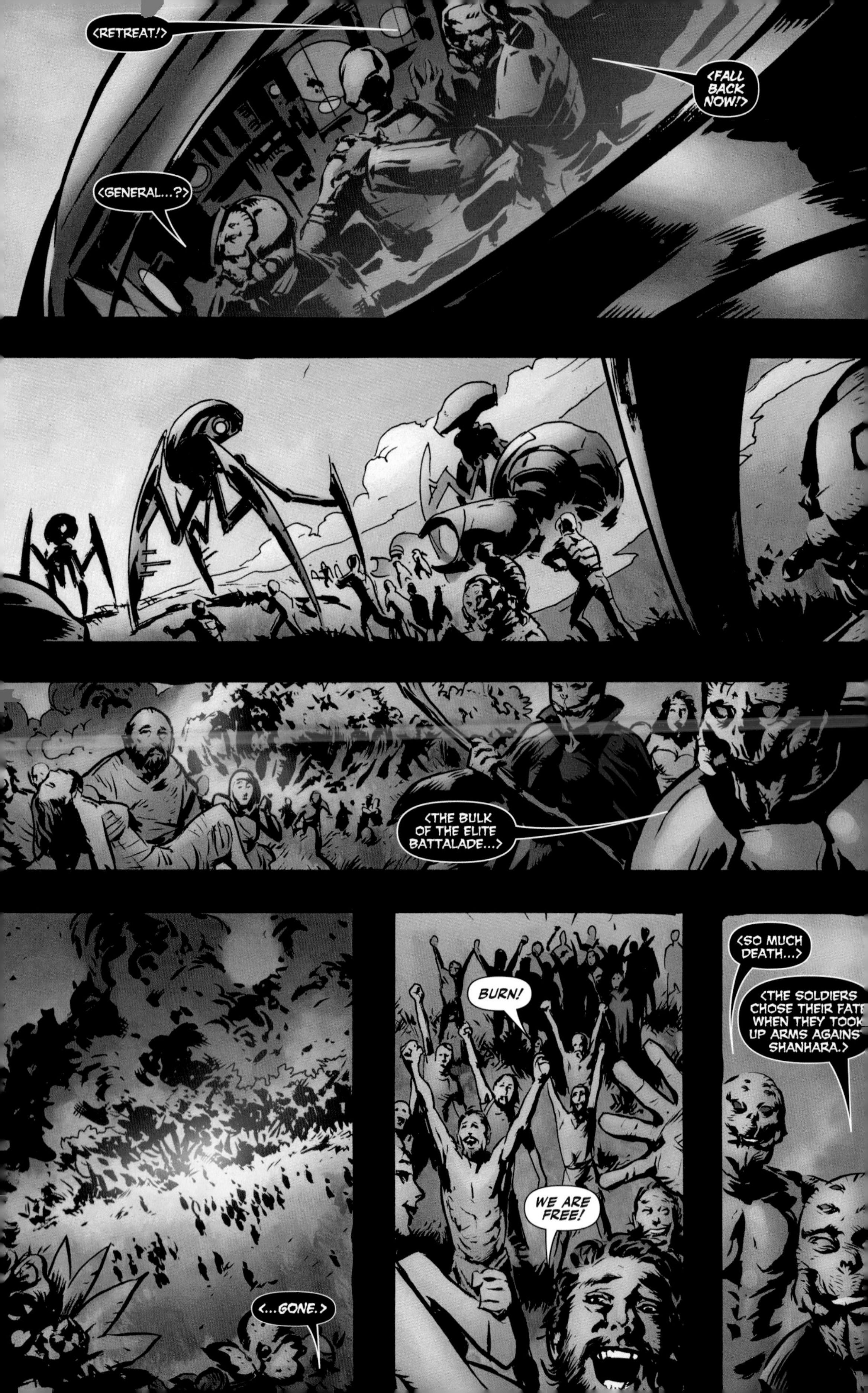

<RETREAT!>
<FALL BACK NOW!>
<GENERAL...?>
<THE BULK OF THE ELITE BATTALADE...>
<...GONE.>
BURN!
WE ARE FREE!
<SO MUCH DEATH...>
<THE SOLDIERS CHOSE THEIR FATE WHEN THEY TOOK UP ARMS AGAINST SHANHARA.>

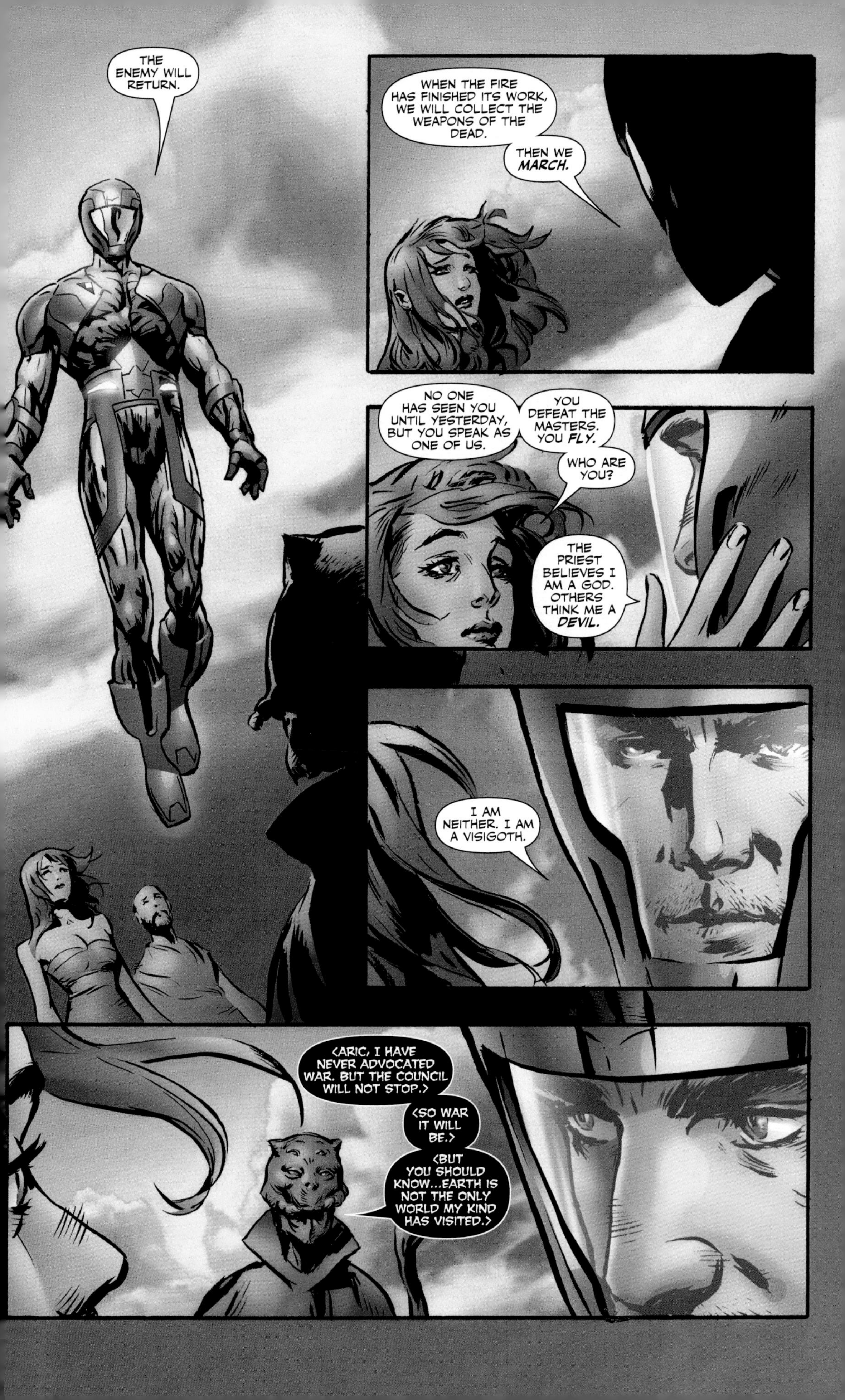
THE ENEMY WILL RETURN.
WHEN THE FIRE HAS FINISHED ITS WORK, WE WILL COLLECT THE WEAPONS OF THE DEAD.
THEN WE MARCH.
NO ONE HAS SEEN YOU UNTIL YESTERDAY, BUT YOU SPEAK AS ONE OF US.
YOU DEFEAT THE MASTERS. YOU FLY.
WHO ARE YOU?
THE PRIEST BELIEVES I AM A GOD. OTHERS THINK ME A DEVIL.
I AM NEITHER. I AM A VISIGOTH.
<ARIC, I HAVE NEVER ADVOCATED WAR. BUT THE COUNCIL WILL NOT STOP.>
<SO WAR IT WILL BE.>
<BUT YOU SHOULD KNOW...EARTH IS NOT THE ONLY WORLD MY KIND HAS VISITED.>

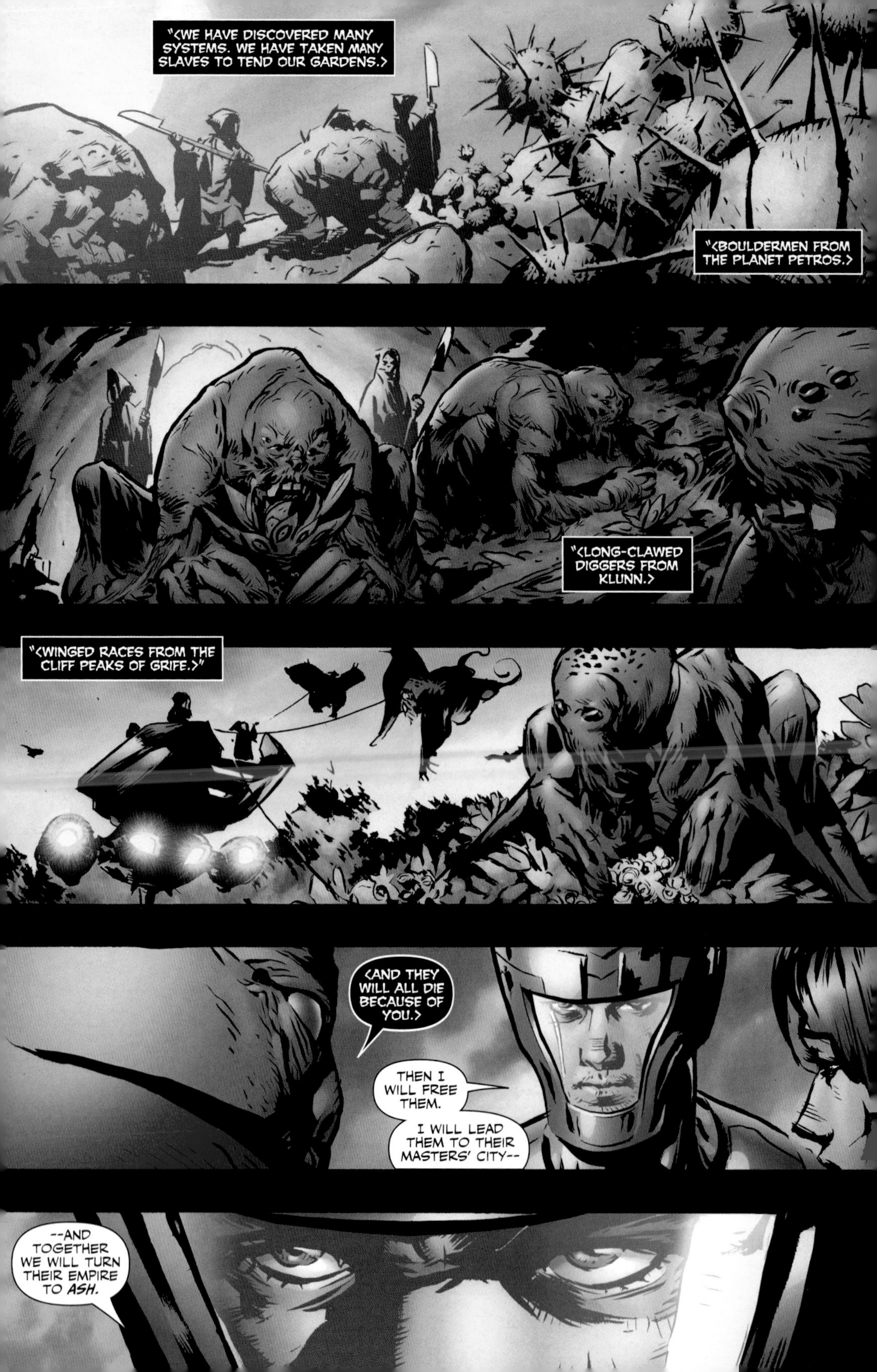
"<WE HAVE DISCOVERED MANY SYSTEMS. WE HAVE TAKEN MANY SLAVES TO TEND OUR GARDENS.>
"<BOULDERMEN FROM THE PLANET PETROS.>
"<LONG-CLAWED DIGGERS FROM KLUNN.>
"<WINGED RACES FROM THE CLIFF PEAKS OF GRIFE.>"
<AND THEY WILL ALL DIE BECAUSE OF YOU.>
THEN I WILL FREE THEM.
I WILL LEAD THEM TO THEIR MASTERS' CITY--
--AND TOGETHER WE WILL TURN THEIR EMPIRE TO *ASH.*

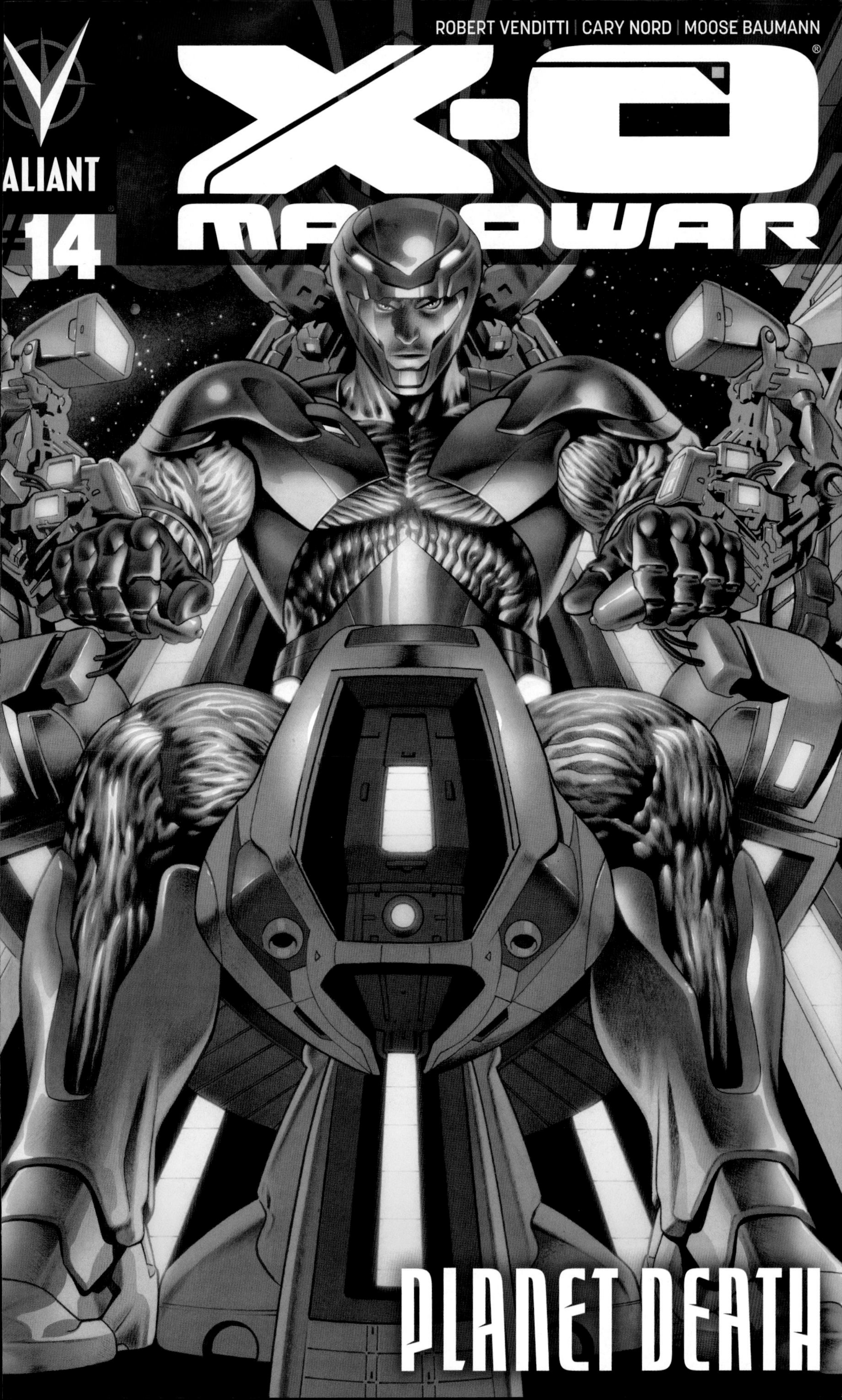

ROBERT VENDITTI | CARY NORD | MOOSE BAUMANN
VALIANT
#14
X-O MANOWAR
PLANET DEATH

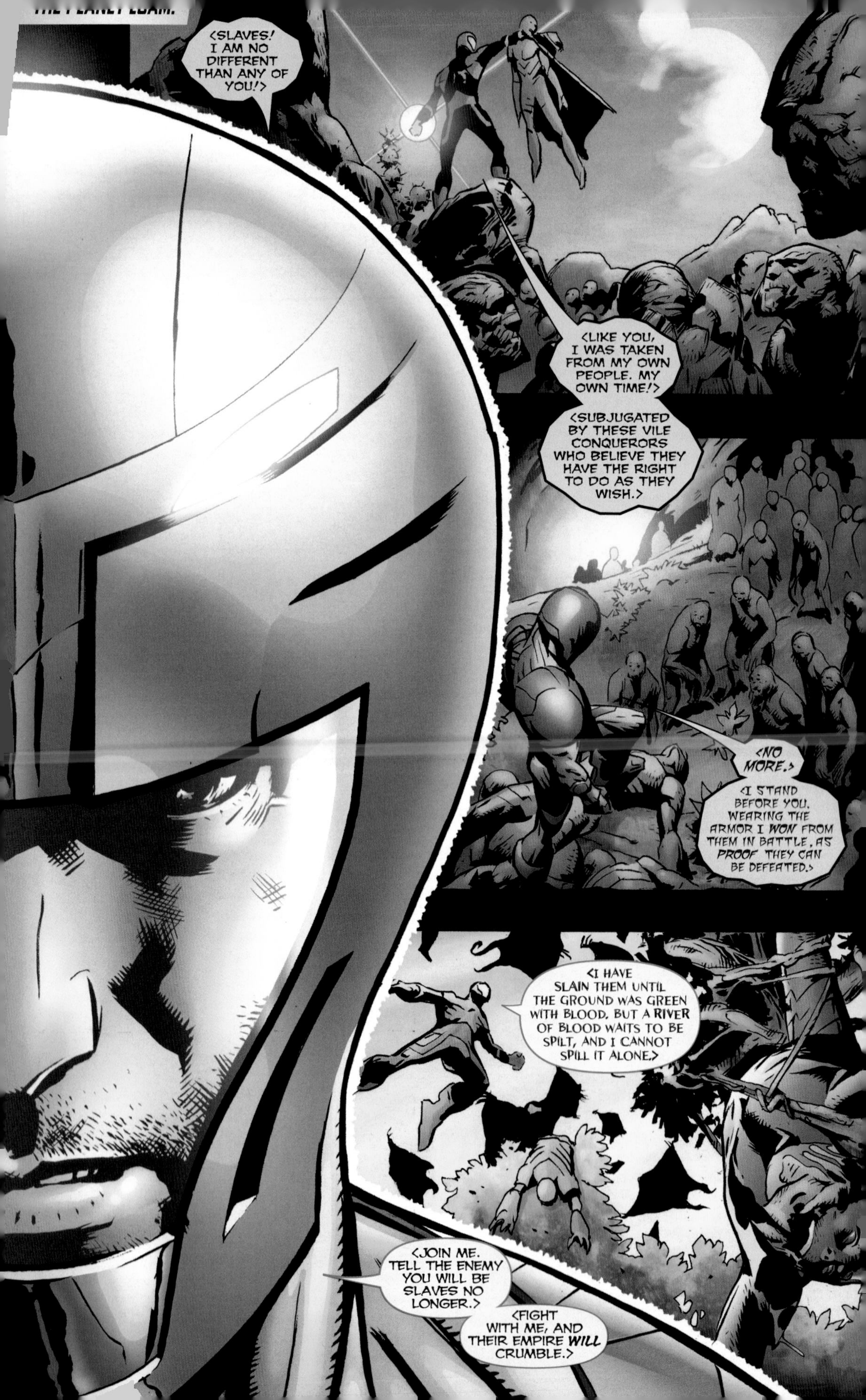

<SLAVES! I AM NO DIFFERENT THAN ANY OF YOU!>
<LIKE YOU, I WAS TAKEN FROM MY OWN PEOPLE. MY OWN TIME!>
<SUBJUGATED BY THESE VILE CONQUERORS WHO BELIEVE THEY HAVE THE RIGHT TO DO AS THEY WISH.>
<NO MORE.>
<I STAND BEFORE YOU, WEARING THE ARMOR I WON FROM THEM IN BATTLE, AS PROOF THEY CAN BE DEFEATED.>
<I HAVE SLAIN THEM UNTIL THE GROUND WAS GREEN WITH BLOOD, BUT A RIVER OF BLOOD WAITS TO BE SPILT, AND I CANNOT SPILL IT ALONE.>
<JOIN ME. TELL THE ENEMY YOU WILL BE SLAVES NO LONGER.>
<FIGHT WITH ME, AND THEIR EMPIRE WILL CRUMBLE.>

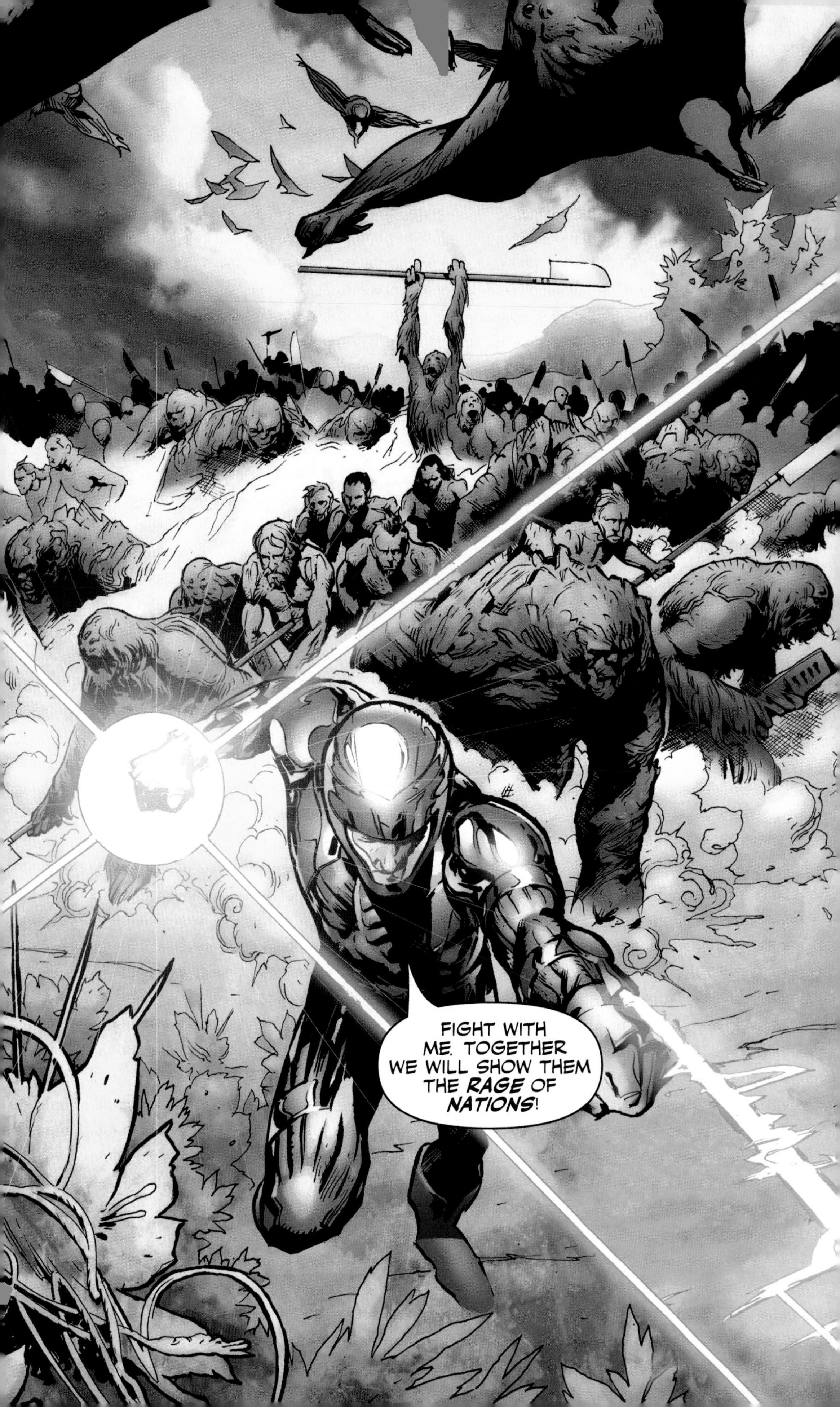
FIGHT WITH ME. TOGETHER WE WILL SHOW THEM THE *RAGE* OF *NATIONS*!

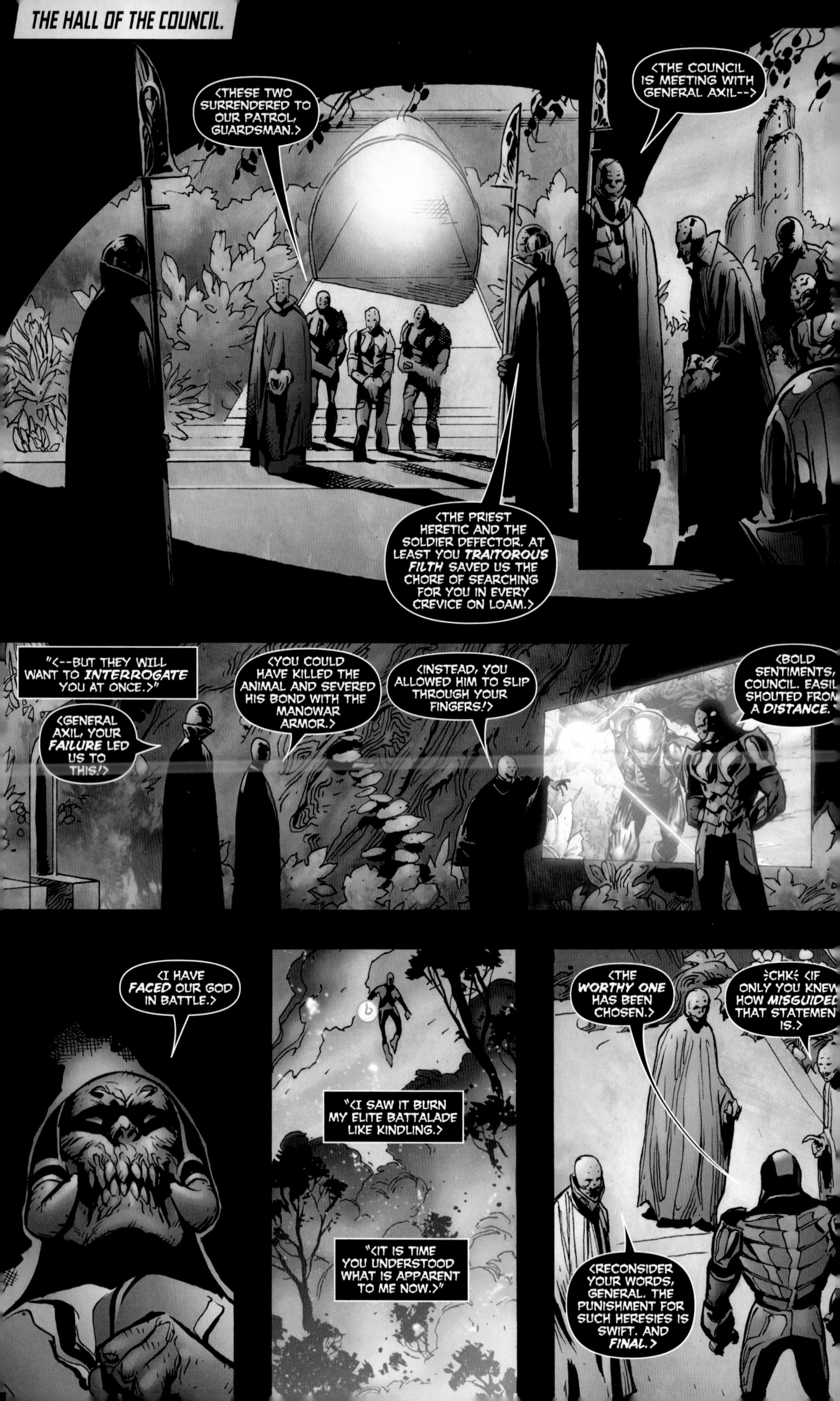

THE HALL OF THE COUNCIL.
<THESE TWO SURRENDERED TO OUR PATROL, GUARDSMAN.>
<THE COUNCIL IS MEETING WITH GENERAL AXIL-->
<THE PRIEST HERETIC AND THE SOLDIER DEFECTOR. AT LEAST YOU TRAITOROUS FILTH SAVED US THE CHORE OF SEARCHING FOR YOU IN EVERY CREVICE ON LOAM.>
"<--BUT THEY WILL WANT TO INTERROGATE YOU AT ONCE.>"
<GENERAL AXIL, YOUR FAILURE LED US TO THIS!>
<YOU COULD HAVE KILLED THE ANIMAL AND SEVERED HIS BOND WITH THE MANOWAR ARMOR.>
<INSTEAD, YOU ALLOWED HIM TO SLIP THROUGH YOUR FINGERS!>
<BOLD SENTIMENTS, COUNCIL. EASIL SHOUTED FROM A DISTANCE.
<I HAVE FACED OUR GOD IN BATTLE.>
"<I SAW IT BURN MY ELITE BATTALADE LIKE KINDLING.>
"<IT IS TIME YOU UNDERSTOOD WHAT IS APPARENT TO ME NOW.>"
<THE WORTHY ONE HAS BEEN CHOSEN.>
CHK <IF ONLY YOU KNEW HOW MISGUIDED THAT STATEMENT IS.>
<RECONSIDER YOUR WORDS, GENERAL. THE PUNISHMENT FOR SUCH HERESIES IS SWIFT. AND FINAL.>

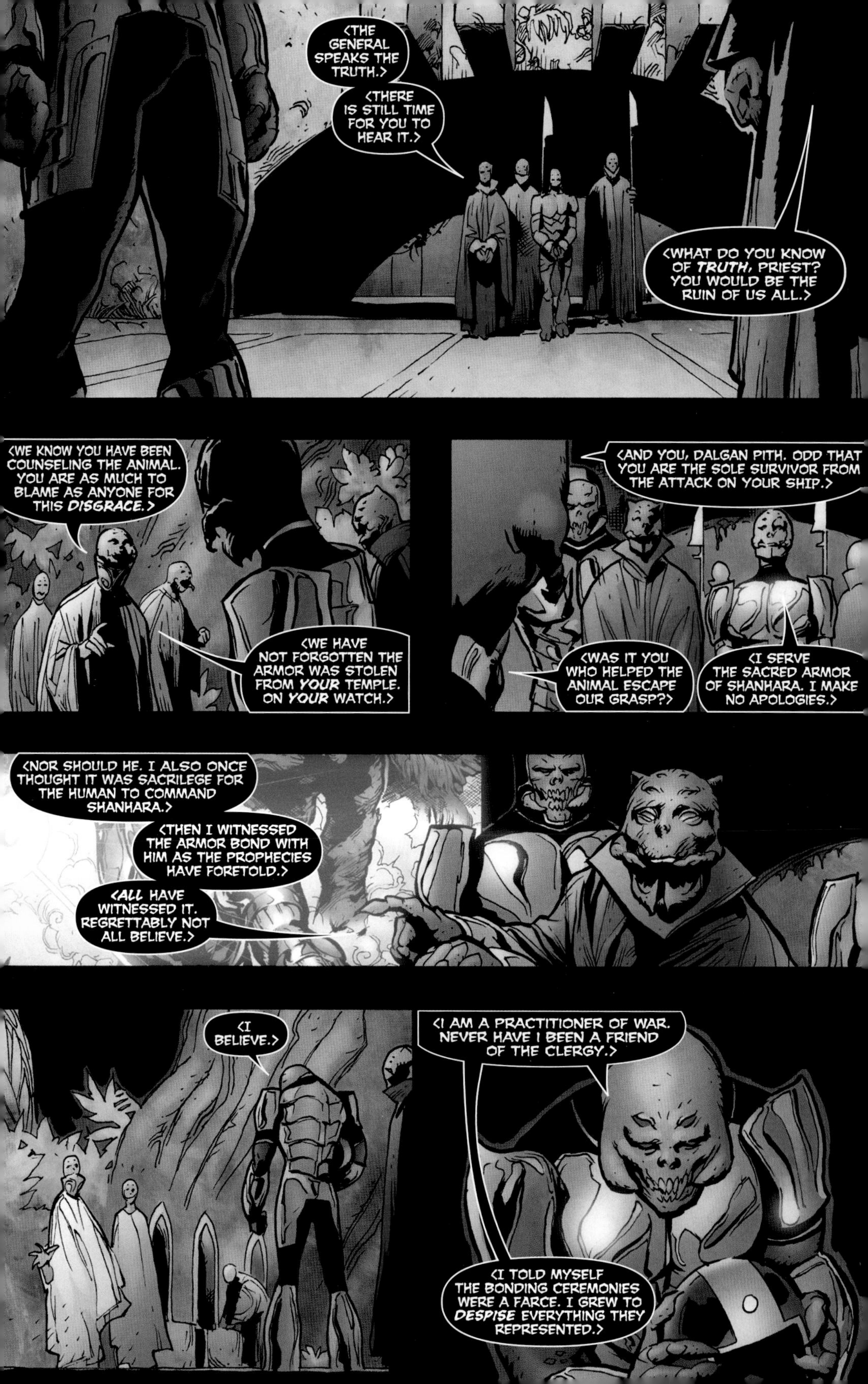
<THE GENERAL SPEAKS THE TRUTH.>
<THERE IS STILL TIME FOR YOU TO HEAR IT.>
<WHAT DO YOU KNOW OF *TRUTH*, PRIEST? YOU WOULD BE THE RUIN OF US ALL.>
<WE KNOW YOU HAVE BEEN COUNSELING THE ANIMAL. YOU ARE AS MUCH TO BLAME AS ANYONE FOR THIS *DISGRACE*.>
<WE HAVE NOT FORGOTTEN THE ARMOR WAS STOLEN FROM *YOUR* TEMPLE. ON *YOUR* WATCH.>
<AND YOU, DALGAN PITH. ODD THAT YOU ARE THE SOLE SURVIVOR FROM THE ATTACK ON YOUR SHIP.>
<WAS IT YOU WHO HELPED THE ANIMAL ESCAPE OUR GRASP?>
<I SERVE THE SACRED ARMOR OF SHANHARA. I MAKE NO APOLOGIES.>
<NOR SHOULD HE. I ALSO ONCE THOUGHT IT WAS SACRILEGE FOR THE HUMAN TO COMMAND SHANHARA.>
<THEN I WITNESSED THE ARMOR BOND WITH HIM AS THE PROPHECIES HAVE FORETOLD.>
<*ALL* HAVE WITNESSED IT. REGRETTABLY NOT ALL BELIEVE.>
<I BELIEVE.>
<I AM A PRACTITIONER OF WAR. NEVER HAVE I BEEN A FRIEND OF THE CLERGY.>
<I TOLD MYSELF THE BONDING CEREMONIES WERE A FARCE. I GREW TO *DESPISE* EVERYTHING THEY REPRESENTED.>

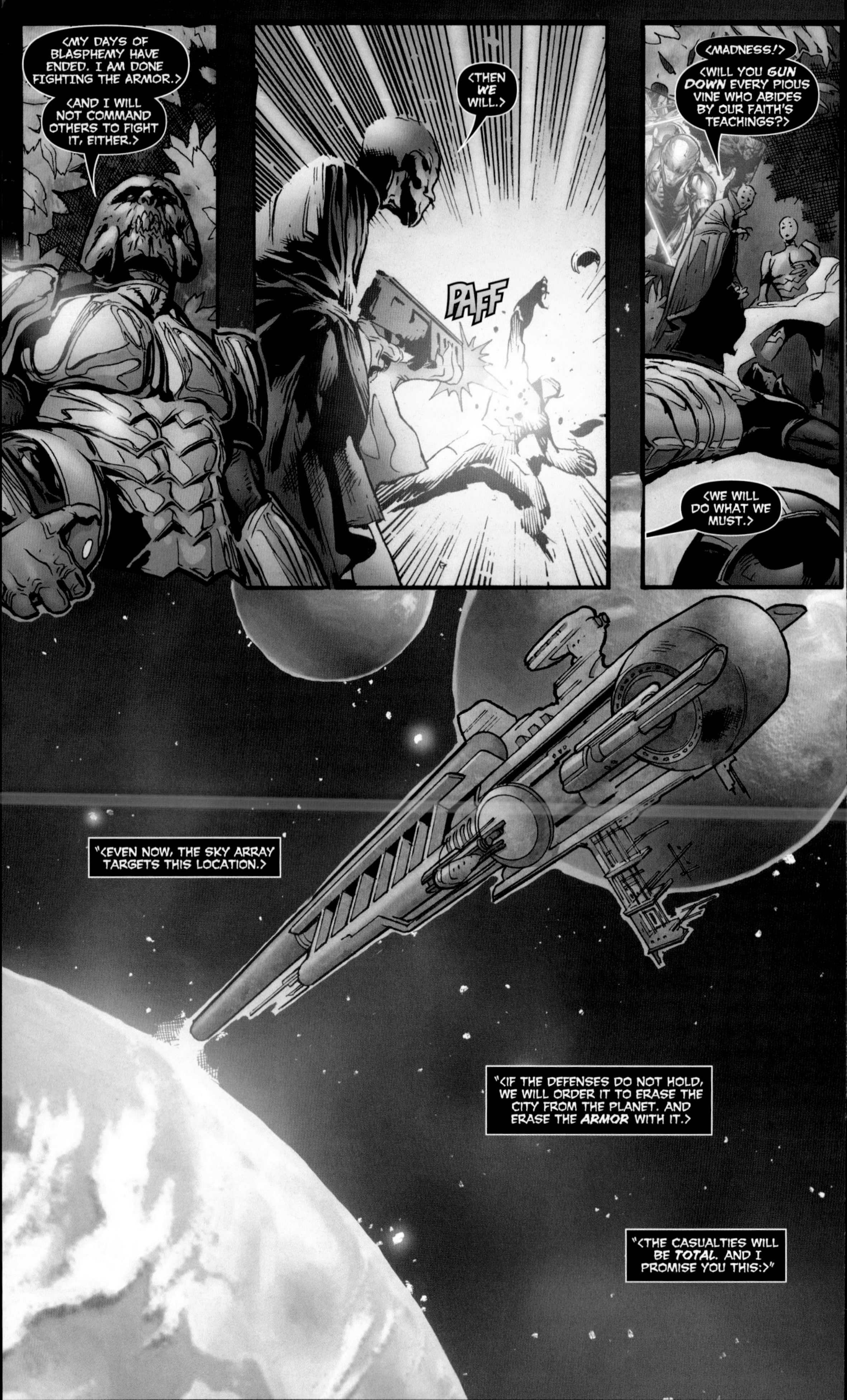
<MY DAYS OF BLASPHEMY HAVE ENDED. I AM DONE FIGHTING THE ARMOR.>
<AND I WILL NOT COMMAND OTHERS TO FIGHT IT, EITHER.>
<THEN *WE* WILL.>
PAFF
<MADNESS!>
<WILL YOU *GUN DOWN* EVERY PIOUS VINE WHO ABIDES BY OUR FAITH'S TEACHINGS?>
<WE WILL DO WHAT WE MUST.>
"<EVEN NOW, THE SKY ARRAY TARGETS THIS LOCATION.>
"<IF THE DEFENSES DO NOT HOLD, WE WILL ORDER IT TO ERASE THE CITY FROM THE PLANET. AND ERASE THE *ARMOR* WITH IT.>
"<THE CASUALTIES WILL BE *TOTAL*. AND I PROMISE YOU THIS:>"

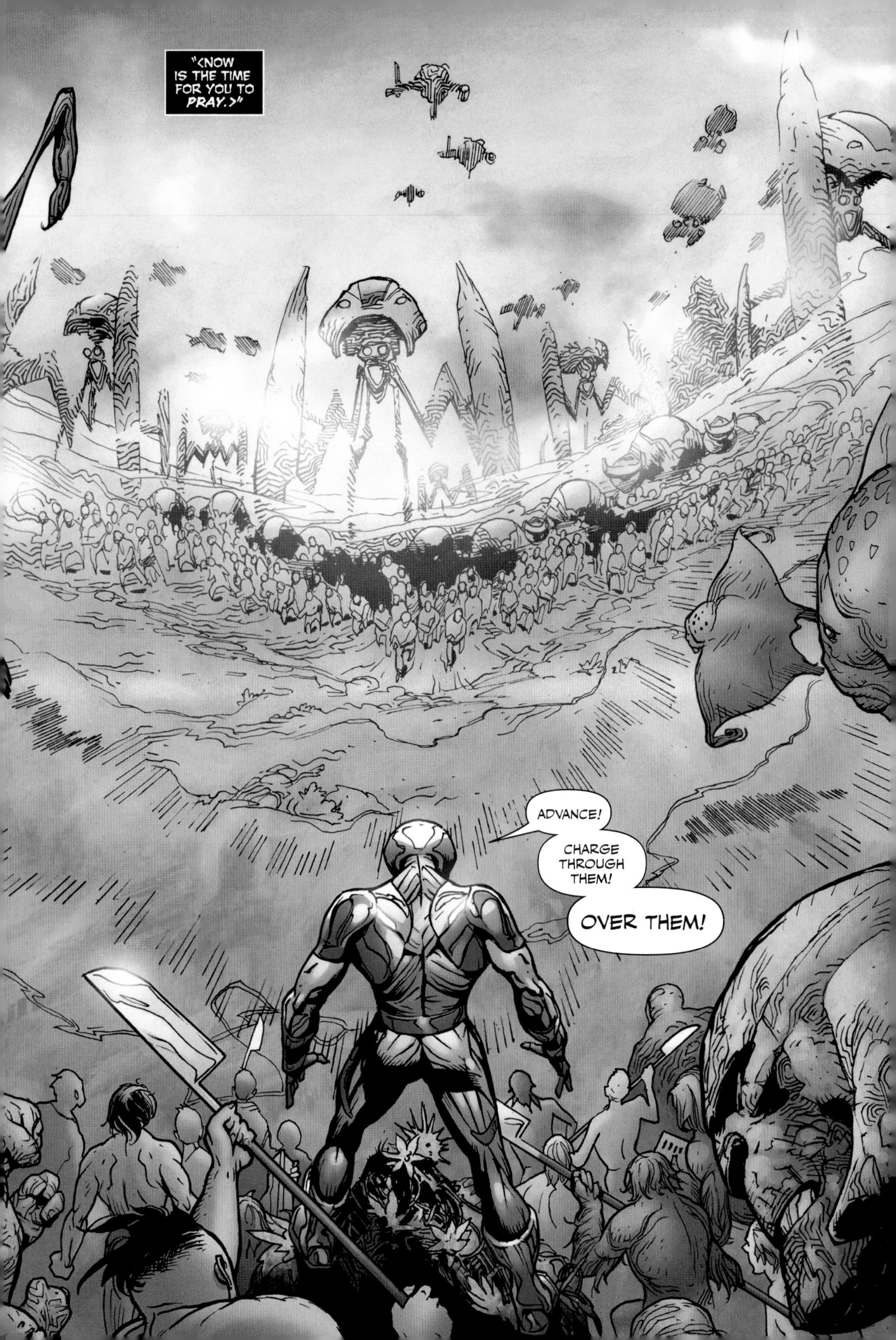
"<NOW IS THE TIME FOR YOU TO PRAY.>"
ADVANCE!
CHARGE THROUGH THEM!
OVER THEM!

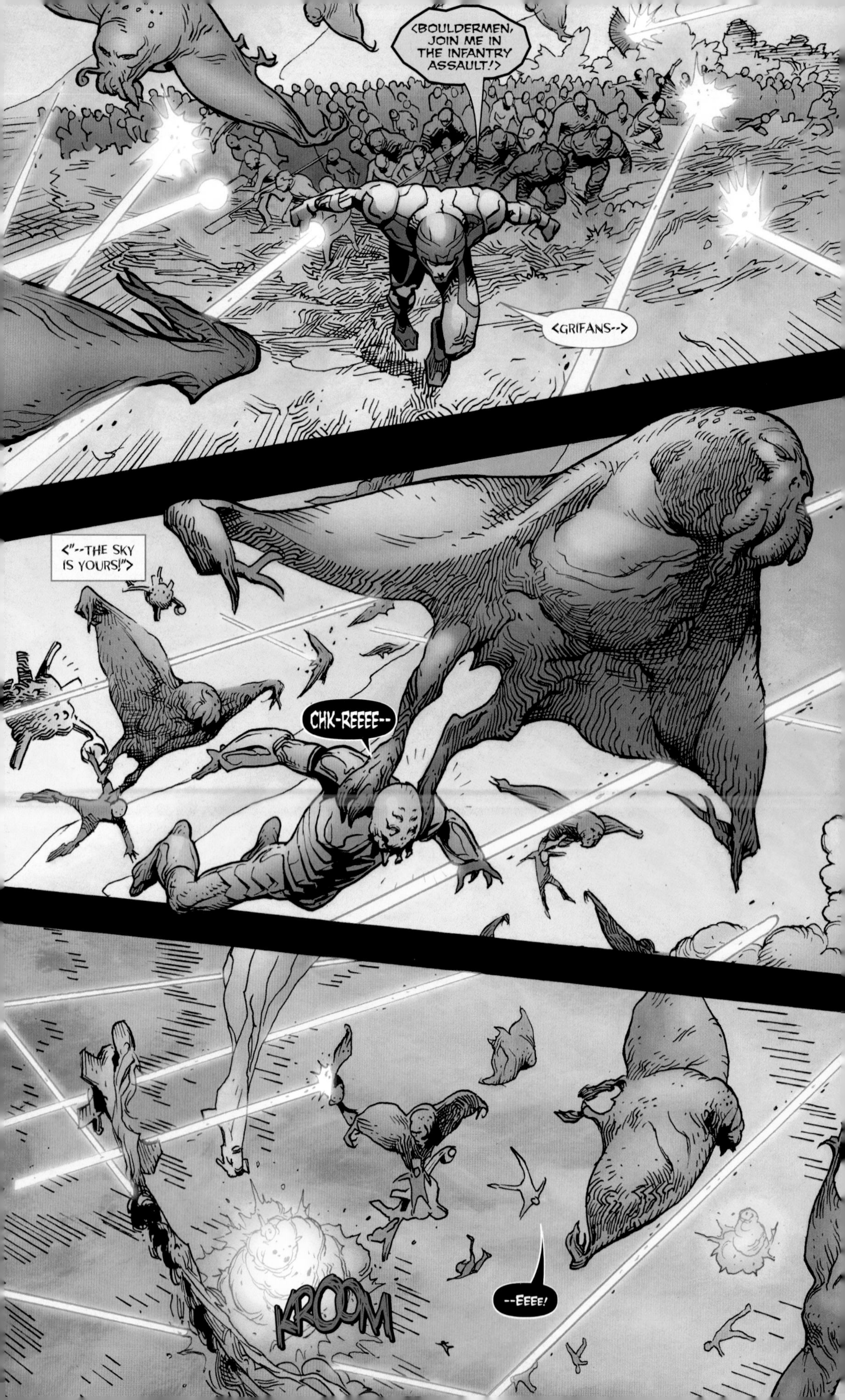
<BOULDERMEN, JOIN ME IN THE INFANTRY ASSAULT!>
<GRIFANS-->
<"--THE SKY IS YOURS!">
CHK-REEEE--
KROOM
--EEEE!

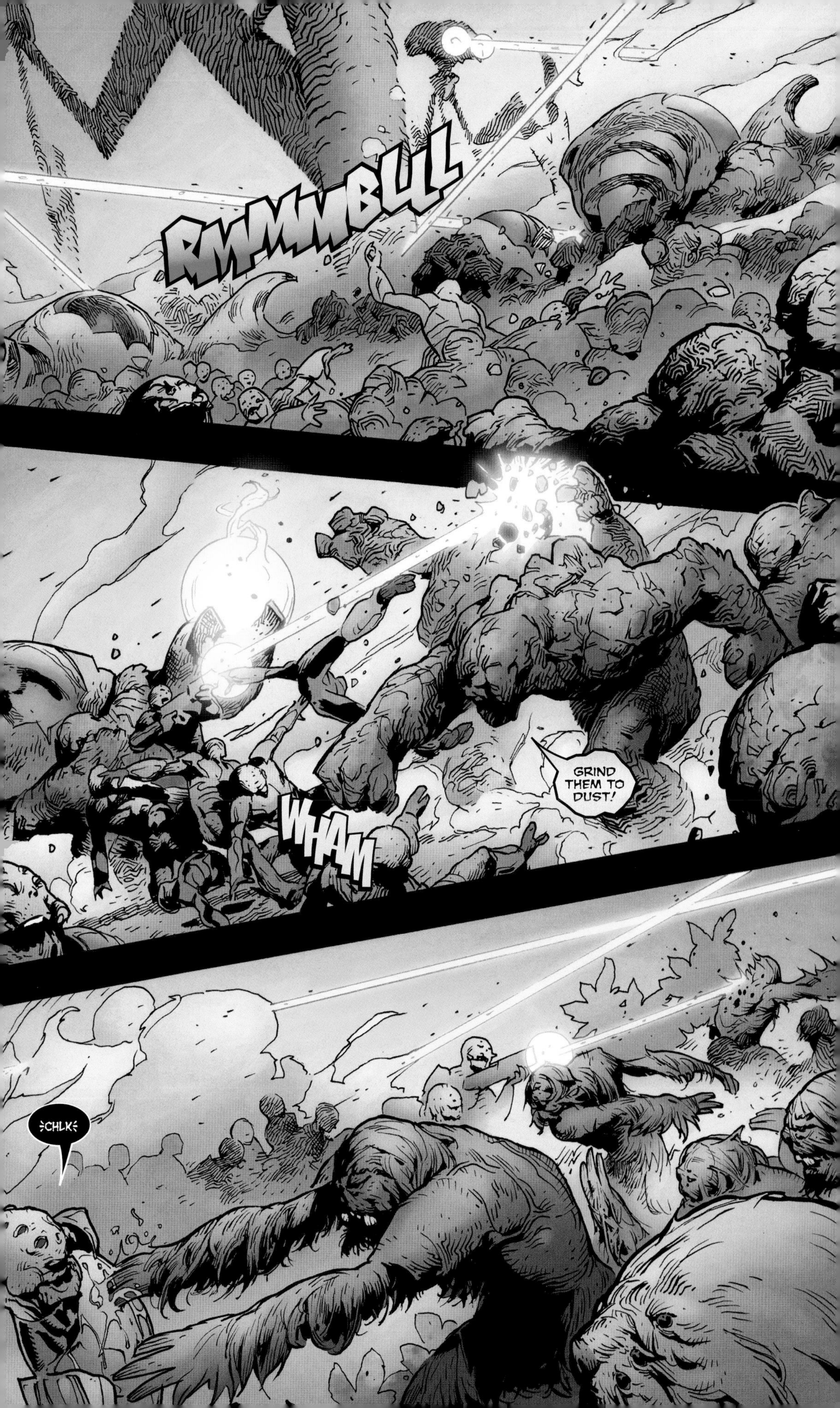
RMMMMBLLL
GRIND THEM TO DUST!
WHAM
CHLK

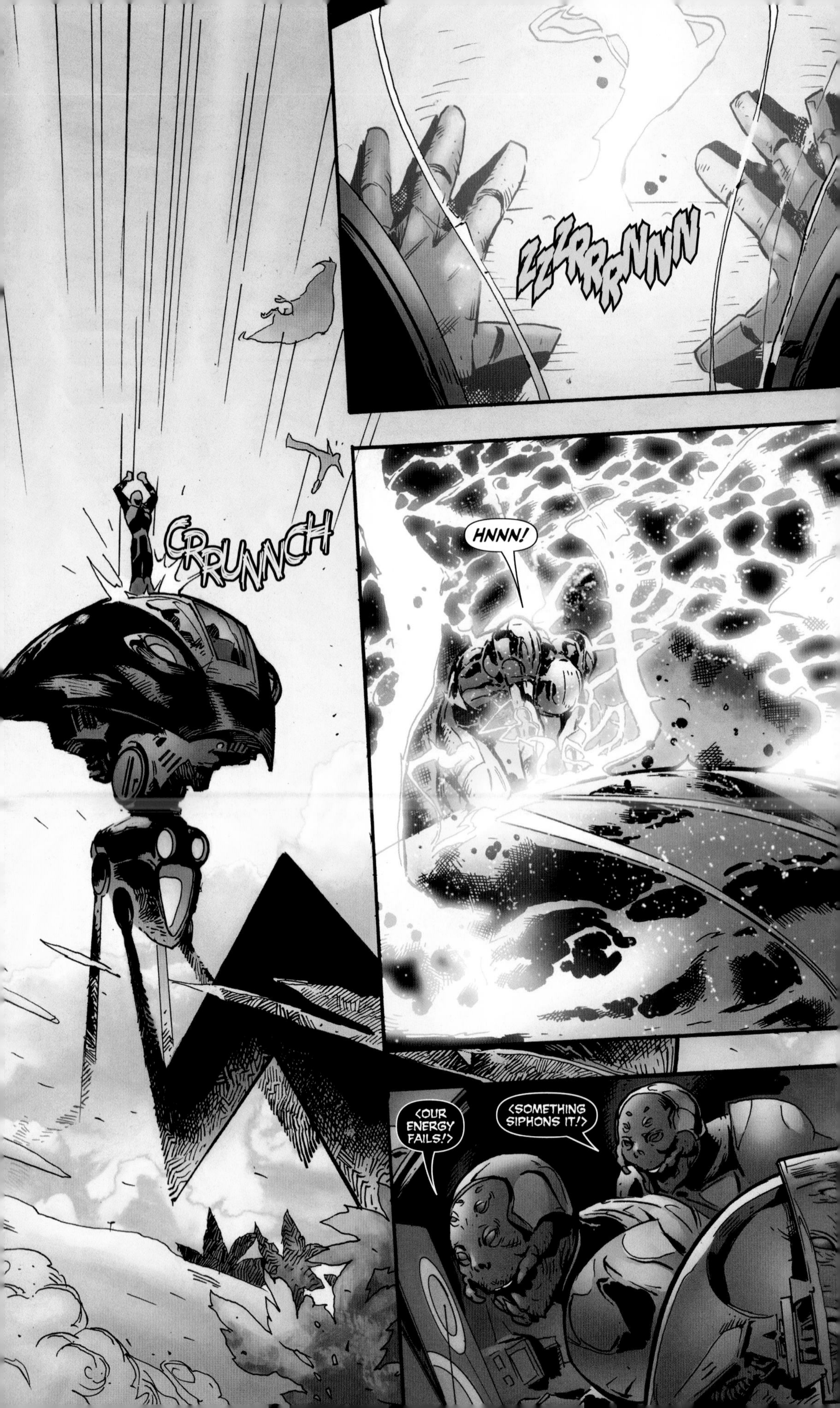
ZZZRRRNNNN
CRRUNNCH
HNNN!
<OUR ENERGY FAILS!>
<SOMETHING SIPHONS IT!>

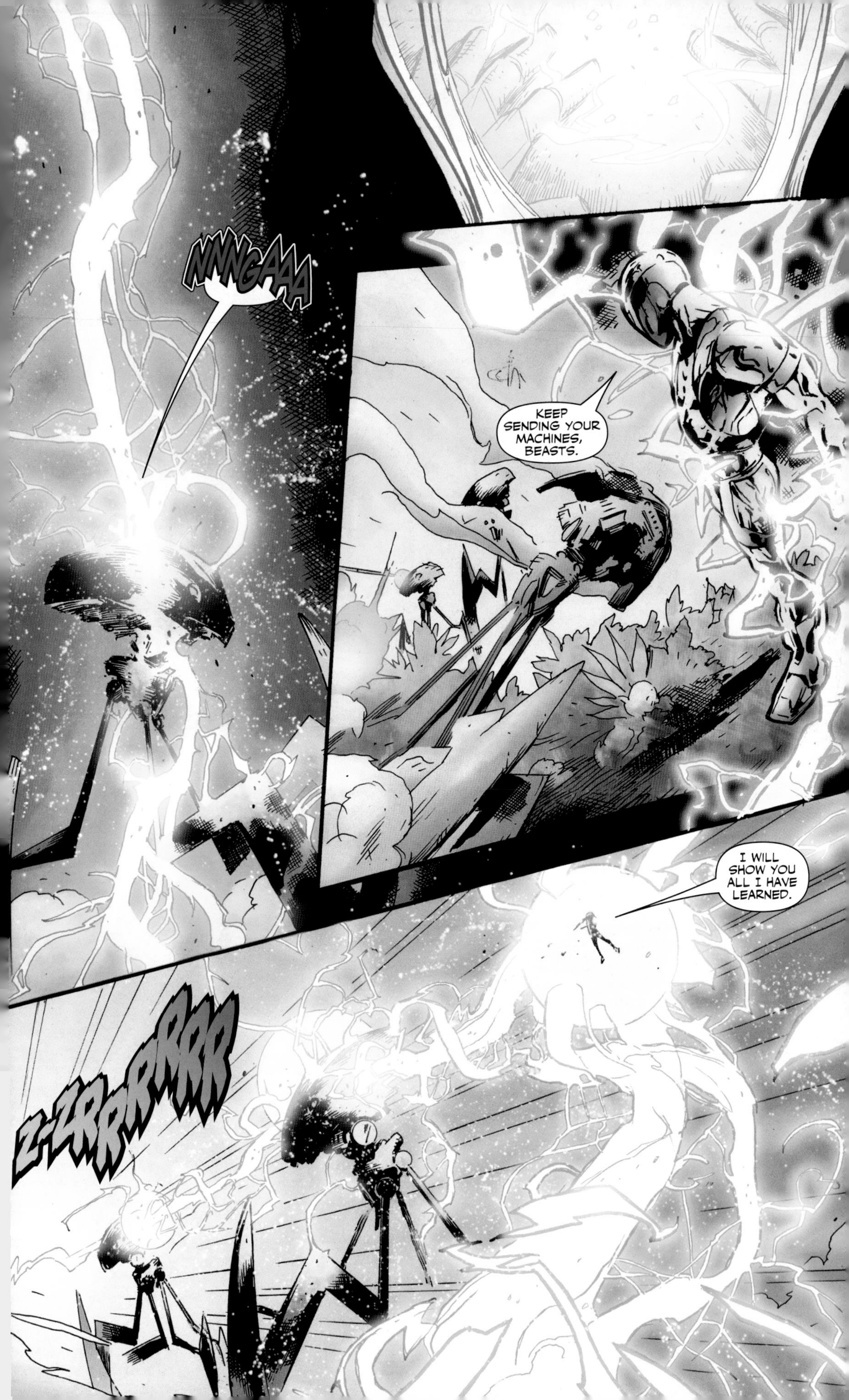
NNNGAAA
KEEP SENDING YOUR MACHINES, BEASTS.
I WILL SHOW YOU ALL I HAVE LEARNED.
Z-ZRRRRRRR

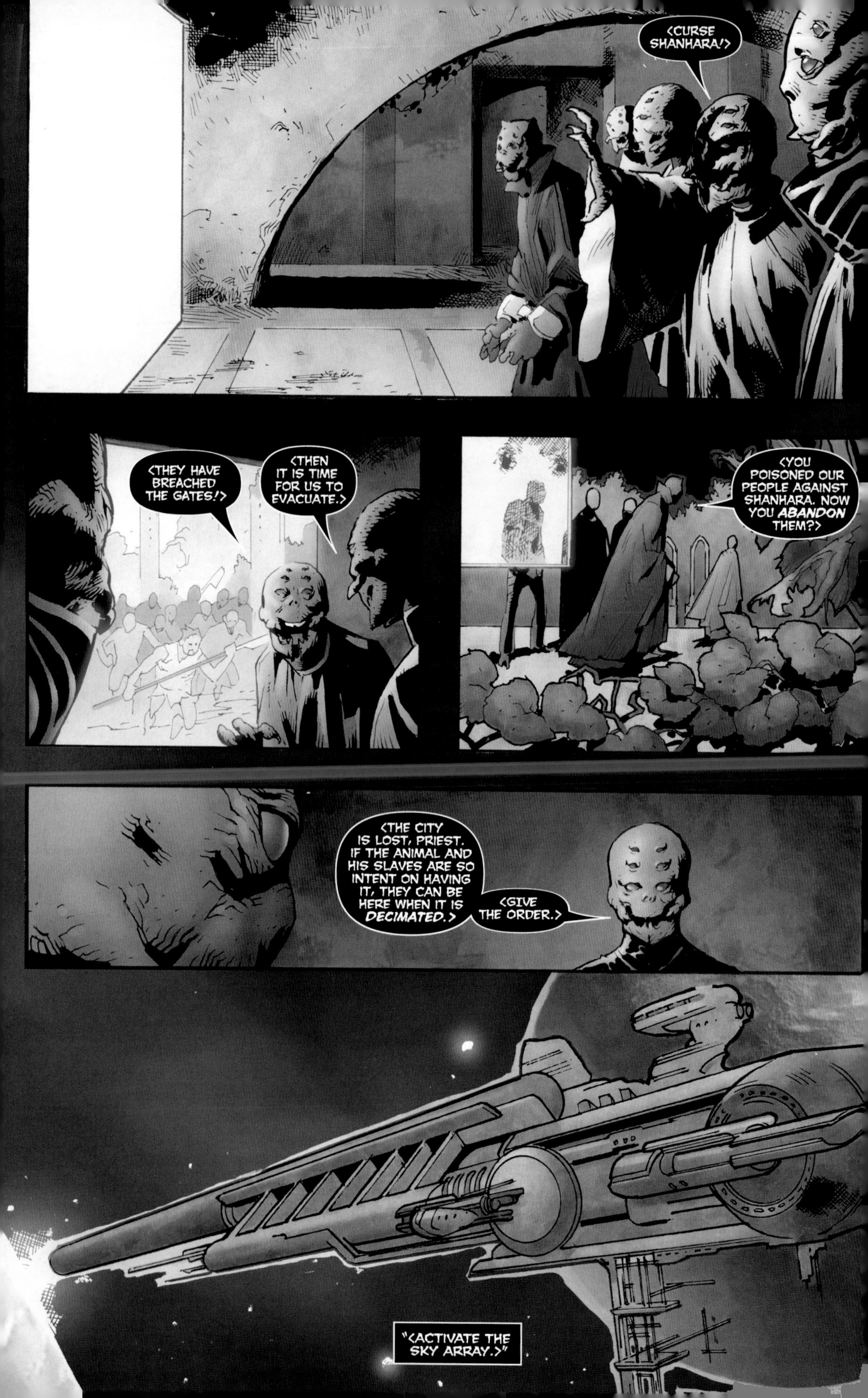
<CURSE SHANHARA!>
<THEY HAVE BREACHED THE GATES!>
<THEN IT IS TIME FOR US TO EVACUATE.>
<YOU POISONED OUR PEOPLE AGAINST SHANHARA. NOW YOU *ABANDON* THEM?>
<THE CITY IS LOST, PRIEST. IF THE ANIMAL AND HIS SLAVES ARE SO INTENT ON HAVING IT, THEY CAN BE HERE WHEN IT IS *DECIMATED.*>
<GIVE THE ORDER.>
"<ACTIVATE THE SKY ARRAY.>"

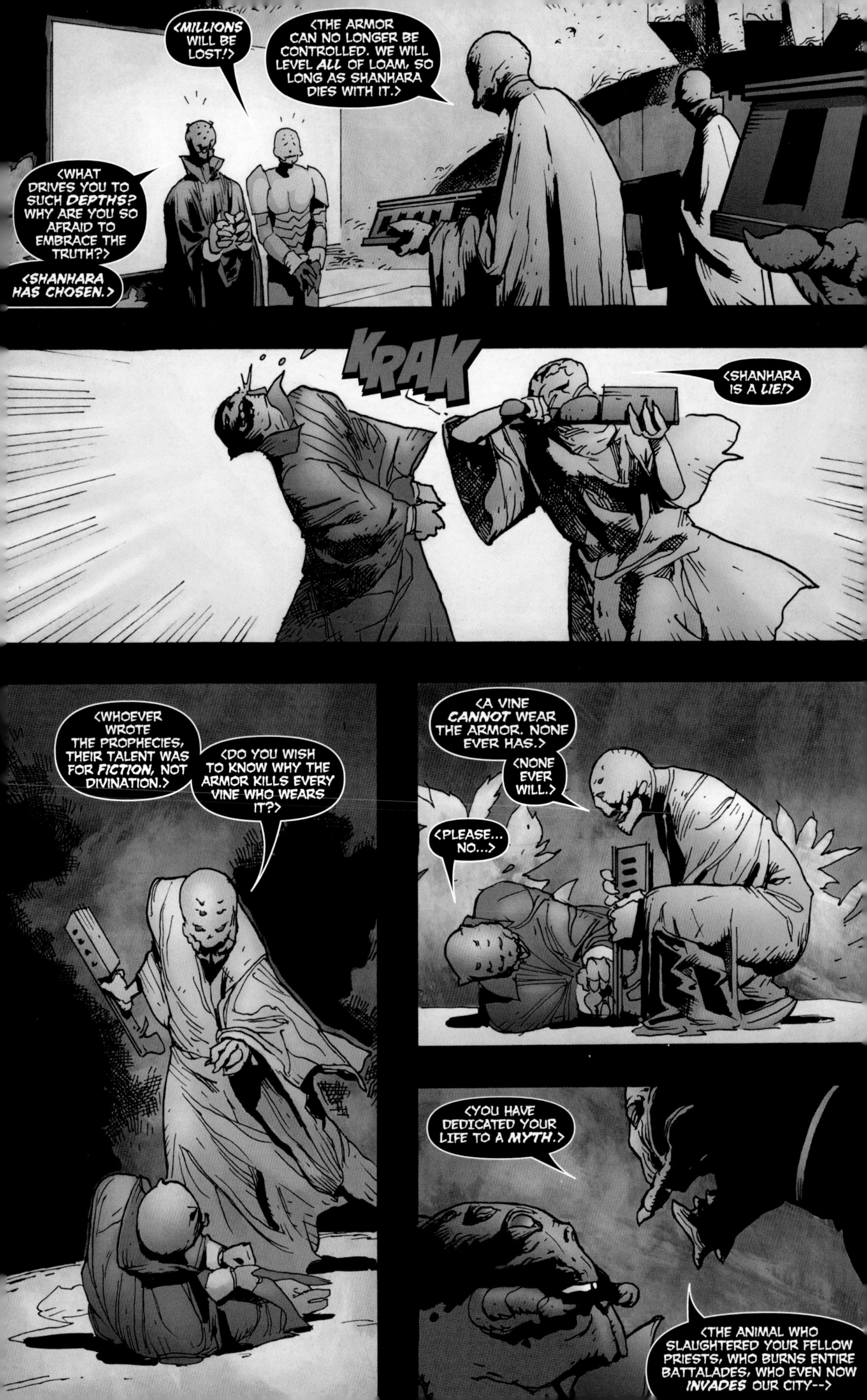

<MILLIONS WILL BE LOST!>
<THE ARMOR CAN NO LONGER BE CONTROLLED. WE WILL LEVEL ALL OF LOAM, SO LONG AS SHANHARA DIES WITH IT.>
<WHAT DRIVES YOU TO SUCH DEPTHS? WHY ARE YOU SO AFRAID TO EMBRACE THE TRUTH?>
<SHANHARA HAS CHOSEN.>
KRAK
<SHANHARA IS A LIE!>
<WHOEVER WROTE THE PROPHECIES, THEIR TALENT WAS FOR FICTION, NOT DIVINATION.>
<DO YOU WISH TO KNOW WHY THE ARMOR KILLS EVERY VINE WHO WEARS IT?>
<A VINE CANNOT WEAR THE ARMOR. NONE EVER HAS.>
<NONE EVER WILL.>
<PLEASE... NO...>
<YOU HAVE DEDICATED YOUR LIFE TO A MYTH.>
<THE ANIMAL WHO SLAUGHTERED YOUR FELLOW PRIESTS, WHO BURNS ENTIRE BATTALADES, WHO EVEN NOW INVADES OUR CITY-->

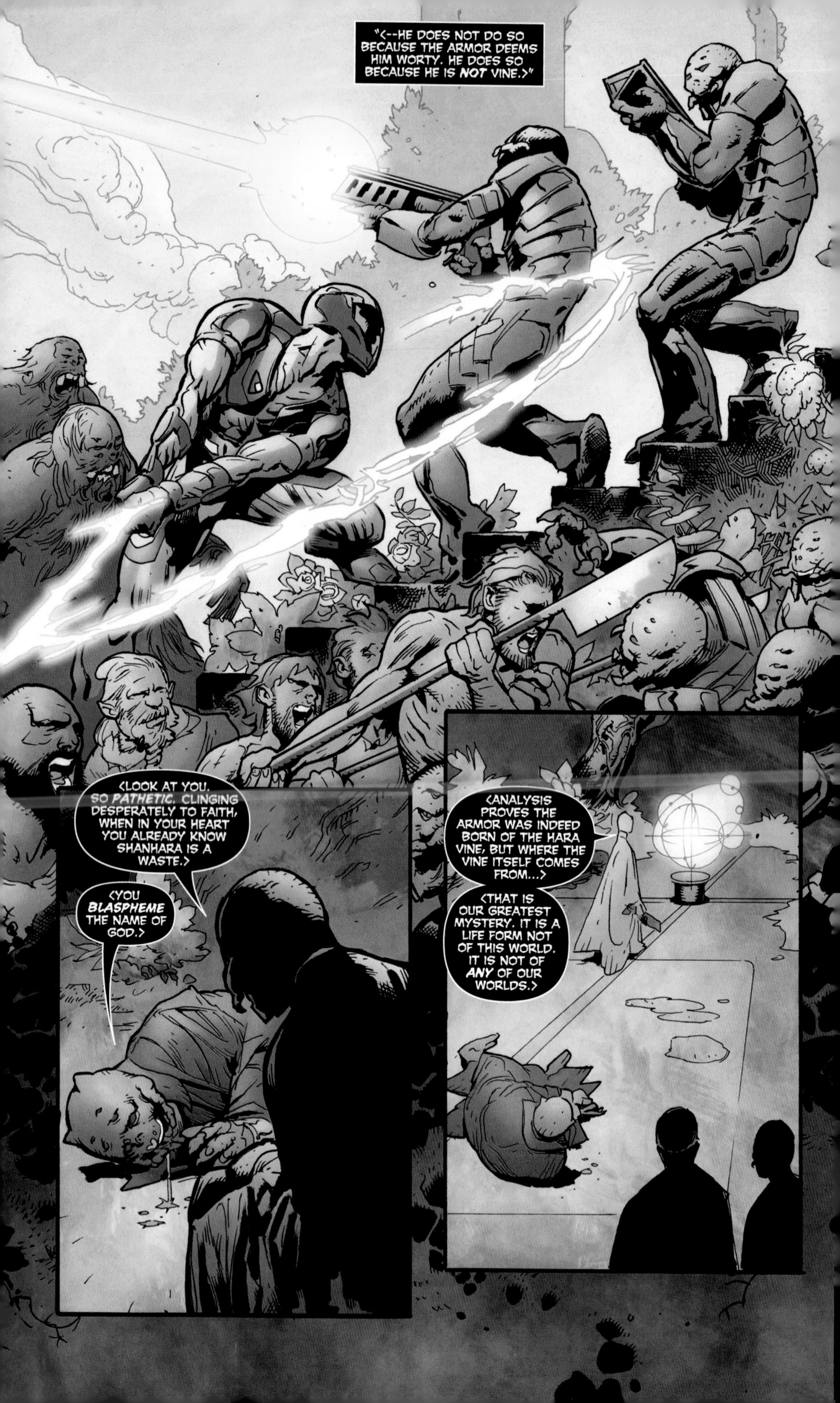
"<--HE DOES NOT DO SO BECAUSE THE ARMOR DEEMS HIM WORTY. HE DOES SO BECAUSE HE IS NOT VINE.>"
<LOOK AT YOU. SO PATHETIC. CLINGING DESPERATELY TO FAITH, WHEN IN YOUR HEART YOU ALREADY KNOW SHANHARA IS A WASTE.>
<YOU BLASPHEME THE NAME OF GOD.>
<ANALYSIS PROVES THE ARMOR WAS INDEED BORN OF THE HARA VINE, BUT WHERE THE VINE ITSELF COMES FROM...>
<THAT IS OUR GREATEST MYSTERY. IT IS A LIFE FORM NOT OF THIS WORLD. IT IS NOT OF ANY OF OUR WORLDS.>

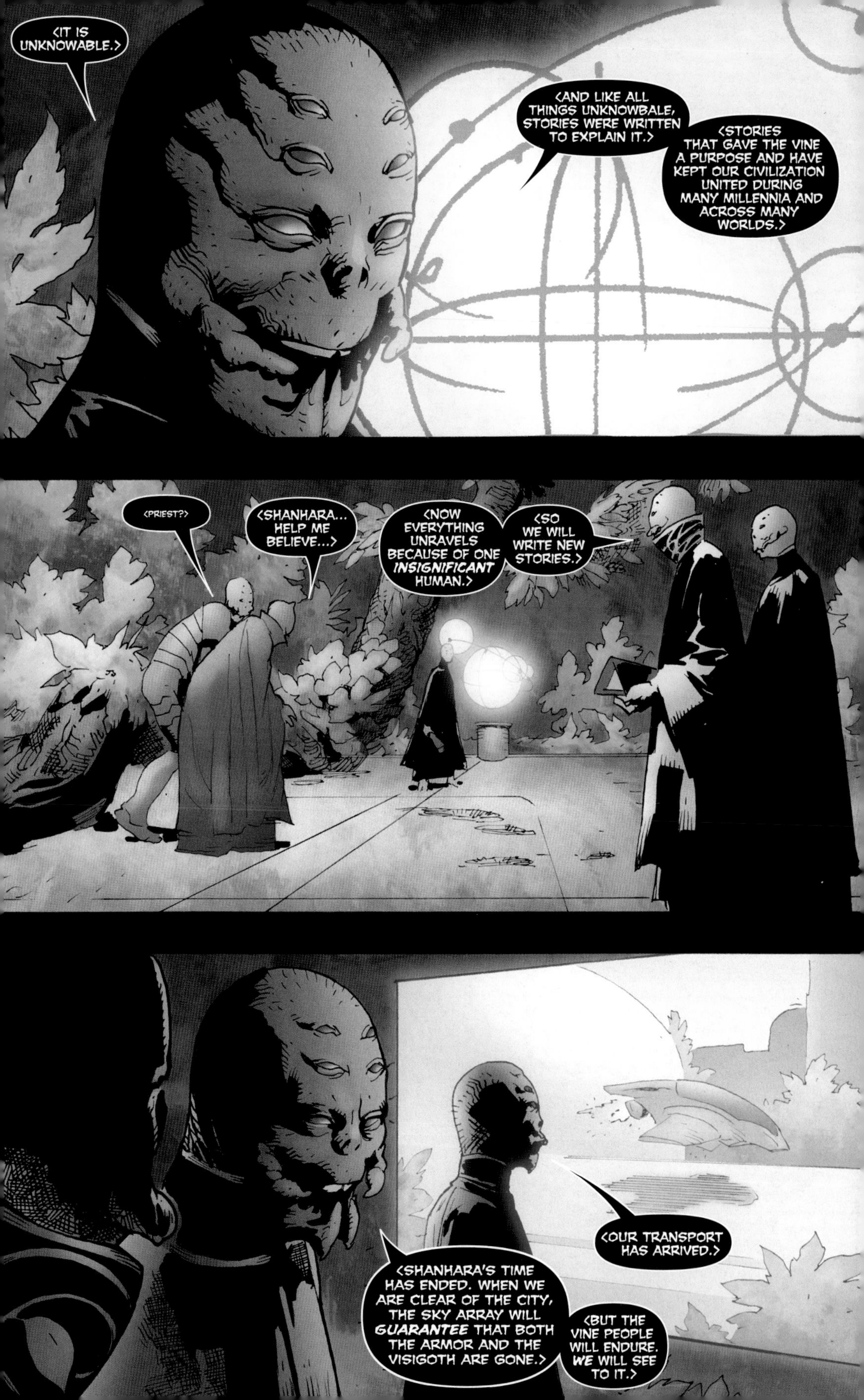

<IT IS UNKNOWABLE.>
<AND LIKE ALL THINGS UNKNOWBALE, STORIES WERE WRITTEN TO EXPLAIN IT.>
<STORIES THAT GAVE THE VINE A PURPOSE AND HAVE KEPT OUR CIVILIZATION UNITED DURING MANY MILLENNIA AND ACROSS MANY WORLDS.>
<PRIEST?>
<SHANHARA... HELP ME BELIEVE...>
<NOW EVERYTHING UNRAVELS BECAUSE OF ONE INSIGNIFICANT HUMAN.>
<SO WE WILL WRITE NEW STORIES.>
<OUR TRANSPORT HAS ARRIVED.>
<SHANHARA'S TIME HAS ENDED. WHEN WE ARE CLEAR OF THE CITY, THE SKY ARRAY WILL GUARANTEE THAT BOTH THE ARMOR AND THE VISIGOTH ARE GONE.>
<BUT THE VINE PEOPLE WILL ENDURE. WE WILL SEE TO IT.>

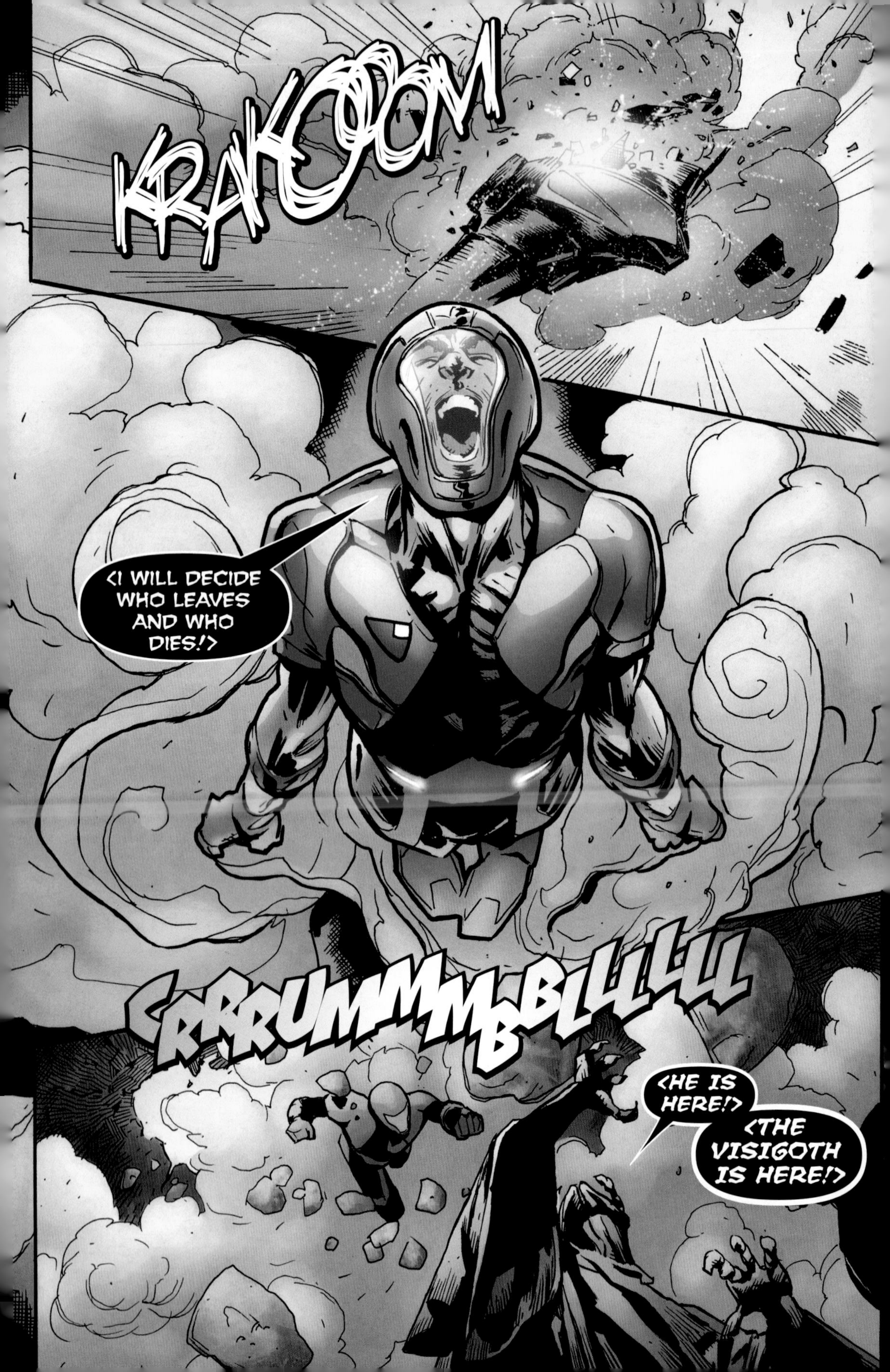
KRAKOOM
<I WILL DECIDE WHO LEAVES AND WHO DIES!>
CRRRUMMMMBLLLLL
<HE IS HERE!>
<THE VISIGOTH IS HERE!>

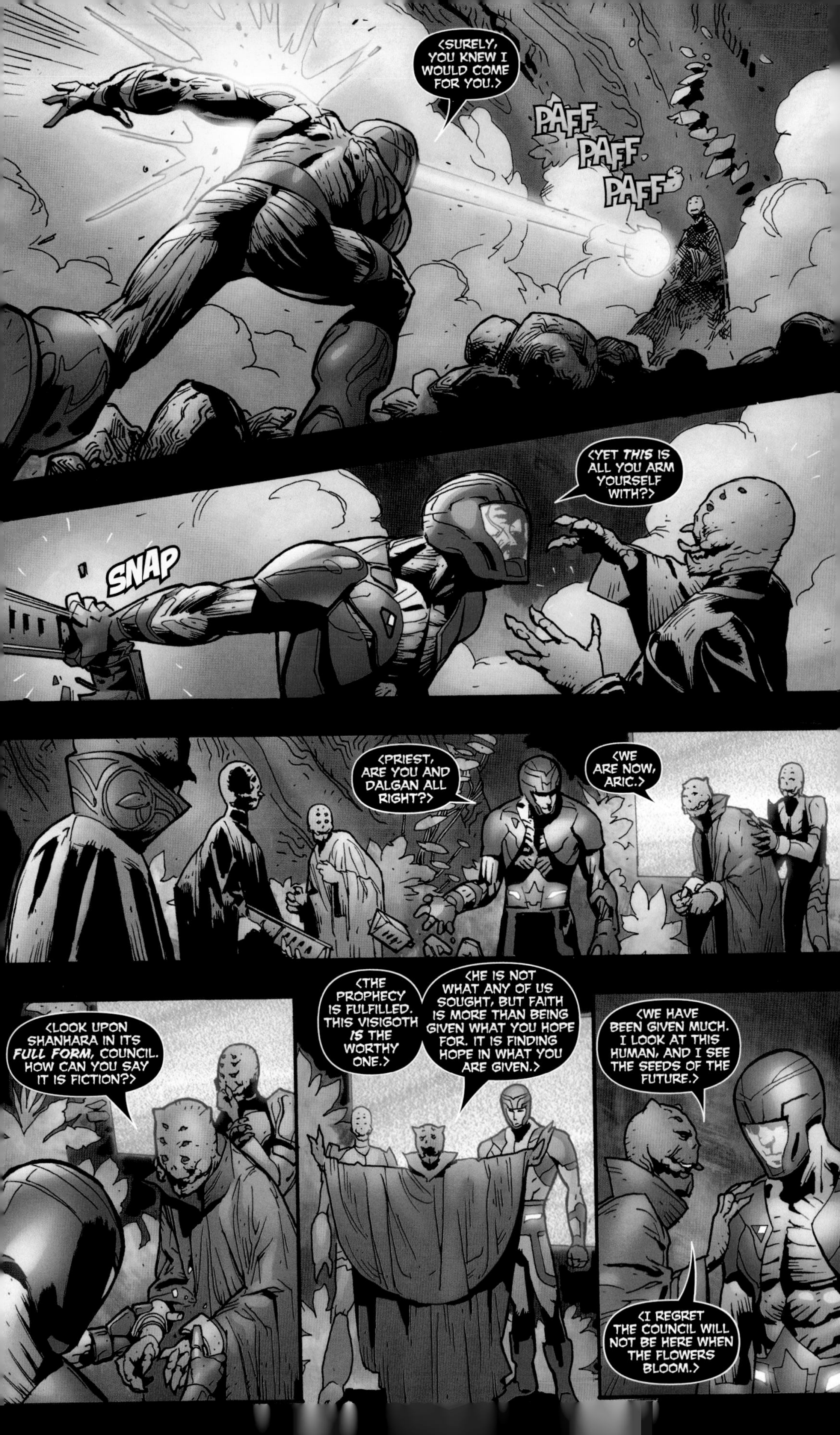

<SURELY, YOU KNEW I WOULD COME FOR YOU.>
PAFF PAFF PAFF
<YET THIS IS ALL YOU ARM YOURSELF WITH?>
SNAP
<PRIEST, ARE YOU AND DALGAN ALL RIGHT?>
<WE ARE NOW, ARIC.>
<LOOK UPON SHANHARA IN ITS FULL FORM, COUNCIL. HOW CAN YOU SAY IT IS FICTION?>
<THE PROPHECY IS FULFILLED. THIS VISIGOTH IS THE WORTHY ONE.>
<HE IS NOT WHAT ANY OF US SOUGHT, BUT FAITH IS MORE THAN BEING GIVEN WHAT YOU HOPE FOR. IT IS FINDING HOPE IN WHAT YOU ARE GIVEN.>
<WE HAVE BEEN GIVEN MUCH. I LOOK AT THIS HUMAN, AND I SEE THE SEEDS OF THE FUTURE.>
<I REGRET THE COUNCIL WILL NOT BE HERE WHEN THE FLOWERS BLOOM.>

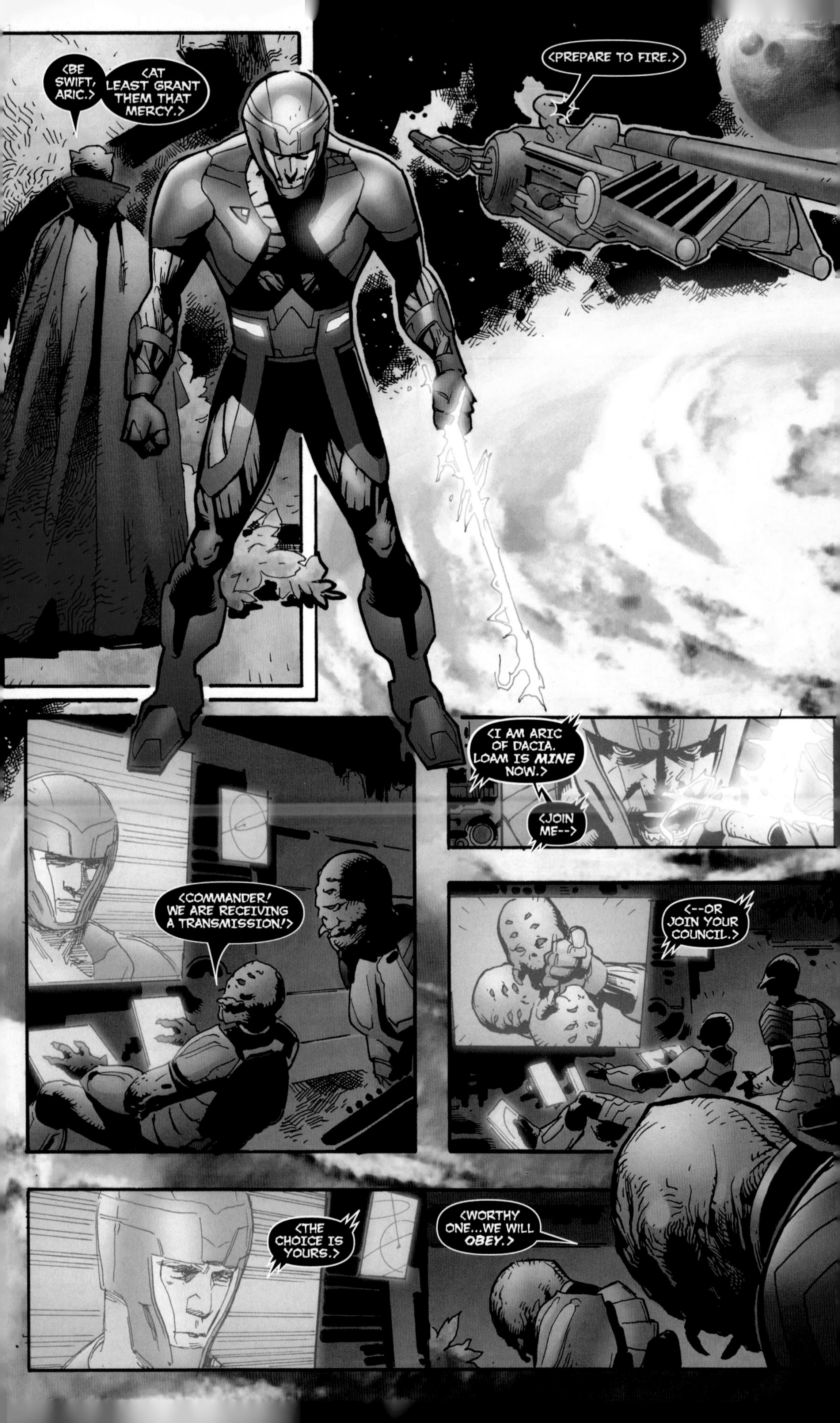
<BE SWIFT, ARIC.>
<AT LEAST GRANT THEM THAT MERCY.>
<PREPARE TO FIRE.>
<COMMANDER! WE ARE RECEIVING A TRANSMISSION!>
<I AM ARIC OF DACIA. LOAM IS *MINE* NOW.>
<JOIN ME-->
<--OR JOIN YOUR COUNCIL.>
<THE CHOICE IS YOURS.>
<WORTHY ONE...WE WILL *OBEY.*>

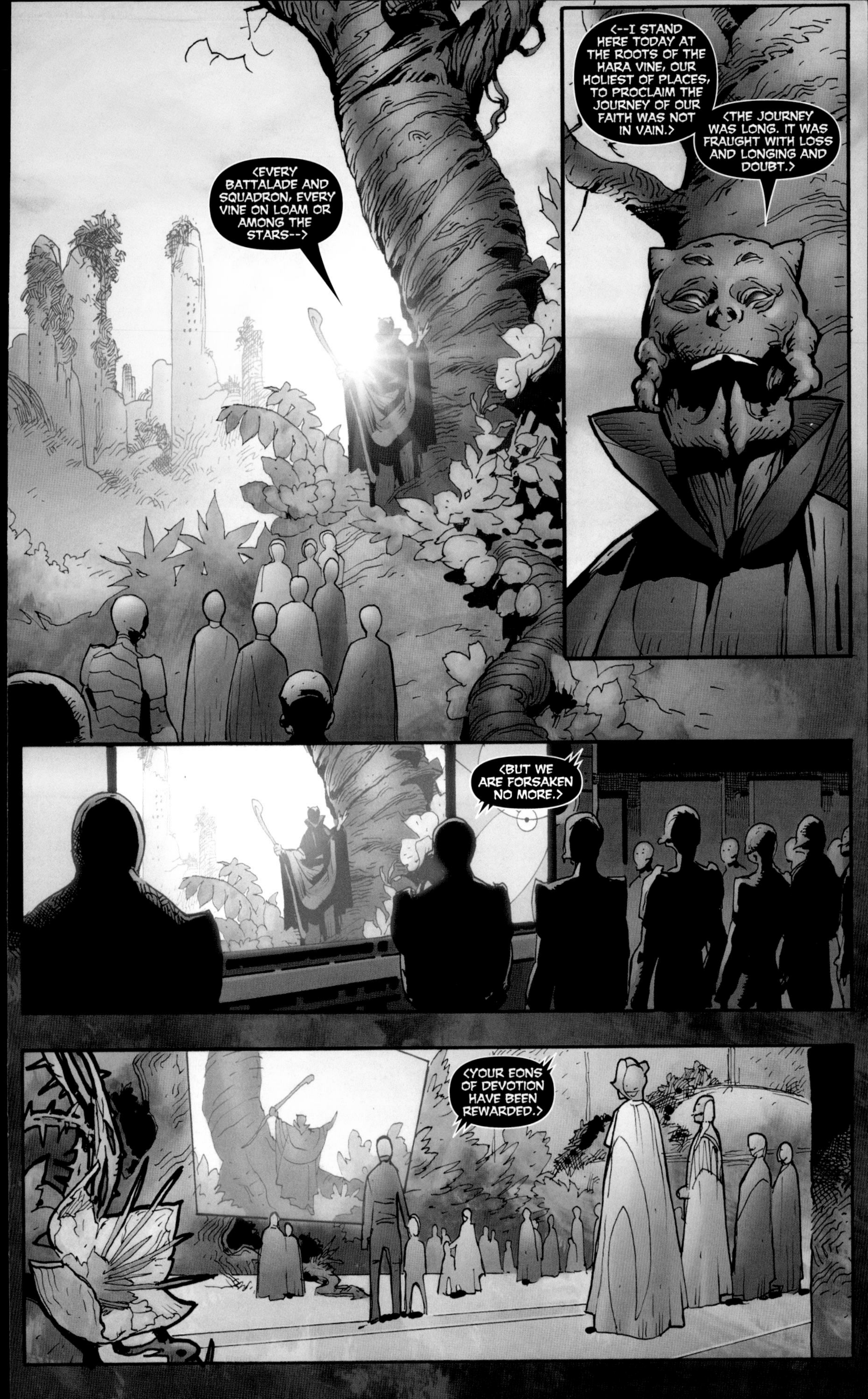
<EVERY BATTALADE AND SQUADRON, EVERY VINE ON LOAM OR AMONG THE STARS-->
<--I STAND HERE TODAY AT THE ROOTS OF THE HARA VINE, OUR HOLIEST OF PLACES, TO PROCLAIM THE JOURNEY OF OUR FAITH WAS NOT IN VAIN.>
<THE JOURNEY WAS LONG. IT WAS FRAUGHT WITH LOSS AND LONGING AND DOUBT.>
<BUT WE ARE FORSAKEN NO MORE.>
<YOUR EONS OF DEVOTION HAVE BEEN REWARDED.>

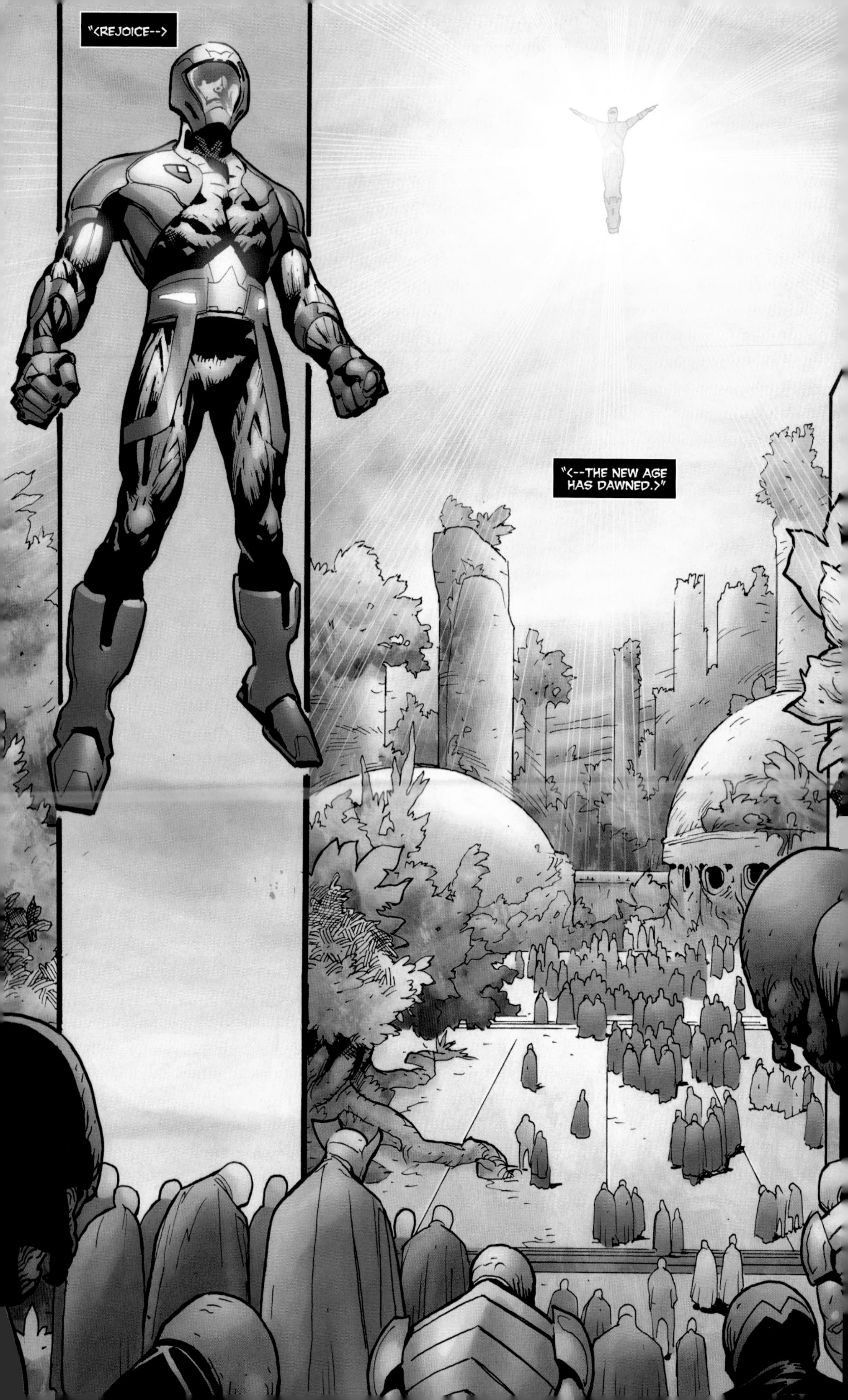
"<REJOICE-->
"<--THE NEW AGE HAS DAWNED.>"

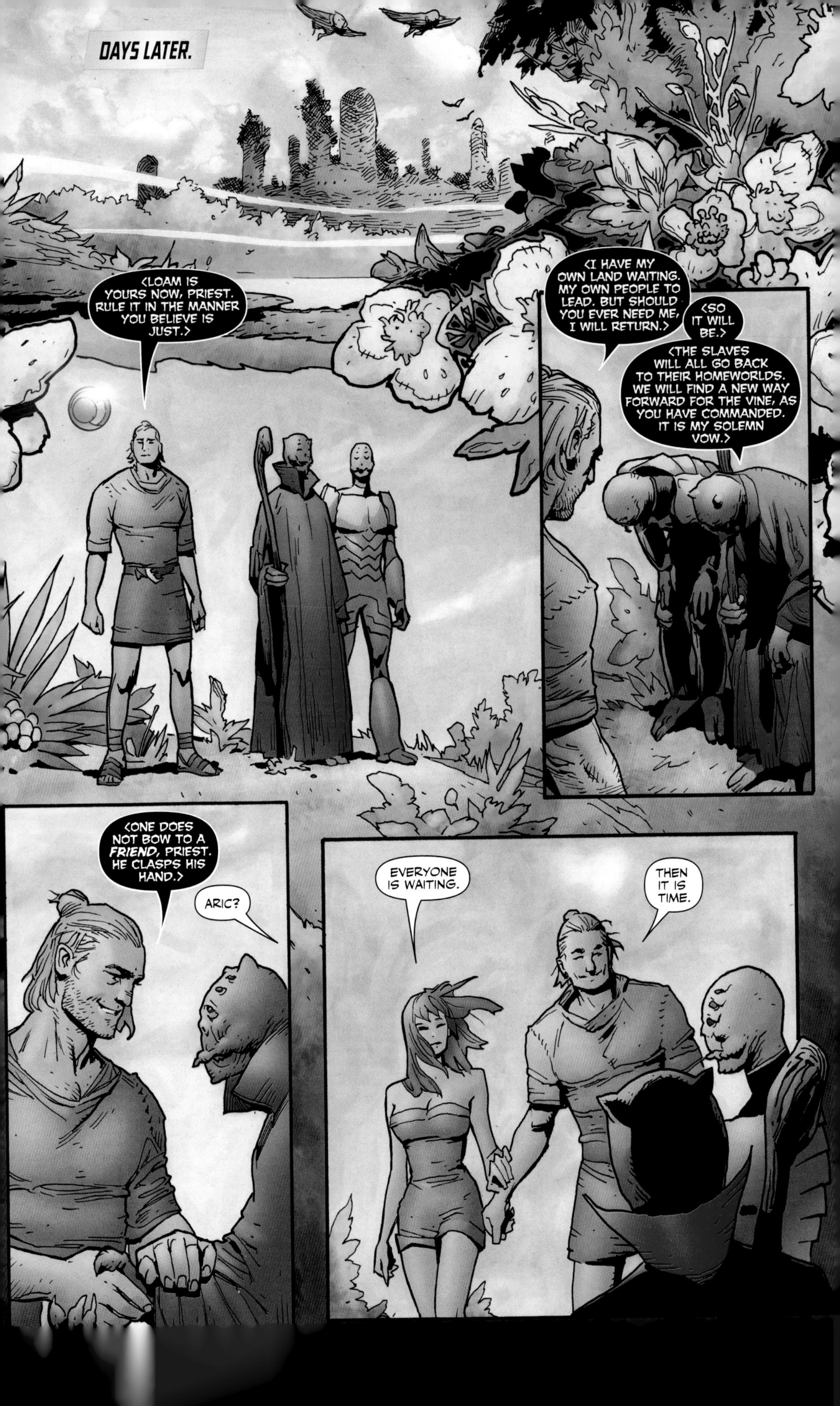
DAYS LATER.
<LOAM IS YOURS NOW, PRIEST. RULE IT IN THE MANNER YOU BELIEVE IS JUST.>
<I HAVE MY OWN LAND WAITING. MY OWN PEOPLE TO LEAD. BUT SHOULD YOU EVER NEED ME, I WILL RETURN.>
<SO IT WILL BE.>
<THE SLAVES WILL ALL GO BACK TO THEIR HOMEWORLDS. WE WILL FIND A NEW WAY FORWARD FOR THE VINE, AS YOU HAVE COMMANDED. IT IS MY SOLEMN VOW.>
<ONE DOES NOT BOW TO A *FRIEND*, PRIEST. HE CLASPS HIS HAND.>
ARIC?
EVERYONE IS WAITING.
THEN IT IS TIME.

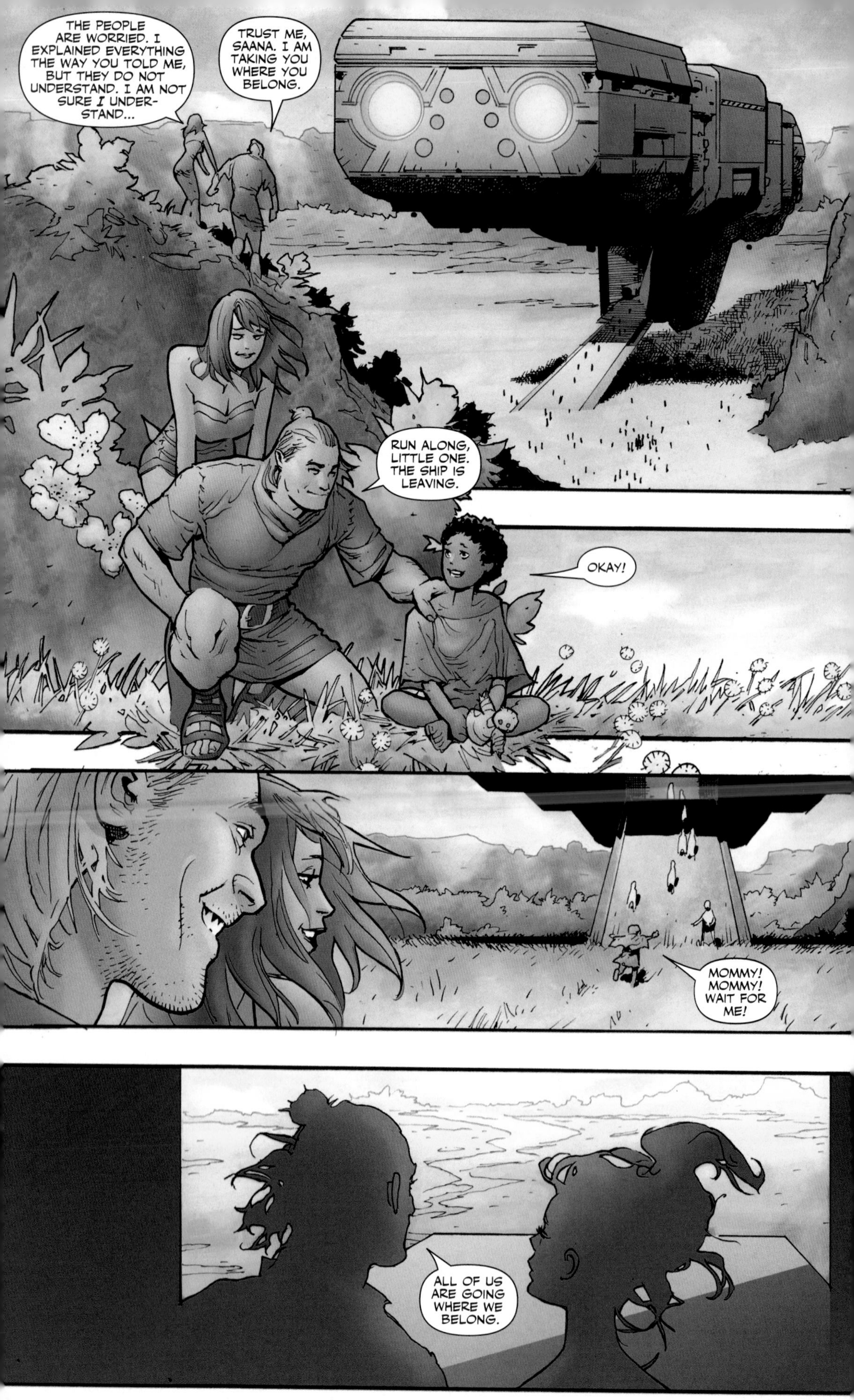
THE PEOPLE ARE WORRIED. I EXPLAINED EVERYTHING THE WAY YOU TOLD ME, BUT THEY DO NOT UNDERSTAND. I AM NOT SURE *I* UNDERSTAND...
TRUST ME, SAANA. I AM TAKING YOU WHERE YOU BELONG.
RUN ALONG, LITTLE ONE. THE SHIP IS LEAVING.
OKAY!
MOMMY! MOMMY! WAIT FOR ME!
ALL OF US ARE GOING WHERE WE BELONG.

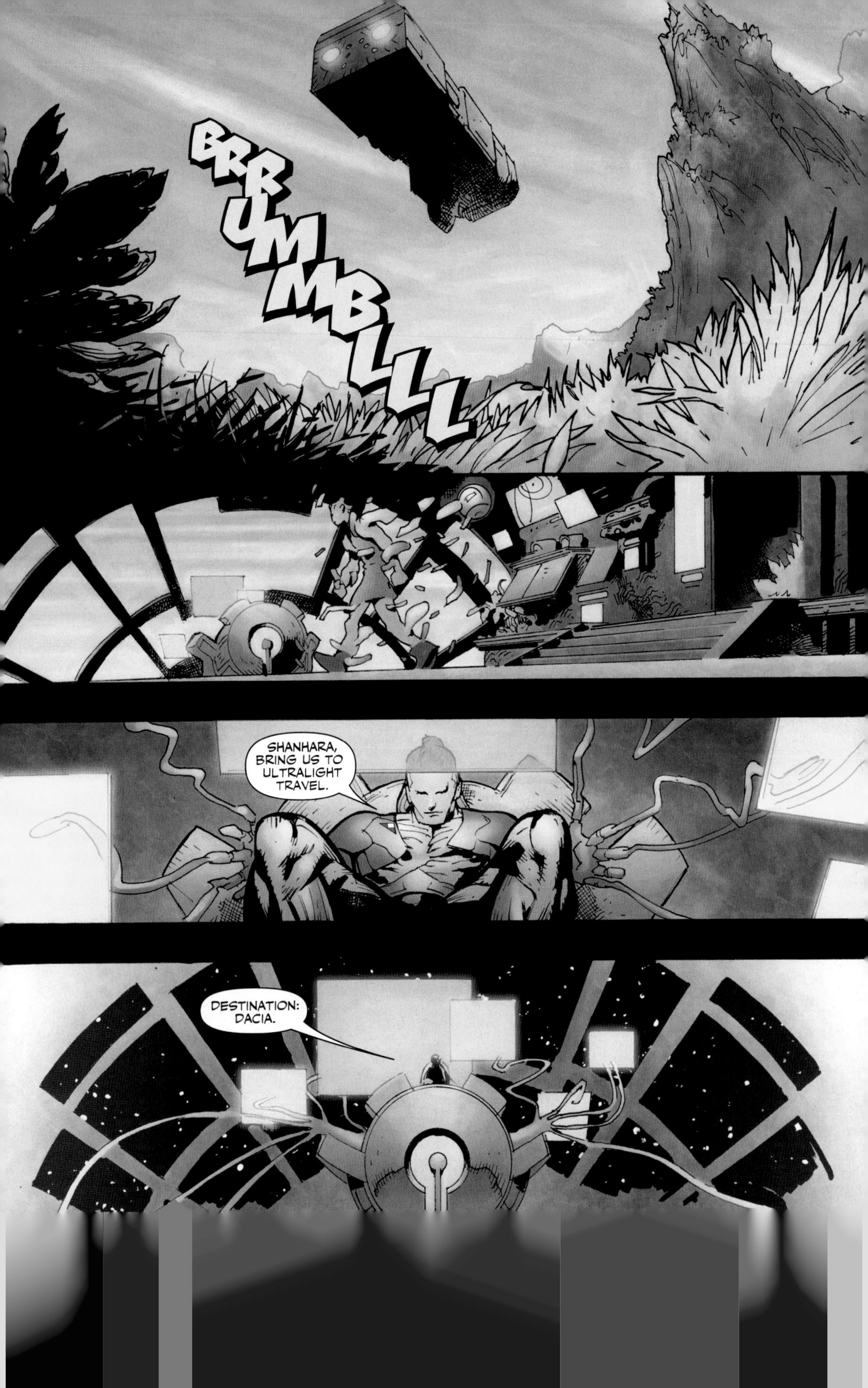
BRRUMMBLLL
SHANHARA, BRING US TO ULTRALIGHT TRAVEL.
DESTINATION: DACIA.

GALLERY

X-O MANOWAR #9 VARIANT
Cover and cover rough by CLAYTON CRAIN

X-O MANOWAR #9 PULLBOX EXCLUSIVE
Cover by CARY NORD

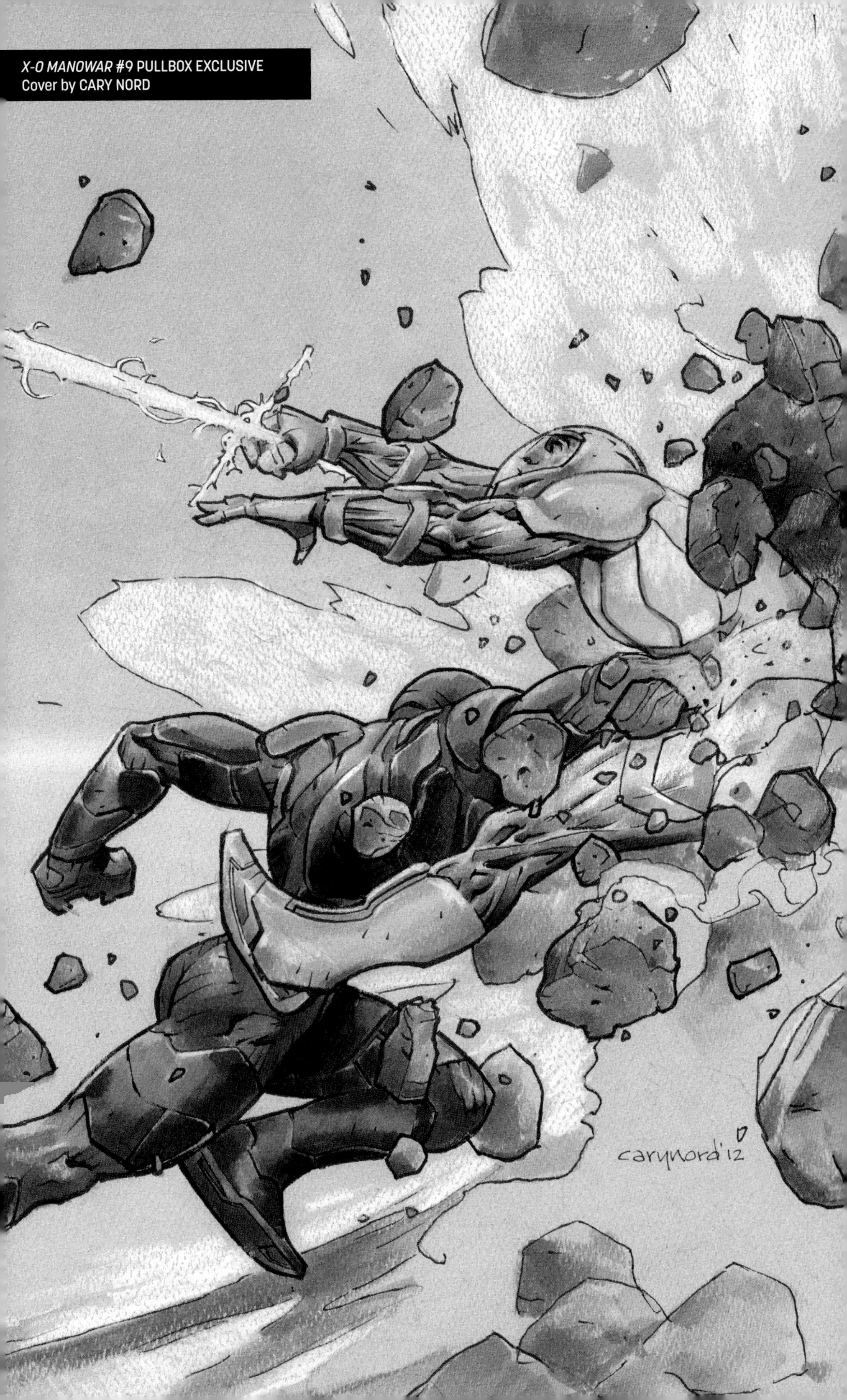
carynord'12

X-O MANOWAR #10 VARIANT
Cover by CARY NORD

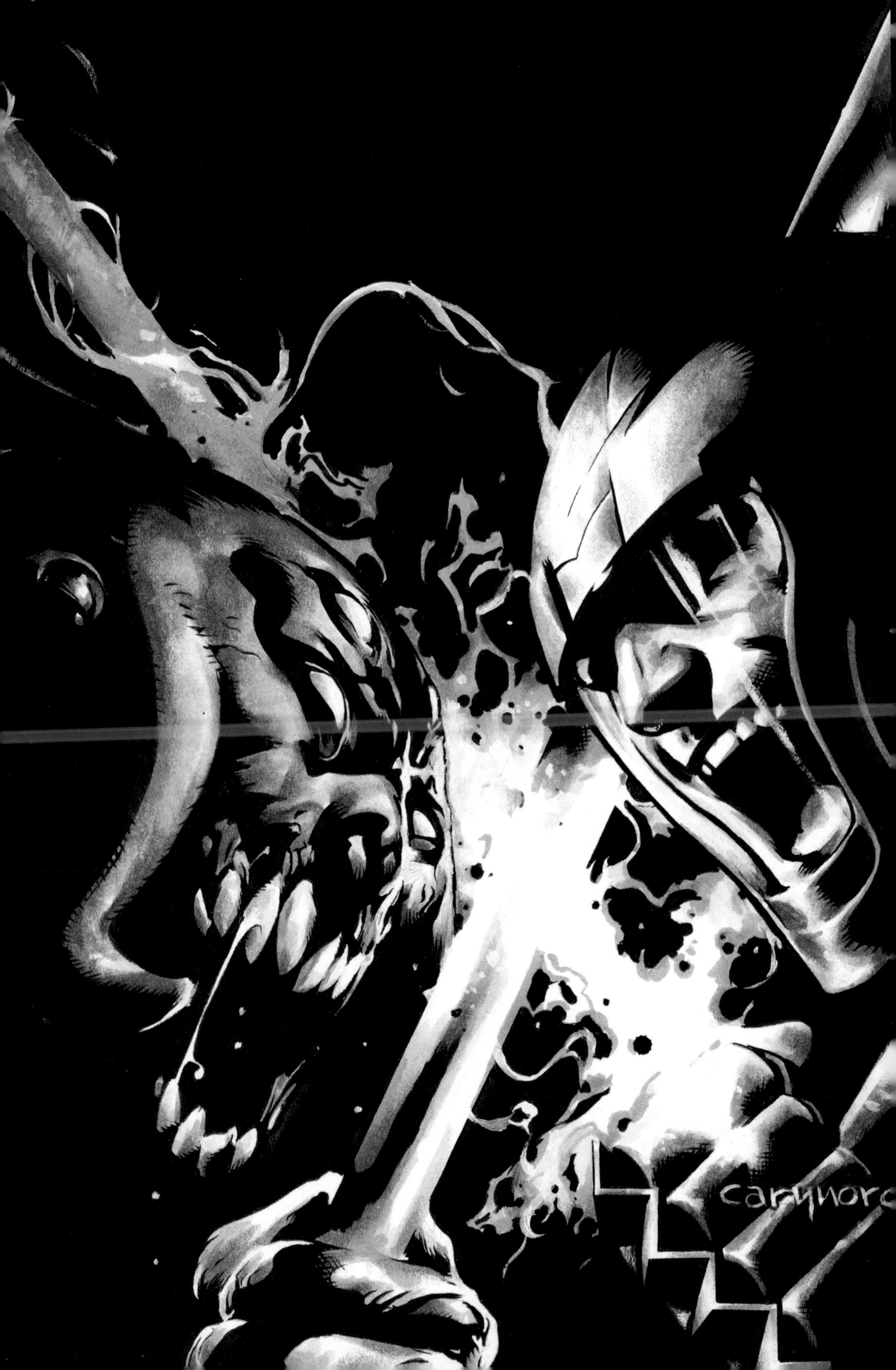

Cover sketches by CARY NORD

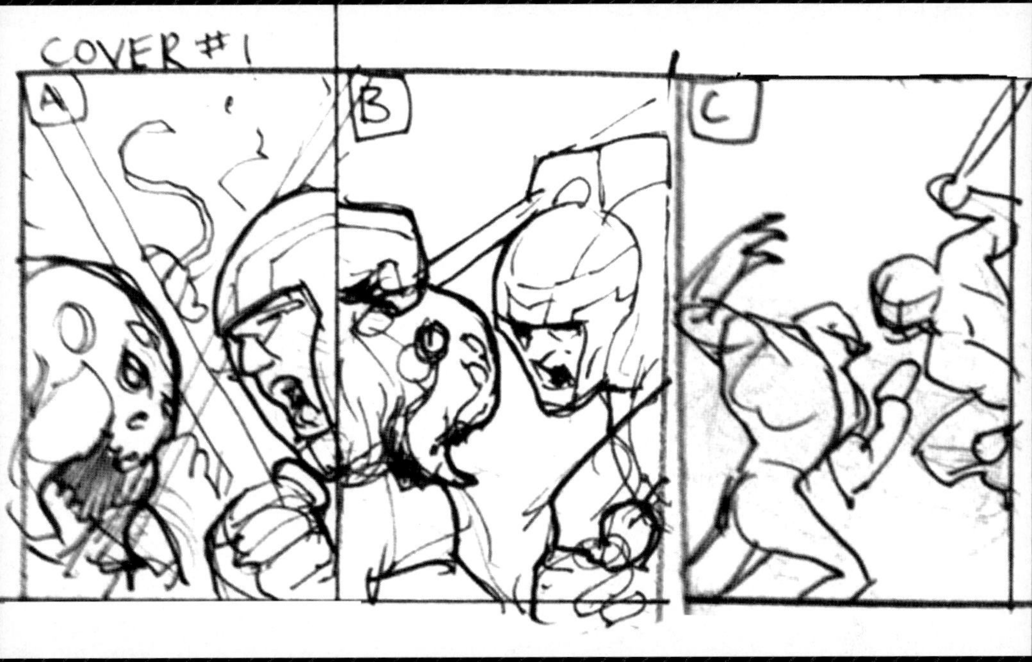
COVER #1
A
B
C

X-O MANOWAR #10
Cover sketch and pencils by TREVOR HAIRSINE

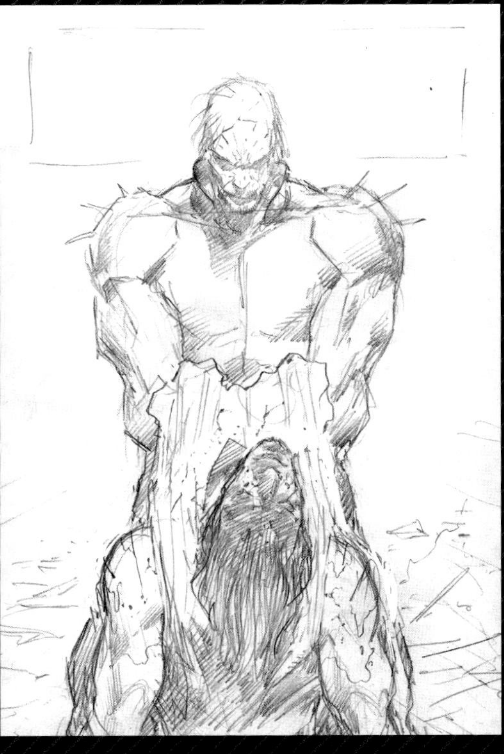

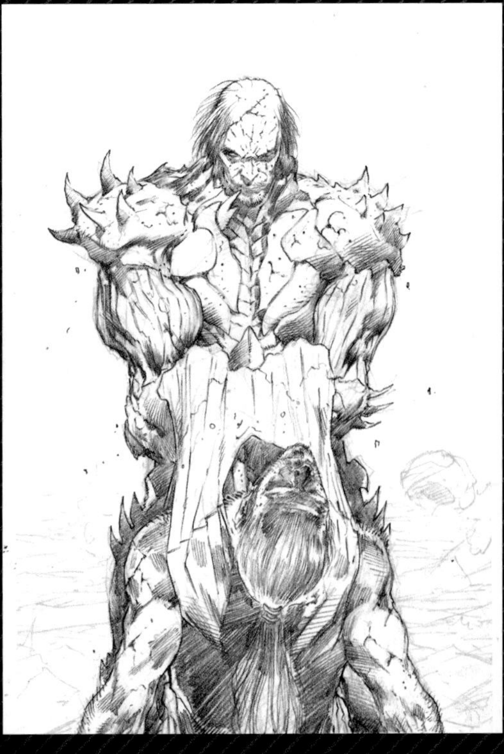

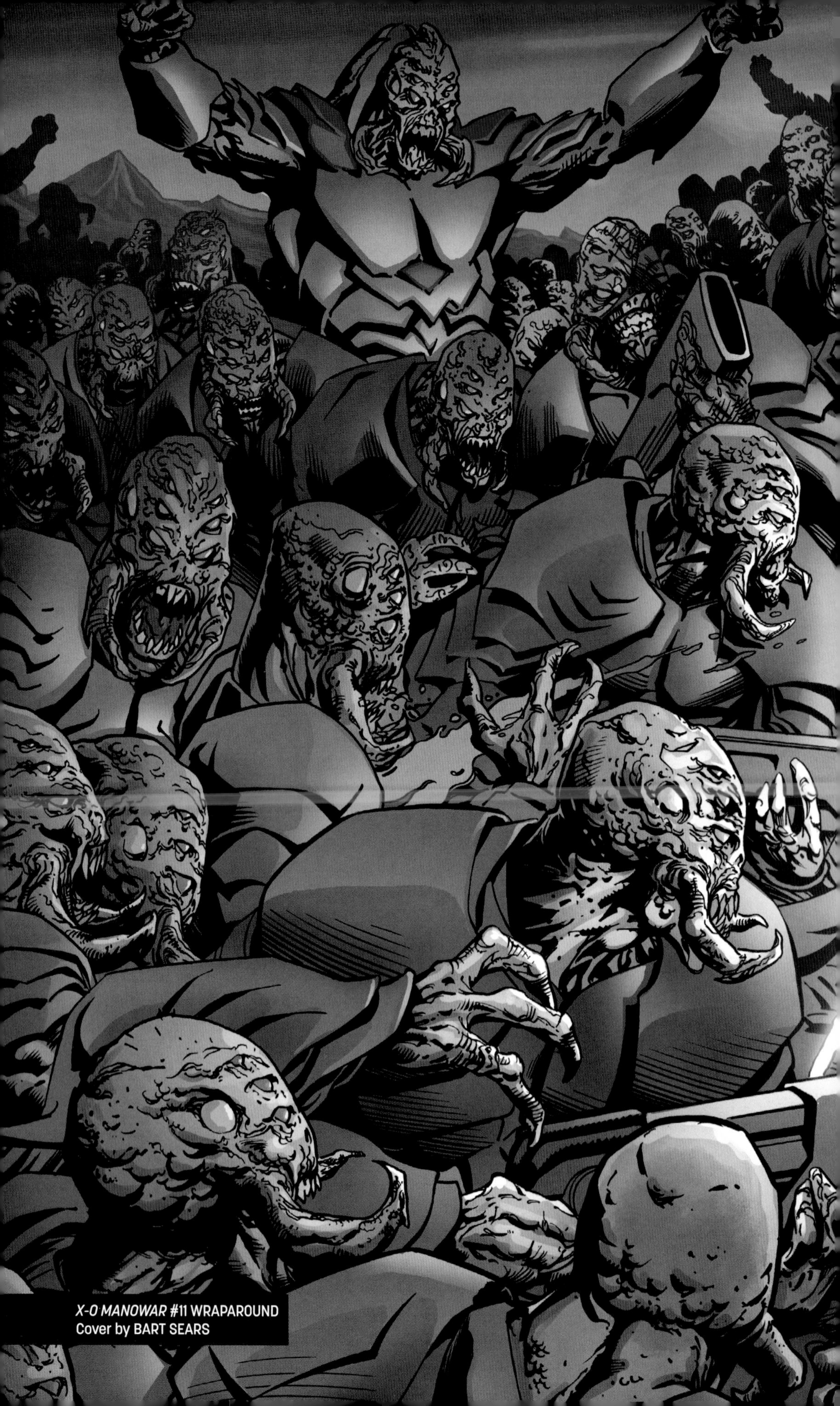

X-O MANOWAR #11 WRAPAROUND
Cover by BART SEARS

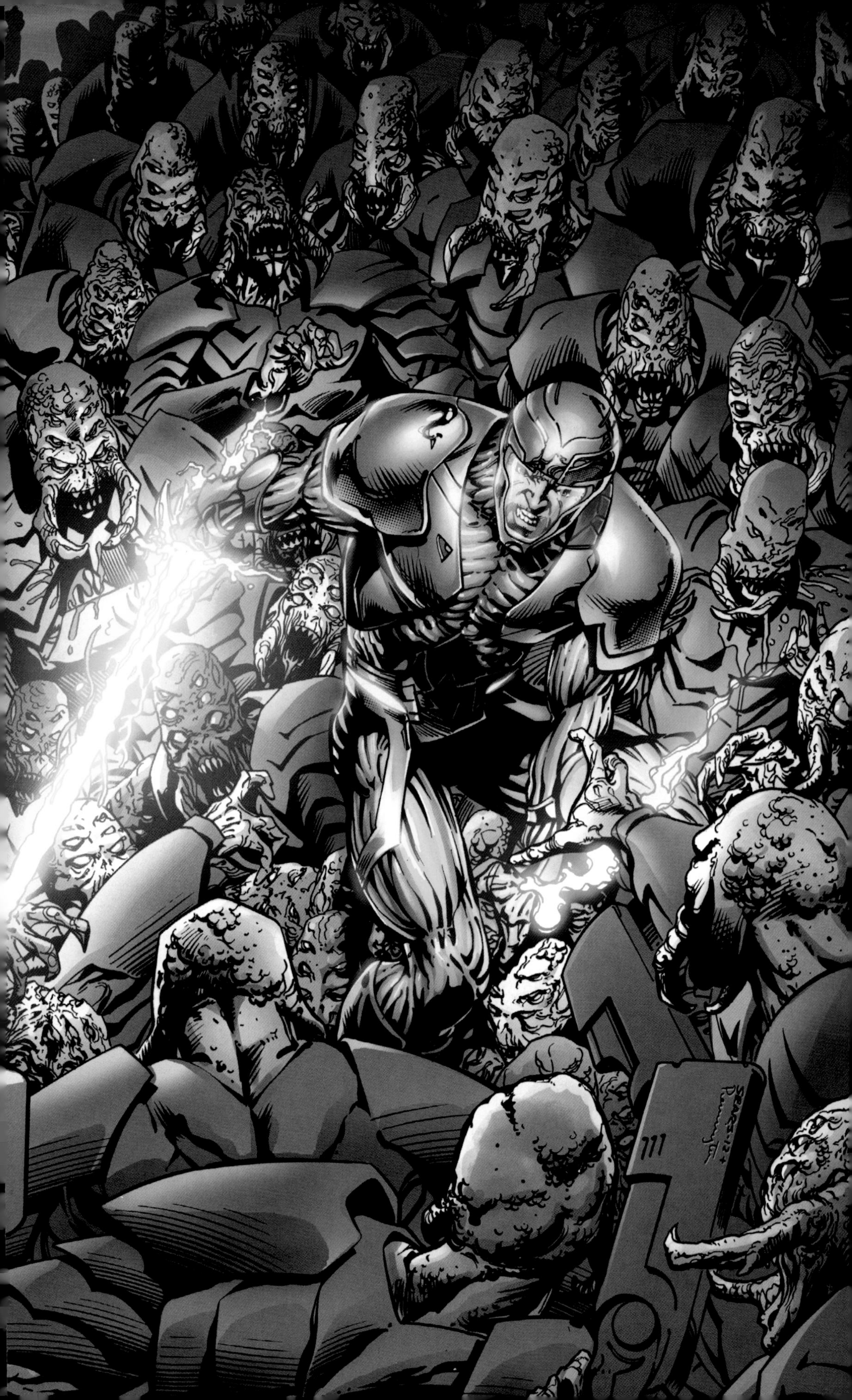

X-O MANOWAR #11 VARIANT
Cover pencils by PAOLO RIVERA
Inks by JOE RIVERA

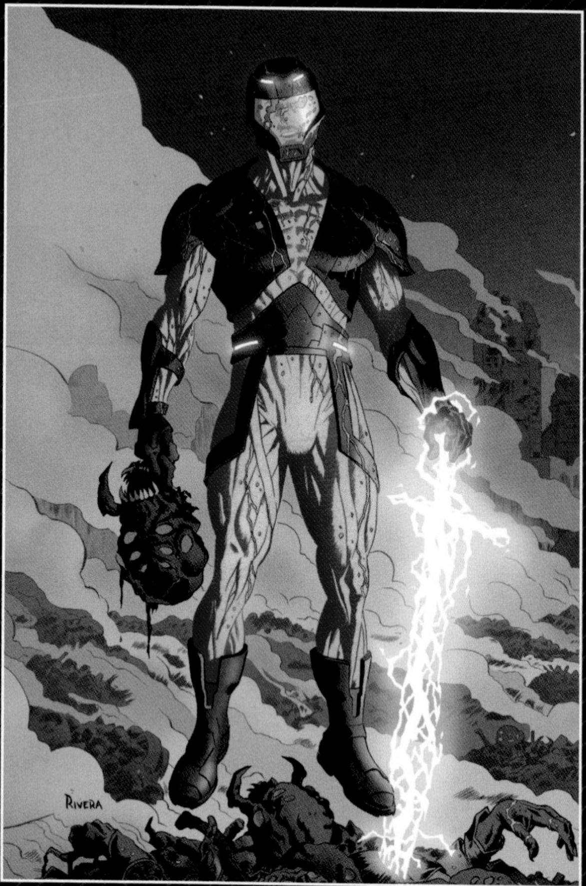
RIVERA

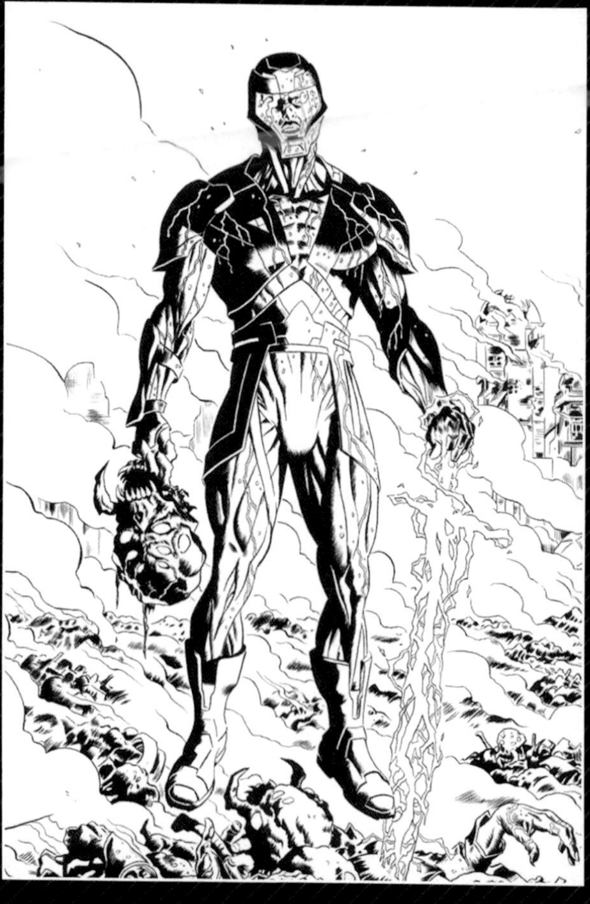

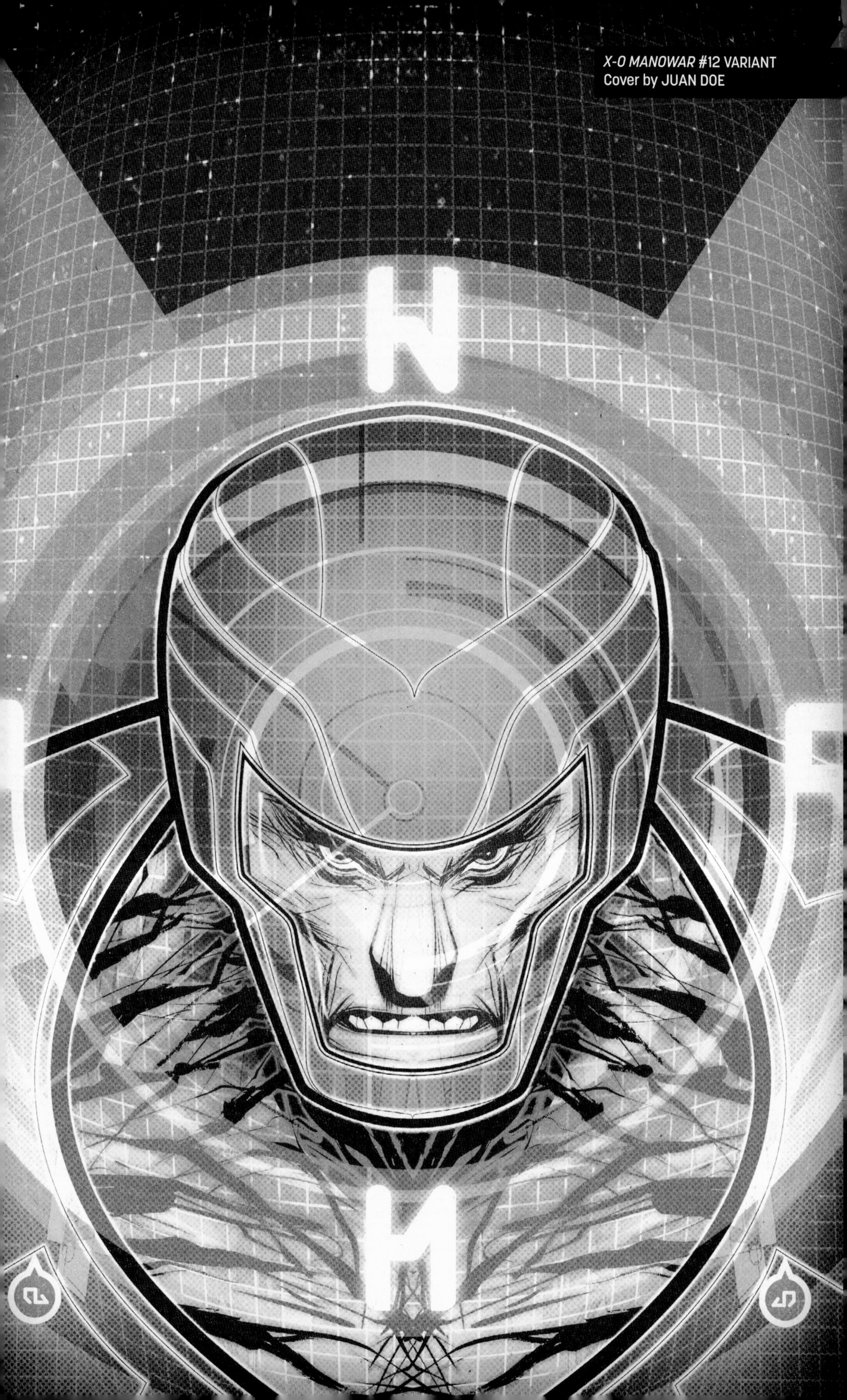

X-O MANOWAR #12 VARIANT
Cover by JUAN DOE

X-O MANOWAR #13 VARIANT
Cover by RYAN SOOK

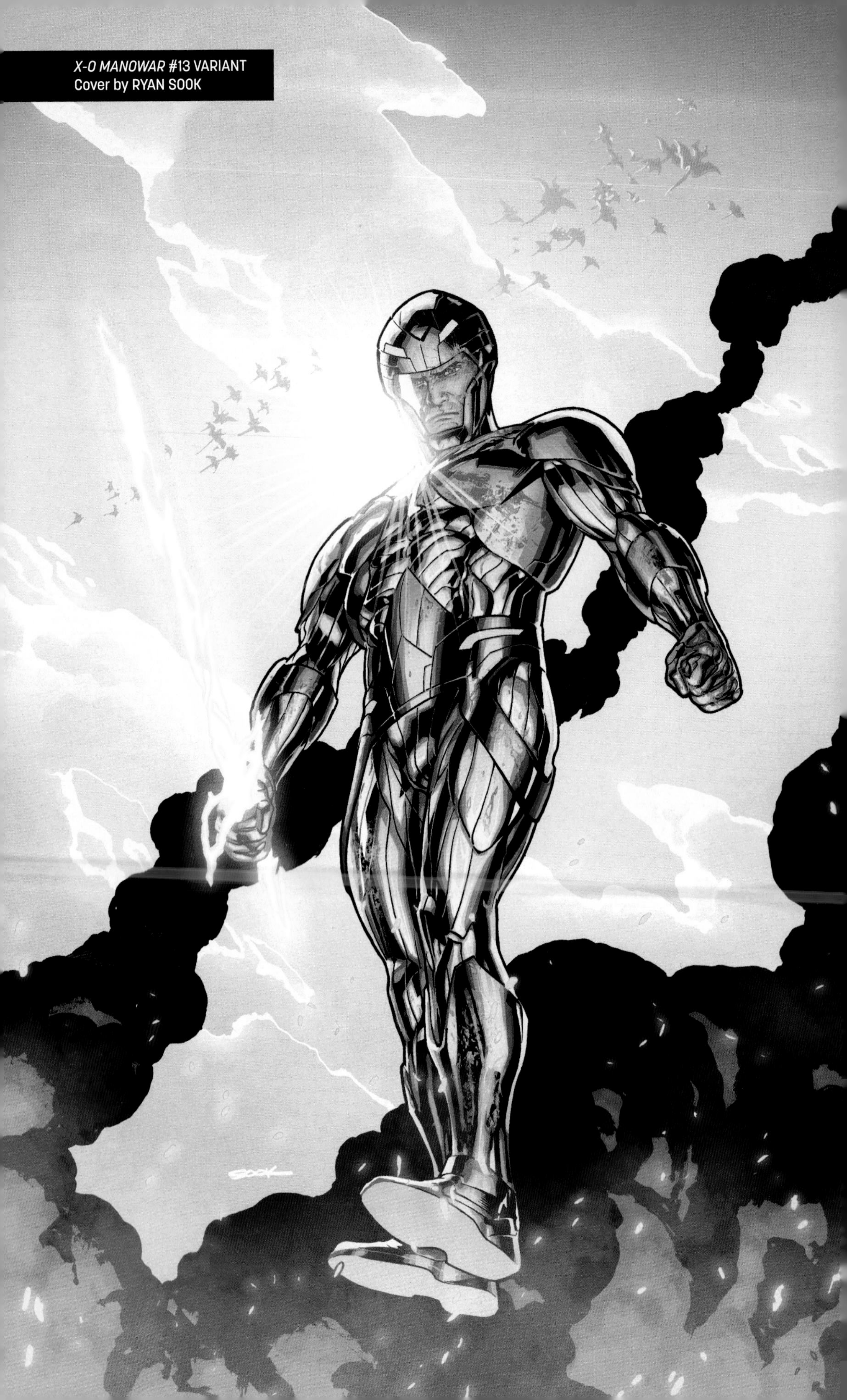
SOOK

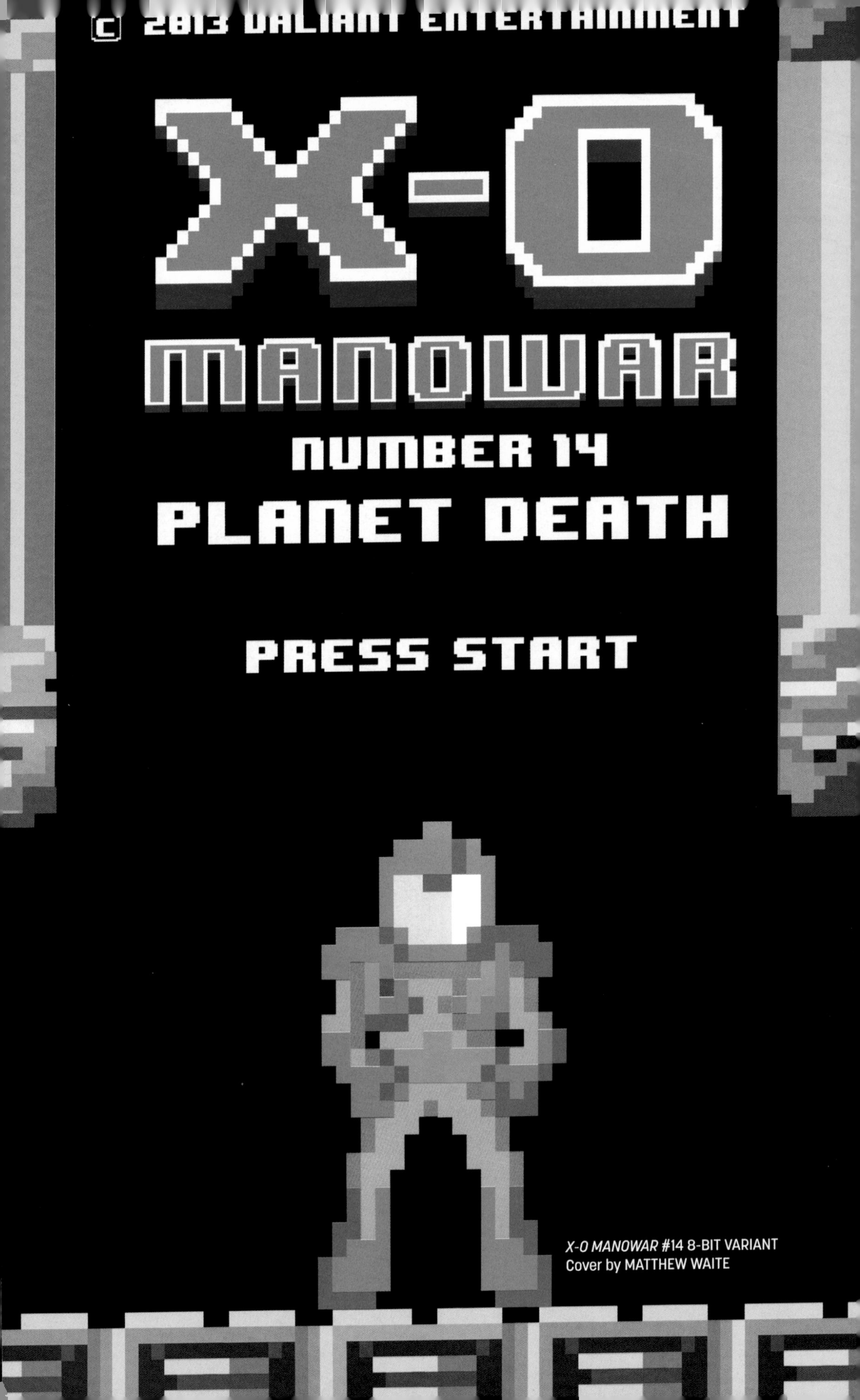
© 2013 VALIANT ENTERTAINMENT
X-O
MANOWAR
NUMBER 14
PLANET DEATH
PRESS START
X-O MANOWAR #14 8-BIT VARIANT
Cover by MATTHEW WAITE

VALIANT MASTERS

"Bloodshot reigns supreme as one of the best characters ever created."
– Ain't It Cool News

VALIANT MASTERS: BLOODSHOT VOL. 1: BLOOD OF THE MACHINE

Written by KEVIN VANHOOK
Art by DON PERLIN
Cover by BARRY WINDSOR-SMITH

- Collecting BLOODSHOT #1-8 (1993) and an all-new, in-continuity story from the original BLOODSHOT creative team of Kevin VanHook, Don Perlin, and Bob Wiacek available only in this volume

- Featuring Bloodshot's first solo mission in the Valiant Universe and appearances by **Ninjak**, the **Eternal Warrior** and **Rai**

HARDCOVER
ISBN: 978-0-9796409-3-3

"Groundbreaking art and epic characters... [Valiant] set comics on its ears..."
– Ain't It Cool News

VALIANT MASTERS: NINJAK VOL. 1: BLACK WATER

Written by MARK MORETTI
Art by JOE QUESADA & MARK MORETTI
Cover by JOE QUESADA

- Collecting NINJAK #1-6 and #0-00 (1994) with covers, interiors, and rarely seen process art by best-selling artist and creator **Joe Quesada**

- Featuring the complete origin of Valiant's original stealth operative and appearances by **X-O Manowar** and **Bloodshot**

HARDCOVER
ISBN: 978-0-9796409-7-1

VALIANT MASTERS: SHADOWMAN VOL. 1: SPIRITS WITHIN

Written by STEVE ENGLEHART, BOB HALL, BOB LAYTON, JIM SHOOTER and MORE
Art by STEVE DITKO, BOB HALL, DAVID LAPHAM, DON PERLIN and MORE
Cover by DAVID LAPHAM

- Collecting SHADOWMAN #0-7 (1992) and material from DARQUE PASSAGES #1 (1994) with an all-new new introduction by visionary Shadowman writer/artist **Bob Hall**

- The first-ever deluxe hardcover collection to feature the origin and debut solo adventures of Shadowman in the original Valiant Universe!

HARDCOVER
ISBN: 978-1-939346-01-8

EXPLORE THE VALIANT UNIVERSE

VALIANT®

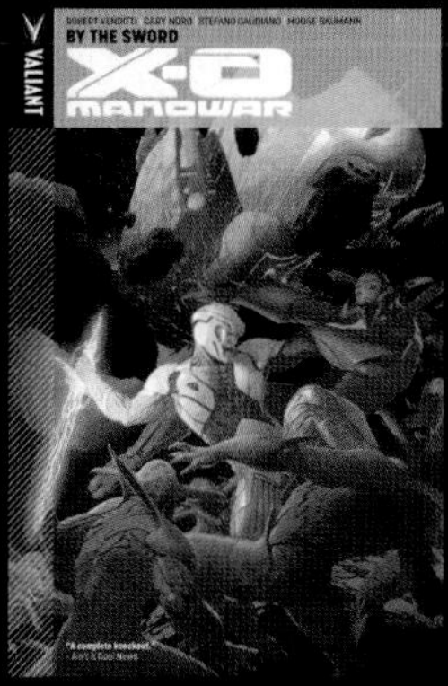
VALIANT
ROBERT VENDITTI | CARY NORD | STEFANO GAUDIANO | MOOSE BAUMANN
BY THE SWORD
X-O MANOWAR

X-O MANOWAR VOL. 1: BY THE SWORD
Written by ROBERT VENDITTI
Art by CARY NORD
Collecting X-O MANOWAR #1-4
TRADE PAPERBACK

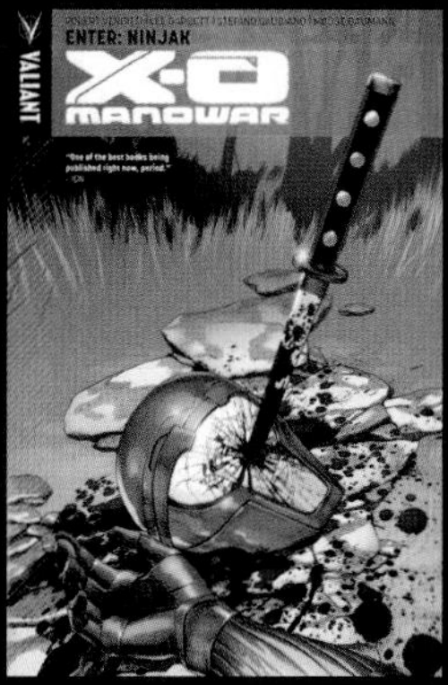
VALIANT
ENTER: NINJAK
X-O MANOWAR

X-O MANOWAR VOL. 2: ENTER NINJAK
Written by ROBERT VENDITTI
Art by LEE GARBETT
Collecting X-O MANOWAR #5-8
TRADE PAPERBACK

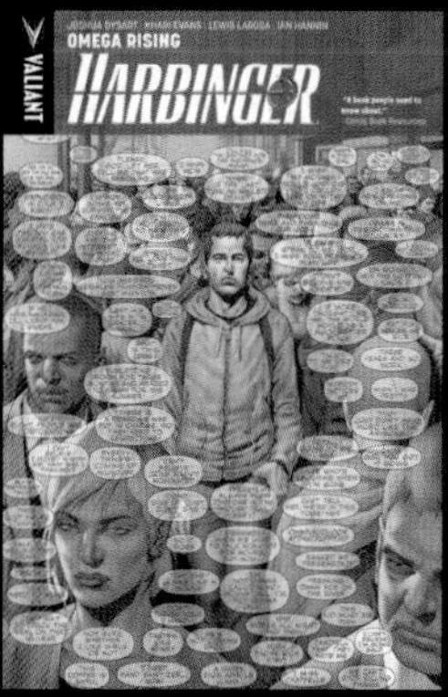
VALIANT
JOSHUA DYSART | KHARI EVANS | LEWIS LAROSA | IAN HANNIN
OMEGA RISING
HARBINGER

HARBINGER VOL. 1: OMEGA RISING
Written by JOSHUA DYSART
Art by KHARI EVANS & LEWIS LAROSA
Collecting HARBINGER #1-5
TRADE PAPERBACK

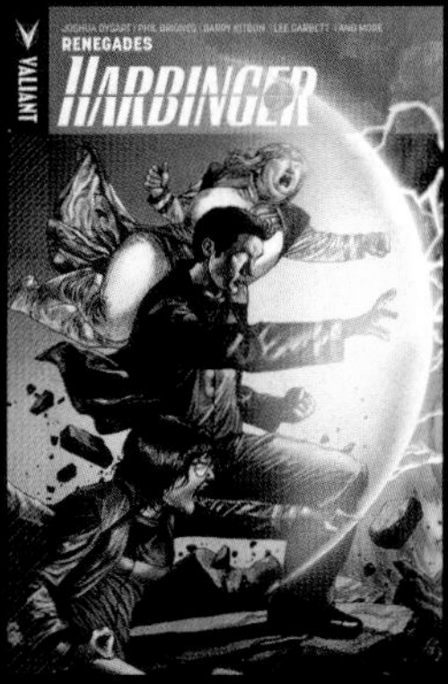
VALIANT
RENEGADES
HARBINGER

HARBINGER VOL. 2: RENEGADES
Written by JOSHUA DYSART
Art by PHIL BRIONES, MATTHEW CLARK, KHARI EVANS, LEE GARBETT, BARRY KITSON and PERE PÉREZ
Collecting HARBINGER #6-10
TRADE PAPERBACK

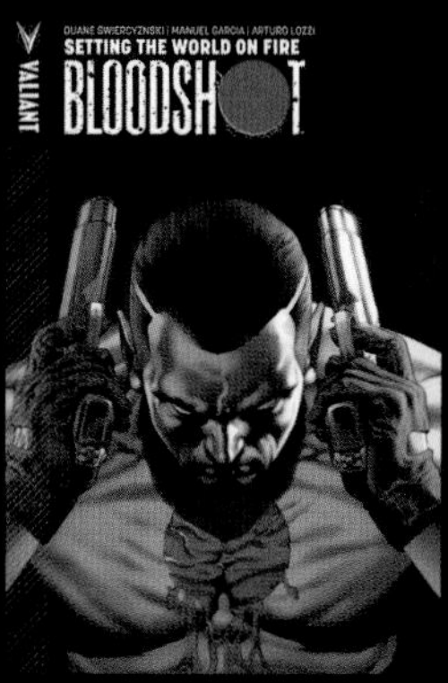
VALIANT
DUANE SWIERCZYNSKI | MANUEL GARCIA | ARTURO LOZZI
SETTING THE WORLD ON FIRE
BLOODSHOT

BLOODSHOT VOL. 1: SETTING THE WORLD ON FIRE
Written by DUANE SWIERCZYNSKI
Art by MANUEL GARCIA & ARTURO LOZZI
Collecting BLOODSHOT #1-4
TRADE PAPERBACK

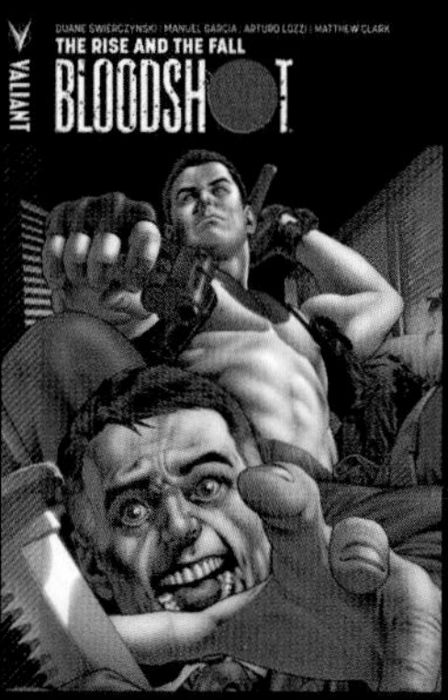
VALIANT
DUANE SWIERCZYNSKI | MANUEL GARCIA | ARTURO LOZZI | MATTHEW CLARK
THE RISE AND THE FALL
BLOODSHOT

BLOODSHOT VOL. 2: THE RISE & THE FALL
Written by DUANE SWIERCZYNSKI
Art by MANUEL GARCIA & ARTURO LOZZI
Collecting BLOODSHOT #5-9
TRADE PAPERBACK

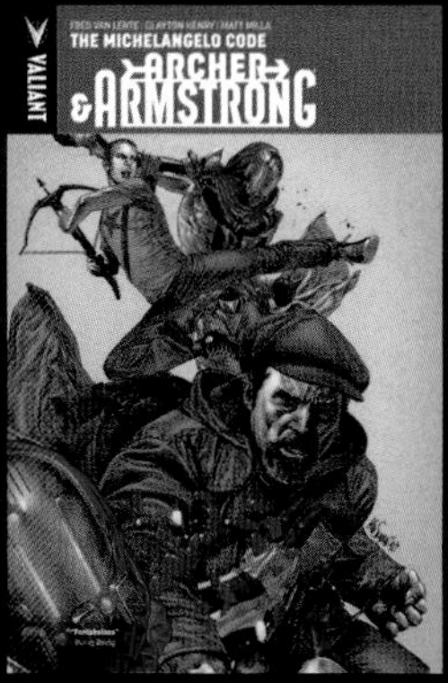
VALIANT
THE MICHELANGELO CODE
ARCHER & ARMSTRONG

ARCHER & ARMSTRONG VOL. 1: THE MICHELANGELO CODE
Written by FRED VAN LENTE
Art by CLAYTON HENRY
Collecting ARCHER & ARMSTRONG #1-4
TRADE PAPERBACK

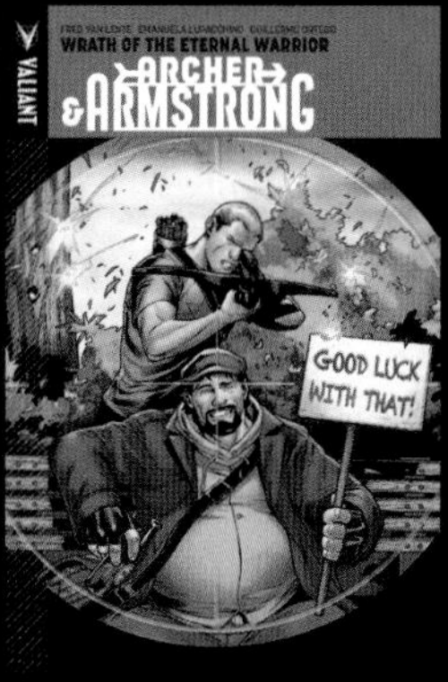
VALIANT
WRATH OF THE ETERNAL WARRIOR
ARCHER & ARMSTRONG
GOOD LUCK WITH THAT!

ARCHER & ARMSTRONG VOL. 2: WRATH OF THE ETERNAL WARRIOR
Written by FRED VAN LENTE
Art by EMANUELA LUPACCHINO
Collecting ARCHER & ARMSTRONG #5-9
TRADE PAPERBACK

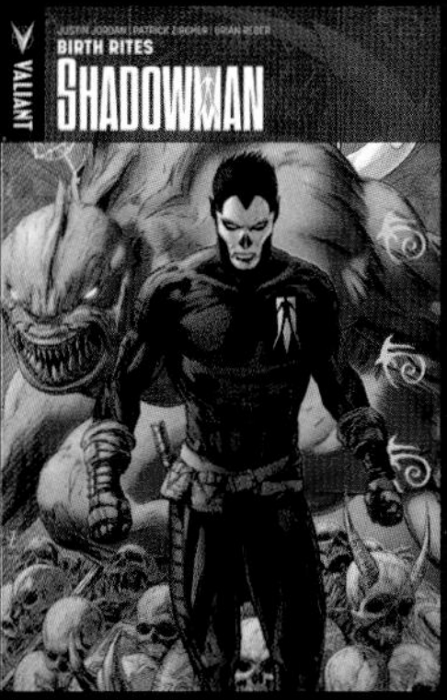
VALIANT
BIRTH RITES
SHADOWMAN

SHADOWMAN VOL. 1: BIRTH RITES
Written by JUSTIN JORDAN & PATRICK ZIRCHER
Art by PATRICK ZIRCHER
Collecting SHADOWMAN #1-4
TRADE PAPERBACK

X-O MANOWAR

VOLUME FOUR: **HOMECOMING**

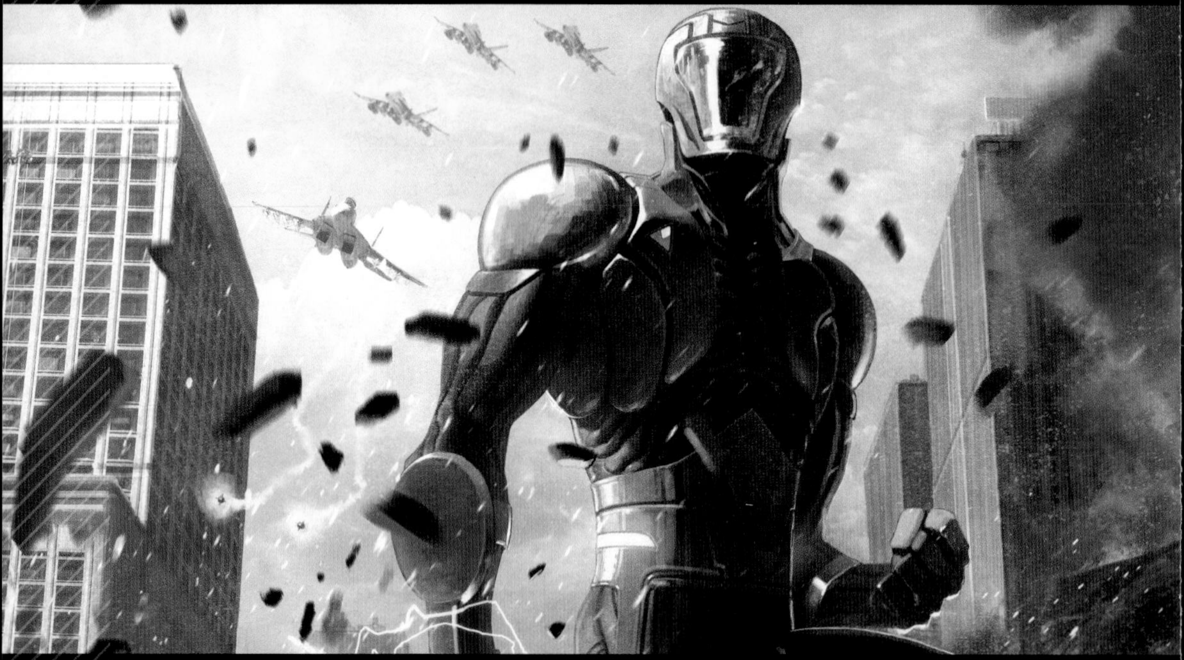

TO THIS KING...A KINGDOM!

Aric of Dacia has returned to Earth with his mind set on reclaiming the ancestral lands of his people. Now, the code of a fifth-century Visigoth is about to clash with the militaries of the modern world, and the only one who may be able to convince Aric to stand down is someone from his past - Gilad Anni-Padda, the Eternal Warrior! As the world watches, two of Valiant's most fearsome heroes are about to meet once again - and the outcome of their latest clash will decide the fate of us all.

X-O MANOWAR VOL. 4:
HOMECOMING

Collecting **X-O MANOWAR #15-18** by New York Times best-selling writer Robert Venditti (*Green Lantern*) and artist Lee Garbett (*X-O Manowar: Enter Ninjak*), the acclaimed series that IGN calls "just incredible" rushes headlong toward a pivotal turning point.

TRADE PAPERBACK
978-1-939346-17-9

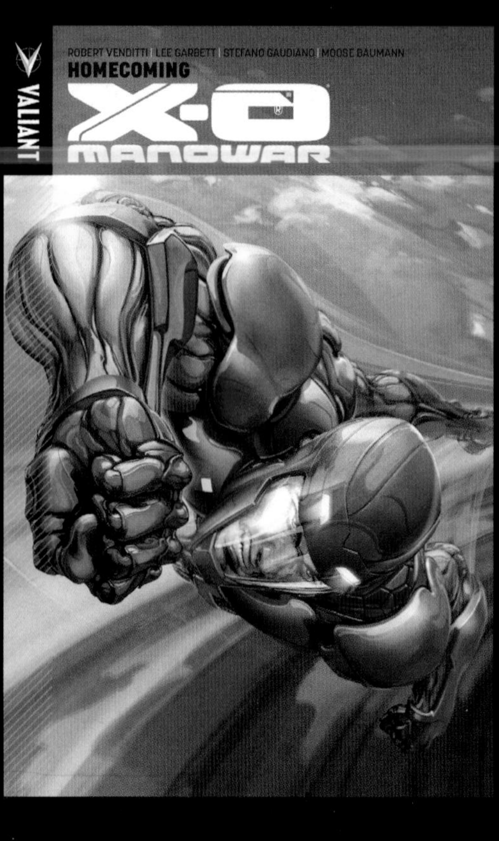
VALIANT
ROBERT VENDITTI | LEE GARBETT | STEFANO GAUDIANO | MOOSE BAUMANN
HOMECOMING
X-O
MANOWAR